ERNEST DOWSON

ERNEST DOWSON AT THE AGE OF FIVE

(*From the original portrait by W. G. Wills*)

ERNEST DOWSON

By

John **Mark Longaker**

UNIVERSITY OF PENNSYLVANIA PRESS
3729 Spruce Street, Philadelphia 19104

To
LENUSCHKA

. . . for all right judgement of any man or thing it is useful—nay, essential—to see his good qualities before pronouncing on his bad.

THOMAS CARLYLE

INTRODUCTORY NOTE

ALTHOUGH by no means a poet of the front rank, Ernest Dowson's place in literature is secure. No anthologist who presumes to select the best poems in the language can possibly ignore him, and no literary historian who is concerned with true poetic values can identify him with a movement and pass on. That his verse profits by selection cannot be gainsaid, but there is more lyric beauty in his slender volumes than is generally believed. He is far more than a one-poem poet: exquisite as the "Non Sum Qualis Eram Bonae Sub Regno Cynarae" is, it is by no means all of Dowson, or all we need to know.

Nor is the view of the vexed and torn spirit, the refugee in cabmen's shelters, East End dives, and dimly lighted cafés around les Halles a complete and balanced portrait of Dowson. It is true that his life was lived amongst shadows rather than light, but on occasion sunbeams filtered through the wall of cloud with which his heredity and environment surrounded him. His life and character cannot be called exemplary, but it can readily be shown that he was far from the wastrel that he is often pictured. Without laboring the point, one who has familiarized himself with the facts can readily conclude that Dowson was more a victim of circumstance than one who deliberately cultivated *nostalgie de la boue* and chose the path which led to evil and destruction. Of admiration for his character and order of life there can be little; but it is easy to like Ernest Dowson, and to wish that something might have been done to give him sanctuary from the world and from himself.

In spite of the fact that the man and the poet cannot be dissociated, in the pages which follow it is Dowson's life and personality rather than his works which are the chief object of consideration. His poetry and prose were of a highly subjective quality, and, as a result, many of the lineaments of his character can be illuminated by a careful interpretation of his works; but it is equally true that much of the dark beauty of his poetry finds explanation only in the circumstances which shaped his life. Nor has there been an attempt to illuminate fully the age in which Dowson lived. Only in so far as he was a part and result of the spirit of the closing decades of the nineteenth century has there been an attempt to recapture the atmosphere of the times. Although he was definitely of the *fin de siècle,* his life and personality cannot be adequately interpreted by identifying him with a time-spirit or movement. To name him decadent tells only a part of the story, a part which has been sufficiently emphasized. If he was the arch-exponent of that group which has been loosely labeled decadent, it must be borne in mind that it was his personality as well as the spirit of the times which made him responsive to the ideal of Smither's press and *The Savoy*.

In my efforts to gather and piece together the facts of his brief and unhappy life, I have encountered widely different descriptions and reports. In fact, amongst Dowson's contemporaries who are alive there exists a rivalry for authority which leaves one bewildered and dismayed. There are many commentators who knew the poet sufficiently well to recall him more or less distinctly, but among them there are few who are in agreement. Each one seems to have a different estimate, a different version, and a different manner of discounting the authority of the other. After listening to some of my informants, I walked about the streets of London muttering the Psalmist's plaint that all men are liars. By long and painstaking consideration of the varied reports and their sources, however, I have reached conclusions which are in some measure dependent on my estimate of the authority of my informants, and which, despite the oral nature of much of the evidence, I am at last willing to accept. It is a mistaken notion that the spoken word is less dependable than the testimony which appears in writing, especially if the spoken word is carefully weighed.

From a considerable mass of oral and written reports, including letters from Dowson's friends to me and many hitherto unpublished letters of the poet to his friends, I have attempted to draw a portrait of Ernest Dowson as I see him without feeling that my vision has been unduly limited by faulty light. Beyond this, few biographers can go. To be sure, there exist some of Dowson's letters which are inaccessible to me at present, and there are stages in his life which remain almost totally unilluminated; but until additional materials are discovered and made available, I can say as did Samuel Johnson when he was questioned about the soundness of one of his accounts in *The Lives of the Poets:* "Sir, I have been entrusted with a share of the truth."

My informants have been many and of widely varied weight and breadth of authority. With a few exceptions, their graciousness in answering my inquiries was in proportion to the quality of their authority. It is not a formal gesture of acknowledgement of obligation which I make in naming some of the men and women who have been kind and helpful to me: most of them have become my regular correspondents and friends. To Robert Sherard, with whom Dowson spent the six weeks before his death, and a fortnight in Paris in 1899, I shall be always grateful for the long afternoons he spent with me in talk about Dowson. To the late Mrs. Dillon-Jones, who was Sherard's first wife and was with Dowson at the time of his death and to whom he spoke his last words, I wish a far happier life in the hereafter than that of her last years in London. It was she who told me much about Dowson's last days. To Spencer and Dulcie Secretan, Dowson's surviving cousins, I am grateful for the generous assistance they have given me. To Conal O'Riordan, who spent the autumn of 1895 with Dowson in Flanders and most of the winter of 1896 with him in Paris, and knew him to the end, I am indebted for much substantial information and for the pleasure of an association with a brilliant literary figure and a charming man. Mr. Arthur Moore, who was at Queen's College, Oxford, with Dowson and collaborated with him on *A Comedy of Masks* and *Adrian Rome*, has given me much specific information concerning their association at Oxford and their method of collaboration. Dr. E. M. Walker, who was a Fellow at Queen's College when Dowson went up, was hospitable and patient under my inquiries concerning the poet's movements at Oxford. Michael Holland, who knew Dowson at Pont-Aven in 1896 and saw much of him later in London, has given me valuable materials, including copies of the Dowson letters which are in his possession. Frank Walton, who with Victor Plarr was Dowson's associate in the annotation of Olive Schreiner's *The African Farm*, has written helpfully to me about "the young poet just down from college." To Captain Vyvyan Holland, I am very grateful for his generous permission to use twelve hitherto unpublished letters which his father, Oscar Wilde, wrote to Dowson from Bernavel and Naples in 1897.

My obligations extend to men of my own generation who did not know Dowson, but who have done much to keep his memory alive and to make materials available to me as well as to encourage me with my work. The young English poet, John Gawsworth, kinsman of Lionel Johnson and recipient of the Benson Medal in poetry, has been a faithful source of information and inspiration. It was he who either directly or indirectly made possible the inclusion of many of the Dowson letters which I have woven into the text, and by his hospitality made my last visit to London both profitable and pleasant. I shall never forget an entire night during which we sat by candlelight in a blackout, talking about Dowson in tones which would have attracted any enemy within a mile. Laurence Dakin, another poet of more than promise, who has written a monograph on Dowson soon to be published, has been a regular correspondent and has given me the benefit of his investigations of Dowson's life without stint. Mr. J. Harlin O'Connell has not only made available to me his fine collection of Dowson materials, but has also given me useful information from his wide knowledge of the 'nineties. Mr. Lessing Rosenwald has been kind enough to let me study at length the two original manuscripts of *The Pierrot of*

the Minute, and to provide me with the reproduction of a page of one
of the manuscripts. I wish to thank my friendly rival, Desmond Flower,
whose edition of Dowson's poems has much merit, for his willingness
to help me solve some of the puzzles which have arisen in my work. The
Faculty Research Committee of the University of Pennsylvania was generous in helping me meet some of the expenses incurred in collecting
materials. My good friends Paul Jones and Edward O'Neill read the
manuscript and offered forthright suggestions for its improvement.

To the following publishers I am indebted for their permission to quote
from books under their copyright: Ivor Nicholson and Watson, for much
material from Victor Plarr's *Ernest Dowson, 1888-1897;* Constable and
Company for passages from W. R. Thomas's article in *The Nineteenth
Century* entitled "Ernest Dowson at Oxford," and from Vincent O'Sulli-
van's *Aspects of Wilde;* Victor Gollancz for quotations from Edgar Jepson's
Memories of a Victorian; Farrar and Rinehart for a few passages from
Ernest Rhys's *Everyman Remembers;* the Liveright Publishing Corporation
for a few brief extracts from Gertrude Atherton's *Adventures of a Novelist;*
Percy Muir for permission to quote extracts from the Elkin Mathews
Catalogue, *Books of the Nineties;* Mitchell Kennerley for permission to re-
produce Charles Conder's sketch of Dowson which was in the collection
of John Quinn; and Grant Richards for materials from Marion Plarr's
Cynara and Holbrook Jackson's *The Eighteen Nineties.*

There are few books which deal with the literature of the closing decades
of the last century to which I am not at least indirectly indebted. Richard
LeGallienne's *The Romantic Nineties,* Bernard Muddiman's *Men of the
Nineties,* Grant Richards' *Memories of a Misspent Youth* and *Author
Hunting,* John May's *John Lane and the Nineties,* Sir William Rothenstein's *Men and Memories,* William Butler Yeats's *The Trembling of the
Veil,* and R. A. Walker's edition of *Letters from Aubrey Beardsley to Leonard Smithers* are only a few of the books which have helped me to view
Dowson and his times more clearly. I take this opportunity to thank the
authors and publishers of these books for whatever use I made of
them. In instances in which the use of footnotes was not absolutely necessary, I have avoided them. Sources of information which are not indicated
directly in the text may readily be found in the Bibliography.

M. L.

Cynwyd, Pennsylvania
November 1943

NOTE TO SECOND EDITION

SOON after the first edition of this book appeared, additional materials, which shed considerable light on Ernest Dowson, were made available. Mrs. Madeleine Brown of San Antonio, Texas, a cousin on Dowson's mother's side, very generously provided me with letters written by her father, Lewis Swan, and Miss Ethel Swan, the poet's aunt, in which there are many references to the Dowson family. Excerpts I have woven into the text in instances in which additional illumination of stages in Dowson's life seemed necessary.

I am also reproducing in an appendix a series of ten Dowson letters which Mr. J. Harlin O'Connell has kindly permitted me to use. These letters, arranged chronologically as nearly as can be determined from their content, reveal Ernest Dowson as far less detached from the events and men of his time than he is often pictured, and an agreeable correspondent.

M. L.

Cynwyd, Pennsylvania
December 1944

NOTE TO THIRD EDITION

THE enduring interest in Ernest Dowson and his poetry accounts for this new edition which makes available materials which have long been out of print. The Letters from Dowson to Conal O'Riordan, only recently accessible and here printed for the first time, provide additional light on the poet's last years.

M. L.

Philadelphia, Pennsylvania
March 1967

NOTE TO SECOND EDITION

SOON after the first edition of this book appeared, additional materials, which shed considerable light on Ernest Dowson, were made available. Mrs. Madeleine Brown of San Antonio, Texas, a cousin on Dowson's mother's side, very generously provided me with letters written by her father, Lewis Swan, and Miss Ethel Swan, the poet's aunt, in which there are many references to the Dowson family. Excerpts I have woven into the text in instances in which additional illumination of stages in Dowson's life seemed necessary.

I am also reproducing in an appendix a series of ten Dowson letters which Mr. J. Harlin O'Connell has kindly permitted me to use. These letters, arranged chronologically as nearly as can be determined from their content, reveal Ernest Dowson as far less detached from the events and men of his time than he is often pictured, and an agreeable correspondent.

M. L.

Cynwyd, Pennsylvania
December 1944

NOTE TO THIRD EDITION

THE enduring interest in Ernest Dowson and his poetry accounts for this new edition which makes available materials which have long been out of print. The Letters from Dowson to Conal O'Riordan, only recently accessible and here printed for the first time, provide additional light on the poet's last years.

M. L.

Philadelphia, Pennsylvania
March 1967

CONTENTS

ILLUSTRATIONS

I

A PAGAN CHILDHOOD

ERNEST Chistopher Dowson was born with only a fighting chance for happiness and success. Heredity and the environment of his home played a more important part in his life than is commonly supposed. When Agnes Rothery observed, "While he succeeded in being very completely and very consistently miserable during the thirty-three years of his life, this misery was in no way caused by impaired circumstances of birth and fortune," she had failed to take into account all of the facts. Surely much of the tragedy of Dowson's life and early death can be traced to his birthright and to the circumstances which surrounded his youth. Although no one will be sufficiently uncharitable to his parents to suggest that they were entirely to blame for his sad life and early death—for they, too, were victims of circumstances over which they had small control—the fact remains that Ernest Dowson had a poor start. In his birthright there were a few advantages, to be sure; but the disadvantages outweighed them an hundredfold. Others have encountered such disadvantages and overcome them, but their number is few. They are the conquerors amongst men, to whom there has been given strength—we know not how—to ride out the storm. Dowson was not one of these.

At the time of his birth on August 2, 1867, his parents were apparently prosperous and well. It is unlikely that they gave a thought to their physical and moral fitness for having children; and if they did, they were agreed that the children which they would bring into the world were marked for happiness and success. In 1867, Alfred Dowson and his wife were sufficiently young to contemplate a future of unmixed success in all their undertakings, including parenthood. Temperamental instability and an inherited predisposition to consumption in both of them were not recognized at the time as handicaps to their well-being or that of their children. Nor were they concerned with their possession of moral courage. Such considerations belong to mature reflection, not to young parents to whom the lines of life have fallen for the most part in pleasant places.

At the time of Ernest's birth, Alfred Dowson and his wife were living at "The Grove" at Belmont Hill in Lee in Kent, which was then far more detached from the boundaries and spirit of London than it is today. The mother, whose maiden name was Swan, was a delicately beautiful woman of Scottish descent with a face both sensitive and intelligent. In later years, she was to impress visitors in her home as retiring in manner, almost to the point of being shy. She was scarcely twenty years old when her first son was born; and the father, considerably her senior, was a personable though indecisive man to whom his forebears had bequeathed a taste for literature along with a dry dock in Limehouse. Although their home, to which apparently an earlier Dowson had given the name "The Grove," was by no means palatial, there was an atmosphere of comfort and distinction about it. Alfred Dowson was later to remind Victor Plarr of the grandfather of Marius in *Les Miserables,* "qui portait sa bourgeoisie comme un marquisat." Unpretentious in its surroundings and furnishings, the home in Kent was free from the atmosphere of the middle class by reason of the interests and manner of its inmates. Their conversation and bearing, as well as a few appointments in the house, suggested an atmosphere of breeding and culture.

Visitors in the Dowson home noticed a portrait of an earlier Dowson who had evidently been an actor in the days of George IV, with what reputation, time and James Boaden do not disclose. They also saw an Italian scene in oils done by Joesph Severn, the man in whose arms John Keats had died. Of Severns, Alfred Dowson spoke as if they had been more than casual acquaintances. There were other indications in the home of an interest in literature and the graphic arts, for the bookcases showed a modest though choice collection of the poets, including the French; and the walls of the library were adorned with drawings and etchings, most of which had inscriptions from the artists to Alfred Dowson. Although pictures, especially drawings in black and white, were evidently a source of considerable delight to the owner of "The Grove," literature was his chief avocation. He was able to discuss English and Continental literature with those who made letters their profession, and it was generally assumed by those who knew him intimately that he had literary projects under way.

The literary atmosphere of the home became more pronounced when Alfred Dowson's uncle, Alfred Dommet, the "Waring" of Browning's poem, continued to write verse during his stay in New Zealand and after his return to London. As early as 1832, Dommet had written a volume of poems and contributed verses to *Blackwood's* which attracted commendation as the work of a rising poet. When he became Prime Minister of New Zealand, he found a new source of inspiration. Such poems as *Ranolf and Amohia, a South Sea Day Dream,* and the verses in *Flotsam and Jetsam,* which appeared in 1877 and was dedicated to Robert Browning, had a fairly wide circulation. Alfred Dowson was proud of his uncle's achievements, and on occasion enjoyed the reflected light which came to him by reason of his relationship.

He had merits and charm of his own, however, with which to cultivate literary acquaintances, for there is a story of how he fitted out a barge with all the comforts of a houseboat, on which the staff of *Punch,* Sir Francis Burnand amongst them, and others who were later to become celebrities, including Swinburne, cruised about on the Thames with more attention to talk than to tide. Although there is no positive evidence, report has it that Alfred Dowson often referred to Meredith, Rossetti, and Browning in a manner which indicated that he had more than a nodding acquaintance with them.

Robert Louis Stevenson, after he had been "Ordered South," mentioned his friendship with Alfred Dowson in his letters written from the Riviera. When Stevenson arrived in Mentone in November 1873, he was uneasy that he might find no one "conversable" at the Hotel du Pavillon at which he planned to stay. In his letter to Mrs. Sitwell, dated November 30, he reported an acquaintanceship with a Mr. Dowson, whom he evidently found "conversable." Aside from the facts that they spoke a common language, came from the same country, and suffered from the same malady, they found each other's companionship agreeable on account of a similarity of tastes and interests. Stevenson told of spending a long moonlit evening with his new friend, whom he called familiarly Dowson, while they listened to Italian music. Although Alfred Dowson was somewhat older than Stevenson, he could be as young as anyone who would talk about literature with him. During December and January when Sidney Colvin was in Mentone, the three of them passed time pleasantly and profitably by taking short excursions to Cap Martin and Mortola, and by sitting in the sunshine appraising the currents of recent British literature. Andrew Lang was another Mentone visitor whom Alfred Dowson met during the early months of 1874. It was not until Stevenson moved to the Hotel Mirabeau overlooking the east bay of Mentone in order to economize that his frequent chats with Alfred Dowson were given up.

The elder Dowson's interest in literature was not confined entirely to discussion and association with literary figures. Occasionally an urge to write overtook him; but this inclination, hampered by a long-standing habit of procrastination, produced little save the translation and amplification of Frederick Fitzroy Hamilton's *Bordighera and the Western Riviera* which appeared in 1883. The translation of the book showed not only an adequate familiarity with the French tongue, but also a sense for prose style. Furthermore, the amplification of Hamilton's work and the notes indicated a considerable familiarity with the Riviera. The popularity of Bordighera as a winter resort for English folk in the 'eighties helped to give the book an encouraging circulation among a limited group who found the translation useful as a guidebook and interesting as travel literature. *Bordighera and the Western Riviera* has little to distinguish it from the mass of travel books which were produced during the latter half of the nineteenth century, but it indicates that its translator was mindful of the literary utility to which his sojourns in the South could be put, and it is marked by an occasional felicity of phrase.*

Had Alfred Dowson been a man of independent means, he probably would have done little save indulge his interests in literature. His only source of income, however, was Bridge Dock, a dry dock in Limehouse which had been in the family for several generations. At the time of Ernest's birth, he was the owner and presumably the supervisor; but from the time that the Dock had passed into his hands he had been willing to allow lessees and his foreman to look after the more arduous end of the business. In 1867 the Dock was a scene of considerable activity. Painting, caulking, general overhauling, and providing ship supplies were the chief services it offered, and many a seagoing and coastwise schooner moved up the Thames for repairs and supplies at Dowson's. As late as 1890, Alfred Dowson issued bills for as much as £158 for one job, with items such as caulking, repainting, scraping off barnacles, and making a dog kennel for the master listed on the bill. But a far-sighted observer, even as early as 1867, would have noticed that Bridge Dock had started to decline. Its antiquated appearance and equipment, although pleasing to a man of Alfred Dowson's tastes, afforded small indication of a prosperous future. The rivers to the north were rapidly taking over the contracts for overhauling on account of superior natural facilities. The Clyde and Tyne had already become the principal centers for building and repairing. Bridge Dock, although still thriving in the 'sixties—for masters out of long habit or immediate necessity brought their ships to Dowson's—was unable to compete with the shipyards in Glasgow, or with the larger and more modern dry docks on the Thames.

During the years immediately following Ernest's birth, however, Alfred Dowson was drawing a fair income from the business, and to him there

* In a letter from Alfred Dowson's brother-in-law, Lewis Swan, to his daughter Madeleine, Swan reported that "Alfred tried to write for magazines, but his stories were always 'returned with thanks,' and did manage to get some accepted in a penny magazine eventually."

were no positive signs to cause alarm. Ship repairing and outfitting had been the family trade for so long that he was both unable and unwilling to see that there might be a time at which such an enterprise could fail. That ships would always need repairs and equipment was a reassuring reflection; and easy-going man that he was when commercial matters were thrust upon him, he took no steps to improve the efficiency of the services which the Dock offered, and showed no interest in selling out when he might still have found a buyer. He leased the Dock to men who did little to improve its services, and for long intervals left the business in the hands of the foreman in whom he had the utmost trust, and who probably knew a great deal more about the essentials of the business than he. A sentimental attachment to the Dock, supported by his own indecision, caused him to close his eyes to what seemed to him to be a remote possibility that the business could fail.

An illuminating description of the Dock, and in large measure of its owner, appeared in *A Comedy of Masks*, a novel written in part by Ernest Dowson, who to all intents was some day to inherit the family property.

In that intricate and obscure locality, which stretches between the Tower and Poplar, a tarry region, scarcely suspected by the majority of Londoners, to whom the "Port of London" is an expression purely geographical, there is, or was not many years ago, to be found a certain dry dock called Blackpool, but better known from time immemorial to skippers and longshoremen, and all who go down to the sea in ships, as "Rainham's Dock."

Many years ago, in the days of the first Rainham and of wooden ships, it had been no doubt a flourishing ship-yard; and, indeed, models of wooden leviathans of the period, which had been turned out, not a few, in those palmy days, were still dusty ornaments of its somewhat antique office. But as time went on, and the age of iron intervened, and the advance of the Clyde and Tyne had made Thames ship-building a thing of the past, Blackpool Dock had ceased to be of commercial importance. No more ships were built there, and fewer ships put in to be overhauled and painted; while even these were for the most part of a class viewed at Lloyd's with scant favour, which seemed, like the yard itself, to have fallen somewhat behind the day. The original Rainham had not bequeathed his energy along with his hoards to his descendants; and, indeed, to the last of these, Philip Rainham, a man of weak health, whose tastes, although these were veiled in obscurity, were supposed to trench little on shipping, let the business jog along so much after its own fashion, that the popular view hinted at its imminent dissolution. A dignified, scarcely prosperous quiet seemed the normal air of Blackpool Dock, so that when even it was busiest, and work still came in, almost by tradition, with a certain steadiness—when the hammers of the riveters and the shipwrights awoke the echoes from sunrise to sunset, with a ferocious regularity which the present proprietor could almost deplore, there was still a suggestion of mildewed antiquity about it all that was, at least to the nostrils of the outsider, not unpleasing. And when the ships were painted, and departed, it resumed very easily its more regular aspect of picturesque dilapidation. For in spite of its sordid surroundings and its occasional lapses into bustle, Blackpool Dock, as Rainham would sometimes remind himself, when its commercial motive was pressed upon him too forcibly, was deeply permeated by the spirit of the picturesque.

Rainham had a set of rooms in the house of his foreman, an eighteenth century house, full of carved oak mantels and curious alcoves, a ramshackle structure within the dock gates, with a quaint balcony staircase, like the approach to a Swiss chalet, leading down into the yard. In London these apartments were his sole domicile; though to his friends, none of whom lived nearer to him than Bloomsbury, this seemed a bit of conduct too flagrantly eccentric—on a parity with his explanation of it, alleging necessity of living on the spot: an explanation somewhat droll, in the face of his constant lengthy absences, during the whole of the winter, when he handed the reins of government to his manager, and took care of a diseased lung in a warmer climate . . . residence even in a less salubrious quarter than Blackpool would have been amply justified, in view of the many charming effects—for the most part coldly sad and white—which the river offered, towards evening, from the window of the dining room.

His den behind the office—a little sitting room with a bay-window facing Blackpool Reach, a room filled with books that had no relation to shipping, and hung round with etchings and pictures in those curiously-low tones for which he had so unreasonable an affection—was what he cherished most in London. He read little now, but the mere presence of the books he loved best in rough, uneven cases, painted black, lining the walls, caressed him. As with persons one has loved and grown used to loving, it was not always needful that they should speak to him; it was sufficient, simply, that they should be there. Neither did he write on these long, interminable evenings, which were prolonged sometimes far into the night. He had ended by being able to smile at his literary ambitions of twenty, cultivating his indolence as something choice and original, finding his destiny appropriate.

Although some of the details in this description must be rejected as fictional, it affords a richly suggestive picture of Bridge Dock and Alfred Dowson in the late 'eighties. Like Philip Rainham, Alfred Dowson's tastes were not toward shipping, and he "let the business jog along so much after its own fashion that the popular view hinted at its imminent dissolution." The business provided him with a sufficient income to meet his needs, which came to include sojourns on the Riviera; and with no great ambition to become wealthy or even to compete with his rivals, he continued to enjoy the picturesqueness of the Dock House and its surroundings without concerning himself seriously over its future.

In the ten years following Ernest's birth, however, Alfred Dowson should have had premonitions of trouble. His income began to decrease with alarming rapidity. As the years passed, he had increasing difficulty in finding anyone who was willing to lease Bridge Dock; for weeks at a time the ways stood empty. And through no fault of his own, for his habits had always been moderate, his lungs began to show such conspicuous signs of being diseased that his health became his primary concern. Hypochondria, supported and aggravated by a disposition toward melancholy, began to take its toll from his energy and spirit soon after he became aware of his diseased lungs. The diminishing income from the Dock began to take on grave portents, and when he, like Stevenson, was "Ordered South," he carried his worries with him. His wife, who had always been of delicate health, also began to show signs of his affliction. The birth of a second son, Rowland Corbet, eight years after Ernest was born, brought small joy to the parents who were already bowed with illness and care. By the time Ernest had reached adolescence, Alfred Dowson and his wife were in the clutch of circumstances over which they could exercise small control.

During this interval, Ernest Dowson's body and character were slowly being formed. His entire youth is a veiled period, for there are no records to which to turn in order to determine the events of his life or his childhood impressions. To his associates at Oxford and the friends of his later years, he spoke only rarely about his childhood and the years immediately preceding his stay at Queen's College. His reluctance to speak about his boyhood was probably more the result of his good breeding than of any desire to hide the facts, although it has been reported that his uncommunicativeness concerning his youth extended almost to an aversion. The only method of determining the nature of his boyhood is to analyze the mature man, and trace the results back to their ultimate causes.

At one time, in a confiding mood, he told Plarr that his boyhood had been pagan, a statement which lends itself to a variety of interpretations. What he probably meant was that there were few restrictions placed on his physical, mental, and moral growth; that his natural inclinations were subject to no discipline. He assuredly was not thrust into a system such as Richard Feverel's, for his parents had none of the strength of will of Sir Austin; nor were they decided on a conventional rearing for their son which would include the academic training and discipline of an English public school. With ill health and financial insecurity beginning to warp their outlook on life, they had little time and energy to formulate elaborate plans for the son's rearing. By the time that he was old enough to go to public school, his parents were primarily concerned about their own health and their dwindling income. His training—or lack of it—was closely related to his parents' plans for themselves, and only in so far as his training could be adapted to their needs and plans was his education considered.

It is possible that Ernest enjoyed the freedom from the discipline of formal education, but his childhood could scarcely have been that of a happy boy. Apparently healthy at birth, he was by no means a robust child, and he never became a boy amongst boys. The pastel of the child at the age of five by W. G. Wills, which hung over the mantelpiece in the Dowson home on Forest Row, may or may not be an accurate likeness of him, but it is easy to read wistfulness in the little face. Unaware as he was of the troubles which were to beset his parents, he must have felt some of the oppressiveness with which the atmosphere of the home was often laden.

The influence of his parents' illness and worries had a more pronounced effect in shaping Ernest Dowson's life than is commonly supposed. Under a different influence, it is possible that optimism and light-heartedness, which are a part of youth, and essential to proper development, would have given him strength of body and character. The atmosphere of his home, however, could do little save direct the inclination toward life-weariness which he expressed before he was out of his teens. It is not to be assumed that his parents' troubles were regularly forced into the consciousness of the impressionable boy, for the Dowsons were not the sort of parents who take dreams away from their children in order to support their own self-pity; but the fact remains that a child feels the tone of his environment keenly, and that he is readily influenced by it. If the boy did not know how grave the illness was from which his parents suffered, and the exact reasons for their recurrent despondency, he surely was affected by the atmosphere of insecurity and despair which became more pronounced as he grew older.

There were frequent trips to the Continent, the reason for which the boy knew only vaguely. He had heard his father speak, no doubt, of the fog which lay thick over the Thames and turned day into night at Bridge Dock; and he had heard his mother gravely say that it was again time for them to leave the cold and damp of London for the sunshine of southern France. To which suggestion, her husband would reluctantly agree, for to go away for another winter meant additional expense and concern about his source of income. Lewis Swan said that "Alfred Dowson was of a most miserly nature, always expecting to wind up in the poor house." There would be delays while Alfred Dowson held to the faint hope that he might remain in London in order to economize and to look after his affairs; but as soon as winter set in this hope dwindled, and his instinct of self-preservation, abetted by the insistence of his physician, carried him across the Channel and into a brighter and more salubrious land.

On these trips the boy was often taken along, and he looked forward to them with a boy's delight. He no doubt realized that his parents were going to France for purposes other than to have a good time, but he could not have been concerned about the exact reasons for their departure. With no friends and associations at home to which to tie his affections, he soon learned to transplant his few interests, and even to look forward to the transplanting. Then, too, although he was unaware of it, his body and spirit needed the sunshine of the South, and his nature rejoiced at the prospect of leaving London behind.

On the Continent, a series of kaleidoscopic impressions came to him. There were trips to Switzerland, and into Italy as far as Florence and Rome. But it was the French Riviera which Ernest learned to know most intimately. As early as the winter of 1873, Alfred Dowson had found the climate and surroundings at Mentone agreeable; but with the progress of his malady and an increasing sensitivity to the presence of his countrymen who formed a considerable invalid colony in Mentone during the winter, he decided that the quiet of Bordighera would be beneficial. Bordighera was within range of the English physician and the well-stocked pharmacy at Mentone, its climate was equable, and pension rates were more reasonable than in most of the Riviera towns. By 1882, when Ernest was in his middle teens, Bordighera had become Alfred Dowson's favorite place of sojourn. At carnival times troubles were forgotten, and for a brief season a spirit of festivity overcame the elder Dowson's bent for worry. Nice, Cannes, and Monte Carlo attracted them away from the quiet of Bordighera, but the piper usually had to be paid. There were instances in which Alfred Dowson could scarely wait to return to the Pharmacie Gros and to the advice of Dr. Bennet, the English physician in Mentone.

Ernest enjoyed the sojourns on the Riviera and undoubtedly profited from them in many ways, especially after he had reached his teens. But in spite of the many new and pleasant scenes which came to him, his impressions were often darkened by his parents' illness and worries. The gayety and sunshine of life in the South were not always his to enjoy. With no boys of his own age with whom to associate, and with little to occupy his time constructively, he must have felt keenly at times the insecurity and despair which his father's manner exuded. Instead of adopting the carefree

manner which surrounded him on all sides, even among the invalids at
Mentone, Alfred Dowson gave himself over increasingly to self-pity and
self-condemnation. He began to blame himself for negligence in attending
to his affairs, and instead of returning to London in the spring refreshed
and filled with new energy and hope, he came back with his body no
stronger than when he had left, and with his spirit still shaken. Worry had
become his greatest enemy. While Ernest was seeing with his boy's eyes
"Mentone lying placidly with its two bays in the westering sun," the elder
Dowson was conjuring clouds out of sunbeams, and seeing nothing but
poverty and suffering ahead.

Youth, however, is never completely denied. There were undoubtedly
advantages as well as disadvantages which grew out of the shifting scenes
of Ernest's boyhood. Travel in itself is a widely recognized specific for
taking one's troubles too seriously. Youth and constantly shifting scenes
kept Ernest Dowson in adolescence from brooding too intently on his
parents' troubles. Even had their influence been more debilitating to his
spirit, he would have managed to reap some benefits from his moving
about on the Continent.

As a boy, he naturally acquired a fluency in the French tongue which his
elders, who had started late in the mastery of the language, could never
possess. Although he had few playmates among the French boys, he was
not always with English-speaking people. His father handled French adequately and encouraged his son to read and speak the language. Then, too,
there were occasionally tutors under whom the boy sat who carried on their
lessons in French. Report has it that Dowson once remarked that at the age
of fifteen he spoke French as fluently as English. In later years he was by
no means bilingual, although on his visits to Paris and Brittany, where he
spent most of his time in his last years, he was never handicapped by inadequate French. Plarr spoke of Dowson's French as dim, but Plarr, it
must be observed, had the bookman's sense of precision. Thomas, Dowson's
Oxford friend, commended Dowson's French not so much for its purity,
but rather for the Gallic spirit with which it was used. When Pierre Louÿs'
Aphrodite was to be translated into English, it was Louÿs himself who suggested Dowson as the one who could do the piece justice; and when Oscar
Wilde, whose taste was very fine in such matters, encouraged Dowson to
accept the commission to translate *Aphrodite,* Wilde knew his friend's
ability to catch the nuances of the French story. Verlaine, Voltaire, Zola,
the Goncourts, and Laclos were only a few of the French authors to whom
Dowson was to apply his talents as translator. Leonard Smithers, whose
notorious press flourished chiefly on account of its excellent translations

from the French, found Dowson his best, if not his most dependable, contributor.

More important, perhaps, than his acquiring a fluency in the language and a feeling for its nuances was his impressionability to the French point of view. The total length of his sojourns in France with his parents has not been determined, but it is certain that the boy was in France sufficiently long to cultivate an attitude toward life and literature which was often peculiarly French. The length of time spent in a country in attaining a racial point of view is not nearly so important as the particular time at which the racial influence is at work. Dowson was in France during his most impressionable years, with the result that he cultivated, with no deliberate intent, mannerisms and an outlook on life which were more Continental than English. While other young Londoners in the early 'nineties were trying desperately to cultivate the French air, Dowson carried it with a naturalness which left him free of all charges of affectation. Although he was frequently to wear black bow ties, slouch hats with brims wider than those usually seen on the Strand, and boots which were not made on London lasts—all of which he delighted in as being French—in his garb and manner there was no studied application to Continental models. To casual observers, he often gave the impression of one who had been born of French parents but who had spent much of his life in England and was doing his best to adapt himself to English ways.

Much of his preference for French life and literature in his later years can undoubtedly be traced to the impressions of his youth. His susceptibilty to French influence was not entirely dependent on the particular time in his development at which this influence was at work; it can also be traced to the fact that he came to like France because it was there that he had spent the happiest days of his boyhood. Edgar Jepson, who knew him well during the 'nineties, has observed: "I think he was happiest in the remote Breton villages, whither he now and again withdrew himself, from which he wrote his most delightful letters. They used to give me the impression that the world went well with him there—as well, at any rate as it could go with him." As time passed, he came to associate his brief intervals of happiness with his sojourns in France; and, as a natural result, he was ready to believe that France was a panacea for ailments of both body and soul. Quite unconsciously during his formative period, Dowson imitated the features of French life which pleased him until they became a part of his nature.

His sincere and abiding liking for things French, and the influence of his tutors, led him to a familiarity with French literature which was extraordinarily wide for one who was born of English parents. His reading in boyhood and adolescence left almost untouched the novels and poems on which the English public school boy was brought up. Scott, Dickens, Thackeray, Shakespeare, Milton, and Wordsworth were not on the lists of readings which his tutors prescribed, nor did he show any inclination to read the standard English authors. With Dumas, Balzac, and Hugo, however, he had more than a casual familiarity. In his late teens he was to ignore Hugo and Dumas, but to continue his reading in Balzac. By the time that Dumas no longer appealed to him, he had become much interested in Gautier and Musset, and had read considerably in Flaubert, Daudet, and the Goncourt brothers. But his favorite in his late teens was easily Charles Baudelaire, whose *Fleurs du Mal* evidently held him under a prolonged spell. Large gaps were later to appear in his knowledge of French literature, which can be traced to the unsystematic manner in which he pursued his reading, but his comparatively thorough knowledge and sincere enjoyment of French authors were distinguishing characteristics when he went up to Oxford.

Although his sojourns on the Continent were largely in that region of the Riviera in which French is spoken, there were times at which his parents tooks up brief residence in Italy in towns sufficiently distant from the French border to make Italian the common language. With the natural impressionability of a boy, Ernest picked up a considerable Italian vocabulary. As late as February 1893, he told Plarr, whom he had asked to recommend him for a position as a librarian, that he was to mention his knowledge of French and Italian. It is likely, however, that this self-evaluation of his capabilities in the Italian language was the sort of optimistic estimate of proficiency which often appears in letters of recommendation. That he had had at one time a fair grasp of the language is probably true, but with lack of use his Italian could scarely be compared with his French. He never read widely in the Italian authors, nor did he ever show a particular preference for Italian art and life.

To some of his friends of later years he spoke as if he retained more than flitting impressions of the principal cities of Italy, especially Florence and Rome; but his familiarity with Italian art and life could never have been great. His parents did little more than visit Florence and Rome, and he never read widely in the culture history of Italy. His father was a man of sufficient background to indicate the significance of the places through which they traveled; and it may be assumed that the boy was made aware of the historical and intrinsic interest of the chief landmarks in Italian art. There was no effort, however, on the father's part to make of his son an

Italianate Englishman, nor could the boy in the brief intervals in which the Dowsons were in Italy gain more than a superficial knowledge of Italian culture. Some impressions of Italy naturally lingered in his memory, but they were not of the sort which, taken singly or as a whole, would provide a distinguishing characteristic in his personality.

It was while the Dowsons were at Senta that the boy was provided for an interval longer than usual with a tutor, an Italian priest, who was not only an ardent Latinist, but also one who possessed a fine enthusiasm for classical literature. Although too much significance cannot be attached to a tutor's brief influence, the fact remains that the boy began to show a marked proficiency in the Latin tongue, and an increasing enthusiasm for the Roman poets. If it is unlikely that the Italian priest who undertook to teach him Latin introduced him to Catullus and Propertius, who were later to become Dowson's favorites among the ancient poets, the tutor at least made possible the interest which his pupil showed when the works of Catullus and Propertius were introduced to him. Whatever the materials and method which the priest followed, he managed to give the boy an excellent foundation in the Latin language and to stimulate an interest in Roman literature. In spite of the fact that *Vitae summa brevis spem nos vetat incohare longam* and *Non sum qualis eram bonae sub regno Cynarae* were far from the boy's mind as he translated generous passages from the simpler classics for his tutor, Dowson was laying the foundation and learning the phrases which were later to be put to apt use in his own verse.

His father encouraged and helped him with the study of Latin literature, for he believed with many of his generation that a solid foundation in Latin was not only a mark of culture but fundamental to intellectual development and attainment. It is remarkable, however, that the boy, undisciplined and little accustomed to assiduous application to anything, attained the proficiency in the language and literature that he did. In fact, his knowledge of Latin literature was sufficiently evident when he went up to Queen's College to cause his tutor at Queen's to suggest that he read for honors. His classmates at Oxford who knew him intimately soon learned of his exceptional knowledge of the Roman poets and his proficiency in the language. Oscar Wilde, it has been reported, respected Dowson's erudition largely because he believed that Dowson held a superior knowledge of Latin literature; and Lionel Johnson, whose attainments in the classical tongues were considerable, found Dowson a kindred spirit, especially in their bond of interest in the ancient poets. Those who knew Johnson and Dowson well in the early years of the 'nineties recall many a heated discussion in Johnson's rooms in which he and Dowson upheld the merits

of their favorite Roman poets. Dowson could readily hold his own with
Johnson in such discussions, quoting stanza and line with surprising fluency
in order to support and illustrate his judgments. Among many of the
members of the Rhymers' Club, Dowson was regarded as a young man of
scholarly attainments on account of his apparently wide familiarity with
Latin literature.

It is idle to try to determine to what extent his reading of the ancient
poets shaped his inclination to write verse. Before he had gone up to
Queen's, when he had just turned nineteen, he had finished a piece, "Potnia
Thea," which with its references to the Cronian Zeus, the Delian barque,
and Paphos' groves undoubtedly drew much of its inspiration from classical
themes. In his later work there are themes, or at least suggestions, which
he took directly from his reading of Vergil, Catullus, Propertius, and
Horace. He himself told his friend Smith that the lines in the Sixth Book
of the *Æneid:*

> *Discedam, explebo numerum, reddarque tenebris.*
> *I decus, i, nostrum: melioribus utere fatis.*

inspired him to write a sonnet. It has been suggested that the Horatian
phrase *Non sum qualis eram bonae sub regno Cynarae* from the first Ode
of the Fourth Book was the sole genesis for the justly famous Cynara poem.
Plarr observed that the poem was suggested to Dowson "by the Cinara of
Horace, celebrated in Book IV of the Odes. . . . Horace suggested, but
Propertius inspired." And Horace's line *Vitae summa brevis spem nos
vetat incohare longam* in the fourth Ode of Book One undoubtedly suggested in part the exquisite poem which begins "They are not long, the
weeping and the laughter."

An examination of his verse indicates that he was inspired on occasion
not only by the themes of the ancients, but also by their manner. Much
has been observed concerning Dowson's classical restraint, and the peculiarly
Latin brevity and clarity in his verse. It is true that there is nothing in
Dowson's work which corresponds to the lushness of Wilde's *The Sphinx,*
or the adjective-laden lines of Arthur Symons' early poems. Dowson's
verse is marked by dignity, simplicity, and clarity, virtues which have often
been referred to as classical. It is likely that Dowson's admiration for the
Roman poets led him to cultivate deliberately their manner. There is ample
evidence to support the notion that his admiration for them was of the
sort which would lead to imitation. Plarr, amongst others, believed that
from youth he strove consciously after the manner of his favorites until it
grew to be a natural characteristic of his style. All of this has ample support,

but the description of Dowson as "the belated counterpart of Catullus, Propertius and the rest" is a large order for any one poet to fill. An examination of Dowson's works in their entirety will convince most readers that any phrase which names Dowson as the "belated counterpart" of any or all of the Roman poets needs considerable modification. The Latin Ernest Dowson was a part of him, no doubt—a part which has been adequately recognized; but such labels as "a nineteenth-century Catullus" are both inadequate and misleading. Dowson enjoyed the Roman poets during an impressionable period in his development, and in their works he found much to admire and imitate until it became his own; but although his familiarity with the Roman poets was one of his distinguishing traits when he went up to Oxford, he was far from being the result of their exclusive influence and was much less of a Latinist than his classmates at Queen's generally believed him.

His reading of French and Latin authors, however, did little to stimulate curiosity in other fields. In the sort of information which was part of every English schoolboy's common knowledge he showed no interest, nor was he given much opportunity to cultivate interest. In later years, his friends were often startled at the wide gaps in his education. Although the poets of the *fin de siècle* were generally disdainful of encyclopedic information, Dowson's ignorance of the common facts of history, geography, and natural science was conspicuous even among the young men of Bloomsbury who preferred patchouli to roses. Plarr recalled that Dowson's ideas of the French Revolution were confined to the belief that the aristocrats died like great gentlemen, wearing satin clothes with red roses in their lapels. To one of his friends, Dowson was to comment wonderingly on another's habit of reading history. His ingenuous notions concerning the great men of the past often gave his acquaintances of later years considerable amusement. The fact that his great-uncle, Alfred Dommet, had been Prime Minister of New Zealand did nothing to stimulate Ernest's interest in government or in England's far-flung possessions. Nor did his father's business at the Dock, where ships passed flying the flags of a score of nations, tempt him to inform himself about foreign lands. He told Plarr that it would be unsafe to visit America on account of the wild Indians who greatly outnumbered the whites; and to Charles Conder, who had lived in Australia, he remarked that the Island Continent was the sort of place in which any Englishman might feel supreme, since most of the native population was pygmy.

In spite of the fact that in his youth he was largely detached from the atmosphere of large cities, he showed no interest in nature. Later, he was to enjoy walking in the country, probably because on his walks he could escape from his surroundings and in part from himself; but in his youth he had no inclination to roam about the fields and woods. Names of trees and flowers appear occasionally in his verse and prose tales, but they are with few exceptions the blooms of books and vases rather than those of the out-of-doors. Dowson's lilies, asphodels, and violets have none of the dew of the garden upon them; they are only a part of a remote background. He liked the word "violet," but it was for the sound of the word rather than for the fragrance and beauty of the flower. The roses which he "flung riotously with the throng" were only symbols to him, not flowers whose velvety petals moved him to joy. Nature for him, said Agnes Rothery, "was only a dreamy symbol of sentiment." On his walks in the country with his friends at Oxford and later, he was frequently to amuse them by the bookish names he inaccurately applied to common trees, flowers, and birds; and by his notions of the menaces which were lurking in every forest. Plarr recalled how Dowson, while walking in the country with him, saw an innocent newt crossing the road. Dowson announced that it was a venemous reptile, and after finding a heavy stick, he proceeded to belabor the harmless little lizard, which escaped unhurt in the sand. He kept the stick in case another of its kind lay in his path, and implored Plarr to protect himself in a similar fashion.

Other pronounced gaps appeared in his training, one of which should at least be suggested. Although he was tutored by a priest for a time, the boy learned no Ave Marias, no Decalogue, no biblical tales. His parents nominally were of the Church of England, but in the Dowson home there were no devotional rites enacted and no insistence on any formal mode of worship. In fact, there was no moral code in the home save a vague sort of application of the Golden Rule. Although the Golden Rule, if conscientiously applied, is sufficient to make many a man noble and strong in virtue, the fact remains that some form of religion is beneficial in homes in which children are trained. The point need not be labored, but it can be observed that Ernest Dowson's boyhood would have been better ordered, and possibly his character would have been strengthened had some creed been professed, even had that creed been burdened with the weight of dogma. Such a suggestion implies no brief for any particular creed, but rather a willingness to believe that some creed, even if mumbled uncomprehendingly, may give to a boy an instinctive feeling of security and peace.

"All these fluctuations and agonies of a hypersensitive, morbid childhood with Hebraic traditions are to me incomprehensible," he wrote to Plarr. Natural religion was "a phase, which at no time of my life have I ever undergone or understood." We have his own word to support the observation that he was never concerned with either formal dogma or natural religion in his youth, but there is no word of his to indicate that his "pagan" childhood was carefree on account of his freedom from religious training. If he escaped the morbidness which sometimes is the by-product of a too earnest devotion to religion in youth, he also missed the discipline and the instinctive feeling of security which are usually part of an intelligently moderated religious training.

If he missed the advantages which are the result of religious training, he missed even more the discipline and the give-and-take which might have come from companionship with boys of his own age. To his brother Rowland who was eight years younger, he could not turn for the companionship which a growing boy needs on account of the disparity in their ages. Of his cousins, Spencer and Dulcie Secretan, and the Hooles, he saw little. If the sonnet, "In Memoriam," to H.C. who died on February 24, 1886, is to be taken literally, he had a boyhood companion whose death touched him deeply; but the friendship could not have been of long intimacy or of the sort which brings lightness of heart. The consciousness of his parents' illness and worries would have been mitigated had he been surrounded in his impressionable years by hearty companions. But the Dowsons changed their place of residence so frequently in both England and France that the boy had little opportunity to moke more than passing friendships. Change was always imminent; and in spite of the advantages which came from a constantly shifting scene, the frequent change of address of his parents gave the boy little to which to tie his affections and interests. His roots could never become strong in one soil, for he was continually being transplanted. Shifting scenes probably kept his attention from being constantly fastened on his parents' troubles, but they denied him the opportunity of being a boy among boys and of strengthening his affections and ambitions in a permanent province. An illuminating picture of Ernest's boyhood appears in Lewis Swan's letter to his daughter Madeleine: "When I visited them [the Dowsons] at Ilfracombe in December, 1880, Ernest was a good-looking, rather shy boy of fourteen, studious, thoughtful and of a serious disposition. . . . He was a sweet but very odd child—taught himself his letters and would lie in bed reading to himself when only six years old. He was spoiled to death—and had no advantages and it's wonderful he did what he did."

By the autumn of 1886, when he had passed his nineteenth birthday, he was widely read for one of his age in Latin and French literature, he had read a few of the English poets with keen enjoyment, and he had a fairly large storehouse of miscellaneous impressions which had come to him from his travels on the Continent. In general information, especially of the sort which becomes part of English public school boys, he was noticeably deficient; and of orderliness and discipline he had nothing. His plans for a profession and the future were vague. The nature of his life and training had left him with no great consuming ambition to reach any of the goals conventionally set by English boys of his class.

The shifting scenes and irregular training of his youth, however, permitted and probably abetted an interest in literature which had come to him in large measure from his father. The instinct to write, which came to him we know not how, evidently was fostered rather than curbed by the life he had followed. There is no record of when he first showed an aptitude with his pen, but as early as August 1886, he had written poems which he was carefully copying into a notebook which he used exclusively for his poetry. It is unlikely that his plan to keep his poems in a notebook and his first efforts with verse were simultaneous. Although the poems which he first copied into the notebook are undated, one can readily believe that at least some of them were written long before the plan of keeping his verse in a collection was carried out.

That he followed a chronological order in copying his poems into the notebook is disproved by the fact that Number Four of a series of sonnets entitled "Sonnets of a Little Girl" which he placed on page 14 in his collection he dated 1885, whereas the poem entitled "Potnia Thea," which appeared on page 5, he dated August 1886. There is no means of determining when he wrote Number One of the "Sonnets of a Little Girl," but it seems reasonable to conclude that he had finished it before Number Four, which he dated 1885. With the exception of Number Four of this sequence of eight sonnets, "Potnia Thea" and the sonnet "In Memoriam," dedicated to the unknown H.C. who died on February 24, 1886, there is nothing to indicate the time of writing of the first thirty-four entries. Starting with the poem "Transit Gloria," the thirty-fifth entry, he followed a consistent practice of dating all of the poems as he copied them into his notebook. This poem he dated May 19, 1887. It may be concluded, however, that the notebook was started earlier, and that the thirty-four poems which precede "Transit Gloria" were written in some instances as early as 1885 and possibly earlier. Some of his friends of later years have reported that it was always their impression that Dowson had started to write verse in his middle teens.

Too much significance, however, need not be attached to the particular time at which the earliest poems were written. Until additional evidence can be provided, it is enough to observe that by 1886, or at the latest, May 19, 1887, Dowson was sufficiently conscious of his talents to keep a manuscript book into which he apparently copied only the poems which satisfied him. The variety in theme and manner of the poems which come before "Transit Gloria" indicates plainly that his inspiration was dependent on no momentous event in his life, or on no single literary influence. Sonnets, four-line stanzaic schemes, and verse-patterns with refrains appear among the thirty-four early entries; and the themes, save for the sequence of "Sonnets of a Little Girl," show considerable variety.

The quality of the early entries varies to such an extent that were it not for their position in the notebook, one might readily believe that they were written at widely different periods in the poet's life. Such a piece as "Potnia Thea" is plainly immature, whereas the lovely poem "A Mosaic," with its sentiment which suggests Francis Thompson's "Daisy," and the series of eight "Sonnets of a Little Girl"—especially Number Eight—are undoubtedly on a plane with his finest mature work. In fact, were it not that Number Four of these sonnets appeared in *London Society* in November 1886, its chronological position in the notebook might readily be questioned. When it is borne in mind that his sonnet sequence, and at least five of the other entries were written by a boy who was not more than eighteen, their merit and beauty become even more remarkable.

His interest in literature and talent in poetry were evidently sufficiently pronounced to cause his father to consider the advantages which might come to him from university training. Obviously the boy lacked discipline and the sort of education which the sons of men of his class possessed. It is probable, too, that Ernest had shown an increasing curiosity in what other young men of similar interests were doing. Application was made for a scholarship, which, as Alfred Dowson probably knew, his son had small chance of obtaining with the irregular preparation he had received. The Jodrell Scholarship at Queen's College, Oxford, went to another; but at Michaelmas Term, 1886, Ernest Dowson matriculated as a commoner at Queen's.

II

FIVE TERMS AT OXFORD

U NTIL W. R. Thomas contributed his article "Ernest Dowson at Oxford" to *The Nineteenth Century* in October 1928, Dowson's sojourn at Queen's College, like his youth, was regarded generally as a veiled period. Arthur Symons in his memoir of the poet dismissed this period in Dowson's life with a single sentence, which, besides being inadequate, is misleading; and Victor Plarr, who knew him well at the time immediately following his departure from Queen's, reported briefly and inaccurately: "He received no regular education, unless we count his one half-mythic year at college." It was Plarr who referred to his college days as "his mysterious sojourn at Queen's. . . ." W. R. Thomas, however, who was one of Dowson's friends at Queen's, did much to correct the impressions left by Symons and Plarr, and to recall Dowson's life at college in more detail. Arthur Moore and Sam Smith, both of whom were students at Queen's while Dowson was there, have added to the information which is now available concerning his stay at the University. Additional investigations, made among tutors and students who were at Queen's during the late 'eighties, have not been fruitless. Dowson's "one half-mythic year at college" has under investigation become five terms in which his movements, in outline at least, are fairly clear.

Why his father selected Queen's as the college to which Ernest should go is a question which cannot be answered. It can only be assumed that Alfred Dowson had some association with the college, not as an alumnus, but through friends who had made Queen's College their Alma Mater. One of Dowson's friends of later years, who is often given to extremes, reported that "Queen's was a poor, lousy sort of place when Dowson went up"; and Compton Mackenzie has one of his characters in *Sinister Street* refer to the college as "that terra incognita." It is true that no celebrities had come out of Queen's in the days immediately preceding Dowson's going up, and that the boys who lived in the back quadrangle were scarcely of the fashionable set; but despite its small endowment in the late decades of the nineteenth century, the college numbered among its faculty and students men of substance and intellect.

Dr. Magrath was provost at the time, and T. W. Allen and E. M. Walker were fellows. They represented the more conservative thought of the time; they were sincerely convinced of the unmixed good of the Oxford system of training young men to become familiar with the classics, to discipline their minds through the proper application to detail, and to make them responsive to their obligations to home, church and country. Although the pattern was not rigidly applied, their standards were set; and if anyone was unwilling or unable to conform to the established order, he was soon made to feel that the University had nothing to offer him. The attitude of the lectures and tutors toward the individual students varied. Some of them were almost unaware of the existence of extraordinary personalities in their student body, while others were evidently interested in the individuals who made up the college roll. Mr. Allen, when inquiry was made of him concerning his recollections of Dowson, replied: "Yes, I knew such a person. His private life will not bear investigation." Dr. Walker, however, who was to become a distinguished lecturer in the years following Dowson's sojourn, recalled the young man intimately and sympathetically, and spoke as if he had always been concerned about him. If Dowson was ever an object of Magrath's attention, there is no record of it, and there can be no testimony now from this source.

The conservative thought fostered by the faculty at Queen's College found willing disciples among many of the students, but by 1886 there had entered into Oxford at large a questioning spirit which was not always in harmony with the tenets of the traditionalists. The University had always had its liberals, but as the century began to draw to a close their ranks increased until the tone of Oxford was more frequently echoed in its questionings than in its serene discipleship to the established order. Oxford of the 'eighties, Plarr observed, "was pessimistic; it affected here and there to worship Buddha, and it read its Schopenhauer and much else." Although there were those who still seized upon Pippa's Song in the Browning poem as their refuge, and who presumed "not God to scan," the more active minds among the undergraduates were not given to the recitation of the last lines of Tennyson's "Crossing the Bar" as a prologue to their discussions. The issue of the attempted reconciliation of the discoveries of science and the faith of the fathers had penetrated Oxford, leaving in its path a considerable group of agnostics and pessimists. What Hardy had so poignantly declared in "Hap," "Nature's Questioning," and "The Impercipient" was seeking expression in the minds and discussions of many young men who were never to read the *Wessex Poems*. Schopenhauer evidently helped to crystallize undergraduate opinions into convictions; and finding little of their faith in dogmatic religion and the ultimate good unshattered, many young men began to turn to the arcana of Oriental shrines for temporary distraction or for something to which to tie, while others gave themselves over to cynicism and atheism. There were others among this questioning group who, after becoming aware of the spiritual and intellectual plight into which their inquiries had led them, turned abruptly from further questioning and embraced the Roman Catholic faith. This group had become sufficiently large at Oxford to constitute a movement.

There was another force at work at the University during the late decades of the century which was in large measure the result of the prevalent inclination to question the primary cause of man's existence. The esthetic movement, which undoubtedly strengthened its roots in Oxford soil, might readily be considered an outgrowth of the pessimism which Schopenhauer had clarified for the mind of the age. Estheticism as a philosophy held out a marked appeal to minds which were convinced that there was no promise of a hereafter and that life was in general abhorrent. If there were no promise of a hereafter, the proper cultivation of beauty could provide an avenue of escape from the ugliness and cruelty of a material world. And in its careful cultivation, it could become more than an escape: it could become a constructive philosophy which would transcend mere hedonism. Stoicism and asceticism were rejected largely by reason of the fact that young men are poor disciples of any philosophy which demands resignation. Estheticism seemed a more positive sort of agency for immediate happiness than the other avenues which presented themselves; and furthermore, by a sincere application to the constructive esthetic principle, man could not only escape from the ugliness of life, but make life less ugly for humanity at large.

It was Walter Pater was had given to a considerable group of young men at Oxford their slogans and creed. Oscar Wilde, who had taken his double first at Magdalen in the 'seventies, exercised a limited influence on a small group in the years following the publication of his *Poems* in 1881; but Wilde cannot be named as the standard bearer and the chief inspiration of the group who embraced an esthetic philosophy in the 'eighties. His poems were never widely circulated at the University, nor were his personality and literary creed the topic for much discussion. It was Pater's *Marius the Epicurean,* and his discussions of the utility of beauty as an agency for full living which clarified and intensified the doctrines which many undergraduates were ready to adopt. The crassness of a seething utilitarian world could be both mitigated and corrected by the proper cultivation of beauty.

In spite of the fact that Schopenhauer and Pater were providing a considerable amount of the intellectual nourishment for Oxford students in the 'eighties, the old order was far from being broken down. The quadrangles continued to echo with the shouts of boys who were sufficiently young to put their pessimism out of mind when a boat race was in the offing and when examinations were near. No matter what they had concluded in their discussions of religion among themselves, most of the undergraduates were willing to conform to the traditional ideals of the University. In fact, the very boys who had argued against the dogma of religion were often the ones who sat most meekly in chapel, and those who had insisted that life was abhorrent were frequently frank in their expression of a joy in life. Much of the pessimism and the discipleship to cults was experimental rather than a firmly rooted, living philosophy; and it was only among the very impressionable students and those who belonged to no established tradition that the cults of Oxford had more than temporary appeal. Undoubtedly much of the tone of the University had penetrated the back quadrangle at Queen's in spite of the fact that no one figure or movement was outstanding, but Queen's College represented the more conservative colleges, and student thought during the period followed closely the traditional ideals of the University.

When Ernest Dowson walked down High Street on October 25, 1886, to present himself for matriculation, he had just turned nineteen. He had attained a height of about five feet and seven inches, and a weight which did not exceed one hundred and twenty pounds. Dark brown hair grew over a forehead which was narrow though high, beneath which large hazel eyes were set somewhat closely together. The mouth and chin showed sensitivity rather than strength, as did his unusually long hands. Slightly stooped in posture and of small breadth of shoulder, he gave the impression to those before whom he appeared to matriculate that he was not strong. E. M. Walker reported that he looked ill from the time he arrived until he went down. Although there were no positive signs of disease, the pallor of his countenance, his slight frame, and his mannerisms set him apart from the other students.

The basis for his admission to the college was clear neither to those who were to become his friends nor to those who now devise the standards for matriculation examinations. If Lionel Johnson had to be coached in "smalls" before he could take "mods," Dowson was surely in a worse state of academic deficiency at the time of his matriculation. It is barely possible that at his father's direction and with the prospect of a Jodrell Scholarship he had made a frantic last-minute effort to fill out some of the gaps which had resulted from his irregular training; but it is more likely that his admission to Queen's was based not on the results of an intensive period of cramming but on his attainments in French and Latin, and on recommendations concerning his literary interests. Apparently the basis for admission as a commoner in the 'eighties was sufficiently flexible to allow students to matricualte without a preparatory school training or its equivalent. One of Dowson's friends of later years had observed that "Dowson would never have gone up had he been forced to take matrics."

The lack of formal education of the public school sort evidently offered no great handicap to his studies at the University, but the irregular training he had received presented drawbacks which were equally important. His unfamiliarity with boys of his own age and their ways made him appear shy and unresponsive. If he seemed unfriendly to his fellows at the start, it was because he was unfamiliar with their ways and ideals. His apparent distaste for company was the result of his sensitivity. Boys of his own age who had been trained in the public schools and in the security of substantial British homes existed in a different sphere from his. Of their games he knew little, and, as a result, it was difficult for him to share their lively interest. To one who had been virtually detached from participation in the traditional English sports, it seemed unusual if not altogether tedious to show enthusiasm over the manner in which a boy kicked an inflated ball. The competitive instinct was almost totally lacking in his nature. This indifference to the outcome of a contest or struggle he probably inherited from his father, and during his youth there had been small opportunity for him to cultivate the sort of satisfaction which comes when one measures his brawn and skill against another's. He had learned to play tennis, possibly on the Riviera, a game at which he never developed proficiency and in which he was unwilling to exert himself to win.

Then, too, the boys with whom he came into contact during his early weeks at Queen's were as unfamiliar with the books which he had read as he was with their favorites. This is no damaging charge against the quality of his reading, for the books with which he was familiar were in most instances of the sort about which only those of literary background and taste were informed. And with the small topics of conversation which interested his fellows he was generally not concerned. Those who recall their impressions of him during the months immediately after his arrival have reported that he seemed different from his classmates, but in no way insensible to their company or interests. He would stand on the outskirts of their circles, listening to what was being discussed, with a strange little smile on his face which some mistook for irony and others interpreted as a sort of envy that he was unable to participate in their talk. Although some of their talk probably sounded inconsequential to him, he was not patronizing in his attitude toward their conversations; it is likely that the smile which some of his fellows detected had more of polite attentiveness in it than irony.

Although he was not the sort to be given to homesickness, for he had often been left alone or with relatives by his parents, he must have been lonely in the early weeks after his arrival at Queen's by reason of the unfamiliarity with the scene into which he had been so abruptly thrust. His room in an attic at the top of Number Five, back quadrangle, had little save its detachment from the coming and going in the rooms on the lower floors to distinguish it. In fact, the attic rooms of the back quadrangle were so detached from the commotion on the lower floors and from faculty supervision that students who lived at the top were often tempted to violate the dormitory regulations on account of their infrequently visited quarters. Dr. Walker has told me of how a student in one of the attic rooms kept a dog with him for a whole year before he was finally discovered by a proctor. The dog ate and slept in plain view in the room, and after the proctors had retired for the night, the student allowed the dog to run on the roof between the windows and the high balustrade. Attic rooms, by reason of their detachment, were often the scene of merrymaking; but during Dowson's early months in the back quad he was generally alone when he reached the top of Number Five.

The low-ceilinged rooms were neither commodious nor well appointed. His parents had given little thought to his comfort at college, and he had neither the money nor the inclination to affect tastes which were foreign to his nature. In fact, it was an uncle, Alexander Swan, known as Uncle Sandie, who gave Ernest £20 to met his matriculation expenses. His collection of books was small and without especial interest. For rare and beautiful editions, he evidently had no particular desire. The walls of his quarters had nothing to distinguish them in pictures or tapestries; and his tea set was the sort which could be procured at the shops which had a parasitical existence near the College. No rare incense burned in the attic of Number Five, nor were there odds and ends from his travels on the Continent which would add warmth and personality to the rooms. It was the general impression of those who were later to come to Dowson's attic for an evening of talk that he had just moved in or that he was about to move out. Evidently the habit of traveling light to which he had become accustomed during his sojourns in France persisted in his Oxford days

His quarters were by no means uncomfortable or barren, but they lacked the decorations and knick-knacks which usually gladdened the heart of an undergraduate.

The detachment of the attic in Number Five probably had advantages to its occupant, for he was not only unconcerned with much that was going on in the rooms below, but he was also engaged with literary projects which had no particular bearing on university life. The month after his arrival at Oxford, *London Society,* a literary periodical of fairly wide circulation, in its November issue printed a poem entitled "Sonnet—To a Little Girl" under which stood the initials E.C.D. Its lines indicate more than excellent workmanship in the Shakespearean sonnet form. In them there are depth of sentiment and a feeling for word and image. This sonnet, which is listed as Number Four in a sequence of eight poems, was the only one of the series which was printed during Dowson's lifetime, with the exception of Number Eight, which appeared in the November issue of *The Savoy,* 1896, and was later included in *Decorations* in 1899. The others, all of which were written in 1885-86, remained unpublished until 1934, when Mr. Desmond Flower included them in his edition of Dowson's poems. With the possible exception of Number Eight, none of them is more representative of Dowson's early work than the sonnet which appeared in *London Society.*

> Even as a child whose eager fingers snatch
> An ocean shell and hold it to his ear,
> With wondering, awe-struck eyes is hushed to catch
> The murmuring music of its coilèd sphere;
> Whispers of wind and wave, soul-stirring songs
> Of storm-tossed ships and all the mystery
> That to the illimitable sea belongs,
> Stream to him from its tiny cavity.
> As such an one with reverent awe I hold
> Thy tender hand, and in those pure grey eyes,
> That sweet child face, those tumbled curls of gold,
> And in thy smiles and loving, soft replies
> I find the whole of love—hear full and low
> Its mystic ocean's tremulous ebb and flow.

In Dowson's manuscript book the poem is dated 1885. That the sonnet was written by a boy of eighteen makes it remarkable not only in that there is a demonstration of mastery of the form, but also in that the theme is scarcely of the sort which one expects from a very young man. The general theme underlying the sequence, with the exception of Number Eight, is the beauty of innocence. Such a sentiment has found expression in many poets, including Wordsworth and Francis Thompson. It is not difficult to find an explanation for Wordsworth's use of the theme, or to understand Thompson's wistful response to little girls which is illustrated in "Daisy" and "Sister Songs," for Thompson at the time he met the child who inspired "Daisy," saw in himself one from whom all innocence had fled and who was sadly refreshed by the charm of little girls. But for a boy of eighteen to find "the whole of love" in the soft replies of a child, and hold children in such reverence, is unusual in that young men—especially those who have been nurtured on Baudelaire's *Fleurs du Mal* and Swinburne's "Dolores"—are rarely concerned with the appeal of innocence.

Were it not for the fact that Dowson returned to this theme in both his verse and prose, and that episodes in his later life bear out the sentiment and conviction expressed in the sonnets, one might be tempted to believe that this poem and the others in the sequence were little more than a well handled literary exercise. The suggestion that Number Four was only a sort of *façon de parler* would gain support by recalling Edgar Jepson's remark that there was a cult of little girls at Oxford during the 'eighties. The students, so Jepson recalled, were in the habit of taking the professors' small daughters on the River and inviting them to tea. Little girls were the mascots, they appeared at student rituals and celebrations, and they were generally held in an esteem which Oxford knew neither before nor since. This cult of little girls was not confined only to Oxford. Stevenson's letters from Mentone during the mid-seventies show how completely he had been captivated by the eight-year-old May Johnstone. "Kids are what is the matter with me," he confided to his mother. William Ernest Henley's adoration of little girls was well known among his contemporaries; and even George Meredith was known to walk far out of his way so that he could listen for a while to the prattle of little girls. If one were so inclined, one could present quite a formidable list of literary figures of the late nineteenth century who were unable to resist the unaffected charm of little girls, and who gave expression in prose and verse to their pleasure in being with them.

Dowson's sonnets in which he celebrated the beauty of innocence, however, were written largely before he had been influenced by any existing cult at Oxford. Furthermore, the authors who were his favorites at the time at which he was writing the sequence gave him neither the inspiration nor the model for the sentiments which found expression in Number Four and the others. It is also to be observed that had Dowson written these

poems as an imitative exercise, or as the spokesman of an undergraduate
cult, he probably would have emerged from the stage of mere imitation
and carried his offerings in time to other shrines. The beauty of innocence,
however, was not a passing source of inspiration. In his most mature works
he returned again and again to its ennobling power. It is possible that some
of his reverence for little girls was affected somewhat by what Jepson
called a cult, but there is nothing to indicate that Dowson's regular homage
to childhood was other than a sincere expression of his instinctive trust
in the power and beauty of innocence.

Until more adequate records of the period in Dowson's life at which
the sonnets were written are discovered, it is idle to try to determine the
specific sources of inspiration for the poem. Although the sequence was
grouped in his manuscript book under the general title "Sonnets of a
Little Girl," there is no dedicatory note, nor is there anything to indicate
where they were written. Line eight of Number Four might indicate that
it was childhood at large which appealed to him, for here in the early half
of the sonnet, the child is a boy. It is only in Number Two that there is a
direct reference to a little girl. The fact that there is a consistency in the
description of the child's features—grey eyes and golden hair appear twice
in the series—may or may not indicate that there was a specific source of
inspiration for the sequence. That he had a child with such features in mind
when he wrote the poems is no more likely than that he drew a composite
though concrete ideal as the child in whom he found "the whole of love,"
and who was his "amulet . . . ritual . . . and mystic prayer." Whereas many
of his friends inquired of him concerning the source of inspiration of the
Cynara poem, no one apparently questioned him about the little girl who
inspired the sonnets, probably owing to the fact that all save one of the
poems were for his eyes alone in his manuscript book.

Although his classmates were soon to learn that he wrote verse and
prose, he evidently did not take any of them into his confidence concerning
the poetry he had written and continued to write, or concerning its source
of inspiration. He who felt the strangeness of his new surroundings keenly
was not inclined toward self-revelation. During the autumn months he
stood on the outskirts of the student circles, listening attentively but without trying to cultivate friendships, and then going to his attic at the top
of Number Five to look across Queen Lane at the tower and cemetery of
St. Peter in the East before settling down at the well-worn table to write
on the story which he had under way, or to revise a poem.

Sometime during the winter he finished a poem which, curiously
enough, he did not copy out in his manuscript book, but which he sent in

to *London Society* with encouraging results. In March 1887, *London Society* printed "Moritura."

> A song of the setting sun!
> The sky in the west is red,
> And the day is all but done;
> While yonder up overhead
> Ah, too soon!
> There rises—so cold—the cynic moon.
>
> A song of a Winter day!
> The wind of the north doth blow,
> From a sky that's chill and grey,
> On fields, where no crops now grow—
> Fields long shorn
> Of bearded barley and golden corn.
>
> A song of an old, old man!
> His hairs are white and his gaze
> Long bleared in his visage wan,
> With its weight of yesterdays;
> Joylessly,
> He stands and mumbles and looks at me.
>
> A song of a faded flower!
> 'Twas plucked in the tender bud,
> And fair and fresh for an hour,
> In a lady's hair it stood;
> Now—ah, now,
> Faded it lies in the dust and low.*

In theme and manner, there is little to distinguish these stanzas from mediocrity; and were it not for the fact that they reveal some of the life-weariness which was to become a frequently recurrent sentiment in his later poems, they might be dismissed as an expression of the sort of melancholy which young men at times affect. The "song of a faded flower," however, was to him without artifice; it represents one of his earliest attempts to make articulate a sentiment to which he remained faithful to the end. Although he showed some of the natural vivacity of youth, his associates at Queen's were able to detect a tiredness in his manner which a few mistook for diffidence and indolence.

Before the first term was spent, Dowson had attracted the attention of

---

* This poem was later included in *Decorations: in Verse and Prose*, 1899. Dowson made a few slight changes in the punctuation and wording for its second appearance.

many of his classmates and a few of the second-year students. One day in the late autumn as W. R. Thomas was crossing the back quad, which was known among the students as the Rabbit Warren, Arthur Moore overtook him to ask abruptly, "Have you met Dowson?" When Thomas replied that he had not, but that he was interested in knowing what the extraordinary fellow was like, Moore agreed to arrange for a meeting. Moore recalls that he first talked with Dowson over a game of whist, into which Dowson had been drawn possibly by reason of the fact that a fourth man was needed. Moore wrote in a letter to me:

I well remember that, after the final rubber, Dowson and I adjourned to my rooms (over the Taberdar's Room in the back quadrangle), and that it was daybreak before he left me. I believe that we discussed little else but Henry James on that occasion; and I recall that it was not long after that I read a paper on the subject of this author to a College Literary Society (the "Addison") of which we were both members.

This was the beginning of a friendship which was mutually profitable, for they were later to collaborate on two novels, and to remain friends and fairly frequent correspondents until the time of Dowson's death. Then, too, it was the beginning of Dowson's first attempt to mingle freely with young men of his own age who professed literary interests.

Soon after the meeting between Thomas and Dowson had been arranged, a small luncheon club was formed which included Moore, Thomas, and Sam Smith, who was later to translate *Lysistrata,* to which Dowson came regularly in spite of the fact that most of the group were second-year men. The members of this informally organized club took turns at playing host; and when the time came for Dowson to take his turn, he received his new acquaintances graciously. Although he did little to lead or direct the conversation, he spoke without shyness and with a certain dignity about the topics on which he had something to contribute. When the subject of conversation shifted to a province in which he had slight information or interest, he sat silent, with his strange little smile which some mistook for patronage, but which was in reality his only way of showing attention.

His conversational accomplishments at the gatherings of the luncheon club and the other groups with whom he mingled during his stay at Queen's were without particular distinction. Though with small gift for paradox and epigram, he was keenly appreciative of neatly turned phrases. Frank Harris, who was later to see much of him in London, reported: "Any curious, arresting epithet pleased him beyond measure. I said something about 'eventful originality' at which he jumped up and clapped his hands and crowed with delight, repeating again and again 'eventful . . . eventful

originality!' " Such a demonstration of appreciation of an arresting epithet
was unusual with Dowson, for his responses to strikingly apt phrases were
generally more mildly expressed, but he had more than an ordinary pleasure
in witty and brilliant talk. His own talk, however, showed no effort to be
either witty or profound. When he was genuinely interested in the topic
under discussion there was a spirited quality in his talk which had in it
boyish enthusiasm and an ingratiating determination to make himself clear.
His voice, never strong, became high-pitched in moments of rising earnestness; and his laugh was neither musical nor contagious. Like his smile, his
laugh was often mistaken for an expression of patronage, for it rarely
suggested mirth. But he was good company by reason of the earnestness
with which he discussed his opinions and the attentiveness with which he
listened to others who conversed about topics in which he had only mild
interest. Late in his life he often appeared distracted when anything which
had no immediate bearing on his interests was discussed, but during his
Oxford days he was a gracious participant in all manner of conversations.

His attentiveness to what his acquaintances discussed was the result of
his innate good breeding and his eagerness to become more familiar with
the ways and ideals of young men of his own age. By the end of the first
term, he had acclimated himself in some measure to the Oxford air. The
feeling of being different from his fellows was rapidly being submerged
in the interest which he began to share with his acquaintances of the
luncheon club. Away from the atmosphere of a home which had often
been depressing, he began to show the natural vivacity of youth; and before
the first term was spent, he had a nodding acquaintance with most of his
classmates, and a feeling of friendliness for a few with whom he had exchanged more than casual remarks. He learned from them the essentials
of good sportsmanship, and began to experience the thrill which comes
from the expression of loyalty to one's school. He never became the typical
undergraduate, but before the first year was out he adorned himself in
Queen's blazer, striped flannels, and washing tie; walked out on occasion
in a brown bowler and spats; ran with his college boat on the towpath; and
yelled "Stop that cab" with the zest of the most loyal Queen's man.

After some of the strangeness of his new environment had worn off he
seemed eager to adapt himself to the Oxford pattern. The process of
adaptation—a new experience for him—was in itself agreeable and salutary. The year at Queen's, after the early adjustments were made, was
undoubtedly one of the few happy experiences in his life. Thoughts of
past and future were dispelled by the lively interests of the present. The
attic at the top of Number Five no longer seemed detached from the
quadrangle below; some of the students who moved across the paths were

his friends, ones who had sat in his rooms for long hours talking with him
about topics in which he was vitally interested. Here Moore, Thomas, and
Smith often came to air their views on this book or that lecture; and here
the philosophical creeds which appealed to undergraduates were examined
in the light of their limited experience along with a consideration of the
chances the Queen's boat had of defeating its chief rivals. The occupant of
the attic atop Number Five was still a figure apart in many ways, but by
the time the grass of the quadrangles had begun to put on its new green,
he was no longer the shy, aloof young fellow who had walked up to the
Domestic Bursar in the sere days of Michaelmas Term.

There is more than a faint resemblance to Dowson at Oxford in the
character of Adrian Rome, a personality which Arthur Moore and Dowson
were later to portray in their second novel. If Moore's memory has not
failed him, it was he, not Dowson, who described Adrian Rome in Chapter Three of the novel as follows:

A striking personality, and in many ways a puzzling man: it has been said of
him with some shrewdness by a keen observer, that in whatever country he might
find himself, he would pass for a foreigner: and yet—although this may sound
inconsistent—there was in Adrian Rome, physically no less than morally, material for the making of a good cosmopolitan. . . .

The clock in the little belfry above the college chapel chimed the hour, linger-
ing on the notes with the gentle deliberation of old age, making its warning a
hint rather than a command. It was half-past eight, and Rome reminded himself that he had invited one or two of his friends to take coffee with him. On
nodding terms with most of the men of his college, he was intimate with few;
he had not gone out of his way to make friends, and it was one of the defects
(advantages he might have said) of his education that he had had no early opportunities for forming juvenile intimacies, the chains of which university life
would have welded more closely. He belonged to no camp; he could not have
been classified either as an athlete or a reading man; his set (if indeed he could
have been assigned to anything so definite) was composed rather of the free-
lances of college life, the men who made no great profession of ability, who did
not regard themselves too seriously, who were tolerated, nervously, rather than
approved by the authorities. He belonged to a literary society which showed
symptoms of developing into a whist club, to a whist club which was suspected
of being a society for the encouragement of poker. A member of the Union, he
had been spurred by a moment, a mood, to deliver himself, nervously, of one
brilliant, audacious speech; but he could never be induced to repeat the experiment, or even to propose a motion. . . . Briefly while general repute set him
down as eccentric (without thereby intending a compliment), the few men who
knew him spoke of him as clever, and even as a genius.

ERNEST DOWSON AT OXFORD

It is not difficult to read biography into this portrait of Adrian Rome. Much that Arthur Moore has reported about his friend and collaborator only corroborates one's first impression that the character of Adrian Rome at Oxford was largely Ernest Dowson as Moore saw him at the time of their early association. For Moore, Thomas, Smith, and the others who were to become intimate with him during his first year at Queen's had met him more than halfway, and they were in time to understand the reasons which lay behind his shyness in mingling with his fellows. That Dowson considered his lack of opportunity to form "juvenile intimacies" an advantage rather than a defect cannot be proved, for in spite of the fact that "he had not gone out of his way to make friends" when he came up to Queen's, it was only because he was unfamiliar with the environment into which he had come. His apparent distaste for company at the start was not the result of any conviction that there were advantages in moving about alone; it was rather the result of his diffidence. And although "he belonged to no camp," he began to show an increasing willingness to conform to the Oxford pattern.

The delight of associating with young men who shared some of his interests led him to try to share some of theirs. In his attempt to recognize advantages in the ideals and aspirations of most of his classmates, however, he was frequently unsuccessful. For exact detail, which was part of the Oxford objective, he could not be made to care. It has been said by those who knew him well that he disliked anything in the form of common knowledge, and eschewed the role of deliberately seeking information. The practical advantages of being well informed offered no appeal whatsoever; to him, education was an end in itself, and its worth was largely undermined when it became an agency for penurious or practical ends. Although his tutor rarely stressed the practical advantages which might be derived from the studies his student had undertaken, he did insist on a certain amount of care in Latin composition and on the assimilation of some facts. In a moment of eagerness to fulfill all his obligations to the University, he joined the Union—later to urge Thomas to join since "it was the only place in Oxford where you can wash your hands"—but he took no interest in its affairs. In fact, some of his friends remonstrated with him against his "lamentable indifference towards the affairs of his country."

Although the University was unsuccessful in its efforts to make Dowson a well-informed man, it augmented and fostered the interests which he had cultivated in his youth; and in his application to the studies he liked he found much satisfaction. The Roman poets to whom he had been introduced in the years preceding his matriculation continued to appeal to him; and under the guidance of his tutor, Latin literature took on additional interest and significance. Horace, Catullus, and Propertius became his favorites, and during his first year at Queen's this list was added to until he was familiar with even the minor poets of the Augustan age. His classmates never knew where he had learned his Latin, but report had it that he knew the poets backwards and forwards. The truth of the matter was that his Latin was by no means exact. His prose compositions, Thomas recalled, were done *currente calamo*, and rarely found favor among those who supervised his study. Few men have ever studied Latin from a more cultural angle than Dowson; his study was approached from an entirely different point of view from that which was customary with his classmates. It was the substance of the literature which he sought; for the mental discipline which came from giving nouns their proper case endings he had no patience.

His increasing familiarity with the Roman poets evidently pleased the authorities, for in time they suggested to him that he ought to read for honours. It was unusual at the time to suggest to anyone who had matriculated as a commoner that he read for honours. Only students who had distinguished themselves by ability and sincere interest were considered for such an arrangement. The exact manner in which Dowson distinguished himself for such consideration can only be surmised: his friends have reported that he held a considerable reputation among the more scholarly students at Queen's for his wide knowledge of the Roman poets, his even wider familiarity with French authors, and his sincere interest in literature. That these merits, brought to the attention of the authorities, might lead them to encourage him to read for honours is not unlikely. The prospect of getting out of the commoner class held out a temporary appeal to him, and for a time he seemed entirely willing to try to reach the higher goal.

To get ready for Honours Moderations, however, necessitated a compromise between his notions of what he should follow in his reading and what the authorities prescribed. His reading had been of such a scattered and apparently purposeless nature that it could not be made to fit into a systematic preparation for the examinations. He soon realized that if he were to be prepared for the examinations, he would have to change his tactics in reading and at least modify his notion of what he considered a good education.

There were gaps in many provinces which would have to be filled. His reading in French, although fairly comprehensive, had always been of a sort different from that required of undergraduates. For the French classical dramatists, Corneille, Racine, and Molière, he had never cared much;

and for Rousseau not at all. In his Oxford days he ignored Victor Hugo, but of Gautier, Musset, and Maupassant he was very fond. Guy de Maupassant, he told some of his friends, he had met at one time in France in a country house. The novels of Emile Zola, then pretty much under the ban at Oxford, were especial favorites of his. His friend Thomas recalled that he and Dowson were so much impressed by what they considered the sincerity and power of Zola's *La Terre* that they decided to send the author an unsigned letter of commendation and thanks. If Zola was Dowson's favorite novelist while he was at Oxford, Charles Baudelaire remained easily his favorite French poet. Verlaine, who was later to become his chief inspiration—and in the minds of some of his friends, the chief perverter—was as yet unknown to him. His copy of Baudelaire's *Fleurs du Mal* was filled with marginal notes, all of which indicated that he had read and reread the poems with feeling and discernment. Commendable as such an interest undoubtedly was, it was scarcely of the sort which would fill any of the pronounced gaps which stood between him and adequate preparation for Honours Moderations.

Nor were his interests in English literature of the sort which would lead to successful ratings in the examinations. Ignoring Shakespeare and Ben Jonson, he read John Webster, De Quincey's narratives, Poe's tales and poems, Hawthorne's tales, and the early works of Henry James. Of the English poets Swinburne was his favorite. Thomas reported that it was at Dowson's urgent request that he first read Swinburne. "The Suggestion Book of the Queen's Library still contains a request in my handwriting," said Thomas, "for *Swinburne's Works*. The suggestion dates from that first year of Dowson, and was his own idea. I remember his copy of *Hertha* and *Dolores* heavily scored." "Dolores" was to Dowson at the time one of the finest poems in the language. No doubt he was commended by his tutor for his familiarity with Swinburne and John Webster, but it is probable that Dowson was reminded, albeit indirectly, that his examinations would include questions on figures of more generally recognized worth than those with whom he spent his time.

In the weeks before the Long Vacation, however, his horizon was unclouded. Examinations were in the distant future; he had a few friends with whom he became increasingly intimate; and in the social life of the University he had developed a considerable interest. Thomas observed the "the frugal lunches, wet whist afternoons, and poker evenings suited him well. His health was better than afterwards, and his mental trouble had not seriously beset him." Away from the oppressive atmosphere of his home, he had come to share some of the lightness of heart and mind which surrounded him. "I imagine," said Thomas, "that the year was one of the happiest of his life."

According to the reports of his Oxford contemporaries, however, when he returned to Queen's after the Long Vacation of 1887 he had changed. The light-heartedness which had come as the result of his association with carefree undergraduates had disappeared during the course of the summer. Apparently nothing of significance happened to him during his vacation to cause him to adopt a different attitude toward university life. The vacation was spent largely, if not entirely, in England, chiefly with his parents, whose health and spirits were unchanged. His cousin Spencer Secretan recalls a visit which Dowson made at his home during the summer, and how he and Ernest decorated the lawn of the Secretan home with Japanese lanterns in order to celebrate the Jubilee of 1887. Like many others, Ernest enjoyed the festive spirit which grew out of the occasion without concerning himself greatly about the reason for celebrating. He joined the Secretans in the crowd which watched the procession to Westminster Abbey, and on his return to his cousin's home in Reigate, Surrey, where he evidently visited for some time, he was in the best of spirits. If he was sad and embittered during his visit at Reigate, his cousin saw nothing which suggested unhappiness.

He wrote several poems during the summer, one of which, a sonnet entitled "To Nature," with the subtitle, "Morituri Te Salutant," and dated in the manuscript book August 1887, indicated that he had reached through his reading or experience the belief that Nature was an abhorrent harpy, who was a false mother to her children. In terms more positive than were usual for him, he denounced Nature, and vowed that no song of his should ever celebrate the shameful triumphs of her laws. He was completely aware, he stated, of all of Nature's treachery and vileness; and he would never again be betrayed into believing her beauty other than a mask behind which lurked a malign force. The spirited vindictiveness of the sonnet would suggest that he was indulging in no mere literary exercise in penning its lines, and that his source of inspiration was far more concrete than his reading in the pessimistic philosophers; but no one, including his cousin Spencer Secretan, is able to suggest any substantial reason for his vituperative attack on Nature.

Nor do the letters which he wrote during the summer to his Oxford friends indicate any event or influence which might have embittered him. In his letters to Thomas, he mentioned two short prose narratives which he had finished and was sending to the magazines. The tone of the letters was cheerful and even optimistic in the manner in which he wrote about his prospects of having the stories accepted. To Moore he reported on his reading, in which there had been nothing extraordinary for one of his tastes. Toward the end of the summer he wrote to Thomas about his reading of a book which had recently appeared, Olive Schreiner's *African Farm*, in which he told Thomas he found "a crying attack on Christianity." From reports which deal with a later period in his life, we know that he found much to interest him in Olive Schreiner's work, but the change which came over him during the Long Vacation cannot be traced entirely to the influence of a book.

Evidently ill health, aggravated by congenital melancholy and pessimistic literature, and the atmosphere of insecurity in his home worked together in variable proportions and combinations to cause him to regard university life quite differently from the way he had looked at it during the preceding term. When he returned to Queen's in October 1887, he was no longer the shy young man who had come up the year before, nor was he the apparently carefree undergraduate of the Spring Term. Those who knew him most intimately noticed the change in him at once. "Early in the term," remarked Thomas,

I noticed his marked depression. We both took it seriously. I was tinged with pessimism, but pessimism and cheerfulness can live together. In Dowson's case this possibility was gone. Doubtless his unhappiness was largely physical. It has been suggested to me recently by a college contemporary that Dowson would have been helped by modern psychic methods of therapeutics. This would have certainly made him laugh.

If modern psychic methods of therapeutics were unnecessary at this stage of Dowson's development, it is likely that a firm hand in helping him to regulate his life would have been beneficial. Evidently there was no one to insist that good, substantial meals, sufficient sleep, and regular habits of work and relaxation would make him healthier and happier. His friends provided him with neither precept nor example, and the authorities at Queen's apparently assumed that university students were sufficiently mature to regulate their own lives. When the authorities granted Dowson permission at the beginning of his second year to move out of the back quadrangle to 5 Grove Street, they were unaware of his needs, or knowing them, they humored him in his belief that he could lead a happier and more constructive life without the confines of the quadrangle.

His moving from the Rabbit Warren to Grove Street marked a new epoch in his life at Oxford. Evidently all of his interest in undergraduate life was gone. "The novelty of college life had worn off," said Thomas, "and its restrictions proved irksome to one with no experience of school."

Irksome as the restrictions no doubt proved to him, they were exactly what he needed in order to rectify the inadequacies of his earlier training. To one whose childhood was pagan, whose youth was a procession of shifting scenes, and whose training had been irregular and without discipline, the restrictions of college life were of especial utility; but neither he nor the authorities were willing to apply the discipline which is the foundation for a well-ordered life. Although the quarters to which he moved on Grove Street were not without the boundaries of University supervision, those who lived out of college possessed a freedom which the students in the back quadrangle lacked.

It was not only that the novelty of college life had worn off which led Dowson to decide that he would much prefer to live on Grove Street: he had long cherished the notion that a Bohemian life was ideally suited to his temperament and to his objectives. Murger's *Scènes de la vie de Bohème* had done much to corroborate and justify his inclinations and to stimulate them as well. Dowson was no great admirer of Murger as a stylist, but the substance of the book held out a marked appeal. The book itself and its spirit were with him during his second year at Oxford; in fact, the spirit of it followed him through the greater part of his life. It may readily be belived that he spent many hours following in his fancy the movements of Rodolph, Chaunard, aand Marcel. The poisonous quality of the book, which Daudet among others recognized, Dowson failed to detect, largely by reason of the fact that he saw in Bohemia only the freedom from the responsibilities of the more conventional professions, and a life devoted to artistic creation. It is possible that he felt some of the pathos which Murger brought out deliberately in his stories, but he was not oppressed by it. When he reflected on Murger's own statement that "Bohemia is the preface to the Academy, the hospital, or the morgue," he saw none of these destinations. To him, Bohemia was not a preface to any objective or destination; to be within its boundaries was an end in itself. With no well-laid plans for a profession, and with no desire to attain the conventional objectives of success for which other younger men were striving, he was especially responsive to the delights which the Bohemian life portrayed.

The romantic and picturesque aspect of Bohemia appealed to him, but his eagerness to secure a passport to its boundaries was far more deeply rooted than in his delight in the picturesque. The Bohemianism which became a creed to him during his second year at Queen's was a natural development of the philosophies of pessimism and estheticism which he absorbed at the University and from his own reading. The first step in the development of his creed was based on his belief that "Nature and humanity are, in the mass, abhorrent." Such a conviction shared in part by some of his Oxford contemporaries, led young men into varyingly sincere efforts to find a corrective, or at least refuge. Resignation and suicide held out small appeal to young men, although there were instances in which these avenues of escape found followers. Estheticism was a more inviting path to follow in order to find sanctuary from an ugly world; and if it were followed to its end of creative beauty, it could readily become not only an avenue of escape, but a constructive philosophy. Feeling that he had talents which could be utilized in applying such a philosophy, Dowson determined during his second year at college that the estheticism which he believed was fundamental to a worthwhile life in Bohemia was the path to follow. It is unnecessary to attempt to trace all the forces in his own nature and those which came from without which led him to such a conclusion. It is enough to observe that his nature was singularly responsive to the adoption of such a creed, and that his Bohemianism was more the result of earnest thinking than of any romantic attraction which Murger's stories held out.

His feeling that in art he could find a refuge and a constructive philosophy was not without support. He knew that he had talents in the expression of which he had much pleasure, and talents which others had been ready to recognize. The appearance of the "Sonnet to a Little Girl" and "Moritura" during his first year at Queen's, and his increasingly regular contributions to his manuscript book indicated more to him than a province in which he could occupy his spare time pleasantly. Then, too, he was engaged with prose narratives. During the summer he had written to Thomas that he had finished two short stories, and had sent them to the magazines in the hope that they would be accepted. What these stories were cannot be determined, for he never mentioned their titles or themes to Thomas or his other Oxford friends; but it seems reasonably certain that "The Souvenirs of an Egoist," which appeared in *Temple Bar* in January 1888 was one of them. The other evidently was not accepted by any of the magazines to which he submitted it at the time, and although it was possibly one of the five stories which were later bound into one volume under the title *Dilemmas,* there is no evidence to support such a conclusion.

"The Souvenirs of an Egoist" is a touching little piece in which the tenuous narrative thread is plainly incidental to the expression of sentiment. It is the story of a man successful and feted as a great composer and violinist who, upon hearing a barrel organ play beneath the windows of his luxurious home, recalls a period in his boyhood when he had been in want and had had as his only companion a little street girl, Ninette. Remembering that time, he mused,

I sometimes fancy that when the inevitable hour strikes, and this hand is too weak to raise the soul of melody out of Stradivarius—when, my brief dream of life and music over, I go down into the dark land, where there is no music, and no Ninette, into the sleep from which there comes no awaking, I should. like to see her again, not the woman but the child. I should like to look into the wonderful eyes of the old Ninette, to feel the soft cheek laid against mine, to hold the little brown hands, as in the old *gamin* days.

In this closing passage—in fact, in the entire story—there is a subjective quality which indicates the author's trend of thought at the time that the story was written. Although the story is tinged with sentimentalism, its theme was based on conviction. The cultivation of that form of art which led to the plaudits of a wide group of readers would in time prove a hollow satisfaction: the cultivation of art must be independent of the objectives of worldly success. The real satisfaction in a life devoted to art could be found in provinces inhabited only by those to whom art is more than an avenue to fame. The interpretation of the story need not be labored: "The Souvenirs of an Egoist" was only one of Dowson's expressions of belief that the pursuit of beauty and the pursuit of financial security and fame generally followed different paths.

The sentiment, if not the words, which he was later to have the character Adrian Rome express was already well formed by the time he took up residence on Grove Street. Rome's friend, Lord Henry Minaret, argued against the sincerity with which Rome cherished his art. "One shouldn't let such a trifling interest interfere with the order of one's life. . . . Go in for politics seriously—the law, diplomacy, even trade. Be a serious *flaneur*, which is best of all. Take anything you like in the world seriously, except Art." To which Rome replied: "My dear fellow, I will never be the sociable amateur; I will go to perdition first." Such arguments as the one advanced by Lord Henry Minaret, Dowson undoubtedly listened to; and such a reply as Rome's he probably often made. To be "the sociable amateur," or to follow art deliberately as an avenue to fame was foreign to his ideal during his second year at Queen's and for the greater part of his life.

With such convictions concerning the seriousness with which art was to be followed, it is small wonder that he gave no attention to the provinces in which the Lord Henry Minarets of the University found their chief interest. Like Adrian Rome, he had increasing difficulty in seeing the unmixed benefits of university training. More from habit than from a sense of obligation or sincere interest, he continued to attend a few lectures and show a mild form of curiosity over what was going on in the Addison Society. The meetings of the Union, which he had joined during his freshman year in order to try to become a real Oxford man, he no longer attended, nor was he in the least concerned with the prospects for a good Queen's crew. The blazer, striped flannels, and washing tie of the Spring Term were now supplanted by a carelessly kept wardrobe of which a soiled black bow tie was a regularly distinctive feature. During his first year he had given the impression to his acquaintances that he was eager to try to conform to the Oxford pattern, but that he had failed somewhat in achieving his end by reason of his early training; during his second year, however, he gave the impression that he had no intentions toward conformity.

His friends, and doubtless his tutor, tried to persuade him to recognize the value of fulfilling the requirements for a degree even though he was interested only in the profession of letters; but their arguments, no matter how persuasively presented, had small effect. The authorities and his tutor cannot be charged with undue negligence, for in spite of the fact that Oxford has never tried to force knowledge and its regulations on those who are manifestly unwilling to be led, they surely pointed out to Dowson the advantages which would come as the result of fulfilling the requirements for a degree. But he had either no conception of the practical advantages of university training, or notions of his own concerning what he wanted from the University. The books he was required to read he rarely so much as procured; and the prescribed assignments of his tutor he completed with no attention to accuracy of detail or neglected altogether.

It might be suggested that this indifference to the ideal of what an undergraduate should do and be was the the result of crying needs in his nature rather than of any opposition to convention and authority. There were incipient maladies of both body and soul of which he was only dimly conscious, but they were sufficiently advanced to support inclinations which became more and more pronounced during his second year at Queen's. The needs of his nature, aggravated by his reading in the pessimistic philosophers and the art creed which was crystallizing in his mind, could not be satisfied by a consistent application to university routine. His flouting of the regulations after he had moved to Grove Street cannot be traced to any inherent or cultivated rebelliousness to authority: his irregularities during his second year at college were the result, not the cause, of his incipient sickness of body and soul.

To advance the notion that Dowson at twenty tried to build up an elaborate system for outwitting what he considered to be the abhorrence of life by a cunning cultivation of the nirvana which comes from alcohol, narcotics, and bizarre forms of excitement is an interesting but scarcely fruitful exercise in the psychology of undergraduates. It is no doubt true that his nature and convictions encouraged him in his experiments with drink and drugs during his Grove Street days; but these experiments were not the result of a recognition of any need in his nature at the time, nor of any profound calculations of means by which he could ease his struggle against the ugliness of the world. His indulgences at Oxford can be traced to normal undergraduate curiosity rather than to any shrewdly deliberated scheme for outwitting the malevolence of nature.

Too much stress has been placed on Dowson's excesses at Oxford and later. Arthur Symons in his memoir of Dowson gave momentum to the belief that drugs provided a fairly common mode of escape from reality during Dowson's student days:

At Oxford I believe his favorite form of intoxication had been haschisch; afterwards, he gave up this somewhat elaborate experiment in visionary sensations for readier means of oblivion; but he returned to it, I remember, for at least one afternoon, in a company of which I had been the gatherer and of which I was the host. I remember him sitting a little anxiously, with his chin on his breast, half-shy in the midst of a bright company of young people whom he had only seen across the footlights. The experience was not a very successful one; it ended in what should have been its first symptom, immoderate laughter.

Agnes Rothery in the *Virginia Quartely Review* and Frances Winwar in *Oscar Wilde and the Yellow Nineties* gave additional momentum to the notion of Dowson's indulgence in drugs.

Symons' statements in this connections are misleading. That Dowson's taking hashish was only a sort of undergraduate experiment is attested by W. R. Thomas:

The myth that haschisch was Dowson's favorite form of intoxication at Oxford has an extremely slender foundation: the facts stand out very clearly in my memory. In Dowson's second year a Hindu freshman arrived at Queen's. Although he was deservedly an object of derision, yet we were interested in his praises of bhang. Dowson and I were further drawn into the investigation of the matter by Gautier's reference to the drug, and by the well-known passage in *Monte Cristo*. Pills of cannabis indica were accordingly procured from a chemist and consumed after hall. The effect was slight, but on the whole satisfactory. Several of us walked solemnly round the cloisters of the front quad, and noticed that our sensations of time and space were strikingly magnified. When the effect subsided we ate apples, with a general feeling of health and cheerfulness. A second dose, a night or two afterwards produced no results at all. At a third attempt the amount was increased with unpleasant results, which ended in a visit to Claridge Druce's shop in the High and an emetic in his back parlour. In all this Dowson took a very small part indeed. I remember him in the first tests and in the second failure. In the third less fortunate attempt he took no part at all, and that, as far as Oxford is concerned, is the whole story.

Reports conflict concerning the extent to which he drank while at Oxford. Thomas, who has been the most earnest and thorough commentator on Dowson's life at the University, observed:

In spite of his wanderings in France, whiskey was new to him. He had tasted absinthe, but his favorite drink was chablis, diluted from a syphon. Early in his second year, one evening in Grove Street, we tried whiskey, not as a nightcap, but as an after-dinner beverage. With its assistance we discussed literary matters with unusual contentment, and on my departure at midnight Dowson was delighted with the experiment and thought his troubles were over. The next night the panacea was again applied, but this time he sorrowfully pronounced it a failure. He decided that the depression was intensified, even *en route*. For the rest of his time at Oxford he had lost his short-lived faith in whiskey as an ethical corrective. Things like pink noyau at times appealed to his curiosity, but in the use of alcohol his habits were simply those of many undergraduates of that time.

This account of Dowson's mild indulgence may be tinged somewhat by the loyalty which the poet's friend continued to hold for him, for there were rumors, recalled by others of Dowson's time at Oxford, which place a less charitable construction on his experimenting with alcohol. It is true that diluted chablis would not have been much of an experiment for one who had spent so much of his time in France. Chablis probably was his favorite light wine; but the undergraduate in search of fresh sensations is scarcely willing to quaff off goblets of diluted wine when he knows the fuller and more rapid experience which whiskey provides. Report has it that there were experiments other than those observed by Thomas in which Dowson's faith in whiskey as an ethical corrective was probably equally shattered, but in which the effects were more sustained and pronounced. There is no evidence to support the notion that absinthe was his favorite means of seeing the world and himself in a different light while he was at Oxford, for absinthe was not readily procurable there in 1888. Dowson's fondness for absinthe in his later years has led many of his acquaintances, including some of those who knew him at Queen's, to associate this poisonous stimulant with Dowson at all stages of his life. His drinking at Oxford, even though occasionally immoderate, did little to lay the foundation for his later excesses. His experiments in search of fresh sensations and ethical correctives at Oxford were scarcely exemplary, but no great stress should be placed on them as they relate to his later life and work.

He was fond of the excitement of cards, and the evenings at Grove Street were often spent at whist, which at times degenerated to poker and even more rapid devices to insure a turnover of funds. Gambling appealed strongly to Dowson, but his allowance never permitted him to plunge deeply, even had his friends been flush and willing. The excitement, however, was readily attainable whether one had large or small stakes. He was a good loser when luck turned against him, but one of his friends has reported the gleeful satisfaction with which he used to say *"Servi,"* which they had learned to take for the French equivalent that Dowson had drawn a straight, a flush, or a full-house on the first deal and would as a result need to draw no cards. He never became adept at whist or poker, although he played with sufficient shrewdness to hold his own against friendly opposition. There is nothing to indicate that he ever played beyond his means. The few debts which Dowson left at Oxford were not I. O. U.'s to those with whom he had gambled on Grove Street.

Free in some measure from the restrictions which quadrangle life imposed, and no longer eager to share in the common interests of the students, Dowson devoted his life in Grove Street to following his own tastes in reading, to writing poems and stories, and to the cultivation of a *petite Bohème*. There were discussions far into the night in which the creeds of Murger's Marcel and Schaunard were echoed, and even Mimi was there on occasion to provide a much Anglicized and probably frightened companion for the brotherhood of artists. Earlier in the evening they had sung "Farewell, My Own" from *Pinafore,* of which Dowson was particularly fond, but the late hours were usually devoted to discussions about art. In keeping with his means and ideals, the suppers he provided were never elaborate, nor were there any indications of luxury in the appointment of his rooms. His few belongings were never neatly arranged, and although he still showed a sporadic interest in his bowler hat and spats, he obviously had no desire to be thought a dandy when he sat with tousled hair and soiled linen discussing Swinburne's "Garden of Proserpine." Of his own poetry he said little, but concerning his prose narratives he often spoke with his friends and on one occasion at least he was induced to read a passage from one of the stories which he had under way. And after his last guest had departed, before he settled down to transcribe a poem into his manuscript book or to continue his writing on one of his stories, he probably reflected that the Bohemia he had cultivated on Grove Street was more to his taste than quadrangle life and a strict conformity to the Oxford pattern.

Moore, Thomas, and Smith continued to be his closest friends in spite of the fact that they did not altogether approve of the change which had come over him since the Spring Term and that they were not in sympathy with his indifference to university life. There were others at the University at the time who were opposed to his indifference to what the college had to offer him, but who enjoyed his companionship. Lionel Johnson had come up to New College at the same time that Dowson had come to Queen's, and sometime during the Spring Term of 1887 or early the following autumn they had met and found each other's talk stimulating. Johnson had attained quite a reputation at Oxford; in fact, though it was commonly reported that "he had more than once been taken for a schoolboy up for a scholarship examination," he had come up to the University with a reputation as a wit and poet. There is no evidence concerning the degree of intimacy between Johnson and Dowson during the latter's Oxford days, but it may readily be assumed that their friendship in London during the early years of the 'nineties had much of its foundation in the nights spent together at Oxford. It is quite possible that Johnson and Dowson, like Gerald Brooke and Adrian Rome in the novel *Adrian Rome*, "had become intimate on the basis of their common appreciation of Battersea enamel and Catullus," and that their friendship had been cemented by their common belief that the plaudits of the crowd were to be deplored as an objective in the arts. They possessed many characteristics which would naturally draw them together, not the least of which was their dislike of moderation and regularity. But whereas Johnson had an unquenchable desire to be well informed, Dowson considered a mind stocked with facts of small advantage, though there is small doubt that he admired the commodious mind of his friend. It was probably Johnson's influence as much as that of his tutor which caused him for a time to consider reading for honours.

The example of Johnson, however, and the insistence of his friends at Queen's were not enough to lead him to prepare himself for the examinations. The prospect of reading for honours had given him a temporary incentive to distinguish himself in his studies, but by the time the Honours Moderations came around, he was unequipped in either preparation or inclination to pass them successfully. Curiosity led him to apply for the first few papers, which he wrote with small confidence in the results. Unwilling to do anything half-heartedly, and realizing his incompetence for continuing with the additional papers, he decided that he would take no more examinations. When his friends learned of his decision, they argued with him against it; but his mind was made up. His decision to reject the privilege of reading for honours was the result of an ever-growing belief that for him there were few advantages in taking a degree. When Thomas was insistent that he take out the remaining papers, Dowson replied: "I am not for 'Mods' nor 'Mods' for me." To which remark Thomas later observed, "Probably he was right."

He had made up his mind not only that he was unqualified to read for honours, but also that he had had enough of the University. His refusal to take the examinations did not mean that he would be dropped from the rolls: he might have continued his studies at Queen's as he had begun, a commoner; but evidently such a prospect held out no appeal. Although his father's income had appreciably decreased during the terms he had been at college, and several bills of considerable size had accrued in Oxford, Dowson's decision to leave the University was not hastened by any financial emergency at home. Nor had there been any difficulty with the authorities. Nothing of bitterness attended his departure. He had been brought into contact with young men of his own age, he had made a few friends; and despite the fact that he rejected the opportunity to come up for a degree, he felt that he had absorbed the things which the University had to offer him. He was by no means dispirited by his decision to withdraw, nor did he consider himself a failure by reason of his inability to pass the examinations. Although he was rarely given in later years to reminiscence about "the good old college days," when he did speak of his residence at Queen's his manner showed nothing of bitterness or regret.

His departure from Oxford in March 1888, although anticipated by some of his acquaintances, came with a suddenness which left many of his classmates curious about the reasons for his failure to remain for a degree. The rumors which circulated at Oxford after Dowson went down indicate that he was far from a recluse during his sojourn at Queen's. Osman Edwards, an Oxford contemporary, has recalled Dowson as "a very quiet man," but many of the reports indicate that he was far more widely known among his fellows than "a very quiet man" suggests. Some of the reports imply that he was known chiefly on account of stories concerning his irregularities on Grove Street, and a certain notoriety attached itself to his name by reason of the gossip which circulated that he was leaving Oxford to take up residence immediately in the Latin Quarter of Paris, there to devote himself to the picturesque life of a Bohemian. That Dowson himself had given some foundation for such reports is likely, for he had often talked of the delights of Paris, and especially of the brotherhoods of artists which flourished on the left bank of the Seine. That he had laid plans, however, to proceed directly to France has only the questionable authority of dimly remembered hearsay to support it.

Another report which was equally widespread after his departure and which has persisted among some of the men who are Oxford administrators to this day was that he had inherited a considerable property in East London, and that it was essential that he take over the supervision of the property immediately. The only inheritance that Dowson had at the time of his leaving Oxford was the prospect of helping his father make a living from the uncertain revenues of Bridge Dock. Here again, however, Dowson himself had given some momentum to the rumor that he had come into money. His pride in the ancestral enterprise was small, but he had evidently told his acquaintances about his family's holdings in the East End of London, and it was generally believed while he was at Oxford that he was the prospective heir. Knowing that his father was increasingly incompetent to handle the affairs of the Dock, he possibly made a casual remark when he left the University that he had property to look after, which to some of his acquaintances was construed to mean that he had come into a large inheritance.

Then, too, at Oxford as well as in later life, he was almost morbidly sensitive about being thought poor. Although his allowance was small, he had managed at Queen's to give the impression that he was a young man of considerable means. Some of his most intimate acquaintances were, at the time, of the opinion that the Dowsons were well provided with this world's goods, and that his modest quarters and frugal repasts were either the result of a whim or a sign of consummate breeding. Reports of his sojourns in France and Italy, combined with his familiarity with the more refined elements of Continental life, gave added weight to the assumption of his acquaintances that he was to inherit a considerable income. Those who know the facts of his life have never tried to correct the report that Dowson left Oxford in order to devote his time to a flourishing property to which he had fallen heir, with the result that the belief still exists in some circles at Oxford that Dowson's decision to leave the University was thrust upon him by the necessity of attending immediately to his business affairs.

His father's health and the diminishing income from the Dock may have had some bearing on his decision to leave, though there is no evidence to support the notion that he gave up his university career in order to help his father, or on account of his father's straitened circumstances. There was no urgent letter from home in which he was told his expenses at the University could no longer be borne, nor was there any suggestion on his father's part that he was sorely needed in order to keep the family business above water. His father probably knew full well that Ernest could do little to stave off the impending cessation of income. Everything points to the conclusion that Dowson's decision to leave Oxford was the result of his belief that there would be no advantage to him to conform to the pattern and stay for a degree. The decision to leave Queen's was entirely his own.

III

A YOUNG POET JUST DOWN FROM COLLEGE

WHEN Dowson went down from Oxford in March 1888, his interests and attainments pointed only to the profession of letters. Although he resented the thought of devoting his time to any province save literature, he realized the necessity for having at least a small income or some sort of provision for living. The few pieces he had published had given him sufficient encouragement to believe that he could make money with his pen; but in spite of the fact that he held the natural optimism of all young authors who have seen their work in print, he had no delusions about vast monetary rewards which might soon be his. At twenty he had a proper regard for his capabilities, but he understood that with his sort of artistic creed and talent he was scarely equipped to be self-supporting. Literature, however, could be his profession if he were not too insistent on the economic security which such a profession afforded. He would be of some service to his father at the Dock, find adequate provision for his immediate needs by living at home, and in his spare time—which would be much—he could write stories and poems for the magazines, and even publish a volume. Although this plan was not completely defined in his mind, circumstances helped him to fashion his life after such a pattern soon after his arrival in London.

His home-coming after almost two years at Oxford did little to gladden his father's heart, for the elder Dowson had hoped that Ernest, despite the irregularities of his early training, would conform to the Oxford standard and eventually come home with a degree. He neither understood nor sympathized with Ernest's decision to quit the University in the middle of his examinations. Later he was to confess to Victor Plarr "that he was rather afraid of the younger generation, and of Ernest in particular." To keep his son at Queen's had not been without sacrifice, but he had been more than willing to draw on his decreasing income in the hope that through systematic training his son would in time be prepared to settle down to a definite profession. Proud as he was of Ernest's literary talents and achievements, he had come to recognize the instability of literature as a profession for those who were inclined to deplore the level of public taste and to cater to a small, fastidious group. Had his income been large, nothing would have pleased him more than to see his son devote his time and talents to pursuits entirely cultural; but with the passage of years he had become increasingly oppressed with the economic insecurity which his own lack of business instinct had brought to his home. He possibly never reflected on the inclination to instability which he had given to his son during the years preceding the boy's sojourn at Queen's; and, if he did, he was incapable of sharing any of the blame for Ernest's failure to remain for a degree and fit himself for a definite profession. His disappointment at Ernest's failure to take a degree, however, was only temporary, for he had troubles of his own of a more pressing nature to occupy his attention.

During his son's absence, his health had remained unimproved. In fact, since he had assumed the management of the Dock in order to watch more carefully over his affairs, he had worried himself into such a state that his body had small chance to combat his congenital malady. Instead of seeing any of the sweet uses of adversity, he became increasingly enfeebled by it. His manner became mercurial, both in company and with his family. In company, he generally exuded an air of graciousness and geniality, although there were times that he carried an air of fretfulness into his home that none was willing to try to dispel. Actual poverty was in no way imminent, but his failing health supported an increasing inclination to see only a cheerless future. If his work at the Dock kept his mind a times off his ailments, it also contributed to them by giving him a constant cause for worry.

Ernest's presence at home after his sojourn at the University did nothing to ease the situation, for in business matters he was as ill-equipped as his father; and he was in small way capable of dispelling the clouds which, to his father, were lowering from all sides. His reading in the pessimistic philosophers at Oxford was hardly conducive to a gospel of hope and cheer, nor were his own health and spirits of the sort which could give buoyancy to an atmosphere of somberness. He had no prospects of contributing materially to his own support or that of the family, and his inclinations were such that his parents realized the futility of trying to prepare him for a profession or trade in which there might in time be a secure income. In his fashion, however, he felt a strong loyalty to his family; and with nothing more definite to occupy his time than his reading and occasional writing, he set out willingly to try to be of service to his father at the Dock.

It has been reported that he viewed his work at the Dock half-humorously. There was surely nothing in his nature which could respond to the odd jobs which his father saw fit to give him save his loyalty to his family and a small part of his father's pride in the ancestral enterprise. His principal work was to do the bookkeeping, for which he had neither aptitude nor liking. What he was set to do, however, he tried to do to the best of his ability. The ledgers which he kept intermittently for five years showed a surprising neatness and precision for one who was so obviously disinclined toward system and orderliness. His cousin, Spencer Secretan, has recalled Dowson sitting on a high stool in the combination office-living room of the Dock House, working over a ledger and eating his luncheon without descending from his perch. That he ever contributed ideas for the improvement of the facilities of Bridge Dock is unlikely, but he showed a constant willingness to bring to the business the services of which he was capable.

Although he had little of his father's pride in the Dock, he found much that was interesting and picturesque in his surroundings; and on occasion, when acquaintances from the West End came down to visit him, he delighted in pointing out the more colorful details of his environment. The Dock House, extending to the land end of the ways, and surrounded by a palisade-like fence on all sides save that part of the rectangle which was formed by the river, was in itself an object of interest. There was something of mildewed antiquity about its eighteenth-century wainscoting and its leaded panes which looked out over the basin in which the ships were lying, and beyond to the Thames. The street leading up to the Dock House was one of those irregular streets which are to be found in the neighborhood of docks all over the world. Cordwainers, ships stores, sailors' dives, and strange, foreign eating places jostled one another indiscriminately. The cul-de-sac which ended with Bridge Dock and the river was honeycombed with dingy houses, from which the fragrance of tar and paint reached the office in the Dock House. It was a local colorist's paradise to which the young man was not entirely unresponsive.

He liked the Dock especially at night, for when the ships moved up the channel at high water the scene presented pictures which were memorable to him when he was writing *A Comedy of Masks*. He recalled

. . . the streaming, vivid torches, their rays struggling and drowning in the murky water, glimmering faintly in the windows of the black warehouses barely suggested at the side; the alert, swarming sailors, busy with ropes and tackle; and in the middle the dark, steep leviathan, fresh from the sea-storms, growing, as it were, out of the impenetrable chaos of the foggy background, in which the river lights gleamed like opals set in dull ebony.

In the months which followed his departure from Oxford, however, he saw little in his environment which suggested literary utility. Artists came to the region between the Tower and Poplar with their easels, and journalists found copy in the very Dock House in which Dowson worked; but the interest and picturesqueness of his surroundings were of a sort which held small appeal to one who had been lately nurtured on Walter Pater. His nature was peculiarly subjective. He was aware of the interesting features of his surroundings, but stimulation for his mind and inspiration for his art came from within rather than from without. That he was subjective because he was unaware of the objective is hardly the case; his peculiar subjectivity in viewing his surroundings at the Dock was rather the result of the egocentric lines which his nature and training had drawn on his character.

Despite his inability to find inspiration in his surroundings, he showed much more interest and had more information about the Dock than is commonly supposed. His lack of interest and information in things maritime has been somewhat exaggerated. The picture of Ariel in Limehouse needs considerable retouching. When he took Victor Plarr to see the Dock, he amused his friend by his apparent ignorance of all nautical terms.

"This is the front part of the ship," he called to his friend as he ran to the bow of a 287-foot schooner which was drawn upon the ways. "This is the back part of the ship," he announced later when they both were standing in the stern. "Though I'm always here," he remarked ingenuously to Plarr, "I've never learned the proper names for things." Such speeches, coming as they did from a young man who wore a black butterfly necktie which he delighted in as being French, amused Plarr and others who were taken on inspection tours of Bridge Dock. One wonders, however, whether Dowson, even with his mind filled with Baudelaire and Swinburne, was so totally uninformed about "the proper names for things" with which he had been associated since his boyhood. It is perhaps more reasonable to conclude that he, who disliked the thought of being considered well informed, found pleasure in exaggerating his lack of technical information about ships and their ways. A few years after he had reported to Plarr that he had never learned " the proper names for things," he described Philip Rainham in *A Comedy of Masks* as one who, after a lifetime spent around ships, had never mastered the difference between the port side of a vessel and the starboard. He smiled at Rainham's ineptitude in a fashion which causes the reader to believe that he was completely aware of the charm which the character's lack of information about his own business afforded. Then, too, in *Adrian Rome,* Dowson was able to give not only "the proper names for things" which belonged to the sea but also was able to give many authentic touches to the *Anonyma,* the boat in which the principal character cruised among the Channel Islands.

It may be concluded that Dowson's apparent lack of interest and information in things maritime which he demonstrated to Plarr and others was somewhat of a whimsical pose. It was the fashion among young men who had been nurtured on the gospel of Pater to profess an ignorance of everyday matters, especially if they were in any way associated with trade. It is probably true that he was unable to tell off-hand how many barrels of pitch it would take to caulk the seams of a 200-foot schooner, but one who had been in contact with the jargon of seafaring men as much as he, could scarcely escape learning some of their terms and assimilating a considerable amount of information about ships. Nor was he an exclusively dry-land sailor. During the summer of 1889 he went on a short cruise with one of his father's patrons, to whom he referred in a letter to Plarr as "respectable old buccaneer." The prospect of ocean breezes—"not too much of 'em, I hope"—was evidently agreeable to him, for he reported that the cruise would probably revive him from "the intolerable ennui" of his work in the office. Surely on such a trip, with only seamen for company he could not readily close his eyes and ears to what went on around him. It was probably his realization that his friends cared little about the technicalities of dry-docking that caused him to profess an ignorance of nautical terms and the details of his father's business. This, combined with his eagerness to discuss matters which were genuinely interesting to him, led him to create a role for himself in the playing of which he protected his own interests and amused his friends.

Without being rebellious to the thought that he should try to be of service to his father, he became increasingly eager to get away from his ledgers and start for the Strand. There was little consorting with the picturesquely unkempt figures who moved about the waterfront. In this stage of his life, he much preferred the well-appointed bars and restaurants in the West End to the dingy, smelly dives near the wharves. Morally, his surroundings at the Dock had little effect on him; in fact his experiences in Limehouse had a very small share in forming his character and giving direction to his life and art. He referred to himself facetiously as the intellectual docker, and left the general impression that he was a figure completely apart. When the novelty of working at the Dock had worn off, he found it increasingly difficult to fulfill his obligations to his father; and as time passed, his services became irregular. He had a normal sense of loyalty to his parents, but his sense of responsibility was never lively. He sought escape from all obligations which exacted regularity, patience, and decision. Like Adrian Rome, in his novel, "he had a nervous horror of making up his mind." Although his work at the Dock rarely called for momentous decisions, he much preferred to avoid the responsibility of supervising even the most trifling details. "The intolerable ennui" which oppressed him after the novelty of his work at the Dock had worn off was not so much the result of boredom as his dread of responsibility.

When his work for the day had been finished, he found no avocations which were related to his duties at the Dock, nor did he try to train himself for a more efficient kind of service. His bookkeeping, though neat, followed no standard method, the utility of typing and stenography was unconsidered, and in the economics of the business he had neither interest nor comprehension. Although he knew much more about drydocking than he professed amongst his friends, his essential interests were elsewhere. As soon as he closed his ledgers at the Dock House, he went straightway to the Strand where in the company which he found at Henekey's and the Cock he could forget that the master of the 247-foot *Indian Ocean,* fretful at the delay and the type of service he had received at Dowson's, had sworn that this was his last trip to Bridge Dock. He had learned in part the knack of making friends during his five terms at Queen's, and in the months following his going down be became intimate with an ever-widening circle of young men, many of whom had been at Oxford during his time.

Among his most intimate friends in the year following his departure from Queen's were Charles Sayle, Frank Walton, and Victor Plarr. Sayle, "that great introducer" as Plarr called him, was a dilettante in literature, whom Dowson probably met at Oxford, and who was to write a sonnet to Dowson, one of the few verse tributes paid to him. On one of his frequent trips to the West End, Dowson encountered Sayle, and with their common interest in literature and bars as a starting point, they became fairly intimate in the early months of 1889. It was in Sayle's rooms in Gray's Inn that Dowson met Victor Plarr to start one of the finest friendships he ever enjoyed. The fact that Plarr had been at Worcester immediately before Dowson went up to Queen's gave them a starting point, and before they had chatted togther for long they found that they had many common interests.

They talked of Pierre Loti, for whose works Dowson at the time had considerable admiration; other French authors were discussed, each delighting in the other's familiarity with works which were generally unknown among the men recently down from college; and Plarr had a dim recollection that during the course of their first conversation Dowson talked about one of

Plato's *Dialogues* in which he "had probably been 'ploughed' " during his residence at Queen's. Although there is no evidence to indicate that they made mention of their own writing when they first met in Sayle's rooms, Sayle had told Plarr that Dowson was a poet, and Dowson probably knew that his new friend had been active in the affairs of the Lovelace Society —the poetry club at Worcester—during his stay at Oxford. They saw much of each other after that first meeting. When Dowson did not encounter his friend at one of the gathering places on the Strand, he often went to Plarr's rooms in Great Russell Street where, as their friendship increased, he frequently spent the night.

Plarr was an ideal companion for Dowson. Even as a young man, he understood the advantages of moderation. Both his actions and speech showed a conservatism of nature which became more pronounced with advancing maturity. In spite of the fact that he told Dowson at their first meeting that he was static—"about four years of age"—he never regarded his youthfulness as an excuse for sowing a bumper crop of wild oats. In an age in which young men recently down from college were generally intent on enjoying the excitement of wine, women, and song, Plarr's conduct showed an unusual sense of restraint. There was never anything of the "holier than thou" in his manner, but in his middle years his air of self-sufficiency, his well-ordered life, and his reserve in speaking about topics of a personal sort caused some of his more lusty contemporaries to recall him as something of a prig. Despite his mildness of manner, however, he could be an excellent companion and a loyal friend. During the early years of the 'nineties, when he and Dowson were on especially intimate terms, there was certainly nothing oppressive about his inclinations toward regularity and moderation. Had there been, Dowson would have been the last man to strike up a friendship with him. In Plarr, Dowson saw a young man who was interested in poetry, widely read in the French authors whom he liked, and one who by reason of his evenness of disposition suggested a spiritual and mental serenity which he himself lacked. In spite of their sharply contrasting natures, their friendship was firmly rooted, and it became one of the most salutary influences on Dowson's life.

When Plarr first met Dowson, he saw a young man who "was singularly fresh, young, eager, sympathetic, his charming face unscathed by any serious sorrows or dissipations." His own genial nature probably made it impossible for him to detect the signs of illness and life-weariness which had struck some of Dowson's acquaintances during his second year at Oxford. He saw a certain diffidence and a boyish shyness in his friend, which he attributed to his good breeding and to "a gracious and insistent

air of modesty." Obviously Dowson was different from most of the young
men down from college, but the difference to Plarr was not to be found in
the vexed and torn spirit which others had readily detected. He found
Dowson very earnest, but not without a sense for fun. Although he never
saw his friend laugh, he could not conclude from his association with him
during the early years of the 'nineties that his body and spirit were constantly being flayed. Plarr's own kindly nature helped him to recall the
early years of his friendship with Dowson in a manner perhaps more penetrating than that of those whose recollections of Dowson's young manhood
are tinged with the shadows of his later years. He saw little of his friend
after 1894, with the result that his impressions of Dowson during the early
'nineties were unaffected by later and less pleasant pictures.

Although Plarr found Dowson "singularly fresh, young, eager, sympathetic . . ." he also saw in his friend an inclination toward pessimism.
This, at the time and later, Plarr was tempted to minimize, largely by reason
of the fact that he too was going through a stage of experimental pessimism
which even then he recognized as only a passing state of mind. It was during the period in which he and Dowson were becoming fast friends that
Plarr and his roommate, Frank M. Walton, who was later to become Librarian of King's College, London, set themselves to the annotation of
Olive Schreiner's *The African Farm* in the manner of German commentators. Under the names of Schnutzius and Hans Tübner, they listed the reflections which passages in the book provoked. Their notes were made in a
spirit of mingled seriousness and frivolity. When Dowson, who had become
a frequent visitor at Plarr's rooms, was told of their pastime—and they regarded it only as such—he was at once eager to have a part in it; and under
the pen-name of Anatole de Montmartre he annotated quite seriously.
Plarr and Walton were in turn amused and concerned at the earnestness
with which de Montmartre contributed his reflections and conclusions. *The
African Farm* he had read during his Long Vacation in 1887; and during
the interval between his first reading of it and the time at which he joined
Plarr and Walton in their game, he had evidently thought much about
Olive Schreiner's doctrines. His remarks, which Plarr carefully preserved,
illuminate much of Dowson's state of mind at the age of twenty-two.

The conclusions which Anatole de Montmarte drew from the provoca-
tive passages of *The African Farm* were too fragmentary and inconsecutive
in their presentation to constitute a philosophical system, nor was there any
striking consistency in the spirit and letter of these marginal notes. To one,
however, who has tried to follow Dowson's line of thought as it was expressed in his early poems and his conversations with his friends at Oxford,

these fragmentary reflections and conclusions have considerable significance. Although these jottings show the plain stamp of immaturity, they do much to refute the notion that Dowson was only a bundle of emotions and senses with no binding quality of intellect. Arthur Symons was later to remark of his verse that it showed only a pure lyric gift which was "unweighed or unballasted by any other quality of mind or emotion." Dowson himself gave support to this belief concerning his verses when he told Arthur Moore that his poems were to be read for their music, and that any attempt to invest them with meaning would prove unproductive. Such a statement, however, cannot be taken literally. In spite of the fact that Dowson cannot be named as a "poet of thought," he cannot be identified strictly with those authors who consider poetry only music. It was after he had read Verlaine's *Art Poétique,* with its opening line "Music above everything," that he told his friends that his poems were devoid of meaning. It is undoubtedly true that Dowson's gift was essentially lyric, but neither his own statements nor those of Symons support the notion that he eschewed thought.

In fact, one of his first observations in the margain of his copy of *The African Farm* implied that intellect was man's only substantial endowment. "Ere our death day," he wrote,

Faith, I think does pass, and Love, but Knowledge abideth. Let us seek Knowledge. At least let us shun emotion as we would hell, for which it is a synonym. Let us live in ourselves and for ourselves. A reasonable self-love without passion or thought of others, and with the end of self-culture before us, is better than a million emotions. Corollary—let us shun emotion and seek knowledge only . . . O. S. seems to admit that the ideal state is to be without hate, or love, or fear, or desire—passionless.

All this, to be sure, sounds most extraordinary in the light of what is known about Dowson's later life, but there can be no doubt that when he wrote of the uses of the mind he had a more sincere objective than to puzzle his fellow commentators.

Anatole de Montmarte introduced himself to his readers by observing that his "most decadent friends regard him as somewhat of a heretic." He must have felt his difference from his friends keenly, for, as Plarr observed, in his first utterance he expressed a peculiarly decadent note in his remark: "The conclusion of the whole matter—a striving and a striving and an ending in nothing." Such a note, written when he was only twenty-two, would seem to bear out T. B. Mosher's estimate of Dowson:

The final impression . . . that one gets from him and his verse is in substance this: behind the veil of personality if you could succeed in raising it—such seems

to be his analysis of human purpose—you would find—nothing. The thought is
not new; it is older than Lucretius—as old as Ennui. An echo from all outworn
hearts; found, indeed, in much greater men and their works—Flaubert will serve
for an exemplar. The mystery of our days and deeds, according to the pessimistic outlook, may be likened to a series of cunningly devised, but empty
audience chambers; or if you prefer a different notion, a secret drawer one dis-
covers by merest chance and forcing it open finds a billet-doux, a faded ribbon,
ashes of roses—Rien!

His next observation of note bore out what he had told Thomas
about *The African Farm* in the summer of 1887: the book was evidently
still "a crying attack against Christianity." Beside one of the explicit attacks he wrote: "Symbolic of the inefficacy of all spiritual, supernatural
help in one's sorest need." Quite evidently he felt that when one could no
longer find himself self-sufficient, he had little to expect by way of help
from a so-called benevolent force. From one of Olive Schreiner's comments
concerning the origin of deity, he was led to conclude: "By a similar process
did the religious sentimental man invent the Immaculate Conception. Cf.
Zola's 'Faute de l'Abbé Mouret,' Book I." Farther down the page, he
wrote: "The first theologic maxim which ever profoundly impressed me
was Stendhal's 'La seule chose qui excuse Dieu c'est qu'il n existe pas.' "
To Olive Schreiner's remark that "Whether a man believes in a human-
like God or no is a small thing," he observed: "This is a profound saying.
Theism, Pantheism, Christianity, Positivism—they lie so close together
that it is like splitting hairs to consider them apart. The vital issue is between optimism and pessimism." It was evidently agreed that pessimism
was the only honest choice and that faith and love could provide no avenue
toward an ultimate good. From a passage in Miss Schreiner's work, he concluded that the hope of heaven and the fear of hell were both ill founded
and destructive to the proper self-cultivation. "Surely annihilation is not
horrible," he wrote, but to him heaven and hell were horrible conceptions.
"I object most strongly to a personal immortality. Immortality! Wretched
ideal. Infinite ennui—I die at the thought." To Olive Schreiner's hypothesis
that "There must be a Hereafter because man longs for it," he replied: "A
very weak argument. A man may long for water in Sahara, but he doesn't
alway get it."

Such a scattered and fragmentary series of observations is at least indicative of Dowson's trend of thought concerning the inner significance of life
during the years immediately following his departure from Oxford. His
jottings concerning his attitude toward women at the time are equally
scattered and equally illuminating. Obviously he took no stock in the thesis

which Coventry Patmore had advanced in "The Angel in the House," a poem which he probably would have put aside as inane. "Helas, helas, for the utter materialism of the feminine nature," he exclaimed. To Miss Schreiner's suggestion that "if wine, philosophy and women keep the dream of life from becoming a nightmare, so much the better," de Montmartre retorted . . . "women are hardly fit for even that. They make it a worse nightmare than ever." When he encountered a passage which displeased him in Miss Schreiner's attitude toward man's regard for women, he exclaimed: "Typical inherent *basesse* in woman's nature—the brutal method, the only method with woman—e.g. the perverse pleasure (to be observed in a hundred cases) with which a woman sets herself to degrade and obliterate the feminine ideal if she comes across a man with any faith in it." And at Miss Schreiner's remark that "Men are like the earth and we are the moon; we turn always one side to them, and they think there is no other, because they don't see it—but there is," he observed: "And the reverse instance is as true—only women don't believe we have another side than the obvious one, even when we show it." The reproductive instinct is the result of

. . . the Evil Will which baits its trap with the illusion Love and scatters the illusion to the winds when its purpose is fulfilled. Cf. Schopenhauer's chapter on Sex and Desire. "L'hameçon est evident, et neamoins on y a mordu, on y mordra toujours" (Renan). . . . Passion is waste—takes away from a man's stability, his self-centralization: its action on general culture, aestheticism, philosophy, many-sidedness, all that makes life endurable, is ruinous. It fastens on life like a cancer.

All these observations have the stamp of immaturity on them, both in substance and expression; but according to Plarr and Walton, Anatole de Montmartre's annotations struck them at the time as being singularly profound. Obviously to him the annotation was more than a game, and his fellow commentators, although both older than he, found themselves at times somewhat disconcerted by the earnestness with which he supported and amplified his marginal notes. He even went so far as to tell his colleagues that "only a deeper study of Schopenhauer and an adhesion to *some* of the tenets of Plato" would ever conduct them to nirvana. He concluded his observations as Anatole de Montmartre by reminding his readers that "he has a deep distrust of the flowers which grow in the Garden of Propertius. And the fruit of that garden he avows to be Dead Sea Apples, whereof, if a man eats, he shall surely die."

Seriously as he took his annotation of *The African Farm,* Dowson at twenty-two was still sufficiently possessed of youth to reject in his daily life the tenets of Anatole de Montmartre. By nature and training not given to viewing life in its brighter hues, he was still a very young man at heart. The very eagerness with which he set to work on Miss Schreiner's book was in itself an indication that he was unwilling to believe in the futility of all striving. He had perhaps more right to affect pessimism than many others of his generation, but even with ample justification pessimism is rarely deeply rooted at twenty-two. In spite of the deep distrust which he expressed of the flowers which grow in the garden of Propertius, he was quite capable of enjoying the pleasures which others of his generation sought out. Without forsaking entirely the tenets of de Montmartre, he probably would have found a certain appropriateness in the quatrain of Hardy:

> Let me enjoy the world no less
> Because the all-enacting might
> That fashioned forth its loveliness
> Had other aims than my delight.

Certainly his life in London in the years immediately following his departure from Oxford was not a desperate seeking after nirvana. Once finished with his work at the Dock, he was in the habit of going promptly to the bar of the Cock on Shaftsbury Avenue. This was usually his first stop on his nightly rounds. Here he quaffed an apéritif or two, after which he delighted in playing billiards with any acquaintance who chanced to drop in. Dinner he often took in Soho, where for a shilling and three pence he could get a full meal including beer. In the restaurants around Sherwood Street he found not only reasonable prices, but also a Continental atmosphere and occasionally interesting companions. Although he preferred the small restaurants in Soho to the more palatially appointed cafés around Piccadilly, he often went to the Café Royal, where he invariably met men with whom he had struck up a passing acquaintance at Oxford, or those whom he had met on his nightly rounds. If a music hall offered an inviting attraction, or if he knew that some of his friends were sure to be found in the circle, he went to the Alhambra or the Empire, though he much preferred the atmosphere of the less fashionable places such as the Tivoli and the Mogul. Despite his cynical reflections about women in the margins of *The African Farm*, he had his favorite *artistes* to whom he paid tribute which was not always silent.

No matter where the earlier part of the evening had been spent, he usually found his way before midnight to the Crown. To the passer-by in the hours before eleven o'clock, the Crown seemed to be nothing save an ordinary public house which catered to the usual run of thirsty Londoners. When the music halls let out, however, the Crown took on an atmosphere which readily differentiated it from the bars along the Strand. Then it became a sort of Mermaid Tavern for the younger generation of artists. From eleven o'clock until the lights were dimmed at twelve-thirty, there was an ever widening group of figures who were devoting themselves sincerely or in appearance to the arts. Here one was sure to find a convivial group, some of whom appeared with ladies whom they had recently applauded for their singing or dancing at the Alhambra, others with their models, and still others with only an eagerness to talk. The liveliest men in the motley gathering of painters, poets, and hangers-on usually occupied the large center table, from the middle of which rose a tall potted rubber plant, while on the settees ranged about the walls were little cliques advancing their belief in art for art's sake and damning the Philistines. Here the most glamorous *artiste* at the Alhambra was judged according to her worth; and as midnight passed with additional gin and water, Walter Pater's dicta were reëxamined and evaluated. Mallarmé and symbolism, Gaelic verse, and the deplorable level of public taste were discussed in preference to the Kipling rhymes which were appearing in Henley's *National Observer* and the latest labor of the Laureate Tennyson. On week-day nights one was almost certain of finding Arthur Symons, Conal O'Riordan, Herbert Horne, Charles Conder, Lionel Johnson, Max Beerbohm, and occasionally Aubrey Beardsley and Hubert Crackanthorpe. Even Paul Verlaine, on his visit to London in November 1893, was taken to the Crown. Despite the thickness of the air, and occasionally of the talk, the place was thoroughly respectable. Dancing girls and models of only the better sort were comfortable amongst the habitués of the bar-parlor, and no one ever became boisterous. As Grant Richards observed: "A visit to the Crown was not a dissipation; it was the end of a day's work, a chance of meeting and talking with congenial friends, of exchanging ideas."

Dowson was soon numbered among the regulars. He "would, as likely as not, be first to arrive," recalled Richards. Here he struck up new acquaintances and established old friendships more firmly. Often he sat with the group at the center table, expressing opinions on occasion which were perhaps less brilliantly phrased than those of some of his acquaintances who made paradox the chief aim of conversation, but were both sincere and discerning. Although Richards has recalled nights on which Dowson was too far in his cups to be a really good talker, there are others, including O'Riordan, who remember his well-mannered participation in the discussions that went on. When closing time came, he was generally the last to make a move toward the door, for to him, perhaps more so than to most of the others, an evening at the Crown was an exquisite pleasure. Reluctant to leave the society of men whose interests were so definitely his own, he often attached himself to groups who were eager to continue their conversation elsewhere.

His delight in the company which the Crown afforded, and the difficulty in getting transportation to Stepney after midnight led him frequently to join the groups which were on their way to continue their discussions at the Temple, or to carry on at one of the supper clubs where the law had no control of time. In summer, there were always groups that moved about the streets for an hour or two before calling it a night. Plarr has recalled how Dowson, with others who were well on the way to inebriation, at times arrived long after midnight in the street outside his rooms, and yelled his name in a chorus which echoed for blocks around. There was nothing of lurid dissipation in these nightly prowlings; it was youth sowing its wild oats with nothing to differentiate it from the week-end "beerings" of the modern undergraduate. A sort of informal club grew out of these nocturnal merrymakers who called themselves the "Bingers." In this group, Dowson was easily the most regular figure.

Had his parents lived nearer the scene of his nightly activities, or had they been able to provide him with modest quarters somewhere in town, his eagerness to prolong his nights at the Crown might have been in part reduced. But for him to get to Maida Vale, where his parents had taken a house, was both expensive and inconvenient; and for him to go by cab or on foot to Limehouse at an hour at which the arm of the law was least alert was scarcely a pleasant prospect, even with the fortification to courage which gin and water could bring. If he wished to spend the evening with his friends, he had the choice of an early departure while he could still catch the "Owl" to Stepney, or a full night of revelry followed by a makeshift bed at the home of one of his friends. Unwilling to impose on the hospitality of his companion of the night, and at times becoming disputatious when his host was insistent that he occupy a comfortable bed, he often dropped into the first chair he found in his companion's quarters and, turning a deaf ear to those who were willing to provide him with a more comfortable resting place, fell off to sleep. Plarr recalled many a night that Dowson slept in his armchair; and in the rooms of one of his friends at the Temple there was a hard sofa which was referred to as Dowson's bed.

In spite of the fact that Dowson's habit of getting only a few hours' sleep sapped his strength, of which he had little to spare, the period from 1889 to 1893 was one of considerable mental and artistic growth. He continued his reading in the French and Latin poets; and through his association with Plarr, Walton, and the men who gathered nightly at the Crown, he came more and more in touch with contemporary literary movements and

ERNEST DOWSON

(*From a drawing by Sir William Rothenstein*)

thought. Although the group at the Crown knew that he was interested in literature and that he had contributed a few pieces of verse and prose to the magazines, no one, including Plarr and Walton, was aware that the young man who worked at a drydock during the day was already expressing his emotions and reflections in exquisite lyric verse. All the while, however, he was transcribing, in a careful hand, finished poems into a manuscript book which he called his "Poesie Schublade." Before 1890 he had found more than fifty of his poems of sufficient merit to include in the book reserved for only the finished pieces. Only two of these poems, including the "Sonnet—To a Little Girl" which had appeared in *London Society* in November 1886, came into print before 1890. The lovely sonnet "April," which was later included in *Verses* in 1896 under the title "My Lady April," appeared in *Temple Bar* in April 1889. With such a small output, it is small wonder that the circle at the Crown, the "Bingers," and his colleagues Schnutzius and Hans Tübner, did not know that there was a poet in their midst. In fact, Frank Walton, who was to see little of Dowson after his role of Anatole de Montmartre had been played, had no notion that poetry was more to him than a passing interest.*

With his acquaintances at the music halls and the Crown, and with the increasing realization that he had a talent with his pen, Dowson was far from a lost soul during his early twenties, nor did he leave such an impression with his friends. His health was obviously poor, and his discourse was frequently tinged with pessimism; but those who knew him at the time are as one in their report that he showed an unmistakable zest for life. Although he was never fastidious in his garb, he evidently was dressed presentably for the Café Royal and the promenade at the Alhambra. There was none of the *nostalgie de la boue* which Horace Vachell, Gertrude Atherton, and William Rothenstein were later to detect. Those who knew him intimately at the time, including Plarr and Walton, found him a delightful companion whose manners and appearance were entirely in keeping with the standards of young men recently down from Oxford. To less benevolent acquaintances—especially those who recalled Dowson chiefly in his last years—he was already possessed of a fatal life-weariness, in spite of the apparent eagerness with which he pursued the delights which London night life amply afforded him. The only conclusion which can be drawn from the evidence which his acquaintances have provided is that his

---

* An amusing story concerning Dowson's unwillingness to inform others about his interest in poetry is related in one of Lewis Swan's letters to his daughter Madeleine: For long, Alfred Dowson had held in high regard the work of a poet whose verse appeared occasionally, signed only with initials, in a fashionable periodical (possibly *London Society*). It was finally disclosed that the poet whose works Alfred Dowson admired so greatly was none other than his son Ernest.

pessimism was more than an academic exercise, but that he retained the capacity for finding pleasure in his associations at the music halls and the Crown, and in the realization of his poetic talents.

His recurrent inclination toward pessimism evidently did not affect his energy, for in addition to his work at the Dock and his nightly rounds, he still found energy and time to become the assistant editor of a magazine, *The Critic,* which had an ephemeral existence in the early weeks of 1890. The evidence concerning his work for *The Critic* is scanty and vague. According to Plarr, an advertisement appeared in one of the magazines, possibly *The Athenaeum,* "calling for a brilliant pen, wielded by a man of high social connections." Plarr himself interviewed the editor of the periodical which needed such a man, to find him one who valued not only social connections and a brilliant pen, but also his own supernatural ability to visit distant lands in his dreams. At the first interview, he told Plarr that he had been to India in one night "and thoroughly knew the look of it and the feel of it." Plarr was evidently impressed with neither the editor nor the prospect of the work; and after slight deliberation, he rejected the opening, and turned it over to Dowson. To the latter, the prospect of having space in a magazine at his disposal seemed attractive, and without giving much thought to the responsibilities which he would assume by accepting the offer "he joined the staff of the journal," reported Plarr, "a weekly of some dimensions, as assistant editor, and contributed certain admirable papers thereto, notably 'The Cult of the Child.' "

The "weekly of some dimensions," however, was neither well founded nor well supported. The editor was evidently a man of small literary ambition and perception; in fact, his ambitions and resources were so meager that the periodical was doomed from the start. It is possible that he felt that if he could secure the services of the right kind of assistant editor, he could make a flourishing periodical out of *The Critic.* Dowson, however, was scarcely the man to build up a magazine by himself. He could not bring himself to write by the clock, nor was he able to gather around him a group of contributors whom he could inspire to turn in stories and articles regularly. Even had he been able to promise potential contributors handsome remuneration for their work, it is unlikely that he could have made *The Critic* a London institution. For the duties and responsibilities of an editor he had small talent. Furthermore, his literary creed was at cross purposes with the policy of a successful periodical. One who deplored the level of public taste, who believed that the appreciation of art was the heritage of a very few, and who himself believed in the necessity of waiting on inspiration to drive his pen was hardly the sort of editor to build up a wide circulation, or to make a pamphlet grow to the thickness of a book. Dowson qualified in some measure for the work which called for "a brilliant pen, wielded by a man of high social connections"; but as a member of an editorial staff which was composed of only two, he had little save his contributions to offer to the magazine's success.

At the start he took his work very seriously, but by the time the third issue was due to appear the novelty had already worn off, and he adopted an attitude which indicated that he had lost confidence in the magazine and his talent as assistant editor. Evidently he got Plarr to contribute an article to the second issue, and encouraged his friend to send in additional work. In an undated letter to Plarr, he inquired:

Have you seen your article in this week's *Critic?* it makes a most imposing front to an unusually meagre inside. I hope you will give us some more copy "at your earliest convenience." . . . *Du reste,* I am more or less a corpse, what with the intolerable ennui of the office and my laborious efforts with the unhappy "Critic."

In another letter, written from Bridge Dock a week or so later, he told Plarr:

I ought to have answered your delightful letter before, but what with Dry Docking and "The Critic"—I am simply "decayed" with work . . . I must try and look you up but feel it is difficult unless I can catch you at "Seafaring" as the "Critic" claims my evenings & I am—for the present—its special correspondent for all Music Halls. It is rather a jest, I find, visiting these familiar places in the character of pressman. If we survive our third number—it seems problematical even that it appears—I shall be greatly amazed. Mais—quoi donc—enfin—craque! Vive la bagatelle!

The periodical which Plarr called "a weekly of some dimensions" lasted beyond the third number; but by March 8, 1890, with the fifth issue, the unhappy *Critic* gave up the ghost. Plarr reported that Dowson "severed his connection with it before very long." The fact of the matter is that Dowson was with *The Critic* until the end. His work as assistant editor had done little to give life to an enterprise which was doomed from the start, but a few of his contributions of a creative sort undoubtedly did much to raise the literary quality of its meager contents. The two pieces selected as representative by Guy Harrison in his bibliography of Dowson's works, "Between the Acts" and "The Cult of the Child," have never been reprinted. It was of the second piece, "The Cult of the Child," that Plarr was led to exclaim: "It was as an adorer of childhood that his lovers and friends, who have kept his memory green, will best remember him."

It is possible that the work for *The Critic* about which he complained to Plarr was both agreeable and beneficial to him, for in spite of the fact that it exacted a certain regularity and sense of obligation from him, he was at least working in a province which he liked. He had never been indolent; on the contrary, he was always eager to be up and doing. The discipline which lasting work for *The Critic* might have brought to his life was denied him, and with the demise of the magazine he became even more confirmed in his irregular habits and indecision. Much as he complained about being "simply decayed" with work while he was the assistant editor, he undoubtedly was forced to regulate his life by reason of his obligations to a magazine which he hoped would flourish. His cynical comments concerning the periodical and his work for it may readily be construed as the natural expression of a young man who wished to leave the impression that his position as assistant editor was lightly borne.

Although the collapse of *The Critic* helped to support his inclination toward indecision, there were occasions on which he made up his mind concerning a course of action and persisted in following his decision in spite of serious opposition. Whether his decisions were the result of impulse or of long deliberation, on a few occasions he followed them without being swayed by the insistent influence of his family and friends. His decision to embrace the Roman Catholic faith was one of the instances in which he surmounted all opposition in order to follow what he believed to be the only creed for one of his inclinations. Some of his friends have reported that it was at Oxford that he decided to become a Roman Catholic and embraced the Church, but substantial evidence indicates that his conversion took place in London, soon after the time that he had written in the margin of *The African Farm* that the Immaculate Conception was invented by sentimental man, and that he strongly objected to a personal immortality.

Dowson's inclinations toward the Catholic Church had no definite starting point. Among some of his friends the opinion has been expressed that Oxford was the inspiration and guiding force; but in spite of the fact that Dowson's experience at Queen's possibly lent its influence in shaping his decision, his formal embracing of the Church did not take place until at least 1891. If the movement toward the Catholic Church which was in progress at Oxford during the decades of the 'seventies and 'eighties was responsible for his decision to become a Catholic, it must be borne in mind that Dowson was by temperament and experience impressionable to the influence of such a movement. Continental in feeling, and observant of the beauty and tranquility which are part of the Catholic faith, he no doubt had often felt the spiritual and esthetic force of the ritual in the atmosphere of the French and Italian churches. The beauty of the architecture and pageantry of the Catholic Church he could not well escape during his boyhood sojourns on the Continent. His parents, with no strong religious convictions of any sort, were still mindful of the culture history of the Church; and in spite of their indifference to dogma, they had not discouraged their son in his regard for the beauty of places of worship. Sensitive to all forms of beauty, and impressionable to the influence of the spiritual quiet which comes to those who kneel before the high altar, Dowson was equipped by nature and experience to recognize in the Catholic Church an unmistakable power.

It is possible that his decision to become a Catholic was supported in part by the fact that some of his relatives were Catholics. In an unpublished letter from Gerald Hoole, an uncle of Dowson's, to Victor Plarr, Hoole remarked significantly: "As you know, Ernest was a Roman Catholic and to some people that is still a 'red rag.' As I had something to do with his joining the Roman Church you can perhaps understand the situation." Such a statement implies that there were relatives who were unsympathetic to Hoole's influence and to Dowson's decision. The Secretans were evidently opposed to any encroachments on the Protestantism of the family, but neither their objections nor Hoole's encouragement had much effect on Dowson's determination to become a Catholic. His mind was made up in large measure independently, without the support of any one particular person or influence.

His sympathy with pessimistic philosophy so plainly expressed at Oxford, and his bold annotations of Olive Schreiner's *The African Farm* would seem to indicate that his experiences in Continental cathedrals had left him impervious to their spiritual force; in fact, many of his comments, written under the name of Anatole de Montmartre, do more than suggest that he felt that the Church had been responsible for blinding many people to the true reality of existence. Without abandoning his feeling that mankind and nature were in the mass abhorrent, he was willing to believe in the existence of an alleviative force. As a completely curative power, and as an agency for immortality, the Church held no appeal to him, nor did its dicta of right and wrong hold any practical significance. The beauty of the ritual, however, and the fostering of spiritual peace were positive advantages which, even with his subscription to the pessimists, he could readily understand.

Dowson's whole line of thought, in so far it can be traced, was entirely compatible with his belief in the Church as an ameliorative force. In most of his works written during the period preceding his conversion and in the reported conversations with his friends, there is a positive declaration of the beauty and nobility of innocence. His occupation with childhood as a theme in many of his early works undoubtedly reflected his belief in the advantage of regarding life with the simple, trusting mind of a child. This thought did not carry him to a declaration such as the "Ode on the Intimations of Immortality," nor did he ever amplify the sentiment that "the child is father of the man"; but even before he had passed the twenty-year mark, he had found "the whole of love" in a child's face; and in Number Three of the "Sonnets of a Little Girl," he declared that the innocence of childhood had become his ritual, his mystic prayer, and the amulet which guarded him from all harm. One who sees an ennobling force in the innocence of a child can readily recognize beauty and power in the simple faith of a Breton peasant. Simplicity and trust are common to both; and the one who finds a sanctifying power in the purity of a child's heart may well discover a similar force in the trustfulness of a devout Catholic.

It is to be observed, furthermore, that young men in their early twenties who have determined that there is a preponderance of ill in the world are still, as a general rule, sufficiently endowed with plasticity of mind and the hopefulness of youth to seek out avenues for making life tolerable. At Oxford, Dowson had built up an esthetic philosophy which gave his mind the satisfaction of direction; and now, a few years later, without relinquishing his notion that the ugliness of the world could be partially escaped and corrected by a worship of beauty, he evolved the belief that the Church could offer him and mankind partial sanctification if not complete redemption. It could inculcate an innocence of heart and mind which in itself was beautiful and would mitigate the bitterness of the recognition of the preponderance of ill.

When Frank Harris reported that Dowson had told him, "I am for the old faith. I've become a Catholic, as every artist must," he gave support to the belief that Dowson found little more than a sensuous beauty in the Church. In a letter to me, Robert Sherard observed: "I always understood that Ernest 'verted' while at Oxford as so many young men of his generation did. . . . It was the picturesqueness of the Roman ritual that attracted him, but he never in his last years ensued his religion or confessed, or communicated. . . ." Victor Plarr was more outspoken than was usual for him when he recalled Dowson's conversion and the reasons underlying it. "I shall never forget the day of his admittance to the Church," wrote Plarr.

He came to me rather excitedly, and yet shook hands with weak indecision. His hesitating handshake, alas! always betrayed a sorrowful fatigue. "I have been admitted," he said, but he seemed disappointed, for the heavens had not fallen, nor had a sign been vouchsafed. The priest who had admitted him had done so quite casually and had seemed bored. Afterwards, it seemed to me, he forgot about his religion with surprising alacrity. Only his poetry bears witness to a romantic admiration of a creed, which, after all, he shares with many Protestants and Agnostics.

Respecting sincere Catholics as I do, I was keenly annoyed with his conversion—with this kind of conversion. It was comparable to the way in which our clever young men of today, with no knowledge of biology, folk-lore, or the rationale of English Constitutional history, became Socialists. But I held my tongue. Our literary life is a long reticence at best.

Plarr's recollections, and those of others who knew Dowson at the time of his conversion and later, would seem to indicate that it was only the beauty of the ritual which won him to the Church and made possible "a romantic admiration of a creed." It is worth observing, however, that one who had read Schopenhauer and Olive Schreiner thoughtfully, as Dowson undoubtedly had, would need something more than the fragrance of incense to cause him to join the Church. When Dowson told Harris that he had become a Catholic "as every artist must," he surely did not mean to imply that artists find their only religion in pageantry and ritual. It has often been said that whereas Lionel Johnson, who became a Catholic in 1891, could give chapter and verse in support of his conversion, Dowson's embracing the Church was only a headlong rush toward new esthetic delights. This opinion leaves the impression that Dowson was only a bundle of emotions with none of the controlling force of intellect. Johnson himself, however, recognized in Dowson's Catholicism something more than a mere subscription to ritualism. When Johnson wrote "The Faun Among the Satyrs" he did not have Dowson in mind. In a letter to Richard Le Gallienne, Johnson referred to "my dearest friend Dowson: who is now, *Laus Deo,* a Catholic." Although the beauty of the ritual played a part, no doubt, in Dowson's conversion, a young man of his trend of thought certainly based his decision to embrace the Church on a more substantial foundation than the appeal of ecclesiastical regalia, censers, and Ave Marias. His conversations with his friends, his annotations of *The African Farm,* and his prose and verse written during the period of his conversion all indicate that he was more of a thinker than many of the reports concerning his embracing the Church would indicate.

William Butler Yeats in *The Trembling of the Veil* wrote to the point when he observed:

Dowson's poetry shows how sincerely he felt the fascination of religion, but his religion had certainly no dogmatic outline, being but a desire for a condition of virginal ecstasy. If it is true, as Arthur Symons, his very close friend, has written, that he loved the restaurant-keeper's daughter for her youth, one may be almost certain that he sought from religion some similar quality, something of that which the angels find who move perpetually, as Swedenborg has said, towards "the day spring of their youth."

Although there probably was something of the romantic in Dowson's admiration for the Catholic faith, it seems incredible that the poet who wrote "Extreme Unction" should have found his conversion so disappointing as Plarr reported. Is it not possible that Plarr and Sherard, recalling how Dowson's later years were spent, failed to consider the seriousness with which Dowson took his conversion? And is it not possible that his failure to lead a virtuous life according to the standards of devout Catholics has caused many of his acquaintances who knew him chiefly in his late years to report the signal failure of his conversion? That he did not give himself over promptly to mysticism, and to frequent ardent conversations with his friends concerning his sanctification and redemption scarcely implies that his conversion was the result of a passing impulse, and a complete failure.

Plarr's remark that "he forgot about his religion with surprising alacrity" is scarcely supported by the evidence. Keen as Dowson's disappointment might have been at the casual way in which the priest admitted him, he continued to attend mass. In an undated and hitherto unpublished letter to Charles Sayle, he wrote:

15 Bristol Gds.

My dear Sayle

We lunch at 1:30. But come to Mass with me first by all means; then I can show you the road. I am afraid the Dominican Ch. Havestock Hill would make us rather late. My usual Church is the Ch. of Our Lady, Grove Road, St. John's Wood. That will not be far from you and is quite close to me. . . .

I will wait outside the garden gate of Our Lady till 11:15, however on the chance of your coming there: if not hope you find your way to us at 1.0.

Tà toi

ERNEST DOWSON

It is to be noted that Dowson spoke of "my usual Church." Such a statement cannot possibly be interpreted to mean that he had found his conversion so disappointing that he promptly gave up his attendance at mass. Sayle had never been to Dowson's home at the time the invitation to luncheon was sent him, and the house at 15 Bristol Gardens was not easy to find for one who was unfamiliar with the region around Maida Vale; but evidently Dowson was unwilling to forego mass in order to make sure that his friend would find the house in time for luncheon.

His attendance at his "usual Church," however, showed no marked outward effects. His conversations with his friends were devoid of religious discussion, and his sense of right and wrong became no more acute by reason of his conversion. To him, religion and morals had little in common. He made no pretense of living a consistently devout Catholic life; in fact, he made no pretense of consistency in anything. In the efficacy of prayer he occasionally demonstrated belief, for it is related that he used to kneel before the image of a martyred virgin in one of the side chapels in the cathedral at Arques, and that he was seen at times at the Farm Street Church in London with his head bowed in prayer. He was among the assemblage at the Church when the requiem mass was held for the repose of the soul of Aubrey Beardsley. He showed, too, a belief in the grace attendant on carrying about with him a token of his faith. In his last years he still carried a little gold cross in his waistcoat pocket, which, according to Ranger Gull, he would produce reverently and dip in his glass before he drank. This action perhaps had in it a significance entirely secular, but it reveals a willingness to find grace in the use of a religious symbol.

If his conversion showed only a few outward effects, it had a perceptible bearing on the content and manner of his writing. Any classification of his works which omits the religious pieces is incomplete. Although he was never a Catholic poet in the sense that Francis Thompson, Alice Meynell, and his friend Lionel Johnson were, he produced several poems and one short prose narrative which had an unmistakable religious inspiration. There is only one poem, the beautiful "Extreme Unction," which he dedicated to Lionel Johnson, which has in it a quality which may be termed peculiarly Catholic. This poem first appeared in *The Second Book of the Rhymers' Club* which was issued in 1894. It was probably written later than February 1892, for at that time Dowson placed his last entry in his manuscript book, and "Extreme Unction" does not appear in its contents. If he was converted in the spring of 1891, his religion was still a source of inspiration to him after February 1892, for there was no reason for his rejecting "Extreme Unction" for his manuscript book when other poems of religious inspiration were included.

Miss Katherine Wheatley has been at pains to point out in The University of Texas *Modern Language Notes* (1923) that Dowson was influenced perceptibly by Flaubert's description of the administration of the last sacrament to Madame Bovary, and it has also been observed that the line "all the passages of sense" was drawn from Pater's *Marius the Epicurean*. Other parallels have been suggested, including Zola's description of the administration of the sacrament in *Le Rêve,* a novel with which Dowson was very familiar. There is no doubt that he knew the descriptions of Flaubert, Pater, and Zola, and that he saw beauty in them; but it may

readily be concluded that it was the beauty and power of the sacrament
itself which moved him to write the poem rather than an attempt to give
a variant phrasing to Flaubert's theme. Superficial as his religion might have
been, it is unlikely that "Extreme Unction" was only an imitative literary
exercise. It is very difficult to reject the sincerity of the last two stanzas:

> Vials of mercy! Sacring oils!
> I know not where nor when I come,
> Nor through what wanderings and toils,
> To crave of you Viaticum.

> Yet, when the walls of flesh grow weak,
> In such an hour, it well may be,
> Through mist and darkness, light will break,
> And each anointed sense will see.

The other poems which belong to the small province of his religious
poetry are "The Nuns of the Perpetual Adoration" which appeared in *The
Century Guild Hobby Horse* in February 1891; "Benedictio Domini" which
first appeared in *Verses* in 1896; and "Carthusians," which did not appear
until 1899 in *Decorations,* although, according to the manuscript book, it
was written by May 27, 1891. There is also a prose tale, "Apple Blossom in
Brittany," which appeared, curiously enough, in October 1894 in *The
Yellow Book.* The theme of the story is an expansion of the sentiment
expressed in "The Nuns of the Perpetual Adoration." It is interesting to
recall that Dowson on encountering his Oxford friend Thomas at the
Alhambra Music Hall on the night of February 14, 1892, gave to the friend
with whom he had argued against religion as a undergraduate a manuscript poem—"The Nuns of the Perpetual Adoration." A smile, not without satisfaction, must have played on Thomas' face as he read the closing
stanzas:

> And there they rest; they have serene insight
> Of the illuminating dawn to be:
> Mary's sweet star dispels for them the night,
> The proper darkness of humanity.

> Calm, sad, secure; with faces worn and mild:
> Surely their choice of vigil is the best?
> Yea! for our roses fade, the world is wild;
> But there, beside the altar, there, is rest.

The publication of these pieces and the time of composition are generally
different, but all evidence concerning the dates of composition indicates
that they were written over a period of at least several years. Plarr's state-

ment, therefore, that after Dowson's conversion "he forgot about his religion with surprising alacrity" seems extreme, as does his implication that the conversion was the result of a sudden impulse. To be sure, it is unlikely that Dowson had read widely in ecclesiastical history, in Catholic theology, or even in the Bible, but it is likewise to be observed that the one who wrote "Extreme Unction," "Benedictio Domini," and "The Nuns of the Perpetual Adoration" had given considerable thought to the advantages he would derive from becoming a Catholic.

The impression must remain, however, that Dowson's conversion inspired him to be neither a religious poet nor a religious man, and that his association with the Church was sporadic and in large measure unfruitful in providing him with "sweet renewal of lost innocence." Even the partial sanctification which he sought was apparently denied him. When his "wanderings and toils" lay most heavily upon him, and "when the walls of flesh grew weak," his spirit, weakened by indecision and the bludgeoning of a relentless destiny, was no longer able to crave Viaticum. When all the testimony of his friends and all his works have been examined, one must incline to the belief that the essential voice of Dowson is not to be found in the last stanza of "Extreme Unction," but in the lines:

> They are not long, the weeping and the laughter,
> Love and desire and hate:
> I think they have no portion in us after
> We pass the gate.
>
> They are not long, the days of wine and roses:
> Out of a misty dream
> Our path emerges for a while, then closes
> Within a dream.

It was at the time immediately following his conversion that another event of far-reaching consequence occurred. He fell in love. The young man who had written in the margin of Olive Schreiner's *The African Farm:* "Let us shun emotion and seek knowledge only. . . . Women are several incarnations behind men (as cats are behind dogs), and they entirely lack a certain spiritual principle which exists even in the most bestial man" . . . that "The Evil Will baits its trap with the illusion Love and scatters the illusion to the winds when its purpose is fulfilled," was ready to believe by 1892 that his love for a little Polish girl would ennoble and enrich his life. Although the effects of his unrequited love for Adelaide Foltinowicz have been overemphasized by most of Dowson's commentators, the fact remains that his art and life were affected considerably by his love for her. Nor was the relationship between Dowson and Adelaide the exquisite impossibility which Arthur Symons and others felt they detected. When all has been discovered and made plain, it will still be evident that Dowson was sincere in his love for Adelaide and that he planned seriously to marry her.

The girl who was to become the great passion of his life was little more than a child when he first saw her. Sometime in 1891, when his habit of dining in Soho was already fixed, he went into a restaurant at 19 Sherwood Street, Soho, which was owned by a Pole, Joseph Foltinowicz, who had given up his trade of tailor by reason of the difficulty of competing successfully with London tailors to become the proprietor of a small eating place at which he and his family could at least have sufficient food. According to most reports, the restaurant was one of the unpretentious sort which flourished in Soho at the time, with little to distinguish it from others of its kind. The food was evidently palatable to those who were not too insistent on a moderate use of garlic, the place was passably clean, and the meals were cheap. A full meal, including beer and a tip for Auguste the waiter never exceeded a shilling and three pence, and the *plat du jour* was usually about eight pence. Arthur Moore, Edgar Jepson, and Marmaduke Langdale among other Bensonian actors made it a fairly regular practice to have dinner at the restaurant which came to be known as Poland. It was while Dowson was eating at Poland that he first saw Adelaide, then just turned twelve, as she sat at one of the back tables with her mother. The girl's freshness and innocence immediately attracted him who during his nights at the music halls had been only mildly affected by the coquetries of ladies who were more nearly of his own age. When Adelaide moved along the tables to talk with the few diners, he saw in her a charm and loveliness which he had never encountered elsewhere.

Dark haired and blue eyed, with a nose which observers other than Dowson found a little crooked, she was quite as decorative as many a poet's inamorata. Edgar Jepson remembered her long, oval face, its warm coloring, and the beauty of freshness and youth. "Poets have sung of poorer loves," he remarked. Although Dowson must have found her features attractive, it was not her beauty which appealed to him, for to her comeliness he never referred. It was her unspoiled, unaffected grace and sincerity which arrested his attention. In spite of her rearing in a neighborhood in which the English of Oxford was rarely heard, she had no trace of cockney in her speech, but a slight accent which came from her association with her parents and gave a note of piquancy and quaintness to her talk. Her innocent prattle gave Dowson immeasurable delight. Evidently he was not alone in recognizing the girl's charm, for the other patrons, including Jepson and Langdale, liked the girl, and often beckoned her away from the table at the rear to come to talk with them.

Their pleasure in watching her and listening to her was only the natural response of young men who find themselves refreshed by the artlessness of youth. To Dowson, however, Adelaide was not one in whom to find only a passing delight; she was a girl to love. The disparity in their ages made no difference to him, for the love he idealized was not the carnal love of a man for his mistress, but the sweet trustfulness which comes from innocence. His devotion to the beauty of innocence he had expressed in the days when he was writing the "Sonnets of a Little Girl," and now that which had been a more or less abstract inspiration took on a concrete, living form. His love for Adelaide Foltinowicz was only the natural result of his devotion to the beauty of innocence. In such a love he could see nothing inconsistent with many of the beliefs he had expressed while annotating *The African Farm*.

Reports vary widely concerning Adelaide and the place where she lived. Plarr, who was well informed about Dowson's movements at the time, refused to comment on Poland and the Foltinowicz family. To him, the entire subject was taboo. Others who knew Dowson intimately have deliberately refused to comment on their impressions of the girl. There are a few of his contemporaries, however, who recall Poland and the Foltinowiczes in a scarcely favorable light. Conal O'Riordan has reported that the odor of the place nauseated him, that the restaurant was not only uninteresting but ill kept, and that the Foltinowiczes represented nothing above the usual immigrant type. It is to be borne in mind, of course, that O'Riordan's preferences in restaurants have never been Continental. Another of Dowson's friends, who is often given to extremes, and to whom garlic is apparently an abomination to be tolerated only to nullify the vile stenches of the ghetto, found a single visit to Poland enough to keep him out of Soho for years. It was among those of Dowson's friends who disliked Poland that the unfavorable reports concerning Adelaide have generally grown, although O'Riordan was unwilling to speak out against the girl of whom he admittedly knew little.

Arthur Moore, who had come down from Queen's the same year as Dowson, evidently found the restaurant and the Foltinowiczes agreeable enough, for he was often in the habit of eating in Soho; and Langdale, with other Bensonians, found the *plat du jour* palatable especially when his wallet was thin, and enjoyed Adelaide's unaffected pleasure at his antics. Edgar Jepson, who had been in Barbados, and was engaging his talents sporadically at teaching and writing, became one of the regular habitués of Poland, eating there with Dowson sometimes as often as four nights a week. That Moore, Langdale, and Jepson found the restaurant and the Foltinowiczes agreeable, of course does not indicate that it was an ideal place in which a young man of good birth and training was to fall in love; but it does at least suggest that Adelaide lived in an environment which was not entirely devoid of salutary influence.

From many sources, including Dowson's letters to his friends and Jepson's recollections in *Memories of a Victorian*, it can be gathered that Poland was an eating place rather than a place for roystering. There was little in its atmosphere to encourage Bohemian revels. The restaurant did its chief business at noon. Usually by nine o'clock the lights were turned down and by eleven extinguished altogether. At times games of cards were played during the late afternoon and early evening, but no real gambling went on. Whist and poker were usually reserved for later gatherings, while halma, bezique, and occasionally chess were the pastimes after dinner. All agree, no matter what their impressions of the food and the hosts, that the place was respectable, and that Joseph Foltinowicz tried to cater to a well-mannered class of people.

Dowson's impressions of Poland became more favorable as his attachment for Adelaide increased. In the early stages of his fondness for her, he was apparently satisfied to consider her a lovely child, for the difference in their ages, and the care with which Madame Foltinowicz attended her daughter, discouraged at the time any declaration of affection. To her parents, there was nothing unusual in his fondness for the girl, for all the patrons found her presence refreshing; nor did they see anything extraordinary in his joining them, after his friends had departed, at one of the back tables in order to talk over inconsequential matters and play à game of halma with Adelaide. To his acquaintances who had usually found him playing billiards at the Cock at six o'clock and at the Café Royal or a music hall from eight till eleven, there was an occasional expression of wonder when it was learned that he was spending the early part of his evenings regularly at Poland; but in spite of the fact that they failed to understand Dowson's preference for Poland to the Alhambra, they attached no significance to his refusal to accompany them. The matter was generally dismissed with the reflection that he had always been a curious sort of fellow. For himself, he saw ample justification for the way he spent his early evenings.

In his own mind he had built up a role for the Foltinowiczes which had a few slender threads of evidence to support it. To him, they were totally different from the restaurant-keeper class of Soho. As his fondness for

Adelaide increased, her parents appeared to him to be folk of breeding, possessed of Continental charm and taste. They were refugees, he learned at one of the back-table conversations, not from Poland, but from Germany, for what reason they never explained clearly to him; but as his attachment to the girl grew and some of his friends tried to discourage him in pursuing it, he intimated that the Foltinowiczes had seen better times, and that their present condition was only a makeshift until the lines of life fell unto them in more pleasant places. That they spoke German and French, which was unusual for Poles of lowly stock, did much to support Dowson's belief that they were of higher rank than their present occupation indicated; and, with an inclination toward wishful thinking, he was ready to believe that if the whole truth about the family were to be disclosed, he would find that his birth and that of most of his friends was no higher than that of the winsome Polish girl. Furthermore, the strict surveillance which Madame Foltinowicz gave to her daughter's conduct left the impression that the family was of gentle manners. In conducting their business they had always maintained a certain dignity and reserve, all of which Dowson saw in the most favorable light.

In the months immediately following his first sight of Adelaide, no one, including the principals in the affair, foresaw the serious turn which his fondness for the girl was to take. His remarks to his friends that he was in love with her were put aside as nothing more than a young man's enthusiastic response to something which held out a temporary attraction. Sentimental as his attachment was, with the passage of time it took on all the emotional intensity of a great passion. It was not until he was in the throes of a love affair which had small chance of ever giving either Adelaide or himself happiness that his parents and friends were able to see the seriousness of it. Even then they remained in large measure uncomprehending, and out of their inability to understand the reasons for his love for a Soho restaurant keeper's daughter who was still a mere child, they helped to fan his passion into a bright flame by reason of their vehement antagonism to it. His parents, relatives, and some of his friends, once they were aware of the serious results which might develop from what they had considered a passing sentimental attachment, only helped to make Adelaide seem more desirable by making him defend her and justify his love for her.

By the autumn of 1892, the situation had already become serious. In a letter to his Oxford friend Sam Smith, Dowson described the difficulties into which his love for Adelaide had brought him.

I go on in precisely the same situation in Poland. I can't somehow screw myself up to making a declaration of myself to *Madame*, although I am convinced that it is the most reasonable course. Any day however with favourable omens it may arrive. She herself is sometimes very charming, sometimes not! But in the latter case it is merely my own abominably irritable temper which is to blame. I have had an interview of abnormal length with Lionel [Johnson], in which he argued with me most strenuously all night. He had been dining at my Uncle's (the Hooles), and apparently this infatuation of mine was openly discussed the whole of the dinner-time *par tous ces gens*. So I do not see how it can go on very much longer without an understanding or a *fracas*—the latter I suppose will be inevitable first—with my people. Altogether *Je m'embête horriblement;* and my only consolation is that if it is so obvious to all my friends and relatives it ought to be equally so to the Poles as well. "Masquerade" [*A Comedy of Masks*] is now under consideration with Bentley: the first publisher it has yet been to. If the result is favourable I really think I shall be inspired to make the disagreeable necessary overtures in Poland. Another year of the stress and tension and uncertainty of these last 6 months will leave me without a nerve in my composition and I am not sure whether I have any now.

It must be remarked in all fairness to Adelaide and Madame Foltinowicz that they did little to bring about and foster the attachment. It is a mistaken notion on the part of some of Dowson's commentators to identify the waitress in Somerset Maugham's *Of Human Bondage* with Adelaide of Poland. Adelaide was neither waitress nor siren; and she certainly lacked at the time of Dowson's early association with her the hardness of heart and the coarseness of nature which Maugham's waitress possessed. It is certain that Dowson was not the poor dupe who was drawn into the net of a scheming, flint-hearted girl by reason of his immoderate fondness for her. Adelaide and her mother set no cunningly devised traps for him; in fact, when the attachment began to show signs of developing into a serious affair, the Foltinowiczes were flattered, perplexed, and reticent in turn.

The girl who was to be "Missie" for the rest of his life was undoubtedly a considerable force in shaping his life and work, but the notion that his actions and his art from the time of his first meeting with her were largely directed by the undulating course of his attachment needs modification. It has been the general assumption that Missie, to whom his first volume of poems and much of his prose were dedicated, was the instrument of his poetic inspiration and of his destruction. On the basis of the evidence available, largely in the letters which Dowson wrote to Sam Smith, there is reason to believe that Missie played a very important part in the direction of his art and life; but Dowson's poetry is of sufficient variety to discount the notion of a single source of inspiration, and his life was influenced by so many forces which were unrelated to Poland that any inclination to find a unity in his art and life in the person of Adelaide Foltinowicz is bound to produce an inadequate and inaccurate interpretation of Dowson's character. There were many long intervals following his early association with Missie in which she played a very small part, or no part at all, in giving direction to his art and life.

Despite the fact that he told Smith in the autumn of 1892 that "another year of the stress and tension and uncertainty of these last 6 month would leave [him] without a nerve in [his] composition," the early years of his attachment for Missie brought him more pleasure than pain. His conversion, too, no matter what the causes or the results, was a step in the right direction; and his companionship with Plarr, Johnson, and the group who gathered at the Crown each night was a source of much delight. Although never a light-hearted young man, Dowson was far from being unhappy in the years immediately following his departure from Oxford. His health showed no untoward signs of giving way, nor did his continued reading in the pessimists completely undermine his ambition. Some of the seeds of the misfortune which was later to overtake him were planted during the years following his departure from Oxford; but in his love for Missie, his embracing the Church, his companionship with young men of similar interests, and his writing he found much which gave him pleasure and hope.

IV

THE RHYMERS' CLUB

THE years from 1890 to 1894, when Dowson was in his middle twenties, were the most productive in his brief life. And it is probable that they were his happiest years. Although sinister signs frequently appeared in his health, in his attachment for Missie, and in conditions at home, their significance was lightened by the joy of creation. In fact, he became so occupied with his profession of letters that for the time his cares of body and soul receded into the background of his consciousness. The growing realization of his art, and the stimulus provided by his intimate connection with an artistic movement encouraged and sustained him. His energies rose with his hopes, and the encouragement which came to him from the recognition of his work helped him to cultivate a mild ambition to be numbered among the great English authors.

Until April 1891 he was unknown as a poet outside the small circle of his acquaintances, and even among some of them he had done little to lead them to believe that literature was more than an avocation. Only three of his poems had appeared in print, and in spite of their merit they had attracted small attention. "The Villanelle of Acheron," which was finished on March 25, 1890, was apparently accepted by the editor of *Atalanta*, but for reasons which can only be surmised the poem was never printed in the magazine. If one excepts the work which Dowson contributed to *The Critic*, only two prose pieces had found their way into print before 1891, "The Souvenirs of an Egoist" in *Temple Bar* in January 1888, and "The Diary of a Successful Man" in *Macmillan's Magazine* in February 1890. Such a slender output, in spite of its obvious merit, was an indication to only a few of his acquaintances that he had either the qualifications or the ambition to become a poet.

His contemporaries have generally selected the lovely "Amor Umbratilis" as the poem which first caused London readers to believe that a poet was in their midst.

"Amor Umbratilis" [wrote Plarr] was one of the first poems which attracted much attention. It was published, if I remember rightly, by Mr. Herbert Horne in *The Century Guild Hobby Horse* together with a batch of the poet's other most noteworthy verses. The MS. of it, in pencil, lies before me now, inscribed on the back of a fierce letter referring to the poet's Oxford bills, which, he told me,

[80]

he had agreed to pay by degrees. "You have not returned the promissory note as arranged—please do so at once." And Ernest Dowson has immortalised this gruffness with one of the loveliest elegies in the language! One wonders if he chose this scrap of paper of set purpose.

"Amor Umbratilis," "The Carmelite Nuns of the Perpetual Adoration" (later entitled "The Nuns of the Perpetual Adoration"), and "Fleur de la Lune" (later entitled "Flos Lunae), were grouped under the general title "In Praise of Solitude" and appeared in *The Century Guild Hobby Horse* in October 1891. It is possible, as Plarr stated, that " 'Amor Umbratilis' was one of the first poems which attracted much attention"; but it seems reasonable to conclude that Dowson had already aroused considerable interest in his work in the preceding April issue of *The Century Guild Hobby Horse,* for it was in that issue that there appeared for the first time the justly famous "Non Sum Qualis Eram Bonae Sub Regno Cynarae."

Although Dowson is not a poet of one poem, it is "Cynara" by which he has come to be most widely known. To his contemporaries the poem was arresting, but it was rarely pointed out during his liftime as his most characteristic piece by either his critics or friends. It was after Dowson's death that Arthur Symons, who in his earlier notices of Dowson's poetry had never given particular attention to the poem, singled it out by observing that it is "one of the greatest lyrical poems of our time; in it he has for once said everything, and he has said it to an intoxicating and perhaps immortal music."

Such an appreciation minimizes the poetic worth of other pieces which possess a comparable beauty and possibly more of the essential Dowson. The fact remains, however, that Dowson has come to be identified largely with his poem. "Certainly no poem is more associated with the period," said Richard Le Gallienne, "and perhaps of all the poems then written it is the one still found most often today on the lips of youth." To identify Dowson with only "Cynara" is obviously unfair, but in this instance, the association is by no means unfortunate. Greater poets have at times been identified with less beautiful and representative poems. Dowson himself considered the poem his best. Six years after "Cynara" had first appeared in *The Hobby Horse* he recited it to Frank Harris as the climax of his poetic talents. From the start he was much concerned about the reception which would greet the appearance of the poem. In a letter to Sam Smith, written sometime in March 1891, he expressed his anxiety. "I have just seen the proofs of my 'Cynara' poem, for the April *Hobby.* It looks less indecent in print, but I am still nervous! though I admire Horne's audacity. I read it, or rather Lionol [Johnson] did for me, at the last Rhymers. . . ."

"Non Sum Qualis . . . Cynarae," which has been called the poem of the decadence and "one of the greatest lyrical poems of our time," has become by reason of the nature of its theme and the beauty of its measure a fascinating topic for a wide variety of interpretations. Although the complete and true story of its genesis will possibly never be told, it is both interesting and illuminating to reflect on some of the interpretations which have been advanced in order to determine to what extent they shed light on Dowson's mind and art at the time the poem was written. If the poem is placed in the strong light of the time in the poet's life at which it was written, some of the suggestions concerning its genesis must promptly be rejected. Many of the interpretations, on the other hand—especially those which are not too intent on a complete and specific identification of passages of the poem with Dowson's own life—are worthy of consideration for their biographical and critical worth.

The most frequently encountered interpretation of the poem is that Cynara was Adelaide Foltinowicz. The fact that Dowson dedicated his first volume of poems, *Verses*, "To Adelaide," announcing in the Epistle, "To you, who are my verses . . ." has led many of the poet's commentators to conclude that Adelaide was Cynara. It is a pretty notion that Dowson, while seeking pleasures elsewhere, always loved Adelaide, even to the point of being remorseful at the time of his unfaithfulness. Miss Marion Plarr, th daughter of Dowson's friend and biographer, in her novel *Cynara* (1933) accepted in large part this conclusion. "Cynara was Innocence and Innocence was Adelaide," she wrote. And Mr. Edgar Jepson, who knew Dowson very intimately during the days in which the poem was being written, in speaking of his first visit to Poland, said: "I was introduced to Missie, the little lady of Dowson's heart and the Cynara of his poem. . . . Had there been no Missie, there would have been no 'Cynara.' " Later, however, Jepson was willing to change his mind and agree with Mr. John Gawsworth that Missie and Cynara had no such positive relationship.

The interpretation of the poem that Adelaide and Cynara are essentially one has simplicity and concreteness to commend it. It must be borne in mind, however, that the poem was written in February 1891, when Missie was only twelve years old and before Dowson knew her very well. When Sam Smith, Dowson's Oxford friend who had often sat with the poet at Poland, heard of Miss Plarr's suggestion that "Cynara was Innocence and Innocence was Adelaide," he exclaimed: "The incongruity of it! One has merely to glance at the poem to ask oneself what a child of twelve, whom the poet had known for hardly more than a year, could possibly be doing

dans cette galère." It is to be observed that Dowson's devotion to innocence (which by the time the poem was written had taken on a concrete
form), contrasted with his occasional pastimes after the Crown had been
closed for the night, might readily become the inspiration for a really
good "sin poem" which he was eager to write. But despite his devotion to
innocence exemplified in Missie, it is incongruous, as Smith pointed out,
that the shadow of a twelve year old girl should fall between him and the
"kisses of the bought red mouth," and cause him to cry out, "The night is
thine." It is more plausible to believe that Dowson's expressed remorse
was more the result of a feeling of deviation from an ideal of love than
from an attachment to a child. Then, too, it must be recalled that in February 1891, when the poem was written, Dowson had not shown more than a
natural fondness for the little girl at Poland. It was more than a year after
the poem had been written that his friends detected a growing seriousness
in his attachment. That "Cynara was Innocence" may readily be the conclusion to the interpretation of the poem, but that Cynara was Adelaide is
not necessarily a sound corollary.

When Miss Marion Plarr adopted the license of the fiction writer in her
novel *Cynara,* she employed the license with considerable discernment. In
an imaginary conversation between her father and Dowson, she had her
father exclaim:

"Why, my dear Ernest, the fellow must have had a head of cast-iron to be conscious of remorse at that stage of the proceedings."

"It's not meant to be taken quite so literally," replied Dowson.

"It's sensational," continued Plarr. "It's the absolute anthem of the morning
after the night before. The grey willies in an atmosphere of rose leaves and
Falernian. Who's Cynara, by the way?"

"She's in Horace. Book Four of the Odes."

"No, really, I mean."

"She isn't anybody."

Such a reply, though admittedly fictional, in spite of its apparent evasive-
ness, is probably a true statement of the case. The passage in the First Ode
of the Fourth Book of Horace which Dowson used for the title of the
poem may have provided more of the inspiration of the poem than any
experience or combination of experiences which he had had at Poland and
elsewhere. "The phrase excited Dowson's imagination to such a degree,"
observed John Gawsworth, "that he honoured it with a new poem." Dowson's letter to Sam Smith, written at the time at which Horne was about
to issue the poem in *The Hobby Horse,* in which he told his friend that a

couplet from Vergil had started him on a sonnet entitled "To a Child, Growing out of Childhood and Away!" gives additional support to the conclusion that Dowson found a frequent source of inspiration in his reading of the Roman poets. If, according to his own report, Dowson found his inspiration for a sonnet in a Vergilian couplet, it is equally plausible that the Cynara poem had a similar source of inspiration. "Is not the Horatian phrase from the first Ode of the fourth book," asks Gawsworth, "the sole genesis of 'Cynara,' as is its title?" Plarr was of the opinion that Horace suggested and Propertius inspired.

At least one more suggestion must be considered before the question of the interpretation of the poem can be dismissed. If the situation in the poem shows similarities to that in the "Cynthia" of Propertius, it shows even more marked similarities to that in a poem which appeared a few years after Dowson wrote his "Cynara." In Arthur Symons' *London Nights,* a collection of poems which appeared in 1895, there is a poem entitled "To One in Alienation." According to Symons' own dating in the collected edition of 1924, this poem was written on July 31, 1892, a full fifteen months after Dowson's "Cynara" appeared. The theme of the poem is so similar to that of Dowson's that the parallel cannot go unnoticed.

> As I lay on the stranger's bed,
> And clasped the stranger-woman I had hired
> Desiring only memory dead
> Of all that I had once desired;
>
> It was then that I wholly knew
> How dearly I had loved you, my lost friend;
> While I am I, and you are you,
> How I must love you to the end.
>
> For I lay in her arms awake,
> Awake and cursing the indifferent night,
> That ebbed so slowly, for your sake,
> My heart's desire, my soul's delight;
>
> For I lay in her arms awake,
> Awake in such a solitude of shame,
> That when I kissed her, for your sake,
> My lips were sobbing on your name.

Symons, who heard Lionel Johnson read "Cynara" for Dowson before the Rhymers' Club and who udoubtedly read the poem when it appeared in *The Hobby Horse,* felt no hesitancy in giving the theme of the poem a different version. He acknowledged no indebtedness: he is, however, reported to have said, "Why speak of the matter? Such a theme was the common property of all poets who wished to treat it." If by "common property" he meant that such a theme had been discussed among the poets who gathered at the Crown or elsewhere before either Dowson's or his poem was written, there is an excellent premise on which to base the surmise that Dowson amplified the Horatian phrase under the momentum of an evening's conversation with his friends. If, on the other hand, "common property" is taken to mean that sort of theme which any poet is likely to discover and utilize without dependence on others, there is no reason to believe that Dowson and Symons were led to treat such a theme on account of a common contemporary source of inspiration. It might also be observed that Symons, who admired Dowson's poem very much, possibly regarded the theme which Dowson had brought to his attention of sufficiently frequent occurrence in the emotional experience of man to consider it "common property."

In the light of all of the interpretations of the poem thus far advanced, no irrevocable conclusion can be drawn concerning its genesis. It would seem, however, that Dowson at the time the lines were written frequently found sources of inspiration in the Roman poets, and that he was possessed of sufficient depth of emotional experience to take an Horatian phrase which had excited his imagination and amplify it with sincerity and beauty. Whether Cynara was his art, his quest for beauty, his religion, Adelaide, or innocence—or a combination and integration of them all—is a question which, if left unanswered, does not detract from the haunting music and the consummate beauty of the lines.

The poem was largely written, according to Edgar Jepson, in the bar of the Cock, Dowson's first port of call on his nightly rounds. There he quaffed his apéritifs before going over to Sherwood Street to dine on the *plat du jour* at Poland and later to play halma with Missie. There was a corner of the bar at the Cock in which his friends often found him seated behind a marble-topped table, writing on the backs of envelopes and letters with a stub of a pencil. When his supply of miscellaneous paper was exhausted, he often jotted down phrasings, and at times whole stanzas on the top of the table. His writing was obliterated at frequent intervals by the damp cloth of the attendant, who with watchful efficiency refilled his liqueur glass. When acquaintances came to the Cock while he was at work, he rapidly put all evidence of writing away, for despite the fact that he believed with the Bohemians that bars were likely places for inspiration, he was unwilling to tell his friends about a poem until it was finished. In his habit of writing in public places there was absolutely no pose. His work at the Dock, though never assiduous, kept him from un-interrupted application to a theme, with the result that his first stopping place after he left Stepney found him scribbling out phrases and stanzas which had been moving about in the back of his mind during the earlier part of the day. That a few glasses of absinthe were essential to a facility with his pencil cannot be proved. It was largely coincidental that he found time for writing during the hour in which he took his apéritifs.

By the time the Cynara poem appeared in *The Hobby Horse* his poetry began to arrest attention; and when the October issue of *The Hobby Horse* appeared, containing three poems by Dowson under the general title "In Praise of Solitude," including the beautiful "Amor Umbratilis," he was recognized as one of the most talented of the young poets. The periodical in which his poems appeared was in itself a recommendation of his merit: *The Century Guild Hobby Horse* was, according to Jepson, the link be-tween the Pre-Raphaelites and the poets of the 'nineties, and it numbered amongst its contributors some of the choicest spirits of the age. Herbert Horne, the editor, was a man of considerable erudition and literary percep-tion; and it was generally admitted that when he considered contributions he selected only the best.

The recognition which came to Dowson on account of the appearance of his poems in Horne's magazine made him eligible for association with some of the best literary circles. He found himself not only warmly wel-comed at the Crown, but by the late months of 1891 he was also intimate with most of the men who made the Fitzroy settlement the art center of London. Horne's house on Fitzroy Street became the chief gathering place not only for the contributors to *The Hobby Horse* but also for those who had distinguished themselves in the arts. Selwyn Image, coeditor of *The Hobby Horse,* Frank Brangwyn, Will Rothenstein, Ernest Rhys, Walter Crane, William Butler Yeats, Lionel Johnson, and Oscar Wilde were fre-quent visitors in the settlement. Plarr once observed that Fitzroy during the early 'nineties connoted far more than a street: it was "a movement, an influence, a glory."

There were other circles in which Dowson was welcomed. Although he was apparently never a member of the Odd Volumes Club he was invited to their dinners on several occasions. In an undated letter to Plarr, he wrote:

I had a charming evening at The Odd Vols last night. I sat opposite Todhunter who had three Irish guests (Rolleston, Percival Graves & Standish O'Grady, a charming Celt). My Lord Mayor came with a gorgeous creature to wait on him—

Lane had three editors & Le Gallienne one. There was no one else there whom I knew—except by sight only—York Powel.

And in a letter to John Lane, he referred again to the Odd Volumes: "Will you be at the Odd Volumes on the 1st. I am dining there with Brodie-Innes and shall look forward to seeing you." Evidently Dowson's company in the early 'nineties was sought by those who made literature a profession.

Much as he enjoyed his associations at the Fitzroy settlement and at the dinners of the Odd Volumes, his chief delight in the early 'nineties was his active participation in the affairs of a group who were in time to call themselves the Rhymers' Club. The delights of billiards at the Cock, a game of halma with Missie, and the gayety of the Alhambra became inconsequential when a Rhymers' Club gathering was scheduled. In fact, the habitués of the Cock and Poland soon came to know the nights on which Dowson would vary his usual rounds. Although the group often gathered in the paneled room above the ground floor at the Cheshire Cheese off Fleet Street, there was no written or unwritten regulations which restricted the place and time of meeting, nor were there any by-laws which might define too narrowly the manner in which the meetings were to be held. To one who had for long cherished the notion of a brotherhood of artists such as the groups which flourished in the Latin Quarter in Paris, the formation of a club of poets held out a marked appeal.

By the time Dowson's poems appeared in the October issue of Herbert Horne's *Hobby Horse*, the Rhymers' Club was an already flourishing society. According to Ernest Rhys, the idea of the Rhymers' Club was set going one night at the Cheshire Cheese by T. W. Rolleston, W. B. Yeats, and himself. They had evidently read some of their own poetry to one another, and profited by the impromptu criticism which their reading produced. It occurred to them that if a small group of poets, not to exceed ten, should gather frequently and read their verses and listen to the criticism of the others, they could spend evenings pleasantly and profitably. Rolleston, Yeats, and Rhys put the idea into motion by inviting friends who were poets, and who shared their notion of the pleasure and profit which could be derived from evenings spent in reading and judging their own verse. The group gathered first for dinner on the ground floor of the Cheshire Cheese, after which they adjourned to the smoking room on the top floor, which in time they began to regard as their sanctum. Each poet was supposed to bring a sample of his wares to the meetings which he was to read aloud to the group and then listen to suggestions from the others concerning how the piece might be improved.

Others who were to be regular members of the group described the origin of the Club somewhat differently. Plarr remarked that the Club had begun as a small group of Dublin poets, and at a gathering in Horne's rooms in the Fitzroy settlement the group was considerably enlarged and a definite objective was discussed for the Club's existence. He recalled that

. . . it was an evening of notabilities. Mr. Walter Crane stood with his back to the mantelpiece, deciding very kindly on the merits of our effusions. And round Oscar Wilde, not then under a cloud, hovered Lionel Johnson and Ernest Dowson, with others. That must have been in 1891, and I marvelled at the time to notice the fascination which poor Wilde exercised over the otherwise rational. Describing the scene from hearsay, my friend Mr. Morley Roberts declared that Wilde wore a black shirt front and that Dowson and Johnson, small fairy creatures in white, climbed about upon it.

Mr. Roberts' picture of Dowson's and Johnson's adulation of Wilde is little more than fancy, as is the implication that Wilde was a considerable influence on the spirit of the group. Wilde was never a member of the Rhymers' Club, and his influence in founding it and giving it a motive for existence was very slight. Swinburne and Rossetti, especially the latter, were subconscious influences on the work of the group, but it was to Walter Pater that most of the members looked for their philosophy. *Marius the Epicurean* had not spent its force at Oxford alone: it had penetrated the conversations at the center table at the Crown and the Fitzroy settlement; it had become the standard around which most of the artists of the decade gathered. "It taught us to walk upon a rope, tightly stretched through serene air," said Yeats, "and we were left to keep our feet upon a swaying rope in a storm. Pater made us learned." Although Pater's influence was pronounced in the conversations and productions of the Rhymers, the promulgation of his philosophy was in no way the chief objective of the Club. The French *symbolistes,* especially Paul Verlaine, had brought an unmistakable influence to bear upon the young men of the group such as Arthur Symons, Richard Le Gallienne, and Ernest Dowson. To Dowson, Verlaine's *Art Poétique* had become an eloquent expression of the true aim of poetry. In fact, toward the middle 'nineties, Verlaine's influence on Dowson was transcendent. Thinking of his own apostleship, he called the Rhymers Verlaine's disciples. When Verlaine came to London to lecture in November 1893 at Barnard's Inn in High Holborn, the Rhymers went in a body; and there was at least one of their number who listened avidly to everything the master said. He even contemplated inviting Verlaine to a meeting of the Club at the Cheshire Cheese, but apparently lacking courage, he contented himself with sitting near Verlaine at the Crown, whither the group took the poet after his lecture, and with talking with him at the Constitutional with Herbert Horne.

The Rhymers' Club was composed of such widely varied personalities, of different ages and different poetic interests and objectives, that any attempt to name a single standard-bearer is certain to be misleading. A casual glance at the names of the members is enough to indicate that such a group was dominated by no one influence. According to Dr. G. A. Greene, who acted as secretary to a club without rules or officers, the following men were official members: John Davidson (who was irregular in attendance and contributed nothing to the books of the Club), Ernest Dowson, Edwin J. Ellis, George Arthur Greene, Lionel Johnson, Arthur Cecil Hillier, Richard Le Gallienne, Victor Plarr, Ernest Radford, Ernest Rhys, Thomas William Rolleston, Arthur Symons, John Todhunter, and William Butler Yeats. In addition to these official members, Plarr recalled a group of permanent guests who included John Gray, Edward Rose, J. T. Nettleship, Morley Roberts, A. B. Chamberlain, Edward Garnett, and William Theodore Peters. Despite the fact that Herbert Horne was not included in the secretary's list of official members, or in Plarr's list of permanent guests, he was an active participant in the affairs of the Club without contributing to its books. Edgar Jepson was another whose name does not appear on Greene's or Plarr's lists, but who attended the meetings fairly often.

Such a varied group undoubtedly provided a representative cross-section of the interests and inclinations of literary London in the early half of the 'nineties. Dowson and Johnson, both of the same age, in their early twenties, were the youngest members; with Todhunter in his fifties, and Rolleston and Greene in their mid-forties, representing the more mature element in the Club. The disparity in ages, as well as a natural difference in poetic interests and aims, made the group impressionable to many influences and representative of varied objectives. To identify the Rhymers' Club with the esthetic movement of the 'nineties, or with decadence, or with any other so-called movement is a convenience for literary historians, but of dubious critical worth. Visitors at the meetings at times went away with the impression that the Club was following one standard-bearer, but at subsequent meetings they discovered a new leader. A few of the Celts of the group gave the impression to occasional visitors that the Club was one of the forerunners of the Celtic Renaissance. On evenings on which Yeats and Johnson were the principal talkers—and they often were—it is quite possible that the Rhymers' Club might have impressed a visitor as a definite part of the Irish Literary Rebirth.

Edgar Jepson, more in fun than in an effort to provide an accurate state-

ment of what he witnessed at the meetings he had attended, found the
Irish influence sufficiently pronounced to observe of the group at large:

They were all very Celtic too, for it was the days of the Celtic fringe. John Todhunter, as you will gather from the name, was a Celt; and Plarr, whose father
was an Alsatian, was a Celt; and Johnson, again the Celtic name, was a Celt—
at one time he assumed a brogue and addressed me as "Me dearr"; and Mr.
Symons, a Dravidian Welshman, was a Celt; and Dowson, who was probably of
as pure Norman London descent as you could find, was inclined to believe that
there was a Celtic strain in him; and Yeats, who was plainly a Firbolg, was the
most Celtic of all, and they all declared that there was a Celtic Renaissance.

Despite the fact that Yeats at the time was an enthusiast for movements
of any sort and that he did a considerable amount of the talking at the
gatherings of the Club, his zeal and enterprise were not enough to give the
society more than an occasional Celtic flavor, even with the fervent support
of Lionel Johnson. Furthermore, Yeats himself expressed the belief that
Rossetti and Pater were the guiding stars of the group, a statement which
would indicate that the most Celtic of all the members was conscious of a
force far different from that which made possible the Celtic Renaissance.
Symons and Dowson would have probably suggested the French poets,
especially Verlaine, as the standard; and John Davidson would have suggested that Nietzsche's philosophy dominated the thought of the society.
Although it has become almost traditional to identify Yeats with the leadership of most of the literary movements of the past fifty years, Yeats's
presence in the group had no great influence on the poetry which the members produced. The Rhymers' Club was the result of many influences and it
expressed its interests in many voices. "It had none of the propagandizing
significance of other such clubs," said Richard Le Gallienne,

. . . and, as a body, was not an energetic institution, nor of long life. Its members lacked any common fusing artistic ideal such as has animated, say, the subsequent imagist movement. Each was doing his own work in his own way,
and the significance of the Club was in its individuals rather than in any col-
lective character.

No one of the group had distinguished himself particularly at the time,
nor was any one truly erudite. Later, to be sure, some of them were to become great poets and critics; but in 1891, Symons, Le Gallienne, Rhys, and
Yeats were not much more than apprentices in their respective fields.
Symons was concerned with music halls and the French *symbolistes*, Le
Gallienne had been fortunate to secure a commission to do some critical
work for the *New Review*, Rhys was keeping informed about current

literature and developing literary perceptions which were to make him a great editor, and Yeats had been studying what he called the Christian Cabala and turning his pen to verse which showed more than promise. Lionel Johnson claimed all branches of knowledge for his own, even the province of Botticelli which Herbert Horne had surveyed with relative thoroughness; but Johnson's reputation for erudition at the time exceeded his attainments. Dowson's practice of using Latin phrases as titles for his poems, and his references to his reading of the Roman poets in his letters and conversations, gave him the distinction of being the Latinist in the group; but Johnson, Greene, and Plarr, none of whom was a scholar in the strict sense, all were probably as well equipped with Latin as he. No one of the group was sufficiently outstanding in reputation or attainments at the time to be the natural choice for leader. Deference was probably given to Todhunter's flowing beard, but even seniority had small effect on a group whose only concern was writing poetry.

The Club, though informally organized without rules and officers, convened at times to consider recommendations for new members and to examine the benefits which had accrued. Formal elections of new members were held, with an occasional blackballing. In *The Trembling of the Veil*, Yeats recalled how Herbert Horne had nearly brought the Club to its end by introducing four Scotchmen, all on the same evening, in order to bring new blood into the group. Evidently aspirants for the honor of membership were called upon to deliver some of their poetic wares, after which the Club voted them in or out. Yeats remembered how one of the Scots read a melodramatic piece about a lifeboat which had evidently been intended for a public school elocutionary exercise, while later another of the candidates for membership described his experiences as a gold-digger in Australia in unpoetic Scots prose. The newcomers, Yeats reported, excelled in argument which was more robust than persuasive. When Horne insisted on their immediate election, the Rhymers, with that complacency of good manners which is characteristic of well-bred Englishmen, voted them in, though they felt at the time that they were ringing the knell of the Club. It took Yeats seven hours to round the group up for an extempore meeting, at which time the Scots, who had not been notified of the time and place, were voted out.

It appears that Herbert Horne, who was not an official member but had a sort of proprietary interest in the Club by reason of the fact that the group was organized at his home on Fitzroy Street, was the chief agitator for new members. He was accustomed to describe the Club as lacking in "blood and guts." His criticism evidently had enough truth in it to cause the members to look around for new faces and fresh voices. Dowson, understanding only in part what Horne meant by "blood and guts," and eager to contribute his share in the movement for a bigger and better Rhymers' Club, was responsible for presenting to the group John Evelyn Barlas, whom he had probably met at Henekey's very late at night, and who had attracted him by his poetry in *Phantasmagoria: Dream Fugues* which the Driver Press had issued at Chelmsford in 1887, and by his anarchistic principles. To Plarr he wrote sometime in January 1892: "The latest Rhymer is one Barlas, a charming poet and anarchist, who was lately run in for shooting the House of Commons." To what went on in the House of Commons, Dowson was totally indifferent, but the fact that a man had been "run in" for opposing authority gave him the impression that such a man could undoubtedly provide some of the "blood and guts" of which Horne spoke. Dowson's attempt to bring Barlas into the circle as a member fell through, however, for after the "charming poet and anarchist" had been a visitor several times, the group tired of him, and he probably of them. Dowson, too, soon lost track of him. In a letter to Charles Sayle, who made inquiries during the spring of 1892 about Barlas' whereabouts, Dowson reported: "To search for Barlas is like the search after the Sangreal."

There is a record of an effort to bring Francis Thompson into the Club, but the author of "The Hound of Heaven" evidently was satisfied to spend his evenings with the Meynells. What Thompson's reasons were for declining membership have not been disclosed, but it is likely that in spite of the persuasive presence of Lionel Johnson, he found the atmosphere which the group created uninspiring.

Reports vary widely concerning what constituted a typical Rhymers' Club evening. Although there was no rule which prescribed the paneled room at the Cheshire Cheese as the place of meeting, by the winter of 1891- 92 it was generally agreed that the old tavern off Fleet Street was both conveniently located and appropriate in atmosphere to the interests of the Club. In fact, when Dowson told his friends that he would meet them at the Club, he meant the Cheshire Cheese. On the evenings on which a meeting was scheduled, the group would gather on the ground floor for dinner; and after paying their respects to Polly, the parrot, which was already along in years but could still screech out half-intelligible phrases from *Hamlet*, the members arranged themselves in the high, pew-like seats for a meal which had little to distinguish it in quantity and quality from their usual dinners. There was nothing of the banquet in these repasts: soups, chops, vegetables, and beer were the fare, with wine on only rare occasions. Le Gallienne recalls a "discreet conviviality" at all the meetings he attended

The talk over the meal usually turned to literary matters, but it was not until the group adjourned to their sanctum on the upper floor that the real business of the Club was begun.

The meetings, according to Edgar Jepson, were more in the English and Johnsonian tradition than in that of the *Quartier Latin*. Each poet had his own beer mug and long church-warden pipe. Jepson, who was a fairly frequent visitor, reported that the meetings appeared as of an almost profound solemnity. On the evenings that he was with the group, he never heard a Rhymer laugh. "Their smiles were rare and constrained," he recalled.

For besides Dowson and Yeats and Johnson and Plarr there were some of the most serious poets I have ever met, at least three of them bearded. There was Dr. John Todhunter . . . an aged man with one of those flowing beards, and G. A. Greene, with a trimmed beard, whom Plarr called *Il Greno,* because he had so seriously soaked himself in Italy, and Hillier and Rolleston, all seething with the stern sense of their poetic mission, and all of them, except Yeats, read their verse in hushed voices. I was never a Rhymer myself, but when I went to their meetings I read my verse—in a hushed voice.

Jepson's description of the manner in which a Rhymers' evening was spent is quite different from that which Arthur Symons, one of the most active Rhymers, has given. In spite of the fact that he attended the meetings regularly, his remarks concerning how the evenings were spent were probably based on a few memorable experiences which were exceptional rather than representative. He recalled how

. . . young poets, then very young, recited their own verse to one another with a desperate and ineffectual attempt to get into key with the Latin quarter. Through few of us were, as a matter of fact, Anglo-Saxon, we could not help feeling that we were in London, and the atmosphere of London is not the atmosphere of movements or societies. . . . This brave venture of the Rhymers' Club, though it lasted for two or three years, and produced two little books of verse which will some day be literary curiosities, was not quite a satisfactory kind of cénacle.

This, of course, was written after Symons had put away childish things and was able to smile at the very young poets, of whom he had been one, who had read their poems at the Cheshire Cheese. Yeats, too, recalled these meetings after the passage of forty years, but he made no mention of a desperate attempt to catch the spirit of the Latin Quarter. His observations bear out Jepson's that the meetings were more in the English tradition than in the French. "The meetings," said Yeats, "were always decorous and often dull; someone would read out a poem and we would comment, too politely for the criticism to have great value; and yet that we read our poems, and thought that they could be so tested, was a definition of our aims." Perhaps the meetings were often dull, but even after the passage of forty years, Yeats remarked:

I shall . . . remember all my life that evening when Lionel Johnson read or spoke aloud in his musical monotone, where meaning and cadence found the most precise elocution, his poem suggested "By the Statue of King Charles at Charing Cross." It was as though I had listened to a great speech. Nor will that poem be to me again what it was that first night.

Although the criticism offered by the members of the Club generally was considerate of the feelings of the Rhymer whose verses were under discussion, it had the virtue of encouraging the more sensitive poets of the group to display their wares and to continue writing. Polite it surely was, but it was as a rule spontaneous and informal. There were times when some of the members were of the opinion that the discussions might prove more profitable if some prearranged program were followed, but such suggestions were rarely acted upon. Most of the Rhymers believed that the Club should be only an agency for reading and discussing poetry of their own making, with the result that the few attempts which were intended to make of the Club a sort of literary society for the formal discussion of literature at large found small response.

One night at Johnson's rooms, after a meeting of the Rhymers, Yeats, with his talent for cultivating organized discussion, proposed that the meetings in the near future be devoted to a consideration of the stages through which poetry had evolved. He pointed out that there were essentially four stages, which, as Plarr recalled, he named "the Diabolic, the Seraphic, the Celestial, and something else." After defining these stages as they existed in his mind to Plarr, Johnson, and Dowson, Yeats suggested that each of the members present prepare himself to discuss a stage at successive meetings of the Club. To Plarr, the zealous Yeats assigned the first stage, which was to include a consideration of the earliest forms of poetry. He was to point out, Yeats suggested, that poetry had its origin among the aborigines, and found its first expression in long lists of laudatory titles, chanted by tribesmen in praise of their valiant leaders. Johnson and Dowson were assigned successive stages, in each of which Yeats suggested a method of approach. Dowson became uneasy at the prospect, not only by reason of the fact that he disliked to hold the floor for a considerable period but also because he had no sympathy with an attempt to make out of the group a formally organized literary society. He was one of the Rhymers about whom Symons spoke when he said that there were those in the group who tried to get into key with the Latin Quarter. Furthermore, Dowson was far more interested in his own poetry and that of his friends than in any systematic and thorough survey of the entire province. Although Johnson was ever eager for scholarly discussion, he and Plarr sided with Dowson in voting down Yeats's proposal for an organized discussion of the history of poetry.

Dowson's eagerness to keep the Club from descending to the level of a conventionally organized literary society was shared by most of the younger men of the group, but his nature was too yielding to hold out long and vigorously against the plans which some of the more mature members arranged for the meetings. Greene was especially active in his efforts to give each meeting a sort of unity of purpose. After scanning the *Dictionary of National Biography,* or a similar work of reference, he compiled a formidable list of dates on which the great English poets of the past had been born in order to provide the Rhymers with a series of Anniversary Nights on which the members would pay tribute to Christopher Marlowe, Alexander Pope, and William Shenstone by bringing in commemoration verses suitable to the occasion. On the Marlowe night, Ernest Rhys was without a rhyme of celebration, and as a punishment for his lack of coöperation he was commanded to produce on the spur of the moment an appropriate poem. After cudgeling his talent for a while, Rhys recited:

ON MARLOWE

With wine and blood and reckless harlotry,
He sped the heroic flame of English verse;
Bethink ye, Rhymers, what your claim may be,
Who in smug suburbs put the Muse to nurse?

Although there are no records of punishment meted out to Dowson for his failure to enter wholeheartedly into the spirit of Anniversary Nights, it may readily be assumed that he was out of sympathy with such methods of spending the time of the meetings. Facile as he was with rhyme, his lack of interest in commemorative verse undoubtedly blighted any enjoyment in merely turning out measures. The roll was never called at the meetings, but it may be concluded that on nights on which commemorative verse was to be produced, he performed his chore perfunctorily, or missed the meeting altogether.

By the late months of 1891, the Club had an additional incentive for existence to which Dowson responded enthusiastically: an anthology of representative poems by the members of the Club was to be published. Yeats was largely responsible for the suggestion that the group issue a volume, and in recalling his reasons for proposing the book, he paid Dowson a very fine tribute. "For long," said Yeats, "I only knew Dowson's *O Mors*, to quote but the first words of its long title, and his *Villanelle of Sunset* from his reading, and it was because of the desire to hold them in my hand that I suggested the first *Book of the Rhymers' Club*. They were not speech, but perfect song, though song for the speaking voice." Certainly anyone with Yeats's sensitivity to beauty would be unsatisfied to hear them only once, and would want to hold them in his hand. The other Rhymers were at once eager to follow Yeats's suggestion, and Dowson himself became one of the most active members in making the publication of the volume a reality. The volume, he realized, would give him not only an additional vehicle in which to circulate his verse, but it would also give the Rhymers a more substantial objective toward which to strive than that of writing rhymes about Marlowe.

Only three hundred and fifty copies of the book were issued by Elkin Mathews and John Lane in the autumn of 1892. Nine of the ninety-four pages in the volume were given to Dowson, six poems in all, the maximum allowed to any one member. Two of the poems included—"The Carmelite Nuns of the Perpetual Adoration" and "Amor Umbratilis"—had appeared in Herbert Horne's *Century Guild Hobby Horse*, but the remaining four appeared for the first time in print. "O Mors! Quam Amara Est Memoria Tua Homini Pacem Habenti In Substantiis Suis," "Ad Domnulam Suam," "Vanitas," and "Villanelle of Sunset," all of which had been written before the proposal of an anthology had been made, were included in the volume.

The publication of the book was made possible by the adoption of a coöperative plan between the contributors and the publishers. Expenses and profits were to be divided in accordance with the space taken by each contributor. The book was scarcely intended to make money for the Rhymers or the publishers; the authors were to be given one copy for each poem contributed. The maximum number of poems accepted from one contributor was not to exceed six, nor could any member be represented by only one poem: three were the minimum, although in one instance an exception was granted: Rolleston contributed only two. It was finally decided that the selections of the poems to be included were to be made by a committee of four, but the Committee's selections were to be submitted to the Club for its approval. In an undated and hitherto unpublished letter, Dowson explained to his fellow Rhymer Plarr the plan for the publication of the volume.

Bridge Dock,
Limehouse

Mon cher Victor

I am grieved at this long absence of yours; but I hope it implies nothing more than convalescence, and that we shall soon have you once more with us. In the meantime, I write to you, as an official exponent of the sentiments of the "Rhymers" at their last meeting, and at their request to ask if we can count on you, as a contributor to "The Book of the Rhymers' Club" which it is proposed to issue, in an inexpensive manner in the autumn. The Rhymers to be represented in it are pretty much as follows:

Yeats, Green [*sic*], Johnson, Radford, Le Gallienne, Ellis*, Ghose*, Symons*, Rolleston, Todhunter*, Rhys. Those names with asterisks attached are those of persons who have not yet *definitely* promised to join in the scheme. May we add your name definitely to those? The expense will be very small as it will be distributed amongst all, in proportion to the pages given to each; and in view of their numbers and the fact that the maximum of space allowed to any Rhymer is 6 pieces; it could not well be anything but inconsiderable: profits of course if any, on the same scale. We count on your consent. Assuming it then as given, I have to inform you that at the last meeting it was arranged, as to order of sending in and selecting rhymes, that Johnson should be, as a central person intending to be in town all the summer, appointed a sort of receiver of all the verse, although the selection is either to be made by the whole Club in council (which seems to me impracticable) or by a committee of 3 to be subsequently stated: 2nd that the maximum of pieces is to be 6 and the minimum 3 (probably)—3rd that each Rhymer is exhorted to send in *double* the number of pieces he wishes inserted—say 12 for 6, 10 for 5 etc. and that he may mark them in the preferential order he gives to them himself; and he *must* state Where and when, if at all, they have been published. 4th that the verses should be sent if possible to Johnson before the 20th instant. in order that they may be put before the House at the next meeting of the Rhymers and the book be gotten under way *quam celerime*. I have now, I think, discharged my duty, in I hope a fashion not too obscure to be unintelligible. We pray you to give your adherence to this motion and send your rhyme forthwith; or better still, recover your health and come back to the Cheshire Cheese before the 20th. This is our prayer. But I see the post goeth. Please remember me very kindly to your people.

Yours ever,

ERNEST DOWSON†

Dowson's belief that it would be impracticable for the Club in council

† Written hastily over the salutation of this letter is a reference to one of his prose tales, possibly *The Story of a Violin.* "I have just finished a story which I have sent to Macmillan, which will doubtless soon return." The original letter is in the possession of Dowson's friend Michael Holland, who kindly copied it for me.

to select the poems for the book was sound enough, for the Rhymers, like most clubs, had a few die-hards who could delay the approval or rejection of a poem for hours. Even with a committee at work, the matter of selection was difficult. Considerable difference of opinion arose in some instances, for the poems which were finally selected for inclusion were not always the authors' favorites. Although there is no extant record which might indicate the number of poems Dowson submitted, it is reasonable to assume that he turned in at least twelve, for his manuscript book at the time that the project of the anthology was under way indicates that he had over fifty choice poems from which to select. Of the members represented in the first *Book of the Rhymers' Club* only Dowson, Johnson, Rhys, Yeats, and Greene had the maximum of six poems.

For the merit of the book at large, it might have been well had some of the poems submitted by Greene been scrapped altogether in order to make room for more of Dowson's. The first poem in the collection, by the honourable secretary Greene, which understandably enough has never been reprinted, is fortunately not representative of the quality of the book as a whole.

SONG OF THE SONGSMITHS

(First Anniversary of the Rhymers' Club)

Here we do meet again,
After a full year's time:
Here we do meet again,
Meet with our old refrain,
Praise of the regal rhyme.
Songsmiths like them of old
Fashioned their speech of gold
In a far, forgotten clime,
We at that ancient fire
With our young bright breath suspire,
And hammer the golden rhyme,
Hammer the ringing rhyme,
Till the echoes tire.

Who is it jeers at our song?
Scoffs at an art sublime?
Who is it jeers at our song?
We who know right from wrong
Worship the godlike rhyme.
Still on the world-wide breeze,
Over the surge of the seas,
Comes like an echoed chime

The voice of all passions that play
In the dim heart of man alway,
With the rush of a rolling rhyme,
The lilt of a lulling rhyme,
To the end of day.

Ours is the prentice-hand;
Yet 'tis in us no crime,
Here in the misty land,
To seek for the fire that was fanned
By kings of the kingly rhyme.
They have gone down to the shade,
Leaving the songs they made
A wreath for the brows of Time.
Still is the great world young;
Not yet is the lyre unstrung,
As it shakes to the quivering rhyme,
Sighs for the resonant rhyme
Of the songs unsung.

Ours are the echoes at least
That fall from the golden prime;
Ours are the echoes at least,
Ours are the crumbs from the feast
At the feet of the queenly rhyme:
Ours is the task to prolong
The joy and the sorrow of song
In the mist of years that begrime;
In the clinging mist of the years,
With reverent toil and with tears,
To hammer the golden rhyme,
Hammer the ringing rhyme
Till the mad world hears.

The closing piece of the collection, by Ernest Rhys, is a better sample of the quality of verse which the volume contains.

AT THE RHYMERS' CLUB

The Toast

Set fools unto their folly!
Our folly is pure wit,
As 'twere the Muse turned jolly:
For poets' melancholy,—
We will not think of it.

As once Rare Ben and Herrick
Set older Fleet Street mad,
With wit not esoteric,
And laughter that was lyric,
And roystering rhymes and glad:

As they, we drink defiance
Tonight to all but Rhyme,
And most of all to Science,
And all such skins of lions
That hide the ass of time.

Tonight to rhyme as they did
Were well,—ah, were it ours,
Who find the muse degraded,
And changed, I fear, and faded,
Her laurel crown and flowers.

Ah rhymers, for that sorrow
The more o'ertakes delight,
The more this madness borrow:—
If care be king tomorrow
To toast Queen Rhyme to-night.

Interesting as these pieces by Greene and Rhys are in the light they shed
on the spirit of the group, they indicate—especially "The Song of the Songsmiths"—that the quality of the contributions to the volume was not always
high. The variety of themes and manners, and the wide differences in quality of the fifty-seven pieces which formed the contents bear out the statement that the Rhymers' Club had little in common save their general interest in verse. The poems which Lionel Johnson and Yeats submitted are
infinitely superior to those of Greene and Radford, but they are not among
their best. Nor are Dowson's six poems his best, though they undoubtedly
did much to raise the general quality of the book. They are, as Arthur
Symons, who had contributed only four poems, remarked, "at once the
most delicate and distinguished poems which it contained." Even before
the volume was issued, it was generally felt among those of the group
who had real taste in such matters that whereas many of the members were
thoroughly competent rhymers, Dowson was one of the few poets in the
Club. After the passing of forty years, Ernest Rhys remarked: ". . . the
one Rhymer whom we secretly believed to be the most potential of the
group was Ernest Dowson."

That which *The Century Guild Hobby Horse* had done to bring Dowson's name as a poet before London readers, the first *Book of the Rhymers'*

Club carried on with noteworthy success. The small issue of 350 volumes was exhausted before the end of February 1892. The book, which Arthur Symons predicted would some day be a literary curiosity, became rare even before the close of the century; but before it became a collectors' item, it circulated in ever widening groups until few Londoners who professed literary interests were unfamiliar with the poems of its principal contributors. " 'The Book of the Rhymers' Club,' published by Lane in 1892, may be regarded as the first concerted attack of the 'Bodley Head Poets' on the British public, though it was not conceived as such and had no prevailing tone," said Le Gallienne. "It had no purpose beyond bringing together in friendly association, after the manner of such old miscellanies as 'England's Helicon' or Davidson's 'Poetical Rhapsody,' examples of the work of twelve poets . . . who had constituted themselves a very informal club . . ."

Dowson shared the satisfaction which the Rhymers felt at the successful distribution of the book. The notices which appeared in the papers concerning the collection and his part in it were written largely by men who were friendly with individual members of the Club, or with the group as a whole, with the result that the reviews were generally favorable. Dowson followed the notices of the reception of the book with an interest which would seem to belie the assumption that he never cared greatly for what readers and reviewers thought of his work. Sometime in February 1892, soon after *The Book of the Rhymers' Club* had appeared, he wrote to Plarr:

> *Bridge Dk.*
> *Limehouse.*

Dear Victor,

Can you forgive me for this extremely unpardonable procrastination. I ought to have answered your kind invitation at once, but I was uncertain whether I should be able to come or not and what with one distraction and another, I let the psychological moment slip. I must try and come some Sunday soon, but while my people are ill, I find it impossible to make any fixtures. Thanks muchly for your cuttings and the letter which is most charming and polyglot! I return you all herewith save the *Daily Chronicle,* which I should like to keep as you have another, and the *Daily News,* which I will send you tomorrow, when I have shown it to my people. I am amused to find that my cursory acquaintance with the Anthology of Anthologies has made such a deep impression on my manner— or can it be that my reviewer does not know what the Gr. Anthology is about? I didn't go to the Rhymers last night, nor to the last meeting but one; chiefly because the meetings were in inaccessible places and the night was cold, and partly because I was in a condition too lyrical even for the society of poets. So I have not run across Green [*sic*]; but you will be glad to hear that the edition is entirely exhausted. I have seen scarcely anyone lately but Gray and Hall; once for a short time Horne, & for a moment, Image: and there have been accidental meetings. In effect I am become far too absorbed to do anything but sit, in Poland, and gather the exquisite moments. For—to quote mes derniers—

> The wisdom of the world said unto me:
> "Go forth and run; the race is to the brave;
> Perchance some honour tarrieth for thee!"
> "As tarrieth," I said, "for sure the grave!"
> For I had pondered on the rune of roses,
> Which to her votaries the moon discloses.
>
> "Yea," said I, "for her eyes are pure and sweet
> As lilies ,and the fragrance of her hair
> Is many laurels; and it is not meet
> To run for shadows when the prize is here."
> This said I, knowing all the rune of roses,
> Which in her hour, the pale, soft moon discloses.

I will write soon. I hope your Mother makes good progress.

Ever yrs,

ERNEST DOWSON.

P.S. Dear Image! How charming his notice is. I had already obtained it.*

I have deliberately quoted this letter in full, for in Plarr's *Reminiscences* the letter appears with many deletions, which, in some respects, are more illuminating of Dowson's state of mind at the time than the passages which Parr chose to quote. Dowson was evidently pleased by Image's notice, and he was sufficiently interested in the reviews in the *Daily Chronicle* and *Daily News* to want to keep them for a time in order to show them to his parents. Obviously he was attentive to what the reviews had to say about his part in *The Book of the Rhymers' Club*. But in the same letter in which he showed such interest in what others thought about his work, he wrote out a poem in which, after weighing the benefits which are attendant on a struggle for fame, he came to the conclusion that fame was but a shadow. In the last stanza of the poem, which was not to appear until 1896 in *Verses*, under the title "Sapientia Lunae," he made plain that the laurels for which others ran were not comparable to the prize which he felt he had found in his love for Missie.

In spite of the fact that he expressed his unwillingness to compete for the laurels of fame, he continued to show a considerable interest in the

---

* The letter contains only the first and last stanzas of a four stanza poem which Dowson later included in *Verses* under the title "Sapientia Lunae." The stanzas appear in somewhat different phrasing in *Verses*.

reputation of the Rhymers' volume, and in the activities of the Club. In the autumn of 1892, soon after the death of Tennyson, he wrote to Plarr: "Were you at the Rhymers last night? I wish I could have managed to be of the party. I suppose it is settled that we are to hold the Laurelship as a corporate office. . . ." In other letters, he told Plarr that "The book is good—better than I expected, although the binding leaves much to be desired," and that some of Plarr's poems which had been rejected he considered at least as good as the poems which had been selected for the book. On October 24, 1892, he wrote to his friend:

I searched for you at the Independent Theatre the other night, but you were not. Meeting there, along with many other persons, the poet Green [*sic*], I undertook to send out notices for a Rhymers' meeting au Cheshire on Friday next the . . . Will you take this in lieu of a post-card and endeavour to come. I have a quaint old German coming . . . whom you will appreciate.

If Dowson cared little about the fame which might attend his association with the Club, he was at least active in its affairs. Then, too, for one who considered fame only a shadow, he showed a remarkable aptitude for gaining recognition amongst an ever-widening circle of readers.

Under the impetus which a successful volume of verse provided, the Rhymers' Club continued to hold meetings until the summer of 1894. The prospect of publishing a second volume kept the group together, but the meetings became less frequent and the attendance began to drop off. Between the time of the appearance of the first volume and *The Second Book of the Rhymers' Club,* Dowson lost some of his interest in the activities of the Club, probably on account of the irregularity of his attendance. Illness, chiefly colds and rheumatism, frequently prevented his venturing out; and in midwinter, the inconvenience of a trip from Stepney or from Chadwell Heath, where his parents had taken a house, often kept him at home. Even in the months in which the Rhymers had been most active and the weather mild his attendance at the meetings had been unpredictable. Increasingly ominous signs appeared in his letters to his friends in which he explained vaguely the reasons for his absence. As early as May 19, 1892, he had written to Plarr from Bridge Dock:

Mon cher Victor

Why do I never see you? Are you always away or am I, or where are we? "Mais où sont les neiges d'anton"? I hear from Horne that you of the Hobby Horse are all enrhumé, but I hope this does not apply at all seriously to you? I myself have had one of the worst rheums within my memory, but today I am recovered. On Wednesday (tomorrow) I shall dine at home. Will you look in upon me? But perhaps I will call tonight at Fitzroy St. and perhaps,

I will see you. I hope, all the affairs prosper. Mine do not flourish? or only by fits and starts; alternations, which wear me out more than uniform frustration would do. I saw Hillier on Sunday; it seems agreed that the Rhymers should meet au Cheshire, on Friday but nobody has arranged to send out the notices. Will you or Johnson do this, as we have not the list of addresses? It is ages since I managed to go to one, as a rule now I am too chronically irritated to go anywhere, except at rare precarious intervals when there happens to be nowhere to go, and nothing to do.

I am making rhymes in the meantime and trying to write a short story.

Is your muse fertile just now? Or are you too fortunately occupied otherwise to woo her? Well, well,

t   à   t

ERNEST DOWSON*

"The rare precarious intervals" when there happened "to be nowhere to go, and nothing to do" became rarer by the winter of 1893. Poor health and the debilitating alternations of hope and despair at home and Poland .left him with little energy to be an active participant in the project of the second volume of Rhymers' verses. His irregularity at the meetings caused him to begin to harbor notions that the members had tired of him. Half bitterly he expressed his belief on one occasion that he was never missed at the meetings, and that the Club would do just as well without him.

When George Greene wrote to him for his contributions to the second book he left the letter unanswered for days, not only because he had other things of more importance on his mind, but also because he lacked the assurance that the Rhymers really wanted him to contribute to the book. He was evidently reassured, however, for to Plarr he reported—in a somewhat half-hearted manner—that he would try to hunt up the necessary half-dozen poems and send them to Greene, adding, "I should think that the Star Chamber will have decided by this time to dispense with me."

After his poems were finally submitted to Greene, he began to take a renewed interest in the Club and its second project. He went so far as to suggest to those who had been appointed to see the volume through the press that it should be better bound than the first book, and showed concern over the poems which he had submitted and over the quality of the contributions of the others. In an undated letter to Plarr, he wrote:

Bridge Dock, Limehouse

Cher Vieux,

Do you like the enclosed verses enough to include them in the Book in lieu

* One of the few dated letters which Dowson wrote. The original is in Michael Holland's collection.

of "Benedictio Domini"? Johnson to whom I conveyed the weighty packet seems to like them the best of my budget. He was very amicable and we drank much absinthe together. I voted for 6 of your poems with much difficulty for I liked them all so much that I wished to see them all included. I placed the "Cinerarium," "Breton Beggar," and "Nejnun" first—of L's I think I most admired the Cavalier and Mystic. Verlaine is after all still in London. I am dining with Horne and Horne Père at the Constitutional tonight to meet him. So that if I have the courage I will even suggest to the Master that he should honour his disciples with a visit to the Cheese. A bientot—with all amenities to Mesdames Votre Mère et votre femme et à cette chère Bébé.

T. à toi.

ERNEST DOWSON*

With the "Star Chamber's" selection of his own verses he was dissatisfied. "They have chucked my *Lady's Hands,* and my *Terre Promise* for two verses which I like less. Mine will be a poor show," he told Plarr in a later letter. Those who made the selections, however, chose wisely, for the poem which Dowson called *Lady's Hands,* which was later printed in *Verses* as "Ad Manus Puellae" is surely not on the same plane with "Extreme Unction," "To One in Bedlam," "Non Sum Qualis Eram . . . Cynarae," "Growth," "The Garden of Shadow," and "You Would Have Understood Me Had You Waited," the six poems which the committee selected. Of these, "To One in Bedlam" had appeared in Hubert Crackanthorpe's *Albemarle* in August 1892, and the Cynara poem had appeared in *The Century Guild Hobby Horse* in April 1891. The others appeared in print for the first time. "Extreme Unction" was sent in immediately before the book went to press, and at Lionel Johnson's insistence, it was included instead of "Benedictio Domini."

Had *The Second Book of the Rhymers' Club* contained only the poems by Dowson, it would have justified its existence. "The poor show" which he told Plarr his poems would make did much to give the volume its distinction. The six poems which the "Star Chamber" decided to include are undoubtedly among Dowson's finest works. The second book was better bound than the first, as he had suggested; but with the exception of a dozen pieces, including Dowson's, the quality of the contents was small improvement on that of the first volume. It contained forty more pages than the first collection, and five hundred copies, instead of 350, were issued under

* Written over the salutation of this letter there is the note: "N.B. let me know what you think of Moore's story in Dec. Macmillan." The verses to which he referred were "Extreme Unction." They were written on the back of the letter. The date of the letter can be ascertained by recalling the time of Verlaine's visit to London in November 1893. Michael Holland, who has the original letter, has copied it for me.

essentially the same coöperative terms which had made possible the publication of the earlier volume. The book did not fare badly, either with the reviewers or in circulation, though report has it that some fifty copies were still on Mathews' hands a year after it was issued.

The Second Book of the Rhymers' Club was the swan song of the Club. When the summer began to call many of the members away for their holiday, meetings were given up; and by the autumn no one apparently was sufficiently energetic to bring the group together again as a club. Yeats offered one explanation for the Club's demise. "The Rhymers had begun to break up in tragedy," he wrote, "though we did not know that until the play had finished." Thinking largely of a few of its members rather than of the group at large, he remarked that unlike the Victorian poets, almost all the Rhymers were poor men, "and had made it a matter of conscience to turn from every kind of money-making that prevented good writing." The poverty of a few of the members, however, was surely not the principal reason for the disbanding of the Club. Although sufficiently sincere in their apostleship to beauty, the Rhymers, for the most part, were not the garret-living, dry-crust-eating group suggested by Yeats's remark. In fact, with most of them the devotion to beauty was sufficiently tempered by practical considerations to permit them to turn their hands to more lucrative work than writing poetry. When Yeats traced the tragedy of the Rhymers' Club to the suggestion that the form of lyric which the members followed appealed by its very nature to unstable men, he failed to take into account the fact that the Rhymers followed no single literary creed, and that most of the members were pretty stable. Exclude Johnson, Davidson, and Dowson from the group, and those who remain—Plarr, Greene, Symons, Le Gallienne, Rhys, to name only a few—were hardly the victims of a poetic creed, much less tragic figures. The tragedy which Yeats observed in the demise of the Club was only a natural drifting apart among men who with the passage of time developed different interests. Then, too, it is probable that Herbert Horne's judgment that the Club lacked "blood and guts" had much to do with its dissolution. It is remarkable that such a heterogeneous group with nothing but a common interest in verse should have existed as long as it did.

Dowson's irregularity at the meetings in the winter and spring of 1894 had very little to do with the disbanding of the Club. Although an active participant in its affairs in the months preceding and immediately following the publication of the first book, he gave to the group little of its tone. He was always more susceptible to others' influence than an influence himself.

Diffidence and indecision led him to avoid the responsibilities of leadership. He followed the Rhymers, not they him; and when the Club showed signs of having had its day, he had neither the will nor the ability to revive it.

In spite of the fact that he showed a lively interest in the Club for almost two years and contributed the finest poems contained in the two books which the Rhymers issued, he was never one of the principal talkers at the meetings. When the group numbered more than a half-dozen, he preferred to sit silent; and there were times at which he could not be persuaded to read his own poems. Ernest Rhys recalled the last time he saw Dowson at a meeting. "He came late, and broke three clays in succession in trying to light up. Then, asked if he had any rhyme to read, he pulled one out of his pocket, looked at it, shook his head as much as to say it wouldn't do, and thrust it back again." Frank Harris recalled how Dowson, with no encouragement, recited poems to him; but Harris was not a group, and his recollection of Dowson's eagerness to recite his own verse may be built on an isolated experience in which Dowson's reticence had been mitigated by the reassuring effects of brandy. When Dowson could not be persuaded to read, Lionel Johnson, who was alert to Dowson's finest tonal effects, read the poems. And Greene, who evidently belonged to the tradition which enjoyed poetry as an elocutionary exercise, was readily prevailed on to clear his throat and read in a hushed voice the pieces which Dowson passed over to him. It was not that Dowson liked to be urged to read: he realized that some poets could read their own verse in such a way that its beauty was enhanced or at least preserved, while others spoiled their finest effects. Although Gertrude Atherton and Michael Holland say that they can never forget Dowson's reading "Cynara" in the moonlight at Pont-Aven, he never managed to make any of his poems sound as good as they really were, much less to improve on them by his recitation. He often remarked that he "had no gift that way." On the other hand, it is possible that he winced more than once when Greene adopted his best histrionic manner to read "You Would Have Understood Me Had You Waited."

It was after the meetings had adjourned, and Dowson, with a few of his particular friends in the group, had gone to Johnson's rooms at 20 Fitzroy Street, or to one of the pubs beyond the Temple on the Strand, that he lost the restraint which had kept him silent during the greater part of the evening. It was not that he needed brandy in order to enter into spirited conversation; it was rather that he disliked large groups in which men spoke without interruption for minutes on end. In Johnson's rooms, or in the back bar at Henekey's, he was always in the thick of the discussions. It was then that he declared his poetic aims, argued with Johnson about philosophical creeds, and damned the Philistines. The apparently shy young man who had sat attentive but silent with his mug of beer at the Cheshire Cheese became more and more spirited as the night turned to morning. There were occasions when the conversation lasted until well toward dawn and beverages other than beer were drunk that he became disputatious; and Johnson, not to be outdone, would raise his voice until Jepson and Plarr would try to instill in them a sense of consideration for the neighbors.

Already at this time Lionel Johnson had cultivated the habit of spending his waking hours at night. He often arose and had his breakfast when London was getting ready to call it a day. Dowson had come to find Johnson's habit of staying up all night entirely agreeable, for he liked to talk with his friend, and by spending the night talking with Johnson he was not put to the inconvenience of trying to get to Stepney or his parents' home after midnight. When after an hour or two at Johnson's rooms the others were willing to say good-night, Dowson almost invariably stayed on. Jepson recalled how one morning toward dawn, he and a few others had bid Johnson and Dowson good-night; and Johnson, with the exaggerated hospitality of one who had been a generous host with liquor, insisted on lighting his departing guests' way down the flight of stairs. Jepson and the others had almost reached the bottom step when Johnson, with flaming lamp describing erratic circles in the air, came bouncing down behind them, closely followed by Dowson. Neither was hurt, nor were they sufficiently sobered to give up their disputations for the hours until dawn. Such experiences were memorable to Jepson, quite naturally, but it cannot be assumed that on the nights following the meetings of the Club Dowson and Johnson regularly got drunk. It was an exchange of ideas they sought, not an orgy.

In spite of the post-sessions at Johnson's rooms and elsewhere, Dowson's associations with the Rhymers, and theirs with him, were mutually beneficial. The Club, although somewhat disappointing to him in its failure to catch the spirit of the Latin Quarter, provided him with an outlet for his interests and talents; and it encouraged him, by its commendation and publication of his verse, to pursue his art. Furthermore, it gave him a feeling that he belonged to a definite group. In an age characterized by movements, cults, and societies, he wanted to be attached to some group whose interests he could share. A solitary figure during most of his youth, he wanted the association of men of his own age, or at least those who spoke his language and dreamed his dreams. Although the Rhymers were not his ideal brotherhood, they gave him a positive contact with what he considered to be a worthwhile artistic group.

Then, too, through the Rhymers he found new friendships and cemented old ones. Arthur Hillier, with whom he had taken a walking trip in Brittany in the summer of 1890, and to whose cottage in the wood he often went in order to catch up with his writing and to avoid the increasingly oppressive atmosphere of his home, became his very good friend largely through association at the Rhymers'. His friendships with Hillier and Greene, with whom he was later to translate the three-volume *History of Modern Painting,* were both pleasant and advantageous. Although he was never especially friendly with Arthur Symons, it was Symons who was later to take his verse and prose for *The Savoy,* review his poems favorably, and finally become his first editor and biographer. Through the Rhymers' he became more intimately acquainted with such figures as John Gray, later Canon Gray, author of *Silverpoints;* the earnest and talented John Davidson; and the young American actor-poet, William Theodore Peters, who in November 1892 was to produce Dowson's single dramatic piece, *The Pierrot of the Minute.* Perhaps the most intimate association which the Rhymers' Club bred was that between Dowson and Lionel Johnson. They were both of the same age, both had embraced the Catholic faith, and they were both genuine poets. That neither was given to regularity in habits and to a desire for the plaudits of the general run of reviewer helped to cement a friendship which undoubtedly had as its chief bond a sincere admiration and respect for the other's genius. On many matters they disagreed, according to report, and at times seriously quarreled; but even after years of separation, they were able to pick up their friendship without a strain. Their influence on each other was not always beneficial; in fact, Dowson's nights at Johnson's rooms were good for neither his health nor Johnson's. When the disadvantages of their friendship are weighed against the advantages, and when it is borne in mind that each of them often kept worse company, it may be concluded that Dowson's association with Johnson was not without benefits.

Although he never referred to it, the passing of the Rhymers' Club must have caused him regret. The profit he derived from his association with the Club he paid back with interest. He was not of the "Star Chamber," as he was pleased to call the members who took it upon themselves to dictate the Club's policies, and he was never an active participant in the discussions which went on at the meetings, but his value to the group was always recognized. Those who have recalled the meetings always had Dowson in the foreground of their memories, not because he was a mainspring in the general run of the Club's activities, but on account of the memorable quality of the poems which he had brought to the meetings. Years after the Rhymers had disbanded when its survivors were asked: "Who were the outstanding members of the Club?" the answer invariably included Ernest Dowson, and well toward the top of the list. It was Yeats who, forty years after the Rhymers had gone their separate ways, recalled Dowson as the poet who had made him want to preserve the poetry of the members of the group in a volume.

V

PROSE WRITER, TRANSLATOR, AND PLAYWRIGHT

DOWSON'S contributions to the Rhymers' Club were only a small part of his literary activity in the early 'nineties. From 1891 until 1895 he was regularly engaged with literary projects of varied sorts. The twelve poems which appeared in the two Rhymers' anthologies, though representative of the high quality of his poetry, are by no means indicative of the volume and variety of his work. Most of the poems which were to be collected and printed in 1896 under the title *Verses* were written before the Rhymers began to disband, and there is foundation for the belief that a considerable number of the poems which were to appear in *Decorations* in 1899 were finished before 1895. His work from 1891 to 1895 marked him scarcely as a prolific writer, but it marked him as both versatile and energetic. There is some truth in Arthur Symons' remark that "he was always without ambition, writing to please his own fastidious taste, with a kind of proud humility in his attitude toward the public, not expecting or requiring recognition"; but Dowson's projects and activities during the early years of the 'nineties reveal a young man who was not unmindful of his literary reputation. Although unwilling and unable to cater to popular standards, he was at the same time alert to the responses of both critic and public.

As early as 1891 he was not entirely satisfied with his small and infrequent appearance before the public. Certainly it was a mild sort of ambition to gain recognition which led him to suggest to Plarr that they produce a joint volume. In an undated letter to his friend and fellow Rhymer, he wrote:

Mon Vieux,

Seriously—what of my suggestion concerning the mutual-of-some-of-our-poems-presently-publication question? If you don't mind!—at least if we can't do it now, we might select about twenty, ten of yours & ten of mine, arrange them, get a happy title—have them typed and discover what the cost would be. A thin little booklet of some twenty-four pages would contain them—ought not to cost more than £10. Perhaps Image would design us a cover. Give this your attention.

Roses and Rue
by two authors.

or Suaviola or Vine Leaves and Violets or "Apple Blossoms from Oxford."
'Jean Thorel' who can't read English shall write us a French preface in the delightful French fashion stating how fine and large the poems are. You will be
able to put in your 'Disciple' sonnet: and reproduce those charming, idyllic
verses which were wasted on 'Seafaring.' I wish by the bye I might have a copy
of those: I have lost that number which contained them.

Write to me if you have time: I shall not see you this week I expect unless it
be on Saturday.

'Tout votre,'

ERNEST DOWSON

Plarr was evidently interested in the proposal, for in Dowson's next letter,
written apparently a week or so after the suggestion of a joint volume had
been made, he was still enthusiastic about the plan in spite of certain
obstacles which presented themselves.

Church End,
Thursday Night

Mon cher Vieux,

Thanks for yours; the spirit in which you accept my suggestion is precisely my
own; £10 is a chimerical sum to me; but let us prepare our garland for the day
(surely it must come) when this impecunious tyranny is over worn. Of the titles
I like not much the Teutonic ones; they are quaint but not harmonious. Best seem
Suaviola or Gossamer—as affording least handle to the banality of critics: better
I like 'Vineleaf & Violet'—and best perhaps 'Rose and Pine'—both of which
titles would certainly drive the same critics wild. If the former of those two like
you perhaps the appended meaningless verses would come in. It is the only poem
I ever wrote straight off in less than an hour. But *why* 'Rose and Pine' and *why*
'Vine Leaf and Violet'—? will the critics observe! I have been looking over my
'Posie Schublade' as represented by a small MSS book and it will be with difficulty that I shall find ten worthy of the company of the best of yours. I will
bring up about 15 if I can of the least bad & you shall reject five. Let me know
if you will be in Saturday afternoon: either this Saturday or the next I go to
Brighton; but if I am in town the next one, and you, I should like to see you.
Horne was really exceedingly charming & kind last night; we had no one else,
not even the genial MacMurdo; and at 11:30 we strolled Alhambrawards but
were too late for his divinities so he accompanied me eastwards as far as St. Mary
le Strand. I was with Shore on Tuesday: he is very anxious to meet you; therefore if you permit it I will bring him round to you one evening next week. Tomorrow night I dine with Hillier at the grandmaternal mansion; but he is I
believe alone—I was in Poland tonight; why did you not drop in to coffee? . . .

Appended to the letter were the three stanzas—the only poem Dowson
"ever wrote straight off in less than an hour."

Violets, and leaves of Vine,
Into a frail fair wreath,
We gather and entwine!
A wreath for love to wear,
Perfumes as his own breath,
To crown his brow divine,
All day till night is near:
Violets and leaves of Vine
We gather and entwine.

Violets and leaves of Vine
For love that lives a day,
We gather and entwine!
All day till love is dead,
Till eve falls cold and gray,
There blossoms yours and mine
Love wears upon his head!
Violets and leaves of Vine
We gather and entwine.

Violets and leaves of Vine
For love, when poor love dies,
We gather and entwine!
This wreath that lives a day
Over his cold pale eyes
Kissed shut by Proserpine
At fall of night we lay
Violets and leaves of Vine,
We gather and entwine.*

A third letter, also heretofore unpublished, indicates that Dowson was still interested in the joint production.

Bridge Dock
Limehouse, E.

Mon cher,

Thanks for the charming verses: I like them, really, very much; a great deal better indeed than that they treat of, whether supplied in the form of Alhambra, Gaiety or Pantomime. Yes, I admire the poem, the last two lines of the 5th stanza especially, and the ingenious rhymes, *partout*. You must give it to the 'Rhymers'? and to 'Violets and Vine Leaf' of course.

It has given me the first intelligible notion of yours, and the Fritzroyal, ballet worship which is vouchsafed me. . . . I still am unable to join you: but I have an

* By the time this poem appeared as "A Coronal" in *Verses,* Dowson had made several changes in the punctuation and wording.

impression of your temper; and respect it, as, at least, a form of intoxication.
I send you, in return, my latest Versicles: the merest 'symbolism'; almost too
slight for criticism! It's an attempt at mere sound verse, with scarcely the
shadow of a scuse in it: or hardly that so much as a vague Verlainesque motion.
It's an inferior production. I hope we shall meet soon: if you are near the Club
on Sat, would you mind calling in for me on the chance? Very likely I may not
be there, however, so do not go out of your way for that. I have done nothing,
seen nothing, nobody, the week. Simply sat here and otherwise, 'plumbing the
depths of repression': in various bottomless, black pits of pessimism. And so I
suppose I shall continue to do usque ad finum. Well: au revoir. A beintot.

T. V.

ERNEST DOWSON

In spite of the fact that Dowson liked the poems which Plarr submitted
for the joint volume "really, very much," and that Plarr probably liked all
of the "least bad" pieces which Dowson sent him, "Vine Leaf and Violet"
never appeared. Ten pounds was evidently a chimerical sum to both of
them at the time, and there were the usual obstacles of joint production to
blight the enthusiasm of the young poets before the project was well started.
Although Plarr was later to smile at the titles which his friend had proposed, at the time he too was caught by such mellifluous titles as "Suaviola,"
"Roses and Rue," and "Vine Leaf and Violet." Plarr recalled that it was he
who suggested "Vine Leaf and Violet," and if such a title were Plarr's
original idea, Dowson surely approved it. His fondness for "V" sounds he
often expressed. Symons recalled his saying that he considered the line of
Poe, "The viol, the violet, and the vine," of surpassing beauty. The poem
which he wrote to serve as the introductory piece to the collection finally
made its belated appearance as the initial poem in 1896 in *Verses* under the
title "A Coronal with His Songs and Her Days to His Lady and to
Love."

Not all of Dowson's projects, however, proved abortive. In addition to
the poetry he wrote, some of which appeared in *Temple Bar* and *The Albemarle,* he was frequently engaged with prose narratives. Almost all the
short prose tales which were collected and issued under the title *Dilemmas*
in 1895 had been written and printed in magazines long before they appeared in book form. *Macmillan's* and *The Century Guild Hobby Horse*
printed four of the five pieces which were later included in *Dilemmas;* and
in October 1894 *The Yellow Book* took his story "Apple Blossom in Brittany" which has never been reprinted. It was in 1893-94 that William
Heinemann issued in three volumes the novel *A Comedy of Masks* on which
Dowson and Arthur Moore collaborated. A second novel, *Adrian Rome,*

also a joint production of Dowson and Moore, was published by Methuen and Company in 1899; but most of Dowson's share of the novel had been written before 1895. In addition to his work in prose, he finished the poetic drama *The Pierrot of the Minute* before the end of 1892, and was busily translating from the French with the Lutetian Society.

For a reason which eludes adequate explanation, Ernest Dowson preferred his prose to his verse, and he even went so far as to tell some of his friends that it was as a prose writer that he felt he had done his best work. Arthur Symons reported that Dowson was the only poet he ever knew who cared more for his prose than his verse; and his Oxford friend Thomas said that his chief literary ambitions lay in the fields of the drama and the novel, that "poetry, when it came, was an outburst, a digression." To Thomas and Moore, who often talked with him about literature while he was at Oxford, he seemed more interested in the early works of Henry James and the novels of Zola than in his favorite poets, Bauldelaire and Swinburne; and it was about the prose pieces which he had under way rather than his poems that he showed most enthusiasm. His "Poesie Schublade" into which he placed his verse, he bègan at least as early as May 1887; but of it he never spoke to his friends until the joint volume with Plarr was contemplated. To Conal O'Riordan, who was to know him well in the middle of the decade, he often said that he dared not call himself a poet when he thought of other men, but he did hope that O'Riordan thought that his prose had distinction. Frank Harris reported that on one occasion Dowson compared himself to Poe: ". . . a master of both prose and verse . . . his prose better than his verse, as mine is." It was probably by reason of the fact that he talked more about his prose than about his verse that his friends were led to regard him chiefly as a prose writer until the series of three poems "In Praise of Solitude" appeared in *The Century Guild Hobby Horse*.

Sherard recalls how Dowson in his last years was more and more inclined to the tenable conclusion that poetry may and often does exist in prose. The rich cadences and imagery of such pieces as "Absinthia Taetra," "The Visit," and "The Princess of Dreams" which appeared in 1899 in *Decorations: in Verse and Prose* indicate plainly that he was not merely experimenting with a theory, but that he had felt the beauty of impassioned prose. It cannot be observed that Dowson was essentially a poet in all of his prose works, but as early as 1890 he was aware of the poetic effects which could be attained in the short prose tale.

The stories which appeared from 1890 to 1895 are not short stories in the usual sense of the term. They show no skilful integration of character, setting, and plot in order to attain a unity of effect. In fact, they are devoid of real plot, of dramatic development, and stirring action. Furthermore, the characters are generally vague. His men and women are figures rather than characters, and as such, they bear a faint resemblance to Hawthorne's. They are rarely exhibited in the full career of action. The action is either in the past or is implied for the future; the present rarely comes into bold relief. Most of the space in the tales is taken up by a throw-back into the past, leaving the present without action save the results of events in the past. All of the tales are subdued in color, like paintings in *grisaille,* even when springtime in Brittany provides the setting. They are chaste, restrained records of suffering, of devotion and unselfishness, with nothing of the yarn spinner's gusto, and with little on which the reader can take a firm grasp. They linger in the memory only vaguely, for there is nothing in their development which stands out concretely and boldly. To retell them in summary is somehow to lose not only their manner but their substance. An occasional flash-like intensity of feeling and a fragile beauty of manner characterize these pieces and account in part for their appeal. Stories they can hardly be called: they illustrate a form of narrative which is virtually a *genre* to itself. "Studies in Sentiment," the sub-title which Dowson gave to the collection *Dilemmas* in which most of the pieces were collected, is perhaps as expressive a label for his short prose tales as any that can be produced.

To examine a few of these "Studies in Sentiment" will indicate their particular flavor. As early as January 1888, while Dowson was still at Oxford, "The Souvenirs of an Egoist" appeared in *Temple Bar.* In February 1890, *Macmillan's Magazine* printed "The Diary of a Successful Man"; and in August 1891, "The Story of a Violin," which was later entitled "An Orchestral Violin" when it appeared in the collection *Dilemmas. The Century Guild Hobby Horse* printed in Volume VI, 1891, "A Case of Conscience," and in Volume I, 1893, "The Statute of Limitations." All these tales were published in *Dilemmas* in 1895. "Apple Blossom in Brittany," which appeared in *The Yellow Book* in October 1894, was not included in *Dilemmas,* probably because it had so recently appeared in a magazine.

"The Diary of a Successful Man" is illustrative of the sort of prose Dowson wrote in 1891. Printed originally in *Macmillan's Magazine* in February 1890, it became the first of the tales in the collection *Dilemmas.* As the title indicates, it was written in diary form, a device which might presumably curb the smooth-flowing, consecutive quality of the writer's style. The story, however, is of such a nature that a consecutive time-sequence is unnecessary; and the device of following the manner of diary entries is not followed with sufficient consistency to hamper the stylistic effects which were the author's chief objective. The story tells of two young men, sincere friends, who fall in love with the same girl; and who, in order to remain friendly with each other, decide to allow her to choose between them. Thus one will sacrifice his chance for happiness in order that the other may wed the girl. By a misinterpretation of her answer, however, the one whom she chooses departs, feeling that his friend and the girl will be far happier if he leaves for distant lands. After twenty years, during which time he tries to banish all thoughts of the girl from his mind, he returns to the scene of his early love. There in time he learns that she had indicated him as her choice, and that despairing of his return, and unwilling to marry his friend, who had proved unfaithful to him, she had taken the vows of the *Dames Rouges*. Together he and his friend sit in the cathedral, to which the nuns come to sing behind the screen of the gallery, "so near, and yet so far away" from the red-garbed woman to whom they both had long before offered their love.

Vespers were over and a server, taper in hand, was gradually transforming the gloom of the high altar into a blaze of light. With a strange sense of completion I took my place next to the chair by which Lorimer, with bowed head, was kneeling, his eyes fixed with a strange intentness on the screen which separated the outer worshippers from the chapel or gallery which was set apart from the nuns. His lips moved from time to time spasmodically, in prayer or ejaculation: then as the jubilant organ burst out, and the officiating priest in his dalmatic of cloth of gold passed from the sacristy and genuflected at the altar, he seemed to be listening in a very pasion of attention. But as the incense began to fill the air, and the Litany of Loreto smote on my ear to some sorrowful, undulating Gregorian, I lost thought of the wretched man beside me; I forgot the miserable mistake he had perpetuated, and I was once more in the past—with Delphine— kneeling by her side. Strophe by strophe that perfect litany rose and was lost in a cloud of incense, in the mazy arches of the roof.

> Janua coeli,
> Stella matutina,
> Salus infirmorum, Ora pro nobis!

In strophe and antistrophe: the melancholy, nasal intonation of the priest died away, and the exquisite women's voices in the gallery took it up with exultation, and yet with something like a sob—a sob of limitation.

In neither the situation nor the characterization are there qualities which give the story merit and appeal, but in the manner there is unmistakable distinction. It becomes rich without approaching heaviness; the multitude of adjectives never outweigh the images they are designed to create, nor are the effects of sadness and despair in any way overwrought. Despite the diary device, the prose reaches and often preserves a lyric quality in sustained passages. Soon after the tale appeared in *Dilemmas*, a reviewer observed to the point:

Mr. Ernest Dowson has treated these exquisite sensibilities, these fragile delicacies, with a marvellous sympathy, an unerring sureness of touch. Times and again a single violent adjective, a single straining to the forcible, would spoil the whole effect, and the phrase always rings true, the epithet is right. . . .

Although there is nothing in the substance of the tale which is memorable, the delicate beauty of its manner makes it a fine achievement in poetic prose.

The other pieces which appeared in the magazines before 1895 and were collected in *Dilemmas* are equally lacking in substance. In fact, it is only by frequent rereadings that one is able to identify the tenuous themes with the titles under which they were written. In none of them is the sentiment quite so touching as that in the "Souvenirs of an Egoist" which Dowson had written as an Oxford student, nor is there any appreciable change or development in his later manner. The tales written in 1890 are quite as fine as any he was to write in the middle or toward the end of the decade. The most frequently recurring sentiment in these pieces is that which appeared so regularly in his verse: the beauty of innocence.

It was this theme which found additional treatment in "Apple Blossom in Brittany." Certainly Dowson's single contribution to *The Yellow Book* which has come to be considered in some circles the essential voice of the decadent 'nineties had little to do with its fame or with its general tone. In spite of the fact that such names as Henry James, George Saintsbury, and William Watson appeared in the early issues of *The Yellow Book*, it soon became associated with Aubrey Beardsley's drawings and the verse of those who preferred patchouli to the fragrance of English meadows. "It would be difficult to exaggerate the distress—yes, the distress—that Beardsley's work in *The Yellow Book* caused in the hearts of the old-fashioned and conventional," observed Grant Richards. *Punch* showed its unqualified disapproval. Although it was the deliberate intention of the founders of *The Yellow Book* to do something daring, the improprieties and so-called decadence of the periodical were at least according to present-day standards very mild indeed.

In all the discussions which went on during *The Yellow Book's* existence, Dowson had small part. With no acute moral sense, he had difficulty in seeing how art and morals had any clear relationship. He had written a good sin poem, "Cynara," with no conscious effort to shock or offend; and he was willing to believe that his friends, many of whom were writing for

The Yellow Book, were equally free from any attempt to give distress to even the most prudish. To him, the magazine was an interesting receptacle into which he could place some of his work, nor did he try to shape his work so that it might be better adapted to that tone which, presumably at least, had given the periodical its vogue.

The tale he sent to Harland for the issue of October 1894 was not in keeping with the general reputation of *The Yellow Book,* or with Dowson's posthumous reputation as the arch-exponent of decadence. "Apple Blossom in Brittany" is the sort of tale which, morally at least, might readily have been approved for publication by the editorial board of *The Youth's Companion.*

The central figure, Campion, to be sure is somewhat world-weary, but his intentions and actions are noble; and when he agrees with the comely seventeen-year-old Marie Ursule, with whom he had for long been in love, that it would be better for her to go to the nuns at the Ursuline Convent on the hill above Ploumariel than to marry him and to live in the rush and confusion of London, his nature becomes even heroic. This tale is a nearer approach to the standard form of the short story than any of his earlier pieces, for in it there is a protagonist who is confronted by an obstacle which by force of character and his own convictions he is able to surmount. Furthermore, there is more descriptive detail of the sort which has come to be called local color in this narrative than in the earlier pieces. Brittany, the scene of several of his tales, does not become completely real; but the settings at Ploumariel in the early part of the story escape from the vagueness which marks the backgrounds in the other tales.

All of Dowson's narratives tempt the reader who is fairly familiar with the facts in his life to autobiographical interpretation. This is especially true with "Apple Blossom in Brittany." That Campion's love for Marie Ursule was essentially Dowson's toward innocent girlhood may readily be observed; especially in the light of what he had written in his earlier pieces and his love for Adelaide Foltinowicz. It is idle to try to identify Dowson too strictly with Campion of the story, but many of the thoughts that Campion expressed concerning the beauty of innocence he found in Marie Ursule were undoubtedly Dowson's own. Furthermore, Campion's decision to encourage Marie Ursule to become a nun so that her innocence would never be sullied and so that he might always retain the image of the young girl in his heart illuminates much of Dowson's own attitude toward Adelaide. Not long before the story was issued, he had written to Plarr about Adelaide:

Die Kleine instead of changing, altering, repelling, as I feared/hoped might happen, in the nature of things, seems to grow in grace and favour daily. What a terrible, lamentable thing growth is! It "makes me mad" to think that in a year or two at most the most perfect exquisite relation I have ever succeeded in making must naturally end. Yes, it makes me mad! One ought to be able to cease caring for anyone exactly when one wishes; it's too difficult: or one ought to be able to live directly in the present. . . .

Aside from its illumination of Dowson's mind, the story has a delicacy of phrase and movement which gives it an artistic interest quite independent of the narrative element. Effortless and apparently artless, the style is not only lucid, but refreshingly simple. It is as if the author had caught some of the simplicity of manner of Marie Ursule and the folk who lived under the apple blossoms near Ploumariel.

The reception which greeted Dowson's prose tales as they appeared in the London magazines during the early half of the 'nineties was evidently sufficiently encouraging to lead him to contemplate the publication of a collection. As early as the autumn of 1893 he wrote to John Lane, who had become associated with Elkin Mathews, as follows:

> *Bridge Dock*
> *Limehouse, E.*
>
> My dear Lane
>
> Forgive my writing to you personally to enquire as to the fate of certain stories which I sent to you in your *corporate capacity* a month or two ago.
>
> But not having heard any news I have latterly been getting rather nervous as to whether they ever arrived? And I believe the letter I sent with them was included in the package.
>
> I should be very glad if you would let me know this—and assuming they reached you, what is your decision, and whether I shall come and fetch them away.
>
> Will you be at the Odd Volumes on the 1st. I am dining there with Brodie-Innes and shall look forward to seeing you.
>
> Sincerely yours,
>
> ERNEST DOWSON

The matter of accepting the stories was evidently not settled at the dinner, but soon afterwards Dowson received a letter from Lane to which he replied as follows:

> *Bridge Dock*
> *Limehouse, E.*
>
> Dear Sirs
>
> I am obliged for your letter with reference to my stories. Would you kindly let me know about how much more material you would require to make up a volume uniform with 'Keynotes'? There is a story of mine, recently published

in the 'Hobby Horse,' which I could include, if it should meet your approval—and I have one story nearly completed, and another unpublished, which I could send you shortly.

If this would not be sufficient, I am afraid I should not be able to add anything more until the summer, for I am at present engaged upon a translation, which occupies, and will occupy, all of my time until the beginning of May. If you would prefer the matter to stand over till then I could no doubt manage to add a few more. The two new stories I propose sending you are both rather longer than the longest of those now in your hands. The story in the 'Hobby Horse,' however, is not in more than 2,500 words.

Yours faithfully,

ERNEST DOWSON

That Dowson thought highly of his stories is additionally attested by his eagerness to have them issued in a volume uniform with *Keynotes.* This collection of stories which had been written by Mrs. Clairmont, who used the pen-name "George Egerton," had attained a wide circulation, not only by reason of its literary quality but also because Lane had been unstinting in its manufacture. Beardsley had done a fine title-page on which a tall, darkly handsome woman was the arresting figure, and Lane had selected a heavy paper of lavender tint. The book attained such immediate popularity that Lane was later to decide to issue a "Keynotes" series among which such works as Arthur Machen's *The Great God Pan,* Ella D'Arcy's *Monochromes,* and Fiona Macleod's *The Mountain Lovers* were published. It is possible that Dowson's suggestion that he would like to have his stories published in a volume uniform with "George Egerton's" *Keynotes* started the idea of a series in Lane's mind.

The title of his proposed collection he selected only after considerable reflection. Long before the stories were approved for publication in book form, he had written to Arthur Symons:

Bridge Dock

Thursday, Nov. 18, 1894

My dear Symons:

Did I meet you the other night at the Temple or did I dream it? I am just going off to visit [?] Elkin Mathews. I am wavering between 'Blind Alleys' and 'Sentimental Dilemmas' as a title for my stories.

Ever yours

ERNEST DOWSON*

* This hitherto unpublished letter I found inserted in what was apparently Dowson's presentation copy of *Dilemmas* to Arthur Symons, which was put up for sale at the Freeman Galleries, Philadelphia, May 16, 1940. There are certain features of the letter which lead me to raise the question of its complete authenticity. The handwriting is to all appear-

Evidently Mathews and Lane were agreeable to issuing a collection of Dowson's stories, but it was not until the autumn of 1895 that *Dilemmas: Stories and Studies in Sentiment,* the title which he finally selected, appeared. The "two new stories" to which he referred in his letter to Mathews and Lane were either never submitted or they were rejected by the editors, for the five tales which were included in the collection had all been printed in the London magazines before 1894. Richard Le Gallienne read the tales for Mathews and Lane, and made the reader's report.

The reception which greeted *Dilemmas* was for the most part encouraging to the author. Numerous reviews appeared soon after the volume was issued. The critic in the *Daily Chronicle* observed: "Mr. Dowson embodies with great skill and charm the conception of life as 'a series of moments and emotions,' and of certain crises arising therefrom which have an artistic interest of their own largely independent of the longer 'story' of which they form a part." It is no doubt true that the chief appeal of the pieces in *Dilemmas* is "largely independent of the longer 'story'." The reviewer for *The Pall Mall* missed the point of the tales in *Dilemmas* entirely when he remarked: "Unquestionably good stories, with a real human interest in them. . . . The book as a whole is a powerful delineation of the almost incredible meannesses to which men and women may be driven by love of self." It was neither the aim nor the result of the tales to delineate the "almost incredible meannesses" in men and women who are driven by love of self. Much as Dowson abhorred nature at large, he never made direct attacks on its erring wayfarers. It was his role to pity rather than to scorn. Even the weak, deceitful Lorimer in "The Diary of a Successful Man" is a figure to whom the reader must respond sympathetically. Although some of the reviews which appeared soon after *Dilemmas* was issued missed the essential quality of the tales, their very appearance, and their generally commendatory flavor, were welcomed by the author who, despite his uncompromising attitude toward reviewers, was not indifferent to their offerings.

When his novel, *A Comedy of Masks,* written with Arthur Moore was about to appear, he showed considerable concern over what the reviewers might say. In a letter to Plarr in September 1893, he wrote:

A Comedy of Masks appears on Friday—nominally—but I see no reason now why it should be actually any further delayed. You must command it from

---

ances Dowson's—though a hurried and careless Dowson. In fact, one of the words which may be "visit" is entirely illegible. The date of the letter, "Thursday, Nov. 18, 1894" is certainly not written in his usual manner. If the letter is entirely authentic, it is one of the few that he dated so completely.

Mudie's. I tremble at the prospect of being reviewed—I am painfully conscious of the innumerable blemishes and alas! the weakest points are in the first volume so that I fear sleep will overcome the reviewer before he reach any of our less banal passages. What fools we are to write—or rather to publish! Mercifully Lionel does not review novels, and as to the opinion of the average novel-reviewing Le Gallienish animal—"we will not think of it."

And after the novel appeared, he inquired of Plarr: "Will you see the November *Bookman?* . . . they have made quite a creditable article of our meagre biographies, although it is news to me that I have been 'steadily making my way in literature.' There is also a good review in it of *Masks. . . .*"

The novel which produced the "good review" in the November *Bookman* Dowson and Moore had started soon after Moore had come down from Oxford. Before Dowson left Queen's, he and Moore had often discussed prose fiction. Moore recalls how he and Dowson sat up until dawn began to streak the back quad talking about the early works of Henry James. When Dowson moved to Grove Street the discussions were continued, but no work of collaboration was essayed at the time. Moore was a member of a family well known in the world of art, the son of John C. Moore, a portrait painter of distinction, and the nephew of Henry Moore, R.A. Another artist uncle was George Simonds, a sculptor. Born in Rome in 1866, and educated at the Bradfield School, Moore, by reason of his Continental experiences and artistic interests, found Dowson an engaging companion during the latter's stay at Queen's. The friendship which had begun at Oxford was revived when Moore came to London to take up in time the profession of law.

Although Moore was neither a Rhymer nor an habitué of the Crown, he saw much of Dowson in the winters of 1890 and 1891, at times in Soho where they had dinner together at Poland. Literary projects were discussed and plans were laid for a brief tour of Brittany during the summer of 1892. Dowson entertained hopes that Plarr might join them in Brittany, for from Bridge Dock, Limehouse, Dowson wrote to Plarr on June 18, 1892: "I hope you will consider the Breton journey seriously: Moore, I am sure, would be very charmed." It was not until the end of July that Moore and Dowson finally got away. They spent the better part of a week at Le Faouet, after which they moved into what Dowson called the "quite unexplored barbarisms to the extreme west of Finisterre." In concluding a letter to Plarr, written sometime in July, he wrote: "Even if we happen to miss in Bretagne, you must visit Faouet: on the left-hand side of the Market place (looking East) from the Lion d'Or observe the house which, whatever happen, I intend to live in." They stayed for a time in Dol, where Dowson admired the cathedral with its handsome fifteenth-century portal and the stained glass of the large window of the choir. Picturesque Lamballe was their next objective, whither they went by way of Pontivy. Much of the tour was done on foot, for Moore was of excellent physique, and Dowson, though of slighter build, was at the time equal to long stretches without showing signs of fatigue. He had walked in Brittany with Arthur Hillier in the summer of 1890, and it was with much delight that he revisited places which were familiar to him, and showed his friend points of interest.

Although no actual writing was done while they were touring Brittany, they discussed the novel which they had decided to write together, and had the outline for its development clarified by the early autumn of 1892. Mr. Moore, who has outlived his friend these forty-two years, has explained the method of collaboration in a letter to me dated October 10, 1939.

. . . Our first step was to prepare a brief synopsis (or "scenario" as I believe they call it at Hollywood). This was of a very sketchy kind, and did little more than indicate the more important of the dramatis personae and their general line of conduct. On this foundation, we proceeded to construct the work by each alternately contributing a chapter (or occasionally two). Each installment, as completed in draft, was submitted by the author to his collaborator, so that he might read, criticize, and "carry on."

In the case of our first published novel (*A Comedy of Masks*) we had fairly frequent opportunities for meeting and discussion. This was unfortunately not so in the case of *Adrian Rome,* the greater part of which was written after Dowson had left England to take up his abode in France, where I was not able to join him except for brief periods during my summer holidays. This interruption occurred between the dates of publication of the two novels. Dowson became increasingly more erratic and dilatory as a correspondent, and it became more and more difficult to extract his "copy" from him; indeed, in the end, I found myself compelled to write the last few chapters of *Adrian Rome* without his coöperation.

It may possibly be of interest to you to know that the title "A Comedy of Masks" was a happy suggestion by the late Lionel Johnson, who read the original MS under its original title "Masquerade."

Our plan of collaboration was I suppose made easy by the similarity of our respective styles. It is difficult for me now to decide with certainty whether any particular chapter was my work or Dowson's; but I find that he batted first in the "Comedy" and I in "Adrian Rome." We did very little in the way of revision of each other's work, alterations being rarely more than a few words in a chapter.

This homogeneity of style is, perhaps, to some extent explained by the fact that we both sat at the feet of the same authors. It was, in fact, the discovery that we were both enthusiastic about the earlier work of Henry James which first brought us together in our Oxford days. . . .

Despite the fact that Moore had difficulty in extracting copy from Dowson for *Adrian Rome,* for their first novel Dowson's chapters were produced with a fair degree of regularity. Moore's statement that he and Dowson wrote alternate chapters, and that Dowson "batted" first, sheds considerable light on the method of collaboration and helps in the identification of certain passages; but it fails to indicate clearly who conceived the individual characters and who determined their destiny. Everything, however, points to Dowson as the creator of the principal character of the novel, Philip Rainham, and of the scenes at Rainham's Dock and Brodonowski's in Soho. Blackpool and Soho restaurants were provinces which he was well equipped, through intimate observation, to describe. When Bernard Muddiman observed in *The Men of the Nineties* that "Dowson wrote of the purlieus round the Docks," he must have had passages in *A Comedy of Masks* in mind, for there is no other instance in Dowson's works in which he so much as referred to the observations which he made around Bridge Dock. The novel was first sent to Bentley under the title *Masquerade,* but it was evidently rejected. By the end of August 1893, however, the authors received the last proofs from William Heinemann; and after some delay over the design for the cover—for which Heinemann suggested a comic and a tragic mask—the novel was issued in mid-September under the title *A Comedy of Masks.*

The plot of the novel has little to distinguish it from mediocrity. Philip Rainham, through his occasional association with the artists who gathered at the Bohemian restaurants, met a young painter, Richard Lightmark, who apparently was a sincere artist and an admirable character. Rainham, lonely in his antiquated dock house in Blackpool, invited the young painter to his picturesque waterfront home in order to provide him with unusual subject-matter for his canvases; and in time he assisted Lightmark not only to meet Londoners who were influential in the world of art but also to become friendly with Eve Sylvester, a girl whom Rainham had long idealized for her refreshing simplicity and innocence. Lightmark, using Rainham's friendship as a password, rose to considerable heights as a fashionable painter, and became engaged to Eve before Rainham discovered that the young man whom he had helped so materially was both a plagiarist and a scoundrel who had seduced a pretty model and left her broken in body and spirit. In spite of the fact that he had ample proof of Lightmark's villainy, a native indecision kept him from stripping the mask from Lightmark. Then, too, he was unwilling to expose him to Eve, who had become much attached to him, because he felt that such a disclosure would cause her pain. But a painter, Oswyn, of a more robust nature than Rainham's, also learned of Lightmark's plagiarism and treatment of his model; and without deliberating about the results, he exposed Lightmark to the critics and to Eve.

There is much in the novel which promptly suggests autobiographical interpretation. Philip Rainham, the principal character in the book, owner of Rainham's Dock in Blackpool, is with few modifications Alfred Dowson, the author's father; and Rainham's Dock is Bridge Dock. As was the case with Bridge Dock, Rainham's was steadily losing trade since much of the repairing was no longer done on the Thames, but on the Clyde and Tyne. The parallel between Rainham and the elder Dowson becomes pronounced when the former is described as a man who had pride in his ancestral holdings, but small business acumen. Then, too, his health was poor. Each winter he was forced to escape from the cold and fogs of London to Bordighera. In London, his chief delight was to mingle with artists, chiefly painters, for whose province he had excellent critical judgment. The parallel might be pursued farther in so far as Rainham's character is portrayed, but the events which surround the fictional character have no readily discernible counterpart in the events of Alfred Dowson's life.

In the character of Oswyn, Dowson undoubtedly placed many of his own convictions. Oswyn represented Dowson's point of view concerning art and artists. Willing to subsist on the barest necessities, Oswyn devoted his life and genius to the pursuit of beauty. For the acclaim which came from the salons and the fashionable critics he cared nothing. The devices which Lightmark had used to become a salon favorite and a candidate for election to the Royal Academy he deplored as hypocritical and unworthy of a true artist. Guesses have been hazarded concerning whom Dowson had in mind when he drew the character of Lightmark, but the only sound conclusion which can be drawn is that both Dowson and Moore had no sympathy for artists who gained recognition by catering to fashionable taste and by using their friends as rungs in the ladder of their ambition. Oswyn, on the other hand, Dowson frankly admired. Ill dressed, unkempt, half-starved, but with the fire of genius burning in his eyes and heart, Oswyn represented the sincere artist and the admirable man to Dowson.

Although the novel is quite readable, there are obvious weaknesses in characterization, setting, and plot. Eve Sylvester is a beautiful child, no more. Even in her fury at the discovery of Lightmark's villainy, she is scarcely a compelling figure. The model whom Lightmark seduced is little more than a symbol of a multitude of poor girls who have been deluded by handsome and deceitful men. Lady Garnett and Mrs. Dolland are agreeably portrayed—old ladies with the foibles and charm of those who know just enough about the arts to hold salons in luxurious surroundings. And Lightmark, in spite of his painter's smock and a few individual mannerisms, has very little to distinguish him from the villains of the stock romances. Philip Rainham is the most highly individualized character in the novel, and even he is not entirely convincing in his indecision. The scenes at Brodonowski's and at Rainham's Dock are authentic and fairly vivid, despite the fact that they lack a richness of concrete detail. In the development of the mediocre plot, the authors skirted the pitfalls of melodrama successfully, but they attained no gripping suspense and small dramatic effect.

The review of the novel in the November *Bookman,* which Dowson called "a good review," must have proved quite encouraging to the authors. The reviewer commented as follows:

While showing some marks of immaturity, some looseness of construction, perhaps the result of collaboration, some over profuseness of description which makes the story needlessly long, this novel of artist life in London is a book of promise and power. When these defects have been mentioned, and one's conscience thus relieved, one can praise without stint, for the subject and the situations are of undoubted interest. The authors have scored a clear triumph in one way. Evidently from the first, they loved their hero Philip Rainham, but most of their readers, I feel sure, were prepared to find him an arrant humbug, this quiet, languid man, who should have built boats on the Thames like his fathers, but who valued his dry dock only for its picturesqueness, neglected business, frequented the society of artists of an advanced school, and nursed his lung. Before the end we have quite come to take their view of him, not merely for the sacrifices he makes, but because his personality gradually and surely asserts a fascination over us. Other characters more conventional are also made alive by fresh and original readings. Lightmark, the selfish, successful, ruins a girl, deserts her, steals motives for his pictures, writes puffs of them in the newspapers, and allows his friend to bear the shame of his worst deed. Yet, somehow, we are led to see the probability of his wife, when she finds it all out and despises him utterly, stifling her impulse never to see him, and wearing for the rest of her life a fair face to the world. Her husband is such a consummate actor that he will help greatly to make the situation possible. Oswyn, too, the shabby, savage, Bohemian painter, at war with society, leading a life of indescribable sordidness, yet keeping his art high above the mud, is made to live by many true and individual touches. The authors' powers are not dramatic, but in one scene, which might easily have seemed improbable, they have risen beyond the usual level of their powers in this direction, the scene where Philip takes on himself the shame that never could have been his, to shield Eve for a little from the knowledge of her husband's baseness. We invite the writers cordially, together or singly, to give us more.

The invitation of the reviewer to the writers "together or singly" to give them more was promptly accepted. In fact, even before the reviewer's invitation had been extended, Dowson and Moore were started on a second novel. It was not until 1899, however, a few months before Dowson's death, that Methuen and Company issued *Adrian Rome*. The method of collaboration was to be virtually the same as that used in writing the first novel: each was to write an alternate chapter, or occasionally two, and in this instance Moore "batted" first. The novel progressed very slowly during 1893 and 1894, largely because Dowson was engaged with poetry, and translations for Unwin and the Lutetian Society. Furthermore, he was often ill, and the situation at home was scarcely of the sort which gave him the time and inclination to work steadily on his share of the novel. Dowson's irregularity in contributing his share must have been trying to Moore, whose working habits were systematic; and it was on account of Dowson's failure to produce his chapters with any degree of regularity that the novel which was begun in the autumn of 1893 was not issued until the autumn of 1899.

Despite the fact that the circumstances surrounding its composition were unfavorable to a well-unified novel, *Adrian Rome* is a better performance than *A Comedy of Masks* on several scores. The theme of *Adrian Rome* is more substantial than that in the earlier novel. The principal character, Adrian Rome, is a young man of pronounced literary talents who, after his graduation from Oxford, comes down to London to give free rein to his urge to write. He enjoys the stimulation which companionship with Bohemian friends and sincere artists provides; and, devoted to his art, he is producing work which is both beautiful and sincere. At twenty-one he comes into his patrimony, which is ample for him to indulge his whims in yachting, travel, and the salon life of the most opulent patrons of the arts. Swept into the fashionable circles of critics and dilettantes, he is led to believe that his path in life as a salon writer and a gentleman of *ton* is clear. Somewhat against his instinctive judgment, he marries a wealthy girl of passive beauty, although he realizes even at the time that Sylvia, the simple, unspoiled girl of his boyhood affections, would make him a more inspiring and sympathetic wife. It is not, however, until his new life in the fashionable circles has blighted his sincere devotion to his art, and even prohibited him from following his aspirations and ideals, that he understands how grave his mistake has been. He longs for his old Bohemian companions, for the fine flush of inspiration and achievement, and for Sylvia. In his attempt to extricate himself from the prison into which his life as a fashionable writer has led him, he encounters obstacles which are not readily surmounted. In desperation, after many attempts at adjustment have failed, he decides to flee from his imprisonment if Sylvia will accompany him, for to him she symbolizes all that had been sincere in his life as artist and man. Sylvia, hearing of his desperation, tries to join him; but when she comes it is too late: Adrian Rome has drowned.

The tragedy at the end is not well motivated, for the accident which caused his death has small justification in the light of the prevailing circumstances. Nor do the obstacles to Adrian's success and happiness appear so insurmountable to the reader as they seem to him. The reader is in ready sympathy with Adrian in the situation which surrounds him, and wishes for events to grow out of circumstance or his own character which will give him again his devotion to his art and bring him back to his old friends; but evidently the authors felt that Adrian's errors in allowing himself to be swept into salon life and into marrying a woman who stood in the way of his art was sufficiently grievous to permit him no avenue of escape. The development of Adrian's character is a clear revelation of Dowson's attitude toward writers who are distracted from their art by considerations of wealth, social prestige, and the plaudits of dowagers and dilettantes. To Dowson, Adrian Rome readily became a tragic figure; and his recognition of the tragedy in Adrian's life was in large measure a justification and explanation of his feeling about the way his own life was ordered.

The style of the novel shows no marked improvement over that of the earlier work or that of the shorter prose pieces which were written for the magazines. In fact, Dowson's prose style is generally finer in the shorter pieces in which it is unhampered by the necessity of telling a sustained story. Although his manner in the novels is lucid and fairly direct, there is little to distinguish it from merely adequate writing. It is true that there are some passages which rise above mediocrity, but they are not sufficiently sustained to give to the novels a literary quality which makes the story element secondary. In the shorter pieces which were published in *Dilemmas*, however, the style attains distinction consistently, perhaps by reason of the fact that in them the plot is of small significance. In them, there are a choiceness of phrase and a frequent lyric quality which transcend ordinary prose. Victor Plarr observed that

"In his prose, on which he set extreme value, there is sometimes an apparent touch of labour and preciosity. There are petulant Gallicisms, for instance, set down with deliberation. He was fond of quoting Flaubert—was it Flaubert?—

who sat long in meditation in front of a blackboard with alternative words chalked thereon. Dowson would have had me believe that he, too, pondered the *mot juste* for hours.

If his habit of deliberating on the *mot juste* in his prose was similar to that in his verse, for which there is ample evidence, then Dowson's remark to Plarr is readily borne out. Although there are the "petulant Gallicisms" of which Plarr spoke, and "an apparent touch of labour and preciosity," these mild blemishes are outweighed by the rich cadences of his style and his unfailing restraint.

In addition to Dowson's creative work in prose narrative, by the closing months of 1893 he was engaged on translations from the French. Although he did much translating from 1893 until his last days, his translations were chiefly hack work, with occasionally a genuine interest in the artistry which he applied to his commissions. Arthur Symons remarked that Dowson's translations "were never without some traces of his peculiar charm of language." It is true that the zeal with which he entered upon his earliest translations lent to his manner a distinction which is rarely found in ordinary hack work.

The income he received from the prose pieces which had been printed in the magazines and from *A Comedy of Masks* was almost negligible: Sherard recalls that Dowson's royalties for *A Comedy of Masks* amounted to a pittance. When the opportunity presented itself in 1893 to join the group who were undertaking the translation of Emile Zola's works, Dowson was eager to supplement his small income by doing *La Terre* into English. Edgar Jepson reported that the fee to be given each translator who completed a novel was fifty pounds.

Dowson's eagerness to be of the group which was undertaking the translation of Zola was by no means solely dependent on the promised fee. Even as an undergraduate at Oxford, he had developed admiration for Zola which extended to student idolatry. Thomas reported that he and Dowson had the idea of sending the author an anonymous letter of commendation, an intention which was never carried out. The fact that Zola was generally misunderstood at the time in England made Dowson especially eager to espouse his cause. When Robert Sherard, who was writing a life of Zola, met Dowson among others in the Temple in March, 1893, he spoke so fervently about Zola's greatness as a man and author that Dowson was ready to set to work at once in order to open English eyes to the merits of the French author.

His enthusiasm was shared by a small group of his acquaintances who became the main props of an organization called the Lutetian Society. The purpose of the Society was to translate and publish works which appealed primarily to the erudite and conveyed principles and doctrines that were different from, if not always antagonistic to, Victorian ideas of morality. Banded together as a scholarly group who planned only to reach the upper stratum of readers, they felt that their motives could not be questioned. Not long before they started their translation of Zola's novels, Henry Vizetelly had served six months in jail for distributing *La Terre* and paid a fine of £100; but whereas the earlier publisher had issued his translations in moderately priced editions, the Lutetian Society decided that if their translations were issued at high prices the sale would be limited to only the upper classes, and, as a result, they could not be accused of trying to debase public morals. Their conclusion was discerning, but it failed to take into account the fact that the Society needed more than protection if it were to flourish. Books published at prohibitive prices may protect the authors and publishers, but they will not necessarily defray the expenses of the enterprise.

Who all the members of the Society were, no one even at the time seemed to know, although Edgar Jepson remarked in 1935 that he always believed that Teixeira de Mattos "was a good many of them." When Dowson first met Teixeira, whose full name was Alexander Louis Teixeira de Mattos San Payo y Mendes, he of the long name was living at Number 3, Plowden Buildings in the Temple, with a barrister named Swanton and Charles Goodhart, the actor. After the Crown had closed for the night, Number 3, Plowden Buildings was the most likely place to find Dowson. He probably slept in Teixeira's rooms more frequently than in those of any of his friends. From the start, however, Teixeira had small fondness for Dowson. Robert Sherard, who first met Dowson in Teixeira's rooms in the Temple, recalls the manner in which the host was treating Dowson as early as the winter of 1893. "The tenant of these chambers," said Sherard, "endowed with that racial flair which scents dissolution and reveals to those who possess it which men amongst their acquaintances are not going to be prosperous in life, was already treating him with coldness." When Dowson made inquiries about spending the night on the sofa or the floor in order to rid himself of the inconvenience of going to the Dock House after midnight, his host was usually impatient for him to be off. Some clue to Teixeira's attitude toward Dowson may be found in the fact that the former was pretty much of a dandy. He wanted to be considered fastidious in his garb; his high hats were achievements in sartorial excellence. Dowson, on the other hand, was often careless in his dress, even as early as 1893. Then, too, Teixeira's working habits were regular and strict, whereas Dowson's were increasingly unpredictable.

It was owing to Teixeira's dislike for him that Dowson was almost denied the opportunity to become a participant in the Lutetian Society's translation of Zola's novels. When it had been virtually decided that Dowson was to do *La Terre,* Teixeira tried to get George Moore to translate the novel. Moore's refusal of the invitation is unquotable. It was of such a nature, however, that Dowson, who had looked forward to his assignment with enthusiasm, became indignant at Moore rather than at Teixeira, who had applied to Moore without consulting him. There is no record of what Dowson told Moore, but if he said everything to him that he told Sherard he was going to say, then Dowson was not only a man of spirit but of bold, unvarnished phrase.

With George Moore's services unavailable, Dowson was given the assignment of *La Terre,* and the Society set energetically to work. Teixeira himself translated *Pot Bouilli,* Arthur Symons *L'Assommoir,* and Victor Plarr *Nana.* Symons, it has been reported, translated his novel in six weeks; and Teixeira, who was in the habit of starting to work at six o'clock in the morning when assignments hung over him, finished his novel long before the edition was to be issued. Plarr was less energetic in getting through *Nana,* and Dowson had to be pushed. The remaining translators of the Society were ready to deliver their English versions before the date set as the deadline.

Teixeira, largely by reason of the fact that he had many associations with publishers and that he was familiar with methods of handling publishing projects, became the editor-in-chief of the Society, and as such made regular check-ups on the progress of the work. He was concerned not only with the time element, but also with the quality of the translations. He insisted on a completely faithful rendering of the text, in which there were to be no demonstrations of literary initiative on the part of the translator. He set the example in his own work which the others were to follow. While the others, according to Plarr, longed often to dart off into the depths of British decency, Teixeira held them securely to the role of literal translators, even in passages in which the translators themselves were offended.

With th zeal of one who felt sincerely that he was about to reform public taste, Dowson started on *La Terre.* Long before it was finished, however, he was heartily tired of it, and some of his enthusiasm for Zola had waned. Often the artist in him rebelled. A deadline had been set by Teixeira—May 1894 at the latest. By Easter time, Dowson was already far in arrears with his assignment. He had never learned to work by the clock. Undisciplined and dilatory by nature, he was accustomed to wait on inspiration for his literary efforts. To wait on inspiration for the translation of a bulky novel was impossible; and as the winter changed to spring, he realized that if he were to fulfill his assignment with the Society, it would be necessary for him to change his tactics. Over Easter he retired to the home of one of the Rhymers, Arthur Hillier, who had a cottage outside of London. Here he drove himself to complete twenty pages a day. Plarr reported that Dowson "found the task most irksome, and he discussed it with me from time to time, finally deciding to render certain Rabelaisian passages into something less offensive in English—into common cleanly blasphemies at least." In April he wrote to Plarr:

I have been so overwhelmed with Zola . . . I have not done more than 340 pages . . . I suppose you are rurally at your ease now, so far as it is possible to be at your ease and translate Zola . . . Are you going to the *Yellow Book* dinner? I shall, I expect, but I feel that I ought to go to no dinners until this pyramid is pulled down.

The "pyramid" was pulled down, although the work was not finished at the time which Teixeira had set. As a piece of literary prose, Dowson's translation of *La Terre* has little save its clarity to commend it. The effect may be illusory, but the early passages seem more facile and spirited than the main body of the work. Had the translation been of rare literary merit, however, it would have brought Dowson no more than it did. The assumption of the Lutetian Society that there was a sufficient group in the upper stratum who were hungry enough for Zola's work to pay two guineas a volume for it was somewhat optimistic. *La Terre*, printed for private distribution, was never completely subscribed; and the other translations of the Society were likewise under-subscribed. Sherard, whose interest in Zola at the time was zealous, reported that the whole performance was a disappointment to him, and a publisher's failure.

It was through Dowson's association with the Society, however, that a second assignment in translating was brought to him the same year that *La Terre* appeared. At the request of T. Fisher Unwin, Teixeira started on the translation of *Majesty* by Louis Marie Anne Couperus. The work was to be done for a stipulated sum. The translator was to run no risk in its publication and distribution. Teixeira, finding the work trying and having more pressing assignments to complete, enlisted the services of Dowson on the translation, though he was well aware of Dowson's habit of procrastination. It is possible that he offered the work to Dowson in order to salve the latter's feelings over the George Moore episode, or even more likely that he could find no one who was willing to do the work for the pittance that Dowson would take. Dowson produced his share of the work, perhaps not more than a third of the book, for which Teixeira paid him, according to his reckoning, proportionately. Dowson's part in translating Couperus added little to his stature as a man of letters or financially.

Despite the unimpressive results of his translations of Zola and Couperus, he was not deterred from contemplating additional translations. It was during the year following his translation of *La Terre* that he, with two members of the Rhymers' Club, G. A. Greene and A. C. Hillier, undertook the translation of Richard Muther's *Geschichte der Malerei im neunzehnten Jahrhundert*. This huge work appeared in three volumes in which there were 2,304 pages. Volumes I and II appeared in 1895, the third the following year. Henry and Company published the translation, which was done for a stipulated sum. Dowson's share in the work was considerable, and it is certain that Greene and Hillier gave him a proportionate part of the income. The work was tedious to him in spite of the fact that he had developed a lively interest in the graphic arts, especially the contemporary French painters. Although his colleagues and the subject were to his liking, it was only after a struggle and constant joggings by his co-workers that he brought himself to finish his share of the work.

That Dowson's unwillingness to drive himself to finish in a given time what had been assigned to him extended only to his translations is scarcely the case, for his correspondence and many reports indicate that he found difficulty in working under pressure on even the pieces which pleased him. "Many times," said Plarr, "he referred to the difficulties he experienced when writing to order." When William Theodore Peters, the American poet-actor, who often came to the Rhymers' and who was a charter member of "the Bingers," asked him to write a little Pierrot play in verse for him, Dowson consented to undertake it in spite of the fact that Peters wanted the drama at short notice. Once started on the assignment, however, he had reason to regret his decision. Writing to Plarr on October 24, 1892, he said:

I have been frightfully busy, having rashly undertaken to make a little Pierrot play in verse for Peters, which is to be played at Aldershot, and afterwards at the Chelsea Town Hall: the article to be delivered in a fortnight. So until this period of severe mental agony be past, I can go nowhere . . .

Despite the "period of severe mental agony," he was happy for the opportunity which Peters offered him, not only because he needed the small income from such work, but also that for long he had liked the drama as a literary form. While at Oxford, he gave the impression to Thomas that the drama was one of his chief interests; and once in London, he attended the plays with considerable regularity. "Go to see 'A Doll's House'," he wrote to Plarr—"I have been twice and go again. It's the finest play that has been seen for some years. . . ." He delighted in consorting with people of the theatre. Marmaduke Langdale, Lennox Pawle, Charles Goodhart, and many of the Bensonians, he sat with at Poland and the Crown; and it was Peters' association with the London playhouses which brought him and Dowson together. Peters admired Dowson's verse which he had heard read at the Rhymers' Club meetings; and when the occasion presented itself to seek out someone who would do a little poetic play for him, he came directly to Dowson. Peters evidently had the knack of getting him to work in record time, for "the little Pierrot play in verse" was done in the two weeks allotted.

In his letter to Plarr of October 24, 1892, Dowson continued:

I would this play were done: half of it is completed and I have seven days more, but the second half is mightily oppressing me. And I am horribly afraid that when it is written I may be worried with rehearsals and enforced company with terrible South Kensington young ladies and fashionable Chelsea mesdames.

His qualms about being forced into company which he disliked were ill founded, for Peters, who was to be not only the Pierrot of the piece but also the director, had no intention of trying to make Dowson a Chelsea favorite. When the play was turned over to Peters, Dowson's obligations to it were virtually fulfilled. Although he probably attended the first performance at the Albert Hall Theatre, there is no record of his impressions of what happened to his verse when Peters read the lines of Pierrot and Miss Ida North played the part of the Moon Maiden. None of his contemporaries has reported on the reception which greeted the play at its initial production, in spite of the fact that he undoubtedly sent invitations to a few of his friends. Although he was unwilling to assume the responsibility for many of the details of the production, he was evidently sufficiently pleased with the play to want others to see it. In a letter to Lane, he wrote:

Bridge Dock
Limehouse E.

My dear Lane,

Would you care to see a performance of the play described in the enclosed prospectus—the printing, and *colour* and publication of which I am not responsible for. Peters has arranged to play it on Wednesday next, at 9.0 P.M. In the studio of Miss Curtois, 5A Clareville Grove, Gloucester Rd. S.W.

We should both be delighted if you could turn up there.

If you are unable to come, would you let me have a line by return, as on account of space, the audience is to be a limited one and I have to let the responsibilities know exactly how many people I have invited.

Yours ever

ERNEST DOWSON

There were evidently a considerable number of performances of the play, for Plarr recalled one presentation in which Miss Mabel Beardsley, sister of Aubrey Beardsley, played the role of the Moon Maiden. Peters was sufficiently pleased with the play to keep it in his repertoire: several years after its first appearance he read a long passage before a group at a *salon* of Mademoiselle Arnavons in Paris, at which time Miss Maude Roudebush sang the Moon Maiden's song with music by Noël Johnson. Dowson, too, probably thought more highly of his Pierrot play than his reports to his friends indicated. Rushed as he was for time in completing it, he wrote out in very careful longhand two copies, one for Peters and one for Miss Ida North. The two manuscripts, which I have examined thoroughly, show infinite care. Here surely there is ample indication that he, like Flaubert, "pondered the *mot juste* for hours." In spite of the fact that he was satisfied with his work, he apparently did not carry it to a publisher. Save for the Moon Maiden's song, which comes at the end of the play and was printed on page four of the original program, *The Pierrot of the Minute* remained in manuscript until 1897, at which time Leonard Smithers decided to bring it out in a small edition of 350 copies with illustrations by Aubrey Beardsley.

Smithers evidently had no difficulty in disposing of the decorative volume, but it was not until Arthur Symons included the play in the first posthumous edition of Dowson's works that its delicate beauty attracted more than a limited group of readers. And when Grenville Bantock was later to give it a musical setting, the play which had lain for four years without a publisher began to attain a sort of vogue. Mrs. Rosa Newmarch, in comenting upon the work of "the unfortunate poet" who inspired Bantock to such heights, observed:

This graceful phantasy, with its setting which recalls some exquisite scene by Fragonard, is full of suggestion to a composer of quiet imagination, and Bantock has responded with an almost lavish wealth of thematic material. Motive succeeds motive as quickly as thoughts pursue each other in a dream . . . The work is scored for piccolo, two flutes, one oboe, two clarinets (A and B flat), one bassoon, three horns, two trumpets, one trombone, timpani (chromatic), tambourine, glockenspiel, triangle, harp, and the usual strings, *divisi*.

[*Enter Pierrot, carrying lilies. He
stands gazing at the* Temple de l'Amour

My journey's end! This surely is the glade,
That I was promised: I have well obeyed!
A clue of lilies was I bid to find,
Where the green alleys most obscurely wind;
Where tall oaks darkliest canopy o'erhead,
And moss and violet make a softer bed;
Where the path ends, and leagues behind one lie
The courts and pleachèd gardens of Versailles.
The lilies streamed before me, green and white;
I gathered, following: they led me right;
To the bright temple and the sacred grove
This is, in truth, the very shrine of Love.

[*He lays his flowers before Cupid's
Statue: then he goes timidly up the
steps to the temple.*]

It is so solitary, I grow afraid:
Is there no priest here, or devoted maid?
Is there no oracle, no voice to speak,
Interpreting to me, the word I seek?

THE FIRST SHEET OF THE *PIERROT* MANUSCRIPT

(*From the original MS in the possession of Lessing Rosenwald*)

When Plarr learned of Bantock's scoring of the play, he could not help remarking:

How would the retiring poet, who hated the mob and dreaded any battalion which advanced in more than twos and threes, have been staggered by this regiment of instruments! I can see him now, in my mind's eye, musing on the situation with pouting lip and fixity of rounded orb, and afterwards with a shrug and with a kind of half-smile, as though, seeing that he rather suspected humour as such, he nevertheless liked the recognition, the publicity, the glory, and was not sure whether to laugh or not.

And were Dowson to witness the performances of some of the aspiring Thespians in American colleges who "do" Pierrot and the Moon Maiden less as a tribute to him than to their own superlative confidence of merit, he probably would be amused and saddened in turn.

VI

TRAGEDY

DOWSON'S achievements during the early half of the 'nineties, although by no means great, were at least recognized, especially by the circle whose favor he sought. Apparently he was well on the way to success. Still in his mid-twenties, he had attained a literary reputation which was substantial if not wide. In spite of his irregular and dilatory habits, he had produced a considerable amount of verse and prose, most of which had been favorably noticed. The critic who reviewed *A Comedy of Masks* in 1893 for the November *Bookman* had ample evidence for his report that Dowson was "a young man who has been steadily making his way in literature." His poems in the Books of the Rhymers' Club were commended by poets and critics such as Rhys, Image, and Yeats; and Herbert Horne, whose taste was very fine in such matters, considered the poems he printed for Dowson in *The Hobby Horse* among the best contributions that had ever been submitted to him. Then, too, in spite of the complaints of Teixeira de Mattos and others about his indolence in finishing his assignments in translating, his services as translator were constantly in demand. In *John Lane and the Nineties* (1936), Mr. J. Lewis May, after taking a brief glance at the results of Dowson's activities in the early half of the decade, observed that at the time "Dowson was in a strong position." Even Plarr, who was surely more than a casual acquaintance, remarked: "He never, indeed, suffered from that unmerited neglect which is the portion of so many."

To his casual acquaintances, and to a few who knew him well, Dowson seemed to be enjoying a mild sort of prosperity in the early months of 1894. With his associations at the Rhymers', the Crown, and the music halls, and with the commendation which he began to receive for his stories and verse, he apparently developed a sudden pleasure in fine raiment. The soiled black bow tie disappeared, to be replaced by cravats which rivaled those of the Beau Brummells who strutted about the Circle at the Alhambra; his boots were made by a bootmaker who catered to only the fashionable trade; and his hats were in a class with those of Teixeira de Mattos. Teixeira, who had shown distaste for Dowson's appearance during the winter of 1893, became sufficiently impressed by Dowson's apparel to be seen with him on several occasions at the Café Royal. But Teixeira among others must have noticed that despite the quality of Dowson's clothes, they rarely showed proper care. His linen, though fine, was not always fresh; and his manner of wearing his clothes indicated small pride in showing them to advantage. Suits which bore the label of a good London tailor usually looked as if he had slept in them, which of course he often did.

His apparent interest in clothes was in some measure the result of his changing interests in places of entertainment and relaxation. By the late months of 1893, he began to spend less time in Soho and in the ordinary pubs along the Strand. The Café Royal became a fairly frequent stopping-place on his nightly rounds, and at the more fashionable music halls he was a regular patron. He took to riding more frequently in cabs, and to showing a capricious generosity with drivers and attendants in the bars. In his early London days he had always been reluctant to leave gay company, and now, more familiar with London night life, he joined supper clubs to which he and his friends could go after the lights had been dimmed at the Crown. When it came to paying for rounds of drinks, he was often earnestly insistent that he provide for more than his share. What his source of income was during these days of apparent prosperity cannot be determined, but it may be assumed that very little of it came from his father, and even less from his royalties. He was fond of games of chance, even to the extent of remarking to his friends that he "adored gambling"; but his whist and poker were never such that he could make money with them. Money, however, he always seemed to have—at least enough to provide him with what he considered the essentials of a good time.

Then, too, the "terrible South Kensington young ladies and fashionable Chelsea mesdames" about whom he had expressed such alarm when he was writing *The Pierrot of the Minute* began to appear less formidable and stupid to him. When he wrote *Adrian Rome* with Arthur Moore, he was not writing from hearsay only in his description of London salon life. He had seen and talked with the prototypes of Mrs. Vesper, Lady Verrinder, and Miss Lancaster. Although he always felt detached from their interests and ideals he was for a time willing to see their charm as personalities and their utility to young artists who were desirous of fame and money. Apparently he never went alone to the salons of those childless couples who, in their middle and declining years, gave some sort of motive to their lives by surrounding themselves with men and women of wit and talent, and in their way were patrons of the arts. But when some of his friends invited him to accompany them, or insisted that his company was earnestly desired, he went along and enjoyed himself. That he ever contemplated the patronage of those who presided over such gatherings is unlikely, for his attack on the character Richard Lightmark in *A Comedy of Masks* is a clear indication of his attitude toward young artists who made their way through salon associations. More for the sake of the company than for any patronage which such associations might bring him, he went on several occasions to the salon of Sir John and Lady Simon of Kensington Square, as well as to the gatherings of Sir Joseph and Lady Prestwich. The genuinely delightful conversations which went on at the home of Professor and Mrs. Warr he enjoyed, and even expressed regret at his inability to be one of the group more frequently, There is a record, too, that he and Lionel Johnson were in the habit of going to visit a rich old lady who spoke of dancing with Benjamin Disraeli, and who referred to "young Mr. Disraeli and young Mr. Gladstone." That Dowson and Johnson had any thought of making their way as poets through such an association is most unlikely: they went to see her because she was a charming woman.

It was probably at a salon that Dowson was prevailed on to read something from *The Pierrot of the Minute* as part of the evening's program. In the manuscript copy of the play which he had written for Peters, there is a half-sheet attached which has no bearing on the theme of the play and was undoubtedly intended to serve as an introductory speech to his reading of the passage in the play. Written in Dowson's hand, it reads:

Ladies and Gentlemen: the scene of this piece, *The Pierrot of the Minute,* is laid in the parc du Petit Trianon on a summer evening. Pierrot chases a moonbeam in and out of the trees, a moonbeam who has just taught him to love her, laughs at him and eludes him. She says to him: "I jested not, at daybreak I must go."

From that point he followed the lines of the play until he felt he had contributed his share of the entertainment. There is no mark in the manuscript to indicate the closing line of his reading, but it is unlikely that he who refused to read his verse to the Rhymers would read all of his play at a salon.

His associations at the salons reveal Dowson in a light totally different from the much-limned picture of the poet of the cabmen's shelters. In 1893 he was eminently fitted for the role of fashionable poet had his inclination been in that direction. In fact, Plarr observed that he was rapidly becoming "a fashionable writer, his pen much sought after by the shrewd and parasitic." At the time he had written nothing and done nothing which would eliminate him from the eligibles at the most exclusive salons. Although by no means a brilliant *diseur,* he could carry on a conversation in keeping with his reputation as an exquisite poet, and his manner was not without charm. His quiet smile, his unwillingness and inability to appear conspicuous, and his expression, sensitive and at times sad, were consonant with the general impression of good breeding which he left on all those who met him in 1893.

His appearance, with his suddenly developed interest in fine clothes, was quite in keeping with the company he kept; and although he could not be called handsome, his features were far from commonplace. His large eyes, made larger by the thinness and pallor of his face, were arresting not only by their size but by their unnatural brightness. It was probably Dowson's eyes which led G. A. Greene to invite Dowson to lunch to meet the painter Sargent with the thought that the painter would be impressed to the extent of requesting Dowson to sit for him. Sargent, however, was evidently not sufficiently interested, for no portrait was made. Will Rothenstein, Charles Conder, and the French painter Loiseau among others, however, found Dowson's face of sufficient appeal to portray it. The Rothenstein drawing, according to the reports of those who knew Dowson, is a fairly faithful likeness; Conder's sketch, made with obvious rapidity, catches little of the facial detail, largely by reason of the fact that the subject is in profile; and the painting in oil by Loiseau, which, to my knowledge none of Dowson's English contemporaries ever saw, was a piece of Impressionism that caused Dowson to observe that the picture should be entitled "The Portrait of a Murderer." Conal O'Riordan has said that although Rothenstein's drawing is "a very tolerable representation . . . Dowson himself professed to be shocked to think that he looked like that. Why he should have objected to it I do not know." Mrs. Brown Potter, a well-known actress during the mid-nineties, told Dowson that he was the image of Keats. Arthur Symons in "A Literary Causerie" in *The Savoy* for August 1896 also spoke of Dowson's resemblance to Keats. This was probably the beginning of the descriptions of Dowson's face as Keats-like, a description which persists with very slender foundation. It is possible that the largeness and unnatural brightness of the eyes, as well as the faint similarity which existed between Keats's unrequited love for Fanny Brawne and Dowson's love for Missie, led those who had passing glimpses of Dowson to draw such a comparison. There are, to be sure, a few ready parallels between Keats and Dowson, but from portraits of them both, and from descriptions of the latter, one may conclude that their physical similarities were very few indeed.

Although his appearance, manner, and attainments made him eligible to associate with the frequenters of the most exclusive salons, his inclinations in this respect were largely those of Philip Rainham in *A Comedy of Masks*.

Indeed, to Philip Rainham, who had doubtless in his blood the taint of Bohemia, Brodonowski's and the enthusiasm of its guests had a very definite charm. They were almost all of them artists; they were all of them young and ardent; and they had a habit of propounding their views, which were always of the most advanced nature, with a vehemence which to Rainham represented all the disinterestedness of youth. Very often they were exceedingly well worth knowing, though in the majority of cases the world had not found it out. . . . In his mind he would sometimes contrast the coterie with certain artistic houses, more socially important, which he had from time to time frequented; where earnest-eyed women in graceful garments—which certainly afforded rest to the eye—dispensed tea from a *samovar* and discoursed discreetly of the current Academy and the most recent symptomatic novel.

The delight of a visible, orderly culture permeating their manner and their conversation was a real one, and yet, Rainham reflected, it left one a trifle weary, a little cold. It seemed to him that this restaurant, with its perennial smell of garlic, its discoloured knife handles, its frequentation of picturesque poverty, possessed actually an horizon that was somewhat less limited.

That Dowson was usually eager to move to the back bar at Henekey's after an evening at Kensington Square in no way suggests that he was a boor, and that he had developed as early as 1893 a fondness for cabmen's shelters. He had, like Philip Rainham, a delight in the visible, orderly culture which permeated the manner and conversation of the salons; but, like his character in the novel, "it left one a little weary." He was by no means alone among the young poets who gathered nightly at the Crown or at places comparable to Brodonowski's who felt a certain stuffiness in the atmosphere of Lady Prestwich's drawing-room. Lionel Johnson, and even Arthur Symons, opera cape, high hat, and all, preferred the Crown to formal literary gatherings. That Dowson went a step farther on occasion to a restaurant with "a perennial smell of garlic" and "discoloured knife handles" is small proof that his Bohemian taint made it impossible for him to enjoy well-mannered company.

Nor can it be assumed that in his period of apparent prosperity Dowson was exceptionally constrained in the presence of charming and well-bred women. When Horace Vachell told Mrs. Atherton that she was to try to win Dowson over to the pleasure of associating with "nice" women, he left a totally false impression of the sort of women with whom Dowson had consorted in the mid-nineties. "It must be years since he has spoken to a decent woman," Vachell told Mrs. Atherton in 1896, "—if he ever knew one!" In the years from 1890 until he met Mrs. Atherton, Dowson had known not only the charming old lady who talked about "young Mr. Gladstone" and a comely little girl who exuded freshness and innocence, but such lovely ladies as Miss Ida North, Miss Olive Curtois, Mrs. Warr, and a dozen women who were carrying on the tradition of Mrs. Thrale. It is true that he never became especially friendly with any in the latter group, but the fact that he went to the homes of such ladies indicates that he did not need Vachell and Mrs. Atherton to provide him with the novel experience of associating with "nice" women.

Then, too, Dowson had a considerable number of acquaintances who perhaps did not qualify for Horace Vachell's preferred list of "decent" women, but were nevertheless bright, airy spirits against whom severe judgment cannot be brought. Of his acquaintances from that class of girls who enjoyed life to the extent of becoming indifferent to such troublesome things as reputations, none was more attractive and lively than Dulcie. Where Dulcie came from, and even such details as her full name, have never been satisfactorily clarified by Dowson's friends. The girl at the Sceptre to whom J. Lewis May refers was probably a barmaid with whom Dowson had a brief intimacy which went beyond a mere speaking acquaintance, but she was not the Dulcie who moved around with him in his short period of apparent prosperity. A dancer in a chorus at one of the lesser music halls such as the Mogul was a likely place for him to find such a girl, or it is possible that she was a professional model. In spite of the vagueness which surrounds her way of spending her time before midnight, she was, from all reports, a lively companion, decorative, and possessed of not only a sense of humor, but also of comprehension of the talk which went on among young men who were devoted to the arts. Dulcie shared with Dowson his brief prosperity, but there is no indication that she became his companion because of what he might do for her, much less with any thought of marriage. She liked to be in his company, little more; and when she misbehaved or proved unfaithful to him, he showed no chagrin.

Jepson has told of one night when Teixeira de Mattos, Robert Steele, the friend of William Morris and translator of medieval romances, and several others, including Dulcie, went to Conder's rooms on Duke Street to continue their discussion into the early morning. After drinking quantities of wine and listening attentively to the discussion of art and literature, Dulcie became impatient at the small attention which was being paid her. She left the room, to return a few moments later from Conder's bedroom, where she had taken off all her clothes except her shoes. Steele, a newcomer in the group, was at first nonplussed but rapidly getting control of himself, he burst out into a tirade of moral indignation which left Dulcie penitent and the others choking with mirth. Dulcie, unaware of the outburst which would follow her immodest prank, was left alone with the offended Steele while the rest tiptoed down the stairs. Her manner of extricating herself from her plight has never been revealed, but apparently she came off victorious, for she continued to make the rounds with her friends.

Such escapades of Dulcie's amused rather than annoyed Dowson, for his attachment to her was evidently without real depth. He liked her vivacity and spirit; and in her light-heartedness he found much both to envy and enjoy. To her, he was little more than a young man who talked interestingly and took her among interesting people. Long after Dowson had gone to France to take up semi-permanent residence there, Dulcie remained a hanger-on with the group who continued to gather at the Crown. Her rooms, when she stayed at one place sufficiently long to unpack her belongings, were decorated with the drawings of men who were well known in the art circles of the London of 1895, and she was never without the company of lively figures. I have been told that in time she married well, and that the Dulcie who stood in only her shoes at Conder's settled down to the decorous life of housewife. The one man who could disclose her present whereabouts generously insists that his memory is no longer dependable.

Not all the girls who moved in the circle which gathered first at the Crown and later in supper clubs and rooms of their companions were so fortunate as Dulcie. There was the comely Scottish girl, Essie, whom one of the actors of the Benson group brought back with him from one of his tours of the provinces. She was never Dowson's regular companion, but he liked her and she often joined him and the others at the Cock and in Teixeira's rooms. She had not been in London long, however, before it transpired that she was to become a mother. Impatient with the inefficacy of the medicine which a quack had given her to relieve her condition, she took the contents of the bottle at a single gulp instead of in prescribed doses. For days she lingered between life and death. Dowson's concern over her illness was sincere, although he cannot be named as the man who brought Essie to her distressing plight. All during her convalescence, however, he was her sympathetic attendant, often stroking her head and telling her of the delights of France. After her recovery, Essie disappeared from the group; and it is reported that she later married a hardy lad in the North Country.

In an undated letter to Jepson, Dowson described the illness and recovery of a girl whom he called Marie in such a way that one is led to believe that Essie and Marie were probably the same girl. At least, the circumstances which surrounded them were similar, and some of the girls who moved in the circles of the artists found it convenient at times to change their names. The letter not only reveals Dowson's liking for the girl, but it also illuminates a side of his life which became more pronounced as the decade advanced.

Bridge Dock
Limehouse, E.

My dear Jepson,

How are you faring in Arcadia?

We have had an awful time since you left, with Marie, who had a relapse the day after your departure. Then she improved to a certain extent and was persuaded to agree to go back and stay for two or three weeks with her sister. For two nights previously I had not been out of my clothes; Goodhart also has been up there all night. Last Friday—the day before her departure she came out and dined in Poland. She completely broke down there, and Missie made her go upstairs and lie down. We were in despair—Lennox was due at the Elephant to play in the 'Cotton King.'

Finally Goodie arrived—we carried her down and got her into a four-wheeler and drove off with her. That night Goodie, Pawle and I were up till six. I was utterly worn out, so was Goodie. However, somehow or other Pawle and the Doctor got her off at ten the next morning—I was not there—but the accounts were graphic—Pawle had fainted twice during the night, and at the station even the Doctor added his contribution of tears to the ceremony. Goodhart and I wept bitterly when we said goodbye to her at six A.M., Marie of course was sobbing too. It was frightfully pathetic. In the evening Goodie and I went down to the Elephant with Pawle and a wire arrived to the effect that she had arrived safely, been met by sister. We all waltzed around Pawle's dressing room and at the conclusion of the piece indulged so freely in liquor that happening to meet a friend in the Strand we annexed him boldly and carried him in triumph up to the 'Crown.' Later on we fell down and Goodhart and I tore our trousers. We slept anyhow (after having tried unsuccessfully to play whist) all about the place. So much for Saturday. Yesterday Pawle went off to join his Co. at Derby. Goodie and I met in the evening. He had a charming man with him, a twenty-ton opium eater, who had run away with his cousin and is now to marry her. We met at 7 and consumed 4 absinthes apiece in the Cock till 9. We then went and ate some kidneys—after which two absinthes apiece at the Crown. After which, one absinthe apiece at Goodie's Club. Total 7 absinthes. These had seriously affected us —but made little impression on the opium-eater. He took us back to the Temple in a cab. This morning Goodhart and I were twitching visibly. I feel rather indisposed; and in fact we decided that our grief is now sufficiently drowned, and we must spend a few days on nothing stronger than lemonade and strychnine. But the previous strain on our nerves had been terrible. I wish you had seen more of Marie. Her charm was really remarkable—it was not only men but women that it struck. She made an immediate conquest of Missie and her mother who didn't at all take to Hoole's or Marmie's irreproachable fiancees—in fact of everyone who came across her.

But I must say I'm deucedly glad she's gone.

Write and give me your nouvelles—and forgive any incoherences in this scrawl. My hand has a palsy of the first quality, and my head is full of noises.

Ever yours,

ERNEST DOWSON

Such a description of Marie, or Essie, as the case may be, indicates that the girls with whom Dowson spent some of his time in the early half of the 'nineties were scarcely hardened sinners, and that he was not the consort of "cheap harlots" as Yeats stated and Vachell implied. Dulcie and Marie were far from ten-shilling street-walkers; they moved in a totally different sphere from those girls who made vice a business. That Dowson deliberately sought out the most shameless women of the streets in preference to the lively girls who were not averse to a temporary companionate marriage can in no way be proved. Later, to be sure, Dowson's companionships at times fell to a level which cannot be mentioned in the same breath with Dulcie and Marie.

In spite of the fact that Dowson's pastimes in 1893-94 were no different from those of many normal young men of his time, he entered into them with a zeal which can do little save indicate that he lacked stability. That he was willing to tell Jepson that he and Goodhart had drunk seven absinthes apiece is only an indication of a practice, all too prevalent among young men, of boasting about the sowing of wild oats. But Dowson's seven absinthes and nocturnal pastimes had more sinister implications. Edgar Jepson, who saw him at least four nights a week during the fall and winter of 1893-94, was by no means convinced that his friend's excesses were only the result of a natural buoyancy of body and spirit. To most of his friends, however, he gave the impression that he was prosperous and happy; and there were a few who, after noticing his sudden interest in fine clothes, Kensington Square salons, and his relatively lavish expenditures for cabs, girls, and absinthe, began to believe that success had gone to his head. Plarr was led to remark: "To me, part of the tragedy of his life was this—that fame or notoriety, which you will—warred against his essential self. As a boy he charmed. Then came nascent literary celebrity in the Savoy and elsewhere, and he rocked at its approach."

Plarr, among others, evidently had been deceived. None of the tragedy of Dowson's life can be traced to the effects of the fame or notoriety which came to him with his works. It is possible that he left such an impression

on several of his friends by reason of his increasing excesses; but his reckless living in 1894 cannot be traced to the fact that he could not survive
success. His triumphs had been so small that even with the optimism of
young manhood he could not readily be affected by them. A few commendatory reviews, fifty pounds for translating *La Terre,* at best an equal amount
for all of his creative work in verse and prose, including *The Pierrot of
the Minute* for Peters, and an occasional invitation to appear at the salons,
were surely not enough to influence the character of one who was genuinely
modest. Although pleased by flattery, he was never spoiled by it. Any air
of prosperity and happiness which his acquaintances thought they detected
was in large measure a sign that all was not well with him.

When Dowson's triumphs are measured against his reverses in the years
in which he seemed to appear prosperous they sink into insignificance. Had
he been the sort of young man who could detach himself largely from events
which had a direct bearing on his immediate existence, he might have been
able to experience a mild sort of happiness. His sucesses with his books,
however—all of his letters to his friends at the time to the contrary—were
not enough to outweigh his feeling of despair and failure. Already on
January 16, 1893, he wrote to Plarr:

Were you at Headlams's? I was too sick and sorry to come. I fear my affairs
will not bear talking over, or writing about. They are like a Chinese puzzle;
and grow more confused and inextricable the more one considers them. I en-
deavor to possess my soul in patience, but the result is not so much resignation
as a sort of sloth and *tristitia,* "which even monkish moralists have held to be of
the nature of a sin." It is a vile and stupid world; and it will be good to have
done with it.

Such a plaintive cry at a time when he was being commended for his
work on many sides and invited to read his poems at the salons is a truer
expression of the essential Dowson during his period of apparent prosperity than all of the high hats, cards to supper clubs, and invitations to
South Kensington salons might indicate. The fact that his work had been
recognized made life tolerable, no more. Poet that he was, he could not
dissociate himself entirely from the clutch of circumstance and find complete happiness in his art. His love affair with Adelaide, the terrifying
signs of his own failing health, and the illness and despair of his parents
gave him little opportunity to enjoy the success which he had attained and
to contemplate a happy future. Much of his air of happiness and prosperity
in 1893 and 1894 was the result of an attempt to conceal his true feelings. Truly his affairs, as he wrote to Plarr, would not bear talking over.

His attachment for Adelaide which, even at the start, augured more anguish than joy, became increasingly painful. Sentimental as the attachment probably was, the fact remains that Dowson took it very seriously and suffered considerably by it. During the interval in which he was attaining his moderate successes and apparently enjoying the company of Dulcie, Missie was by no means forgotten. There were intervals in which he gave his friends the impression that he had put her out of his mind, for by the beginning of 1894, according to Jepson, he was tiring of Poland,

... though he never would have admitted it ... As Tennyson sang: "Love cannot live forever on a kiss," and he needed little urging to come with me. At Aux Gourmets the cooking was admirable, and you could get an enjoyable dinner, with a small bottle of vin ordinaire, for two shillings. And the company was as good as the dinner: Teixeira, Professor Rothenstein, Dowson, Conder, Mr. Conal O'Riordan, sometimes Beardsley, Langdale, and a half dozen Bensonians ...

It is no doubt true that in his day of apparent prosperity he needed little urging to accompany Jepson to the Gourmets, and that in the company of his friends, among whom Dulcie must be included, he seemed to be tiring of Poland. It was probably in this period that he wrote the pretty "Rondeau," in the sentiment of which there was more than an attempt to catch the spirit of the seventeenth century cavalier poets. By nature easily led, he frequently put off his plan to dine at Poland in order to be with his friends; but there were evenings on which he went to Sherwood Street, and once there, the delights of other companionship were promptly dismissed from his mind. His letters to his Oxford friend Sam Smith which belong to this period reveal clearly how serious his love was. As early as the winter of 1892 he was willing to believe that he had made progress in his love affair, for at that time he wrote to Smith as follow:

I have been existing in a curiously tense state for the last month or so, and for the last week tense is scarcely the word. It is better than the old stagnation, but it is exhausting. Things are coming to a crisis, *cher vieux!* I go to have *tête-à-tête* teas with *Madame!* We talk intimately, we talk of Her—*natürlich*—and we are constantly on the verge of an understanding. Yesterday it was the nearest shave of all. She gave me an admirable occasion. I am sure she expected it. I was just coming out with a protestation, to the effect that my one object and desire in life was to be of service to her admirable daughter—when we were interrupted. We were both curiously moved! I went out and had a gin and bitters and poured it tremulously down my shirt, and passed a perfectly wide-awake night—damning the interruption. This morning I saw that it would have been foolish; but this afternoon I shall be in precisely the same state, and I feel certain that it is only a question of days now. To think that a little girl of barely fourteen should have so disorganized my spiritual economy.

I should like to see you and hear your advice, though of course unless it agreed with my own, however good it were, I shouldn't take it. It is a difficult case. If it were not for the complication of a foreign point of view and foreign traditions —I should be justified in waiting, in holding my tongue. Only when one remembers how very much earlier abroad these matters are arranged—and especially in Germany—the case is changed. An English mother would be scandalised at your proposing for the hand of her daughter before she were 16; a foreign mother might reasonably be equally scandalized if you were attentive to her daughter, without making your mind clear to her, at a much earlier age. But there are objections either way . . . I should like to see you for, verily, this matter grievously weighs me down.

The next letter to Smith, written sometime in the early spring of 1893, not only reveals the seriousness of Dowson's intention to marry Missie, but it also illuminates the writer's state of mind concerning his affairs:

Cher Ami,

Let me preface this by saying that it is strictly private and confidential; and so proceed to inform you of certain recent developments in my affairs. I fancy, when I last saw you, you must have been about the beginning of the rather distressful state of things which augmented itself later on. I daresay I was not very brilliant society then—(I don't remember, frankly, much about our *rencontre*)—and certainly I have been too much absorbed to write letters ever since or I would have written to you. I suppose it will not surprise you very much to hear that I have at last unburdened myself. We were all in rather a stressful state of nerves—and Missie herself rather brought it about by her curious changes of mood—sometimes she was perfectly charming, at others she would hardly speak to me. *Quid plura dicam?* Finally I was goaded into a declaration—of course it was rather an inopportune time, the father having been given up by the doctors—but on the other hand, I don't suppose except for the rather tense state we were in on this account, I should have been so precipitate. She took it with a great deal of dignity and self-possession; I don't think I have ever admired her more. She reminded me very properly that she was rather too young: but she proceeded to admit that she was not surprised at what I had told her, and that she was not angry. Of course I had asked her for no answer—I merely left her with no possible reason to doubt my seriousness in the matter. Finally I suggested that she should forget what I had said for the present—and that we should resume our ancient relation and be excellent friends—and nothing more. Upon this understanding we separated. The next day—after twelve of about as miserable hours as I hope to spend —it seemed to me that I had upset the whole arrangement—a conversation with *Madame* reassured me. Nothing could possibly exceed her extreme kindness and delicacy. She didn't in the least appear to resent, as she might very reasonably have resented, my proposing to her daughter, without her permission a couple of days before her 15th birthday; on the contrary she seemed rather pleased—in short, she was perfect. Moreover she gave me every hope—she said that Missie had told her she would like the idea in a year or two:—only just then she was naturally strung up and disordered by her father's state. According to *Madame* it will arrange itself. You may imagine how this pleased and touched me. All this was on or about the 15th; on Monday last Foltinowicz died—yesterday I attended his funeral. I have seen Missie on or off pretty much as usual during this time—and I have not alluded to the important subject. We are both a little embarrassed—I more than she perhaps—and sometimes she drives me to despair by her coldness. At other times she is charming: *Madame* is always mercifully the same—I think on the whole, the most gentle and delicate minded lady whom I may hope to meet in this disagreeable world. And so, *mon cher ami,* it stands, my affair. *Qu'en pensez-vous?* I entreat you to write to me. I don't know how it will end—I hope at least that the embarrassment, the *gêne* which I have produced, entirely through my own hastiness, will wear off. It has been an exhausting three weeks—I feel as if I had been travelling all the time, sleeping in my clothes, lacking beds and baths. On the whole it is a relief to me to have the air clear—at any rate *Madame* thoroughly understands the situation. For the rest I am not very sanguine; if she liked me less or had not known me so long, I believe, my chance would be much better. She has a very difficult character, but at the same time a very fine one; exceedingly fond of her as I have been, I was amazed to see her during the last difficult week—that immensely trying time which has to elapse between a death and a burial—quite the cruellest part of death—she was intensely distressed and worn out, and perfectly composed. It was the same at the cemetery, when extraneous womankind were dissolved in tears, she stood like a little statue. At the same time I know that when she has been alone, she has had paroxysms of weeping, and this is a child of fifteen. I am afraid I am making large draughts upon your patience. But I may as well exhaust myself completely.

It is a very odd history—Heaven knows how it will end. In my more rational moments however, I am inclined to consider that that is of quite secondary importance; the important thing is that one should have, just once, experienced this mystery, an absolute absorption in one particular person. It reconciles all inconsistencies in the order of things, and above all it seems once and for all to reduce to utter absurdity any material explanation of itself or of the world. I will try and finish some verses I am working on and enclose upon this matter, to-night. I wish you were down here; we must meet soon—but we might have an excellent symposium here, in this extraordinary place of silence, with only river sounds. When you come to Poland, not a word of this, but I hope you will not have anything unusual to notice, except the absence of *ce pauvre monsieur's* cap and coat. What an infinitely dreary thing by the way is a London funeral. We make death more hideous than it need be. As they treated the old Vikings we should be sent out into a stormy sea in a burning ship. That distressing delay, and wearisome *cortège,* and the pit-a-pat of earth on the coffin are cruelties which civilization should spare one. I suppose however that no amount of euphemism will affect the essential horror of the thing or make it a less inexplicable cruelty. I have been interested to note—I have had various occasions lately—the immediate revulsion of life against death, which occurs after the disposal of the body, amongst persons who have been weighed down by the sincerest grief: this is quite universal and well worth consideration. A sort of instinctive protest against the thought of death by healthy life: consciously justifying itself? Or may it not be really the result of a more generous instinct—that actually death is not an essential fact, but an accident of immortality—so that what seems such cruel dishonor to a beloved person, all the corruption of death, is outside his interest or ours, I don't mean that this is rigidly apprehended—but is it not an innate feeling? You really must forgive me this prosing, I shall frighten you from my society. This letter is like *Tristan and Isolde*, it has nothing but love and death in it. I assure you there are still other things upon which I can discourse.

Au revoir

Ever Yours,

ERNEST DOWSON

There were other things on which Dowson could discourse at the time, for it was during this period that he was occupied with the prose narratives which were later to form part of *Dilemmas,* and with his friends at the Rhymers' and Aux Gourmets. But the thought that Missie "would like the idea" of marrying him in a year or two came back to him again and again. He probably reflected often on the theme of the early passage in the Fifth Ode of the Second Book of Horace: "Lalage is not old enough for your advances. Let her be a child a little longer. Have patience, she will come to you by-and-by, and return the love greater than you ever gave to Pholoë or Chloris." By the spring of 1894, a year had passed and there was no material change in his attachment. From Bridge Dock, on Maundy Thursday, 1894, he wrote to Smith as follows:

You are right, I fear, when you draw my horoscope. But the Ides are not yet. *Quod bene eveniat!* One lives and talks as if the making of many books were the end and aim of all things. I am afraid they are the straws one chews to cheat one's appetite. Whether the Ides come a little sooner or a little later, they must come this year. I always have a sort of feeling upon me that I am doing certain things for the last time. Therefore I am particularly anxious for you to come to Brittany with me this year . . . I must have one month more in Brittany before the Ides if only you could manage it. Noah must have had somewhat similar emotions to mine when he began to build his Ark. Out of what am I to build one? I am afraid I must trust to my swimming powers. In Poland there is no material alteration—perhaps we are a little troubled by the approach of anniversaries.

"The . . . exquisite and appropriate impossibility" of the situation at
Poland was recognized not only by Arthur Symons, who never really knew
Missie and Poland, but by Dowson's parents, relatives, and friends. To
him, however, there was nothing which suggested the impossible. He recognized the disparity in their ages—actually not much, but heightened by her
youth—and he no doubt realized that her tradition and his were quite
different; but with his idealization of things Continental, he could readily
make himself believe that at heart he was more a child of the Continent
than of traditional British stock. And there was some truth in his belief.
That her parents were scantily equipped with this world's goods had no
effect on his regard for them; in fact, he knew that he was not so well
provided for himself, and his tastes were simple. Rank and social prestige
conveyed little to him. He understood, as he illustrated in *A Comedy of
Masks* and *Adrian Rome*, how hollow life often became when one tried to
cultivate high friends and deliberate each gesture in terms of the standards
set by those who made a profession of their rank. Furthermore, he was
earnestly convinced that Adelaide's family had more to commend them than
many whom he had seen whose lives were built around the London season.
Possibly he was right, although the responses of his acquaintances who saw
Missie and her parents vary so greatly that his impressions of the Foltinowicz family will never be corroborated or refuted.

Apparently it was the difference in rank which caused his parents and
friends chief concern, but considerations of difference in rank could never
become more than trifling to him. Emotionally intense as his nature was, he
had sufficient intellectual ballast to view the situation from a practical
angle. That the practical advantages which he saw in a union with Missie
were born in large part of a sentimental regard for her is possible, although Dowson's ideal of what might constitute a happy union between
man and wife was built up without a strict dependence on his blinding
love for her. Even before he had met Missie, he had shown his friends
that he cared little for the more conventional ambitions and standards of
life and success. A wealthy wife from a family of high rank, a town
mansion over which she could preside at salons while he tried to charm her
guests with his verse and social grace, holidays at resort hotels on the Continent, and occasional pretty little notices from reviewers who catered to
the fashionable element in the London art circles seemed to him to spell
misery rather than happiness. Missie fitted far more gracefully into his
picture of success and happiness than any of the ladies whom he had met
at the salons.

Nor did he feel that her youth provided insurmountable disadvantages.

He had told his friends, as well as Missie and her mother, that he was willing to wait until she was of proper age, even according to English standards, and there is small doubt that he meant what she said. To his acquaintances, however, his love for a girl in her early teens seemed not only unusual but unsatisfactory to a normal young man who might presumably be expected to want to enjoy the delights of courtship. It was not difficult for his friends to believe that the caresses which Missie might exchange with her lover on the rare occasions when Madame was not in their company were less amorous than filial; Jepson became quite cross at the thought that Dowson was willing to forsake the delights of courtship for the meaningless pecks with which Missie showed her tolerance of his adoration. It probably seemed pretty stupid to Jepson and others for him to sit at Poland playing childish games with a restaurant-keeper's little girl when he might be enjoying the company of young ladies of his own age and station. To Dulcie, whose attitude toward Dowson had become mildly proprietary during the winter of 1893, his manner of spending the early part of his evenings with a child was incomprehensible. Jepson recalled nights on which Dowson, arriving late at the bar-parlor by the Elephant, was twitted by the irrepressible Dulcie about his "petite." Those of his friends who in the early stages of his attachment for Missie were amused at his devotion, which they believed could not be other than a temporary infatuation, became frankly annoyed at its persistence. Rumors, some of which were creditable to neither Dowson nor Missie, began to circulate, the import of which has never been completely dispelled.

It is true that Dowson's devotion to a girl in her early teens and his eagerness to marry her provided sufficient foundation for some of the tongue-wagging which went on, especially among his casual acquaintances, who were eager to believe that any sort of irregularity in love necessarily suggested a psychopathological condition. At a time when many of the artists of London and Paris had come to be viewed with suspicion by almost every rosy-cheeked schoolboy, Dowson did not escape entirely from the insinuations which English respectability felt it its moral obligation to circulate. Men whose lives were regular and exemplary often learned that on account of casual acquaintanceships they, too, were under suspicion. The occasional rumors which were attached to Dowson and which in some ill-informed circles still persist were that he loved Missie because he disliked normal women and that his eagerness to marry her was to be traced to his psychic impotence. Unable to lead a normal life with a mature woman, by reason of mental obstacles, he chose deliberately to live with a child whose demands on him would allow him to preserve a modicum of self-respect.

Despite the fact, however, that Dowson's attachment for a little girl laid a slender foundation for such rumors, there is ample evidence to support the conclusion that Dowson was never a victim of psychic impotence, or any sort of impotence, for that matter; and that he was thoroughly normal in his attitude toward sex. His love for Missie was no cunning device for deceiving himself or attempting to preserve his self-respect. There is no doubt that he wanted to idealize her, that to him she was and would always be different from mature and insistent women, that he wanted to preserve her as an innocent child; but not on account of any libidos or mental and physical debility. It may be inconceivable to some that a man might wish to idealize his wife to such an extent that he wished her to remain an innocent child forever, but such an idealization in certain stages of a man's development is far more common than is supposed.

As a young man Dowson had apparently drawn a distinction between carnal love and a loftier emotion which grew out of his reverence for innocence. The former had its uses and delights, but the love of innocence transcended all earthly pleasure. That he recognized the uses of sexual love can be proved more adequately than in most cases. In fact, this phase of Dowson's life is far plainer than many which propriety need not slight. It has been reported on sufficiently substantial authority that Dowson tried to win Oscar Wilde to the superior delights of normal love after Wilde had been released from prison; and that he was disappointed after he had brought Wilde to a house of pleasure in Dieppe to hear the latter say that his experience "was like a supper on cold mutton." Yeats reported, no doubt from hearsay, that Dowson was in the habit of trafficking with cheap harlots; and Conal O'Riordan, who spent a considerable part of the winter of 1896 with Dowson in France, has spoken of his friend's obvious normality. Sherard recalls that Dowson, in his last years while sharing his rooms in Paris, could not deny his urge for female companionship of the looser sort, and would bring ladies of the night into his quarters without showing the slightest embarrassment. Reports of Dowson's actions in this province are full and vivid; in fact, no one of his intimate friends has ever intimated that he showed signs of homosexuality or abnormality.* There were excesses, and a promiscuousness which at times shocked his friends,

---

* Morley Roberts' picture in *John o' London's Weekly* for September 30, 1933, of Johnson, Plarr, and Dowson "sitting hand in hand before the fire," and Dowson's embracing Plarr, could be ignored were it not for the insinuations which have attended its circulation. If Dowson ever embraced Plarr, it was a Continental gesture, no more. Mr. Roberts' authority on anything that pertains to Dowson is subject to question.

especially in his later years; but in spite of the fact that he mingled with men who sent Bibi la Purée out on the streets of Paris at night to look for likely "navvies," he was evidently content with the normal delights which London and Paris street-girls provided. Only once was he directly accused of perversion, and then by a frowsy trollop, who, seeing him show sympathy for Wilde at the time of the trial, and noting his green coat and flowing tie, called out to her sisters in normal vice: " 'Ere's another of the dirty b—s!"

In the light of what has been reported concerning Dowson's inclinations toward carnal love, one wonders whether his plan for a union with an innocent child did not appeal to him as a practical solution to the problem which arose over his distinction between the forms of love. His letters often suggest that he would have been willing to give up all carnal pleasures had he been assured of the satisfaction which he contemplated in his idealistic union with Adelaide; but it is easy to believe that he would have found such a companionship with her lacking in the beauty he contemplated. Arthur Symons has said that in his love for Missie "there was a sort of virginal devotion, as to a Madonna; and I think, had things gone happily, to a conventionally happy ending, he would have felt (dare I say?) that his ideal had been spoilt." This seems a very reasonable conclusion, for in spite of his eagerness to differentiate between two forms of love, the mature Missie would surely not have satisfied his ideal of the beauty of innocence. His plan, however, to preserve a distinction between the forms of love seemed sound enough to him, especially when he reflected on her youthful loveliness as he sat with her at one of the back tables at Poland playing halma. She would be his perpetual redemption; she would lift him above all that was cruel and sordid by her loveliness.

There is no doubt, however, that for his health and happiness it would have been better to see the ideal collapse than to wait for years in anguished uncertainty for Missie's decision. Already in the early autumn of 1892, he had told Smith that the strain was telling on him. By the spring of 1894, in spite of the fact that in the meantime he had declared himself to Missie and Madame, he could only report bitterly to Smith: "In Poland there is no material alteration." The hope which they had given him that in a year or two all would be favorably settled did little to relieve his anxiety concerning the outcome; and as the second year began to draw to a close and Missie had reached her sixteenth year, and still there was no "material alteration" in Poland, the distress of uncertainty became increasingly acute.

The uncertainty of his relationship was largely the result of his own indecision and of Madame Foltinowicz's frequent bewilderment at his actions. It is the general belief of those who knew Dowson intimately at the time that had he been less delicate in his advances he could have taken Missie away from Poland regardless of her youth and the professed reluctance of her mother to commit herself. There is small doubt that his dallying was in large measure the result of his lack of confidence in his own ideal. After hearing his parents and friends tell him that his intention to marry Missie was fantastic, he was swayed temporarily to their vehemently expressed conviction; but after an evening at Poland, he came away assured that his ideal was both sound and attainable. There were times when it did not appear so readily attainable, but on these occasions he came to the anguished conclusion that he would follow it to the end. Yet he did nothing to relieve the uncertainty. Missie was still young; to be sure, it was her youth he loved, but he would wait. Like Adrian Rome, "He could not quite make up his mind as to what the next move should be; he had, in fact, a nervous horror of making up his mind; he expected the future to arrange itself for him without the necessity of cogitation on his part."

Then, too, his uncertainty of the outcome was the result of Missie's behavior toward him. Although there were times at which she was inconsiderate of the devotion he showed to her, there is nothing to indicate that she and her mother tried deliberately to hurt him. Some of his actions bewildered Madame, who had the point of view of her class and race concerning the manner in which young men should conduct themselves when they professed their love. Often she must have reflected on the extraordinary way in which Dowson wooed her daughter. His intensions seemed serious and honorable enough, but when he came to Poland with his breath reeking of brandy, escorting young ladies such as Marie, Madame Foltinowicz had every reason to entertain doubts concerning the suitability of such a young man as her daughter's husband. It is possible, as Dowson told Jepson, that Marie "made an immediate conquest of Missie and her mother"; but he failed to recognize that his notions of faithfulness and Madame's were at considerable variance. It was probably after such episodes that his future with Missie looked very uncertain and that he complained to Smith: "Sometimes she drives me to despair by her coldness."

Much of his dallying at Poland can be traced not only to his native indecision and Missie's coldness, but also to the fact that he was not well. Had he been of robust constitution, it is possible that he would have brought matters to a head; but the terrifying signs of a fatal malady were already enfeebling his body and spirit. By the early months of 1894, he was coughing and losing weight. Even when he had gone up to Oxford in

1886, Walker noticed that he did not look well. Although he had an uncommon number of colds and sieges of influenza in his early twenties, all of which he shook off only after much difficulty, there had been no positive sign that he was tuberculous. He had more than the usual dread of cold and fogs, his appetite was capricious; and when he was not moving about with an excited rapidity, he was slouched far down in a chair. To many observers, Dowson's manner of slumping in the chairs at Henekey's and the Crown suggested that he was far in his cups, when the fact of the matter was that he no longer had the energy to sit erect. Such signs meant nothing to his friends at the time, or to him. By 1894, however, additional symptoms began to appear which must have been alarming to him. He knew the malady from which both his parents suffered in its most conspicuous manifestations, and there is no doubt that he recognized in his own frail constitution a pronounced susceptibility to tuberculosis of the lungs. It is a mistaken notion that Dowson never knew what ailed him and that even on his death bed he thought he had influenza. He probably left the impression on some of his friends that he was unaware of the malignancy of the disease from which he suffered; but to others he expressed himself graphically about his "half-lung." Before he was twenty-seven, he knew that he was tuberculous. With the optimism of many who are afflicted with this malady, he at times considered his condition only mildly serious; but its insistently recurring manifestations left him debilitated in body and spirit.

It is possible that had he gone promptly to a physician and followed a life of regularity and rest in a more salubrious clime than that of midwinter London, he might have regained enough spirit and strength to combat the malady in its early stages. France had always beckoned to him, and, well or ill, he would have welcomed the opportunity to leave London. It is idle to reflect on what could have been done for his health at this stage of his life had he possessed the means and the will to go to Davos for the cure. Conal O'Riordan and others have said that Dowson was afflicted with a type of tuberculosis which kills its victim rapidly, and that by the time the final symptoms had appeared, he could have been saved or his life at least prolonged only under the most ideal conditions.

The conditions which surrounded Dowson's life in the early stages of his affliction were far from ideal. In fact, they no doubt hastened the progress of the malady. It is true that he did little to try to escape the clutch of circumstance which tightened about him, for he lacked the indomitable spirit of his contemporary who cried out when the odds were all against him that he was the master of his fate and the captain of his soul. But it would have taken a strong spirit indeed to combat even for a time the malevolent forces which by 1894 began to direct their fury against him. With his character weakened by indecision, a weak body made weaker by irregular habits, without great compelling ambition and a strong will to live, he was ill equipped to wage other than a losing fight with the conditions which beset him.

Month by month, he had watched Bridge Dock grow more desolate. A ship on the ways had become increasingly rare. All during his period of literary achievement and apparent prosperity, he was associated with the declining fortunes of his father's business. Although his work at the Dock was never regular, he remained in touch with its affairs, and shared in some measure his father's distress at the prospect of impending bankruptcy. As early as 1890, money had to be borrowed in order to keep the Dock in sufficient repair and to pay the decreasing number of employees for the few small jobs which came to Dowson's. There evidently had not been any effort to bring the Dock abreast of its rivals by necessary modernizations; but the operating expenses had reached a sum which could not be defrayed by the income. Even the foreman, who for long had been loyal to Bridge Dock, became a creditor. By the latter part of 1893, Bridge Dock was almost entirely in the hands of those who had lent Alfred Dowson money for operating expenses. Foreclosure was not immediate because no one of the creditors was eager to take a controlling interest in a business which showed no prospects of income. Alfred Dowson's failure, however, was already written. With his savings over a long period of years placed in the Dock and with his knowledge of how its affairs were managed, the foreman became the owner's successor before Dowson was declared bankrupt.

The failing fortunes of the Dock would have had small effect on Ernest Dowson had his parents been resigned to what had for long been impending. His loyalty was to his parents, not the Dock. That he would be denied his allowance, which had never been large, probably never entered his mind. When he was so inclined, he knew how to make a little money go a long way. But to see his father constantly depressed and failing rapidly in strength on account of financial worries and the ravages of a fatal malady gave him anguish which he could not always successfully conceal from his friends. When the failure of the Dock was imminent and his father was resting after a dose of chloral and ergotine, he would on occasion don his fine raiment, go to the West End, and wear the mask which caused some of his acquaintances to believe that fame had gone to his head.

His father's rapidly failing fortunes and health gave him small opportunity to find the quiet atmosphere which his own physical condition demanded, and his family's frequent moving from one house to another did nothing to produce a feeling of security and peace. As a boy he had been moved about to such an extent that he never had developed even a sentimental regard for the notion of home; and with the passing of years in which his parents continued to change their address, he became increasingly indifferent to the advantages of a settled life. Given his choice, he probably would have preferred to move about from place to place, with few possessions to encumber his movements. For worldly goods he cared little; ownership meant nothing to him. Although an avid reader, he had a very small collection of books, not only because he could ill afford to buy them, but also because his possessive instinct was almost negligible. When he could borrow books, he did so in preference to stocking up with volumes which sooner or later would have to be moved.

Had his parents remained at Lee in Kent, it is possible that he might have cultivated a pride in ownership and have experienced the quiet which comes from a feeling of permanence and from being surrounded by the possessions which, taken as a whole, make a home. From youth, however, he had never been encouraged to accumulate the odds and ends which mark the difference between a place to live and a home. By 1888 Alfred Dowson, no longer able to travel to the Riviera, began to try to find a house which would meet the requirements of both his failing health and fortunes. After spending part of the summer of 1889 in Scotland, he took a house at 15 Bristol Gardens, Maida Hill, where he and his family remained until 1892. For a brief time in 1892 they were back at Lee, but by the summer of 1893 the elder Dowson had taken a house at Chadwell Heath which probably met the requirement of his dwindling income, but was both cheerless and inconvenient to the Dock. The place at Chadwell Heath was no more agreeable to his son, who sometime in August 1893 wrote to Plarr: "The whirligig of time has taken my people to world's end, which is called by the sublunary 'Chadwell Heath'—and there, I suppose, for the present I must pass penitential Sundays with much regret for your ancient, hospitable supper-table." After 1892, Dowson brought few of his friends home for an afternoon or evening. There are reports, however, about the house on the outskirts of Epping Forest, by those who on rare occasions were invited to his home. It was a gloomy place, made more cheerless by the tall evergreens which allowed the infrequent winter sunlight small chance to brighten the prospect, and by a high stone wall, on the other side of which was a mausoleum which seemed to wait expectantly for additional occupants.

Each successive house to which Alfred Dowson moved had disadvantages which he was promptly ready to see. To one who had been able to live comfortably in his early years, the necessity of finding a place which would fit his increasing need for comfort for a modest sum was in itself a tax on his spirit. For both his health and bank account, it would probably have been better had he decided to make the best of the disadvantages and remain in the house in Kent. But a restlessness, heightened no doubt by his illness, caused him to seek healthier and cheaper houses. Although Ernest found several of the places at which his parents lived inconvenient to his interests in the West End, he was in no way responsible for their frequent change of address. With him it had come to the point that he cared little about his place of residence, for he had learned through long experience where he could find friends with whom to sit out the night and in whose quarters he could find an armchair or a cot.

It was to a small flat overlooking Battersea Park that Alfred Dowson brought his family in 1894. The reason usually offered for his taking up such a residence was that it was not only nearer to his business, but that it was healthier and quieter. Although it was never mentioned, a reasonable rental had become a serious consideration. Quiet, especially at night, had taken on unusual importance to him. During the years of failing fortune and health, he had become a chronic insomniac. That he lay awake wondering what mischief his elder son might be up to may possibly be the case, but it is more likely that his own affairs were responsible for his sleepless nights. Driven to desperation by his inability to rest his mind and body, he began to resort to a kind of sleeping tablet in which there was a considerable amount of chloral hydrate. This he found beneficial for a while; but as is often the case with those who find sleeping tablets essential to rest, he found it necessary to take ever increasing doses in order to obtain the desired results. There were times after the family had moved to Battersea Park that Alfred Dowson, after awakening from a sound night's rest, would show signs of hopefulness. But by late afternoon, after he had returned to his wife from a brief application to his affairs at the Dock, he was again prone to see everything in the most dismal light. The Dock was a failure, he was a failure, and life had nothing but pain to offer. Everything he cherished was gone: he had no property that amounted to anything; his health was bad; his family, including his elder son, gave him small pleasure, despite the fact that Ernest had written some excellent pieces and had good literary connections.

His family had seen him depressed so often and for so long that they must have had forebodings of disaster. To them, however, his death came unexpectedly and swiftly. The final judgment of those who made the grim investigation was that Alfred Dowson had died as the result of an over-dose of chloral. The actual facts in the matter will never be known. It is now the opinion of most of Dowson's acquaintances that Alfred Dowson committed suicide. Given to worry, with a pronounced strain of melancholia in his nature, unbalanced by the ravages of a fatal malady and by the failure of the Dock, Alfred Dowson could not resist the temptation to put an end to his suffering. It is possible, to be sure, that accustomed as he was to increasingly large doses of chloral, he took a sleeping potion in good faith that he would awaken on the morrow refreshed by sound slumber, and by reason of the quantity of the dose and the reactions within his enfeebled body, he slept on.

There were few at the time or since who have been willing to put such a charitable construction on the circumstances surrounding Alfred Dowson's death; and in spite of the fact that his family were forever willing to believe the best, they could not help feeling the cloud which his death and its circumstances brought to them.* Dowson never expressed himself to any of his friends on the matter, although some of them have long felt that he knew that his father's death was suicide. Certain of Alfred Dowson's relatives evidently shared the same opinion. As late as 1914, Victor Plarr, after writing to some of Dowson's relatives concerning the reminiscences he was preparing of Dowson's life, announced: "Of the death of the poet's father and mother, I am expressly forbidden to write." Whatever Dowson's convictions were, his father's death affected him more than his friends at the time realized.

With the death of his father, he, now the head of the family as the elder son, was confronted by responsibilities with which he was ill equipped to cope. What his plans were for providing for his mother and younger brother Rowland, and for giving the home a guiding hand, cannot be determined. He had no profession and small income; he had no capabilities which inclined him to try to salvage the Dowson interest in the Dock, and he had no talent for restoring serenity and order to the bereaved home. Even small responsibilities irked him, and now confronted by the task of formulating even makeshift plans for three lives, including his own, he was gripped by indecision, and events took their own course. His plans for his own life were vague and shaken by past events, and he was bedfast with a severe influenza for days after his father's funeral. Severity in judging his inability to bring order and peace to the lives of his mother and brother must be entirely reserved, for try as he might, his nature and his disease-racked body left him impotent in the role of the head of the family.

* It was reported among the Swans that Alfred Dowson died of an abdominal hemorrhage.

There were, however, a few half-hearted attempts to find work which would provide him with a steady though small income. Both irony and pathos surrounded his efforts to find some sort of position. Saddened and ill, the author of "Cynara" and "Amor Umbratilis," "Extreme Unction" and "Beata Solitudo" went in answer to advertisements to the homes of rich men who wanted companions who could read German and play the violin, neither of which requirements he possessed; to librarians who might be willing to allow him to keep the books in order; and to publishers who might give him a regular salary for translating. Those whom he considered prospective employers, however, had either nothing to offer, or were unimpressed by his application for work. The year before his father's death he had applied for a position as librarian and secretary which was to pay £160 a year and an unfurnished apartment on the premises, but even with the recommendations of Plarr and Charles Sayle, he had failed to get the post. Now, with his spirit shattered by recent events and frequently recurring signs of diseased lungs, his very manner of applying for work did little to reassure employers that his services might be of use to them. It was not that he was exacting in his requirements for the kind of work that he would do; it was rather that he had very limited qualifications for positions which provided steady incomes, and that he lacked aggressiveness and decision in presenting himself as one who could be of service. Even before his small confidence in himself had been shaken by conditions at home, he had always been modest in viewing his qualifications for securing a position which paid an adequate salary. In February 1893, he had written to his friend Sayle, who had evidently recommended him for a position:

15 Bristol Gardens, W.

My dear Saile [*sic*],

Indeed, very many thanks: I have not ceased blushing since your letter came, I wish only that the vestrymen of Newington may not be too bitterly disillusioned. Should your kind recommendation induce them to elect me. I do not suppose there is any very real chance of obtaining this office, although Plarr, whom I saw yesterday, tells me that it is not a particularly high qualification which is necessary—as I should have said, indeed, myself. But it is just worth trying.

By the way, a post which it would certainly be fruitless for me to aim at, I see in the Athenaeum, is vacant—the librarianship of the London library, £400. Why do you not apply for this? Or are you grown too attached to Cambridge? . . .*

---

* Quoted from the original letter in the possession of Michael Holland. The letter can be dated by Dowson's reference to the poem in *Atalanta*. "The Dead Child" appeared in February 1893. The rest of the letter reads:

After the death of his father, he was unwilling to apply to any of his friends for recommendations. His pride, made almost fierce by the tragic events in his home, kept him from seeking any sort of favor. In fact, he often tried to avoid his friends, many of whom, including Plarr and Sayle, would have been happy to try to help him, on account of his dread of what he might detect as pity.

His feeling of necessity for finding work with a steady income in order to provide for himself if not for the family was short-lived, however, for within a few months after his father's death, another tragedy occurred which relieved him of any further sense of practical responsibility to the Dowson home. Soon after her husband's death, Mrs. Dowson went back to Lee in Kent. Her sister, Ada Swan, lived in Lee, and the thought of being near her gave Mrs. Dowson a passing comfort. Then, too, the flat overlooking Battersea Park was now intolerable to her, whereas the house in Kent had witnessed most of her rare moments of happiness. It was at the Grove in Lee that her sons had been born, and in its rooms that she had a few associations which were untinged by grief. Her homecoming, however, brought small comfort and peace. Always of fragile health, she had neither the strength of body nor of will to try to find happiness anywhere. Even before the death of her husband, she had begun to harbor notions that she was in large measure responsible for the ills which beset her family; and after his death, she brooded over her part in bringing unhappiness to her husband and sons until the idea became fixed that she was largely to blame. Weakened by the ordeal through which she had recently been and by the same malady from which her husband had suffered, she had little courage of a mental and moral sort with which to combat the obsession which preyed constantly on her mind. If Dowson detected her suffering, he did his best to dissuade her from the notion that she was in any way responsible for the ills which had overtaken her family; but she was in that stage of life in which rational explanation availed little. Some of Dowson's friends who

---

"I hear great accounts of you, and of music, absorbing you: and very likely you are right. But though I hate London more than the pains of hell, I am kept here for a personal reason and must try to keep here although almost any other place would suit me better. Do you know Norman Gale, the man or his work? The last enchants me so much that I am anxious to meet the first. I should like to know what you think of my friend, Gray's poems which will appear immediately under the auspices of the good Lane, if you come across them. I was in 'Atalanta' for this month, with a 'Dead Child.' Some day I hope we shall meet: in the meantime, with again many thanks,

ever affecly yrs

ERNEST DOWSON

P.S. My family desires to be remembered to you; may I say the same to your mother."

had seen her a few months before her husband's death noticed a curious sort of preoccupation in her manner, and in the weeks following his death this preoccupation evidently became more pronounced. She considered herself a failure as a wife and mother; death would in some measure be an expiation of her sense of guilt. Ernest and Rowland could get along better without her than with her. It was only a few months after Alfred Dowson died that she followed him, a suicide.

At the time of the second tragedy, Dowson was at home. According to one informant who had seen him earlier in the day, he had refused an invitation to go to the West End so that he might stay with his mother who, he said, wanted him to take a walk with her, possibly to her sister Ada's, in the afternoon. The walk was never taken. In an unpublished letter in the collection of Mr. Sherard, Dowson's friend was informed of some of the immediate circumstances. "Ernest and she were just going out together and were in the hall; when remarking that she had forgotten something upstairs, she went up to her room. As she did not come back, Ernest went up and found her hanging dead from the bedpost."*

This plain statement of the facts has implied to some who have glanced at it that Dowson, through some ill-chosen remark or reluctance to accompany her, might possibly have been responsible for his mother's decision to free him from the burden with which she believed she oppressed him. It is apparent that she contemplated the walk without pleasure, but it is by no means evident that Dowson's lack of consideration for his mother's wishes and feelings was in any way responsible for her untimely death. All of Dowson's friends at the time who knew him with sufficient intimacy to

---

* Years later, when Lewis Swan who had come to America was insistent that he be informed about the circumstances surrounding his sister Annie's death, Ethel Swan wrote to him in part as follows:

"You persistently ask about Annie's death & and are quite right in thinking it was a tragedy. It was, & that's how we never told you about it. . . . They were very hard up, but no one guessed it. Nell & I were in Scotland & sent them a bunch of Aberdeen 'haddies' which came as a godsend as they had nothing in the house. They were living in a flat over Albert Bridge—& of course poor old Alfred couldn't stand that sort of thing & died rather suddenly with hemorrhage of the stomach, not lungs. Annie and Rowland were alone with him & it upset her brain which was never very strong I imagine. Ernest was playing the fool, translating brilliantly, & then taking awful drugs, absinthe & other things & six months after Alfred's death she put herself away. She & Rowland were in lodgings at Lee, all this was years ago. Stanley saved all he could and bought an annuity for her & took Rowland into Lloyd's. If only she had been a bit stronger in character, she would and could have pulled round. Nell & I, always *much* preferred Rowland, he was a dear boy, but he had just the same bringing up as Earnest, no schooling, just going from place to place, the worst life a boy could have. Afterwards the Dock was sold & he got everything & was quite fairly well off. He was only 17 when he went to Canada, *thankful* to get away from Limehouse and Ernest. The latter

observe his regard for his mother are as one in their insistence that in her presence his manners were gentle and indicative of both love and respect. The death of his mother was the last straw. He loved her fragile beauty, her delicate expression, and her helplessness in times of stress. He never spoke of this love, but it is generally agreed among all who knew him at the time that his sorrow was profound and lasting. Although he had not been the most dutiful son, he had never been the principal cause of his parents' worries. They had remonstrated with him about his waywardness and his apparent unwillingness to settle down to a position with a steady income; they were disappointed when he had left Queen's without a degree, and they were distressed over his attachment at Poland; but Alfred Dowson and his wife were not the victims of his waywardness. In spite of the fact that he often stayed at the rooms of his friends instead of coming home at night, there was no period of estrangement between parents and son. Nor did he ever reproach them for their neglect of his training or for his reverses. His love of his parents was of such a nature that he saw in them not the molders of his own ill lot, but the victims of a malevolent force against which they had struggled in vain. When his mother succumbed to the odds which encompassed her, he lost the small trust he had ever had in an all-wise benevolence.

"I always thought," Robert Sherard told me, "that it was his mother's death, following so closely on his father's, which jostled his little ambition to live and create over the borderline." There is no doubt that after his mother's death, Ernest Dowson was a changed man. Without compelling ambition, without strength of either body or spirit, and without his parents, he took—or rather, he was forced to take—the road which led down instead of up.

---

was always able to earn, for his publishers said his English translations were beautiful. He was a queer mixture, *clever* but fearfully weak character & like a madman when he got drink or drugs. No wonder Rowland *hated* to be with him, but after Annie's death he was generally with us. Doctors hoped voyage & Canadian climate would have kept off consumption, but it didn't, too deeply in Dowson family. He married & had one little girl which he called *Annie*, rather sweet we thought. Both Emily Secretan & I got into touch with his wife, but soon lost sight of them altogether. Emily send the child a Bible. I think a frock or a £5 note would have been more appropriate.

"Now you have the whole tragic story. . . . I think it was misery about Ernest & remorse that she didn't take more care of dear old Alfred made her do it. Ada was at Hospital in Edinburgh & we never told her all the ins & outs—tho' of course she knew most of it. All this is such years & years ago. . . .

"It was a terrible time for us, as you can believe; I had been the last to see her, so had to be at the inquest . . . it's just as well to forget it as much as we can, they have *all* gone, but the heroes are Alfred & Rowland."

VII

PARIS

AFTER his mother's funeral, the arrangements for which were attended to by relatives, there was a long period of emptiness in Dowson's life. Indecision, ill health, and life-sickness all contributed to the void which surrounded him. During the days in which the cruel blows were falling, he had tried to possess his soul in patience; but as he himself observed, "The result is not so much resignation as a sort of sloth and *tristitia.*" Over it all he had not winced or cried aloud, nor had he tried to fight back. His bitterness toward the order of things never became articulate; no fierce rebellion welled up in his heart. A sort of mental stupor held him, from which he apparently made no effort to escape. Thoughts of writing, of his friends in the West End, and of Missie came and went, leaving him with only vague reminders that he was still of the world.

At twenty-seven, however, in spite of his debility of body and mind, he was not without occasional flashes of hope. There were times, amid all of his suffering and emptiness, at which he recalled what he had done at the Rhymers', his little Pierrot play for Peters, and the novel which had been so encouragingly reviewed in the *Bookman.* Thoughts of the sweet innocence of Missie surely began to take on distinctness, and he recalled that Madame Foltinowicz had told him that Missie would like the idea of marrying him in a year or two. Furthermore, if he would pull himself together, he might in time go to live in France, where everything would be different. Such likely reflections, supported by a hopefulness which cannot be entirely destroyed when one is twenty-seven, gave him sufficient will to shake off some of the sloth which had gripped him, and to try to tie together the frayed ends of his life.

The death of his parents had not left him entirely destitute, and his relatives were eager to help him. His paternal relatives, the Hooles and the Secretans, had come into the foreground of his life during the recent tragic events which had affected them deeply, and they were quite willing to give him and his brother the support which lay within their means. The maternal relatives, the Swans, one of whom lived to the end of her life at 53 Burnt Ash Road in Lee in Kent, were not unmindful of the difficulties which beset Ernest and Rowland now that their parents were gone. In fact, Miss Ada Swan, sister of Dowson's mother, showed her affection for her nephew whenever she had the slightest opportunity. At her own request, she was buried in the same plot with him in the Ladywell cemetery in Lewisham, and it was she who ordered and paid for the modest monument which marks his grave. It is a mistaken notion that Dowson's relatives were estranged from him by reason of the complications which beset him and by his wayward ways. It is true that the Secretans were unsympathetic to his embracing the Catholic faith; and the Hooles were much distressed over the seriousness of the affair at Poland, but there never was sufficient friction to cause a cleavage between Dowson and his relatives. Mrs. Holford Secretan, although inclined to disapproval of the way young poets rejected all the Victorian standards of virtue, was proud of her nephew's literary attainments and associations, and would willingly have taken him into her home to treat as her own son. Then, too, Dowson was not altogether penniless after the death of his parents. In the Dock there was still a small interest which possibly could be sold, and there was also an interest in the property in Kent. Rowland, although untrained in any profession, was at least old enough at the time to be self-supporting. In fact, a rapid inventory must have indicated to Ernest and Rowland that there was no immediate cause for pecuniary distress.

Within a half-year after his mother's death, Dowson had managed to devise a makeshift plan for his future. There was still a sufficient instinct of self-preservation to cause him to escape from the void which had encompassed him. The house in Kent was given up, and with the Dock House still open to him, he carried his belongings to the room adjoining the office and attempted to make the quarters tasteful and comfortable. Bridge Dock was after all more of a home to him than any of the houses in which he had lived in the last years of his parents' lives; and so long as the Dock House was open to him, he could find shelter there without going to his relatives, and make some sort of pretense of having work to do. The foreman and his family had always been very friendly with the Dowsons, and in spite of the fact that their quarters were detached from his, he could feel that he was not living entirely alone. He could be of some service to the foreman, who was trying with small success to make a paying enterprise out of the Dock, and in doing so he could supplement his income slightly and keep his mind away from the tragic events of the past year. Reports of Dowson's occupation after his father's death led some of his acquaintances to believe that he had inherited the property and was now the sole owner and supervisor. With no deliberate intent to deceive, he allowed the impression to stand in some places because he had a morbid dread of being thought poor.

After the house in Kent was closed, Rowland went to live with relatives. Here he remained with no satisfactory employment until he was caught by the idea of going to Canada, there to build up his health and fortune as a rancher in the West. It was suggested by some of the relatives that Ernest accompany his brother or, if things turned out well for Rowland in Canada, that he join him later on. Such a suggestion had no appeal to him, even with its prospect of making money and restoring his health. His friends have reported that he laughed at the idea, and he was probably right. As a rancher in the open spaces of western Canada, he would probably have met an earlier fate than that of his brother, who, after years of hardship in the West, died of tuberculosis and was buried in San Diego, California.* With Rowland's departure for Canada, all immediate family ties were severed, and Dowson was left alone to plan his life as best he could.

In spite of the fact that the room which he had taken at the Dock was commodious and comfortably furnished, his arrangement for keeping quarters in Limehouse was short-lived. To him, the room must have appeared like Philip Rainham's quarters in *A Comedy of Masks*.

The dark old room, with its mildewing wainscot, became full of ghosts; and he could fancy that the spirits of his ancestors were returned from the other side of the Styx to finger the pages of by-gone ledgers, and to mock from between the shadows of his incongruous bookshelves, at their degenerate descendant. And these but did give place, amid strange creaking and contortions of the decaying walls to spectres more intimate, whose reprobation moved him more: the faces of many persons whom he had known, forming themselves, with extraordinary vividness, out of the darkness, and in the red embers of the fire, and each adding its item of particular scorn to the round accusation of futility brought by the rest. They were part of his introspection, all those—he was not sick enough to hold them real—but nevertheless they gave him food for much vigilant thought, which always came back to the great interest of his life. Futility!

Realizing his need for companionship in order to free his mind from the phantoms which moved about his room at the Dock, he plead with his acquaintances in the West End to accompany him home, but in spite of their occasional acceptance and the company of the foreman and his family, he was lonely. With Rowland's departure for Canada, he came to the conclusion that he could no longer deceive himself or others in the belief that he was essential to the Dock's existence; and with more decisiveness than

* Rowland Dowson's daughter, child of a marriage in America, christened Annie Dowson, is presumably alive somewhere in America. According to the solicitors of the Dowson family, Baker and Nairne, London, Annie Dowson had a sum of several hundred pounds bequeathed to her which she may recover by presenting satisfactory evidence of identity.
(NOTE: Twenty years after this notice appeared in the second edition, Annie Dowson, now Mrs. A. D. Glanville of Vancouver, B. C., wrote to the author and is in correspondence with Baker & Nairne.)

was usual for him, he determined to sever his connection with its affairs and take up residence in Bloomsbury. Edgar Jepson accompanied him to Lime-house on the afternoon that he went to his room above the office to pack his belongings for his final departure. The operation of packing and leaving was performed with the utmost secrecy, for he was unwilling to tell the old familiars at the Dock of his decision to leave, and to enter into ex-planations. Although he had never liked the place, it saddened him to leave it; and rather than discuss the reasons for his departure with those who had followed his fortunes and those of the Dock for a score of years, he jumped into a cab into which he had placed a slender wardrobe, a bundle of manuscripts including his "Poesie Schublade," a dozen books—most of which belonged to his friends—and was gone. It was at this time that his relatives began to lose track of him.

He found lodgings in Bloomsbury, where he remained until the summer of 1895, at which time he went to Dieppe. His new quarters were agree-able to him, largely because they were in a region frequented by actors, most of whom did their most spirited work in the hours after the theatres were closed. The place at which he chose to take a room was made addi-tionally interesting by reason of its landlady, who, according to general report, had attained the distinction of being the night-time companion of an opulent Hindu who was referred to as the Prince Ansah of Ashantee. It is debatable whether it would have been better for Dowson to have stayed in Limehouse instead of finding balm for his loneliness in such quar-ters. There were advantages, to be sure, in his new residence. He was within walking distance of the Crown and Poland—if such proximity can be considered an advantage—and he was surrounded by men who were not only willing but eager to turn night into day. The necessity for bidding his friends good-night in order to catch the last train to Stepney was gone. The lighthearted nights with the "Bingers" were also gone. But in a new environment, with no responsibilities save to himself, he found relief from the oppressive associations which his quarters at Bridge Dock had insistently produced.

It is possible that his change of address was in some measure responsible for his willingness to try to erect some sort of structure out of the ashes which loomed gray before him, but it is more likely that his interest in literature was the substance out of which he was to begin to refashion his life. And it so happened, fortunately or unfortunately for him, that one Leonard Smithers had established himself as a bookseller and later as a publisher in London. It was from Smithers that he received fairly regular employment. The meeting which gave Dowson to Smithers, and Smithers to Dowson, is one of the accidents in literary history. It probably had more advantages than disadvantages to them both, although this conclusion is subject to question. Leonard Smithers was unique among the booksellers and publishers of the 'nineties: John Lane, Elkin Mathews, Heinemann, Methuen, and the rest were rank conservatives when compared to him. In fact, it is unlikely that the publishing fraternity will ever have a member who even faintly resembles him. Originally a solicitor in Sheffield, with small reputation for probity or talent, he drifted into bookselling with H. S. Nichols of Soho Square. It may readily be assumed that Sheffield was not large enough for a man of his tastes and ambitions. Even before he settled in London, however, he had been the intimate friend of Sir Richard Burton, and it was probably through this association that he cultivated his extraordinary taste in literature. Although Vincent O'Sullivan has stated that it was Arthur Symons who shaped Smithers' inclination to become the publisher of the new school of poets and illustrators, Smithers would have become a London influence without any of Symons' guidance. With a pasty white face —"like the death mask of Nero," said Ranger Gull—eyes set deep in the shadows which surrounded them, and long, twitching hands, Smithers' very appearance suggested a preoccupation with the erotic and the bizarre. Although married twice before he was in his mid-thirties, he was intimate with a round score of women unmarked for either their beauty or virtue in every section of London. From time to time, according to O'Sullivan, he would turn up in Paris, "always accompanied by some appalling Venus . . . hideous to the point that one wondered in what suburb of Houndsditch he could have gone to seek her." His friends in London who found that their appetites for wine, women, and song were unappeased could always rely on him to provide them with some sort of nourishment. His tastes in literature were evidently more refined than his tastes in women, though despite his excellent perceptions he showed small interest in any piece which lacked the quality of the grotesque or unhealthy.

For young men of talent with ample time on their hands, he was always a ready companion. His more conservative associates wondered when and how he did his work. He would sit at the Bodega and the "Marble Halls" underneath Gatti's for hours on end, discussing with young writers and painters matters which were far removed from the practical issues of bookselling. For a long time he occupied quarters at Effingham House on Arundel Street off the Strand, but with his brief day of prosperity he had a shop in the Royal Arcade, and a house of mansion proportions and appointments in Bedford Square. Generally he kept open house for his contributors and friends: one was almost sure of finding something going on at mithers', and more often than not the evenings at his quarters had the features of a revel. His day of prosperity began while he was still at Effingham House, and his reputation, which attained considerable width during the last years of the decade, was by no means slight in 1895. Long before the end of the century his name had become virtually a figure of speech. "One of the Smithers people" was a current phrase in the second half of the decade which was used by the more conservative literati with a definitely opprobious connotation.

It was after Dowson had taken a room in Bloomsbury that he became "one of the Smithers people." Without ambition and plans he was easily led to accept the commissions which the publisher had to offer. Smithers knew Dowson's talents, and with the perception with which he was amply endowed he felt sure that he could put these talents to work for their common benefit. Devoid of a moral sense when matters pertaining to art were concerned, and with no regard for what others thought or said about the private lives of artists, Dowson was happy to undertake any assignment which Smithers had to suggest. It was probably gratitude for what Smithers did for him at a time when he was without hope that caused him to become the most loyal contributor and friend whom Smithers ever had. Arthur Symons, after being closely associated with Smithers for several years, insulted him to his face in a public house; and Beardsley, who drew his chief income from the House of Smithers, snarled at him behind his back. Yeats reported that even in the hey-day of *The Savoy*, he, Jepson, and Beardsley found Smithers' company annoying and tried to keep him at a distance. Beardsley's letters to Smithers, although frequent, show at best a perfunctory friendliness. Vincent O'Sullivan, who owed much to Smithers, has not been silent about the publisher's lecherous character; and Charles Conder and Will Rothenstein, both of whom turned in many an illustration to Effingham House, were never really loyal. But Dowson, to whom it is certain that Smithers paid proportionately less than to his other contributors, was ever grateful and loyal. Late in February 1896 he wrote from Paris to his friend Smith: Smithers "is, all round, the best fellow I know, and it is astonishing to me how many people fail to see this, or seeing it temporarily (instance Conder, Rothenstein *inter alios*) succeed in quarreling with him."

It is no doubt true that Smithers' influence on Dowson was by no means salutary, but it is equally certain that he gave Dowson new energy and hope, and that he advanced money to him on occasion for work which he had every reason to believe might never be delivered. Furthermore, it was Smithers who made possible the fulfillment of the idea of a new magazine, and it was the prospect of contributing regularly to this magazine which gave Dowson a new motive for living. *The Yellow Book* had reached its zenith and was declining; and under the enterprising guidance of Arthur Symons, the idea of *The Savoy*, an art magazine which would appeal to the most refined tastes, was taking on concreteness. When the idea of *The Savoy* was brought to Smithers, he responded with enthusiasm; and it was he who made the periodical possible and gave to it much of its tone. Symons was to be the literary editor, Beardsley the art editor, and Smithers the managing editor and publisher. There was the assurance that such writers as W. B. Yeats, Frederick Wedmore, Havelock Ellis, and Selwyn Image would contribute to its literary contents, and that its pictorial contents would be handled successfully by Aubrey Beardsley, Will Rothenstein, and Charles Conder. When Dowson was asked whether he would support the magazine with regular contributions, he was ready to assure Smithers and Symons that he would do his utmost to make the magazine a success. The prospect of not only contributing to the new magazine, but of also being one of its chief supporting figures gave him the hope and energy which at the time he met Smithers he sorely lacked. His assurances to Smithers and Symons that he would do everything in his power to make *The Savoy* succeed were carried out: Dowson followed its fortunes from the time of its inception to the very end.

With an assignment to translate Balzac's *La Fille aux Yeux d'Or* for Smithers, which the latter planned to issue in a handsome volume with wood engravings by Charles Conder, and with the encouragement that anything he wrote in verse or prose would be considered for *The Savoy*, he began to contemplate means by which he might settle down to work. London offered neither peace of mind nor inspiration. Often he had reflected that if he could only manage to live in France, many of his problems would be solved. When he learned that Charles Conder, who was commissioned to do the drawings for his translation of Balzac's story, was planning to go to France, he was led to believe that he, too, might do better work away from London. O'Sullivan has reported that Conder appeared one morning at Effingham House to tell Smithers that he was going to Brittany to "paint blossoms." Waiting below on Arundel Street was Dowson, who felt that if Smithers was willing to advance money to Conder for the work which was to result from a sojourn in Brittany, then he too might be entitled to some advance for the translation of the Balzac story on which he had started. Smithers, realizing that he had two talented contributors to please, and caught in a moment of generosity, paid for their journey, according to report, and gave them each a little money to defray their living expenses while they worked on their respective assignments with *La*

Fille aux Yeux d'Or. Such generosity encouraged Dowson in the belief that he had something to which to tie his life and talents, and with the money which Smithers advanced and the small provision which was his at the death of his parents, he began to lay plans to move straightway to France.

Smithers' decision to issue *La Fille aux Yeux d'Or* had been in large measure influenced by Conder's enthusiasm for the story. It was Conder's favorite story, and evidently he had no great difficulty in persuading the publisher that a good translation of it with attractive illustrations would bring in ample returns. Conder was one of the talented painters whom Smithers had attracted with the prospects of *The Savoy* and a flourishing press, and with his hospitality at Effingham House. As early as 1893 Conder had exhibited some of his work in Paris with encouraging results, and he had come to be generally recognized among the more advanced critics as an artist of more than usual talent. In his studio he showed a sense of responsibility in the fulfillment of his commissions; but when he was in gay company he could easily be led to forget his painting and give himself over to prolonged excesses. There were times in the summer of 1894 when he and Dowson, accompanied at least on one occasion by Beardsley, walked about the streets of London after the Crown had closed in order to be up for the early boat-train to Dieppe, to arrive without baggage and to return to London in a day or two looking pretty much the worse for wear. Rothenstein recalls that he used to sit up with Conder at times for most of the night in order to help him get over his debauches, which on one occasion had brought on a violent attack of delirium tremens. When Conder was away from the reckless spirits of London and Paris, he was of mild, equable disposition, fonder of women than of wine, and possessed of considerable ambition to get ahead with his art. The seriousness with which he regarded his attachment for his beautiful model Germaine, who was evidently a sufficiently desirable possession for him to become involved in a duel over her, amused and at times annoyed his friends, especially those who were depending on him to come out of his bower of love and settle down to work. He was always more decisive in his movements than Dowson; and when Smithers advanced him money to go to France to make the illustrations for *La Fille aux Yeux d'Or,* he moved straightway to Dieppe, where he finished his part of the commission before Dowson arrived.

It was not until the end of June 1895 that Dowson took up residence at one of the modest hotels near the Cathedral in Dieppe. At that time Dieppe was a popular watering-place for artists and vacationists to whom the very name *La Plage* suggested a Continental holiday. The art colony was chiefly

English, and during the summer of 1895 Dowson saw much of not only Conder, but also the young novelist Conal O'Riordan, Greene of the Rhymers, and Arthur Moore. With them he spent evenings which helped him to regain his interest in writing. *Adrian Rome*, the novel which he had started with Moore, had been interrupted by the events of the year just passed; but now, away from scenes which tormented him and with Moore's encouragement, he set to work to contribute his part to the completion of the novel. It was in some measure his determination to provide Moore with chapters for *Adrian Rome* and to finish his assignment for Smithers which led him after a few weeks in Dieppe to go inland to Arques, where he felt he could work uninterruptedly. Another reason which may readily be advanced for his decision to leave Dieppe for Arques can be traced to the atmosphere which prevailed in Dieppe at the time. Dieppe was more English than French during July and August; and the cricket on the beach, the Varsity blazers on the promenade and in the Casino, and the Londoners on a two-week holiday at the *Hotel des Familles* annoyed him. Sensitive to any manifestation of bourgeois tastes, he finally came to the conclusion that he would be happier and more energetic in the fulfillment of the obligations which had brought him to France if he could escape from the oppressive spectacle which *La Plage* presented. Arques, which was only a few miles from the promenade in Dieppe, and to which he had taken walks with Arthur Moore, appealed to him on account of its detachment from the English holiday crowd and its serene beauty. He found lodgings near the ruins of the old chateau and within the shadow of the Gothic church with its beautiful rood loft and fine stained glass. Within its darkened interior he often knelt to pray; and in the forest northeast of the chateau he took long walks. Although he was away from the group who shared his interests, he found his experiences in Arques comforting. Moore came to see him toward the end of the summer, to find him in fairly good spirits and hopeful that he soon would be able to settle down to the fulfillment of all of his projects

By the end of the summer, however, possibly on account of his loneliness, he determined to return to London. His decision was motivated by two substantial reasons: he was not only lonely, but he had no money; and he felt that the loose ends at the Dock and at Poland could be tied up in such a way that he could return to France for a more prolonged sojourn. What arrangements he planned to make cannot be accurately determined, for his correspondence with his friends at this time was meager; but it seems probable that he should attempt to assure himself some sort of income from his interest in the Dock, that he should try to reach an agreement with Smithers concerning future assignments, and that he should try to com to some sort of understanding with Madame and Missie. To be sure, it was impossible for him to continue at Arques during the autumn and winter, but in the light of what he achieved on his return to London, it is distressing to reflect on his experiences during the brief time in which he tried to adjust his affairs.

First of all, his interest in the Dock was virtually worthless. None of the creditors was willing to risk additional investment in order to buy out the small share of the property which still remained to him; nor was there the faintest prospect of income as a dividend from his holdings. When he had moved out of the Dock house to take rooms in Bloomsbury, he had not, as a few of his acquaintances believed, given up all thought of income from the Dock. Although he was practical enough to understand that the business was not of the sort which would afford him financial security, he continued to cherish the hope that there would come a time when six hundred pounds, which he believed was his remaining share in the Dock, would be paid in full to him, with possibly some accrued income. When he returned to London in the autumn of 1895, he had regained enough spirit to investigate the condition of his holdings. The foreman, who had attained the controlling interest in the Dock, possibly by reason of his own optimism concerning its future and his long attachment with the family, advanced him a little money, which was in no way a dividend of the recent profits. Easily satisfied in such matters, Dowson took the small sum which the generous foreman offered him, with the notion that there was a great deal more to come. To the end of his life he continued to believe that he had six hundred pounds coming to him.

His second purpose in returning to London was equally unproductive. The translation of the Balzac story was far from finished, and Smithers, who combined the instincts of a good business man with those of generous friendship, was unwilling to assure him that he would be his ready provider. As yet Smithers had not reached that level of prosperity and abandon which would allow him to guarantee Dowson anything. He was kindly disposed toward his dilatory contributor, but he could give him little more than the encouragement to believe that if he turned in his work regularly and creditably Smithers would remunerate him for his efforts. It is possible that Smithers, caught again in a moment of generosity, advanced an additional sum to Dowson on account for the completion of *La Fille aux Yeux d'Or*, but there is no indication that Smithers put him on a regular salary as early as the autumn of 1895.

Another source of income, though slight, was in the offing. Richard Le Gallienne had sent his reader's report to John Lane and Elkin Mathews concerning the collection of prose tales which Dowson had been eager to have'publlished as early as 1893. He had written nothing, although he had assured Lane he would try to augment the series of five tales, all of which had been finished before 1894; and Lane, despairing of receiving additional stories, decided on Le Gallienne's favorable report to issue the tales which had been lying about in manuscript for over two years. The publication of *Dilemmas: Stories and Studies in Sentiment* was at best a half-hearted publisher's venture. Even a short-sighted view of the possibility of income from such a source would have indicated that very little could be expected. It is unlikely that Dowson ever thought that the volume would attain the circulation of *Keynotes*, but his fondness for the tales led him to believe that the royalties would supplement his little *Reise* fund.

His financial arrangements for a prolonged sojourn in France, although by no means reassuring, were more satisfactory than the arrangements he tried to make at Poland. His love for Missie remained steadfast, but his plan of action now as always was clear neither to Missie and Madame nor to himself. He wanted to go to France, but he wanted to be near Missie. He wanted to marry Missie, but he felt that she was still too young, and he had no money to take her with him to France. He loved her, but he felt that when she became older his love would die. The agreement which he had hoped to reach with her on his return to London was blighted by his own indecision.

His indecision, no doubt, was heightened by his sensitivity. Had Missie been consistent in her expression of affection for him, it is possible that his equivocal attitude toward his relationship with her would have changed to a bolder course. But she, who had seen little of him since his father's death, had taken on womanhood. She was now seventeen, and already mature for her years. Her mother, after the death of Joseph Foltinowicz, had become increasingly attentive to her daughter's affairs; and together they must have expressed their doubts about this strange young man whose parents had both committed suicide, who drank more than was good for him, and who was known to consort with loose women. When Dowson reappeared at Poland after his long absence, they were unprepared for a demonstration of affection, and he, responsive to Missie's slightest gesture, was unable to outline any plan for the future which their encouragement might have crystallized.

The facts concerning his visits to Poland in the early autumn of 1895 will never be disclosed, but it is certain that any plan which he had vaguely in mind for his future with Missie remained unexpressed or was rejected In fact, on his parting visit they quarreled. If the character Seefang which

he created for his story "The Eyes of Pride" is in any way a reflection of
Dowson's mental experiences at the time, then he had determined as he
left Poland on that evening that ". . . there is nothing so disorganizing as
a great passion. . . . He began to think of his work, and he was surprised
at discovering how utterly he had neglected it during the last six months.
∴. . His art! That he ever should have forgotten it."

It was only after weeks of disappointment in London that he came to
the conclusion that his only means of escape from the vicissitudes which
beset him was his pen. All that he had hoped to achieve in order to give
himself peace of mind for a prolonged sojourn in France had collapsed.
Plarr, who had lost touch with him for almost a year, found him living at
6 Featherstone Buildings, High Holborn, which he had chosen, Plarr believed, "because of poor Chatterton's supposed residence there long ago."
Plarr invited him to his home on the Sunday following their meeting, but
Dowson did not appear. Some time later, Plarr received a brief note from
his friend:

My excuse for not having come to you on the Sunday you will find equally
inexcusable, but it was simply because I was in such a state of nervous and
physical disability that I had not the faintest recollection of having any engage-
ment. . . . I expect to be in this country, much as it tortures and maddens me, till
Christmas or the New Year.

Long before Christmas, however, he left London. His quarrel with
Missie, whatever the cause, accelerated his decision to get away from the
scenes which tormented him; and with the funds which the foreman and
Smithers advanced, and the prospect of more from Smithers and something
from Lane and Mathews for his collection of tales which was soon to be
issued, he felt that he could at least make a start toward settling down to
work in France. His determination to leave London at once was given additional support by the fact that Conal O'Riordan, with whom he had spent
pleasant evenings in Dieppe during the summer, was planning to take a
trip to Belgium, and from there to go to Paris for the winter in order to
finish his third novel. O'Riordan, who had written novels under the pen
name of Norreys Connell, Dowson had seen frequently at the Crown and
Aux Gourmets in 1893, and during the summer of 1895 in Dieppe they
had become friendly. Though at least five years Dowson's junior, O'Riordan
was a precocious little fellow, a cripple, whose bright eyes and winning
manner augmented his charm and distinction as a young man of talent.
Conder was still in France, and when Dowson learned that O'Riordan was
about to start on his tour of Flanders and that he would be delighted to

have his company, he straightway packed his belongings, including a well-interlined copy of *La Fille Aux Yeux d'Or,* and set off with his friend for France.

After stopping for a time in Dieppe, which Conder by this time had left in order to work in Paris, they moved in easy stages eastward to Bruges. In this picturesque old town, which had preserved its medieval appearance more successfully than any other city in Belgium, they found much to delight them. The paintings of Memling, the fine stained glass of the Chapelle du Saint-Sang, and the atmosphere of the Middle Ages which hovered about the market place made Bruges one of their most memorable experiences. It was while they were at Bruges that Dowson received an author's copy of *Dilemmas,* the binding and general format of which must have distressed him. Its appearance bore no resemblance to "George Egerton's" *Keynotes.* There were no illustrations by Beardsley—or anyone, in fact; and the paper was cheap and without distinction. Few books in the 'nineties were so shabbily bound and printed. The proofreading, for which Dowson was not entirely responsible, was abominable. But with the delights of Bruges on every side, his disappointment in the appearance of the book was lessened; and after his first expression of dissatisfaction, he remained silent. From Bruges they went to Ypres where they lodged in one of the old Spanish Houses facing the Cloth Hall, and near to the Gothic Cathedral of St. Martin. After exploring Ypres and its environs, they established headquarters for a time at Lille; but Lille did not detain them for long, for Paris was beckoning, whither they came in November 1895.

Such a tour of Flanders had many advantages to Dowson, not the least of which was the distraction which it offered to his troubled mind. In the beauty and picturesqueness of Flemish towns he was able to forget temporarily the recent events in his life and to feel that the world was not entirely abhorrent. The simplicity of heart and mind which he saw in the peasants around Bruges, and the quaint customs gave him occasional respite from his cares and courage to look forward to a happier time. In Flanders, however, he was never able to shake off for long the spiritual depression into which he had sunk after the death of his mother. O'Riordan, in dedicating his novel *A Fool and His Heart* to Ernest Dowson, recalled the whole experience as "a sorrowful journey through Flanders."

On their arrival in Paris they took rooms at the Hotel de Medici at 214 rue St. Jacques, a place that was modest in its appointments to the point of being poor. To Dowson the location had compensating advantages on account of its proximity to the homes of Paul Verlaine and Henry Davray.

Once in Paris, the spiritual depression which had followed him all through Belgium began to lift. The days following his arrival were pleasant for him, for the charm of novelty and the atmosphere of light-heartedness which the city offered, and the prospect of living and writing in what he considered the art center of the world dulled his memories of the tragic events of the months just passed, and set him to an almost studied application to the carefree life about him. Although he had been in Paris before, he went to the places of interest and amusement with the delight of a newcomer and was eager to participate in the activities of those who gave the Latin Quarter its tone. Apparently Paris provided him with what he needed. His state of mind at the time is well illuminated by a letter he wrote to Sam Smith sometime in December 1895.

You mustn't imagine, as I gather from your letter you perhaps did, that my "crisis" was sentimental. God forbid. I have just answered my *damigella's* last letter and we are on the most affectionate terms—at least I think so—that we have been on for years. You must go and see her when you are in London—*Please* do that, and speak of me as freely as you like, *only do not* speak of my exile as being so prolonged as I presume it will be. I always write to her with the intention of returning in a month or two—and so I may—*for a fortnight!* but I doubt if ever I shall make my home in England again. My great desire is that the Foltinowiczs will carry out their long-conceived idea of returning to Germany. Then I would go there and join them. But I have taken a great dislike to London. I really came away on a sort of mad impulse—which I have not since regretted— because I was financially broke and . . . somewhat sensationally I admit, but not in the state of desperation which I believe is rumoured about me. *Par exemple,* dear Marmie [Marmaduke Langdale, actor], who has written me letters full of the most noble offers and sentiments writes to me in his last, received two days ago: "I have created a sort of mist of trouble, vague as ghosts in a dream, with which I surround you. It forms a sort of halo of sorrow for you and excites the tears and sympathy of those who live and admire you from afar!!!"

Do tell him (don't show him this letter) *do* suggest to him, without hurting his feelings, for I know he has really a great affection for me, and it pleases him to give me an "atmosphere," that I don't want no halo of this kind and extremely object to being wept over, I am not remarkably prosperous nor particularly happy —who is? But I *do not* go about in Paris with a halo of ghosts and tears, having been gifted by God with a sense—common to you and myself but to how many other of our friends?—of humour! I occasionally smile, and even in Paris, at a late hour of the night, and Paris is later than London, have been known to laugh.

Write soon, *mon très cher,* I implore you. And if you see Missie, tell her to write to me often, and if you could convey to her, not *from* me, but as an expression of your own personal opinion that to get a letter from her is my chiefest pleasure in life, you will be doing me a favour, and falling short of the extreme truth which perhaps it is not yet seasonable to say.

The literal nature of his statement to Smith that his premature departure from London was caused in part by his being "financially broke" can readily be questioned, for on his tour of Flanders with O'Riordan he paid his share and never seemed without money. It is possible that he felt that he could live more cheaply in Paris than in London, and that he might be able to find commissions in translating which would supplement his income from Smithers. He was not unknown among the Paris editors and reviewers, and although there is no evidence to support the surmise that he expected a steady income from Davray, a critic on the *Mercure de France* who had commended his work highly, it is possible that in his more optimistic moments he felt that assignments would come his way. There is no doubt, however, that his funds were meager even before he left London, and it is difficult to determine the exact reasons for his eagerness to leave London for a fairly expensive trip to Flanders when he was already "financially broke." The only conclusion which seems in the least tenable is that his statement of financial distress which he gave as the reason for his abrupt departure was his way of evading a discussion of the suffering which made London intolerable to him.

His meager resources, however, had little effect on his mode of life. Sumptuously appointed quarters, modish apparel and restaurants which catered to those of hearty appetites and refined tastes held out small appeal. His straitened financial condition had little to do with his tastes in such matters as lodging and food. He had enough to satisfy his increasingly simple wants: after his brief period of apparent prosperity in London, clothes meant nothing to him, and a snack at a St. Michel bistro satisfied his occasional hunger. As with many consumptives who are not driven to eat, he had to be reminded that food was essential to energy and life; and it was only after considerable persuasion that he could be prevailed on to settle down to a nourishing meal. His room at the Hotel de Medici was provided with only the barest necessities, and some of them, including the bowl and pitcher, he found no great urge to use. The comforts and the nourishing meals which were indicated for anyone in his physical condition were the last things on which he would have spent money. Additional income would have given him peace of mind, no doubt—and perhaps the table cloth which he was later to tell Smithers he sorely missed at the eating places he patronized—but it is unlikely that it would have changed his essential tastes.

Despite the fact that he was soon to complain to Smithers of the conditions in which poverty caused him to live, his distress was in some measure of his own devising—or more charitably and truthfully, the result of forces within his own nature over which he had no control. He had money for absinthe, of which soon after his arrival in Paris he began to drink more than was good for either his pocketbook or his health; his incessant smoking of cigarettes and strong Vevey cigars spoiled the little appetite for nourishing food which he might have developed; and his generosity with thirsty vagrants and streetwalkers might have been curbed without any deleterious effect on his sense for sweet charity. For one who at times passed a whole day with nothing to eat except a roll, a piece of cheese, and a little pastry, to distribute francs to every chance trollop who looked cold and hungry was, in his case especially, a somewhat reckless application of the scriptural injunction that it is more blessed to give than to receive. The girls to whom he gave a few francs were more often than not the objects of his pity and interest rather than of his desire. Stories have been told on sufficiently substantial authority that he would suddenly leave the group with whom he was sitting at a café to follow girls, most of whom he had never seen before, and after talking with them for a few minutes and giving them a franc or two, return to his friends with a sad little smile. One of his acquaintances, who must remain nameless, has told me that he, accompanied by Dowson, after overtaking several pairs of girls and talking with them, became impatient with the dallying tactics of his friend. His animal spirits, finally stimulated beyond control, caused him to tell Dowson that he was going to accompany the next girl they encountered to her quarters and see the thing through. Good as his word, when the next pair were overtaken, he began to make specific arrangements for the manner in which the ensuing hour was to be spent. Dowson accompanied him to the dimly lighted brothel to which they were led, but instead of ascending the staircase to reap the full benefits of his passive conquest, he remained in the vestibule with his lady of the night, listening attentively to her talk and paying the most gallant court to her. She was remunerated for her time, so I have been told, and when his friend rejoined him, he found Dowson kissing the girl's hand as if he were taking leave of a princess.

His experiences with street girls, some of whom he regarded as more innocent of heart than many a so-called fine lady, had a less perceptible influence on his health and pocketbook than some of the chance acquaintances he made on his nightly excursions. As long as anyone would sit with him at a café, or prowl around the streets until the hours immediately before dawn, he was unwilling to call it a night. Such inclinations were bound to throw him into contact with all manner of singular personalities with which Paris has always been filled. Even such figures as Bibi la Purée, the panhandler who knew every noteworthy artist in Paris, Dowson encountered in his early months in Paris. Although he probably never accompanied Bibi on any of his more memorable escapades, for most of them belonged to the early half of the decade, he was seen in his company late one night on the street which leads from the Boulevard St. Michel at the D'Harcourt, brandishing the literary-minded tramp's umbrella, and reciting with inebriated vehemence one of Verlaine's poems. Bibi la Purée was really a remarkable man in many ways; in fact, he had become a Paris tradition by the closing years of the decade; but such company, interesting as it undoubtedly was, could scarcely be beneficial to Dowson.

His energy in the early months of his stay in Paris was not consumed entirely in hobnobbing with down-and-outers. He had not taken up residence in the Latin Quarter long before he found himself in circles which were sincere in their application to art. Then, too, his admiration for French poetry led him to seek out its chief exponents. He soon learned that along the eastern side of the Boulevard St. Michel and on its dimly lighted tributaries there were cafés to which the leaders of the contemporary French literary schools came at certain hours to discuss the verities of art and life with their satellites. Here one learned that Victor Hugo was not an artist at all, but that Vielé-Griffin and Charles Morice—virtually unknown beyond the boundaries of the Palais de Justice and the Luxembourg Gardens—were simon-pure poets. Jean Moréas sat on occasion at the D'Harcourt, deciding for himself and his long-haired disciples what constituted true poetry, and frequently reciting passages from his own verse to illustrate his points. And Paul Verlaine on rare occasions still limped to the François Premier, which had come to be known as the "Café du Maître," and to the dingy Café Soleil d'Or.

Although Verlaine was nearing his end when Dowson and O'Riordan arrived in Paris, Dowson saw him on several occasions. His admiration for the French poet had begun long before he had heard him speak in the hall of Barnard's Inn, Holborn, on November 21, 1893, and before he had talked with him at the Crown and at the Constitutional with Herbert Horne. Although Verlaine had fallen upon evil days since his brief tour of England, and had become almost totally unproductive, Dowson's admiration for "poor Lélian" remained unaffected. He knew that Paris, in which Verlaine had "lived like a fly in a pot of marmalade" and which Verlaine knew "well, too well," had brought misery to the poet other than the "scorched leg" to which he facetiously referred; but the squalor and misery in which Dowson found the Master on his visits to his quarters heightened rather than lessened his admiration. Plarr has called Verlaine one of Dowson's chief perverters, a statement in which there is considerable truth when one is aware of the influence which Verlaine's mode of life had on him. Dowson, to be sure, scarcely needed the example of Verlaine's life to lead him to a renouncement of conventional Victorian ideals; but in Verlaine he saw much that supported and corroborated his beliefs concerning art and life. When Verlaine died early in 1896, Dowson was one of the most sincere mourners at the funeral. He probably witnessed the quarrel between the surviving mistress and the publisher at the graveside, and heard how Bibi la Purée stole the umbrellas of literary celebrities who attended the last rites.

Pierre Louÿs and André Gide, both still fairly young but both already emaciated from irregular living and disease, were among other French writers for whom Dowson had admiration and with whom he struck up a casual acquaintanceship. Louÿs knew some of Dowson's work, both as poet and translator, for it was he who was later to suggest Dowson as the one who could best turn his *Aphrodite* into English. Gide, too, was familiar with his poetry. In a letter to Oscar Wilde, written sometime in 1897, Gide, upon learning that Wilde was seeing much of Dowson, asked to be remembered to him and spoke admiringly of his work. In fact, Dowson was far from unknown among the French writers and critics on his arrival in Paris.

Recognition of his work in France was largely the result of the efforts of Henry Davray, critic for the *Mercure de France,* a journal of considerable size and influence. Trained at Oxford, Davray was a link between the esthetic movement in London and the new literary schools in Paris.* When Dowson's poems appeared in *The Hobby Horse* and in the anthologies of the Rhymers' Club, Davray promptly recognized their beauty; and feeling that they represented some of the finest work which was being done in London, he turned a few of the poems into French along with their English versions and printed them with commendatory remarks. A correspondence had started between them when Davray asked for permission to print the poems; and although the letters between them fail to indicate that Davray ever encouraged Dowson to come to Paris, it seems reasonable to assume that Dowson was aware of the recognition which had come to him in Paris, and that he felt he would find a welcome from Davray and the staff. On his

* Davray had followed the work of the younger English poets so zealously that Ross and Wilde called him an Anglomaniac. He was at least an Anglophile: he spelled his name "Henry," and was exceptionally proud of his wide reading in English literature and his command of the language.

arrival, he found Davray friendly and willing to commend his work to the circles who read the *Mercure* and the groups of *les jeunes* who gathered at his café.

There were also Englishmen and Americans of artistic interests and attainments in Paris at the time, most of whom Dowson had met in London. Charles Conder, who had done the woodcuts for the Balzac story on which Dowson was still working, he often encountered at the D'Harcourt and at Bullier's; Robert Sherard, to whom Paris was more like home than London; Vincent O'Sullivan, also "one of the Smithers people"; and the Americans, Henry Harland, editor of the defunct *Yellow Book*, and Theodore Peters, for whom he had written *The Pierrot of the Minute*, he saw frequently on his nightly rounds of the cafés. Although none of them plunged so wholeheartedly into *la vie de Bohème* as he, they all recognized him as one of them, rather than as one who had severed all connection with British standards. In spite of some of his questionable acquaintances and his irregularities, they welcomed his presence even when he looked pretty much the worse for wear.

In fact, all his London acquaintances who were sojourning in Paris or who came over for short visits were kind to him with the exception of Aubrey Beardsley. Dowson admired Beardsley's work, and was willing to like him as a man; but for some of Beardsley's friends, he evidently had small fondness. Whibley, Whistler's brother-in-law, was one of the few men whom Dowson disliked, probably because Whibley had offended him; and with no admiration for Whibley as a critic or even a conversationalist, he had no reluctance in telling Smithers and others that he disliked him. Beardsley, on the other hand, he admired, and he wanted him as a friend; but after their early nights together in the period of Dowson's apparent prosperity, Beardsley showed his frank distaste for Dowson's company. It was the gravitation of "the Smithers people" which brought them together; otherwise in spite of their common interests, and occasional meetings at the Crown and Aux Gourmets, their circles would never have overlapped. Though Beardsley was in no way a prude, there was a streak of fastidiousness in his nature which caused him to deplore Dowson's untidy appearance and the sort of company he was known occasionally to keep. Such down-and-outers as Bibi la Purée and the girls who moved singly or in pairs in the small streets around the D'Harcourt, Beardsley found disgusting. To see Dowson somewhat thick-tongued and disputatious, as he no doubt was at times, annoyed him quite as much as Dowson's unkempt appearance. When Dowson's merits as a poet were discussed in his company, he was generally scornful. Vincent O'Sullivan has recalled a conversation in which one of the group,

possibly himself, remarked: "But Dowson is a great poet." To which
Beardsley answered: "I don't care. No man is great enough to excuse
behavior like his."

Although Beardsley's remark may have been more just than charitable,
there were instances in which his own conduct might have led others to
judge his drawings and character unfavorably. He was discriminating to
the point of being snobbish about the company he kept, but so long as the
company was to his taste, he had little concern about his behavior. There
is ample evidence to support the conclusion that it was unbecoming for him
to sit in judgment of the weaknesses of others.

Dowson's judgments of the appearance and conduct of his acquaintances
were rarely uncharitable; and although he called George Moore and Arthur
Symons unprintable names, his animosity was only temporary. In his
nature there was no malice. With nothing of the competitive instinct to
lead him to envy, he was pleased by the successes of his associates even
when he was unable to detect merit in their performances and in their
lives. In gossip he had had a normal delight, for he enjoyed hearing about
the manner in which his friends back in London were devoting themselves
pour épater les bourgeois; but those who knew him intimately agree that
he was unconcerned with reports that disparaged and defamed. With a
sense of loyalty to his friends, he was indifferent to their weaknesses, if he
recognized them at all. In his letter to Davray in which he reported one
of Beardsley's escapades, he was the narrator, not the judge.

He [Beardsley] was very amusing on my last Sunday at Paris. We went to see
Lautrec and Beardsley took some haschish for the first time. There was no
result for some hours. Until suddenly, while we were dining with Smithers at
Margary's the haschish began to work very powerfully. Luckily we were in a
cabinet or I think we should have been turned out—for Beardsley's laughter
was so tumultuous that it infected the rest of us—who had *not* taken haschish
and we all behaved like imbeciles.

If Beardsley was ever grateful to Dowson for his solicitude and help
when he was ill or far in his cups—and there were nights in Dieppe
and Paris when Beardsley needed even the unsteady support that Dowson
could offer—he certainly felt under no obligation to think kindly of him.
O'Sullivan, O'Riordan and others who knew both Dowson and Beardsley
in the years in which their paths frequently crossed can recall no instance
in which there was a disagreement between them other than the after-
midnight disputations common among those whose sensitivity is heightened
by drink. There was nothing of the vengeful or vindictive in Dowson's
nature, whereas Beardsley never forgot a slight. He was easily offended,

and many of his friendships ended in feuds on account of slights which were fancied rather than real. This may be the clue to Beardsley's unwillingness to try to like Dowson's poetry and to be pleased by his company. The image of Dowson, shabby, given to absinthe and to consorting with all manner of wastrels, came between him and a sympathetic judgment. It is possible that Beardsley judged Dowson on only a few isolated observations, but the fact remains that he never spoke well of him. To his friends who were disposed to invite Dowson to their gatherings, he remarked that it was unfair to bring a man who looked as if he had spent the night in the gutter and who was so plainly diseased into decent company.

Nor was he more generous when Dowson himself had come into the group. Vincent O'Sullivan has recalled an evening at Bullier's, the students' dance hall in the Latin Quarter, when Dowson joined the circle in which he and Beardsley sat. At the time Dowson was presentably clad, and certainly not intoxicated. Beardsley, as was usual with him when Dowson was of the company, fell into an icy silence, and answered in monosyllables the inquiries which were put to him. Dowson, failing to detect Beardsley's resentment at his presence, or unable to comprehend it, pointed out the young French poet, Julien Leclerq, who was dancing immediately in front of them.

"He looks as if he had just stepped out of one of your pictures," he remarked pleasantly.

"Then the best thing he can do is to step in again," replied Beardsley sarcastically, and with that he bade the group goodnight.

When one reflects on Dowson's solicitude for Beardsley's health, so often expressed in his letters to his friends, and on his attempts to be pleasant to the young artist, one must feel a sympathy for Dowson. Beardsley's attitude toward his co-worker for Smithers never changed, whereas Dowson persisted, half wistfully, in his admiration for the artist's works and in his friendliness. In the Beardsley-Smithers correspondence there are frequent references to Dowson, no one of which is kind. "Good old Dowson," Beardsley wrote to Smithers ironically concerning his co-worker on *Les Liaisons Dangereuses*. But there is almost boyish satisfaction in "good old Dowson's" inquiry of Sam Smith at the time of the publication of *Verses:* "Do you like Aubrey Beardsley's binding block? I am very pleased with it." And all the while Beardsley was explaining the meaning of the two curves of the block which formed a letter Y. The interpretation, he told his friends, was easy to determine: 'Why was this book ever written?"

Nor was Beardsley satisfied with such ill-humored remarks about the volume which contained "Amor Umbratilis," "Extreme Unction," and "Non Sum Qualis Eram . . . Cynarae." When Smithers decided to issue a handsome edition of *The Pierrot of the Minute* and asked Beardsley to do the drawings, he was finally persuaded, much against his will, to undertake the work, perhaps by reason of the fact that his sister Mabel had once played the part of the Moon Maiden. While preparing the drawings, to which he obviously gave considerable attention, he wrote to his friends about being engaged with "a tiresome playlet of Ernest Dowson's." It has been reported that Beardsley was in the habit of referring to the play as "a filthy little piece," but surely the word "filthy," of which it seems he was very fond, was neither an accurate nor a kindly term to apply to such a dainty piece as the *Pierrot* play. If Beardsley's ungracious remarks ever came to Dowson's attention, he took no notice of them. When Beardsley was dying, he went to see him; and when the requiem mass was read at the Farm Street Church for the repose of the soul of Aubrey Beardsley, Dowson was in the congregation. Even had Dowson detected Beardsley's dislike for him in Paris in the winter of 1895-96, it is unlikely that he would have been much affected by it, for the mad pace at which he was living kept him from brooding over such matters as a countryman's surliness. The qualities in his nature which blinded him to the dominant impression of squalor in Verlaine's last days also caused him to be unmindful of the impression which he was making on others with his own appearance. At the time he could have made himself presentable in the best company, but he rarely took thought of such matters. When O'Riordan reminded him, albeit indirectly, that he might feel better if he would wash his hands and face and change his linen, Dowson was always willing to agree and to set himself to a general cleaning up. He took no offense at such suggestions, nor did he profit by them unless they were periodically reiterated. His negligence in his appearance did not reach the point of being offensive during his early months in France; in fact, only a few of his more fastidious acquaintances found his appearance different from that of the Latin Quarter artists at the time; and to him, their notions of what constituted a good appearance seemed only an indication of bourgeois training and ideals.

Of all the men, both French and English, with whom Dowson associated during his first winter in Paris, none provided him with a more wholesome companionship than the young novelist with whom he had toured Flanders. In the character of Conal O'Riordan he must have recognized features which were uncongenial to his tastes but nevertheless exemplary. O'Riordan was an admirably well-balanced young man, one who believed in and applied the maxim of "everything in moderation," and, as a result, was unwilling to embrace whole-heartedly the irregularities of Bohemia. His literary ambitions and his innate moderation had led him to organize his life in such

a way that he could feel that he was accomplishing at least some of the
things he had set out to do. Although he accompanied Dowson at times on
his nocturnal rounds and enjoyed the company of the young artists who
spent their nights in the cafés, he reserved a considerable amount of his
time and energy for the novel which he planned to finish before the summer. All of his moderation in living and orderliness in applying himself to
his work, Dowson deplored as bourgeois. O'Riordan tells an amusing story
of Dowson awakening him at an hour not long before dawn to tell him
with somewhat heavy-tongued insistence that he was bourgeois. The two
young men certainly represented two completely different attitudes toward
life; and still they were fast friends, for Dowson at times realized the dis-
ciplinary effect which the other's presence and example had on his own life;
and O'Riordan, without lending himself to his friend's irregularities, found
himself broadened by the association. That Dowson understood the wholesome effect the younger man's companionship had on him is evident when
one recalls that toward the end of his life, when he was making his last
efforts to get a grip on himself, he plead with O'Riordan to accompany him
again to France.

To O'Riordan he never talked about the tragedies which had come into
his life, or about his attachment at Poland. It was not that the novelist was
of the sort whose own uncommunicativeness discouraged the exchange of
confidences, much less because he had an unsympathetic nature. Concerning
the recent events in Dowson's home, there was nothing to be said; and
concerning Missie, he knew full well what O'Riordan thought. A single
expression of opinion on the matter was enough to keep Dowson from
unloading his affairs of the heart to his friend, nor did O'Riordan try to
dissuade him from his belief that Missie represented all that was lovely and
good, in spite of the fact that he felt, as he was later to tell me, that "Dowson's attitude toward the Geliebte was of course pure fantasy and his death
I consider to have been less a disaster than his marriage to her (were it
conceivable) must have proved . . . the little restaurant where dwelt his
Geliebte . . . had an atmosphere of garlic in which I could not have drunk
a cup of coffee without puking."

There were other issues on which they disagreed, however, without remaining silent. Dowson upheld what he believed to be the sincere devotion
to art which existed only in Bohemia, whereas O'Riordan, discerning beyond
his years, recognized other provinces and attitudes out of which true art
could come. In a letter to me, O'Riordan remarked:

I'm afraid that Ernest (within my knowledge of him) was completely "captivated" by La vie de Bohème. He saw only the picturesqueness, though I never heard him give it that name, and was blind to the squalor. But I have to confess that I have a priggish and bourgeois shrinking for much that is called Bohemian.

Even a casual reading of O'Riordan's novel, *A Fool and His Heart*, written during his association with Dowson in Paris in 1896, and dedicated to Dowson, reveals concretely the author's attitude toward the sort of Bohemianism to which his friend applied himself. At the very start, O'Riordan struck the keynote of the book:

> There lies a land in this stormy ocean of life, which fools think is a free country. Its inhabitants are wrinkled youths, callow satyrs, and sad women; its pleasures are joyless; its sorrows desperate; its mirthful feasts are debauches of depravity . . . for this is the land of Bohemia, where bleach the bones of lost souls.

Although the novel can scarcely be called biographical, there is much in it which illuminates Dowson's attitude toward life and art before and during his stay in Paris. The Unicorn in the novel is a literal description of the Crown in 1895, and the characters are at times reflections of Dowson and O'Riordan.

It was probably by reason of O'Riordan's insistence that if Bohemia had an end at all, its end should be a concrete manifestation of the creative urge, that Dowson was led to the completion of the literary projects which were in large measure his reason for being in Paris. During his early weeks away from London he had done little or nothing save write one story which he wanted to have ready for the first issue of *The Savoy*. His other commissions for Smithers, among them the translation of Balzac's *La Fille aux Yeux d'Or*, remained unfinished. The example of O'Riordan, settling promptly down to work, and turning out a number of sheets each day on his novel, and his own eagerness to be numbered amongst the first contributors to *The Savoy* made possible the promptness with which he finished the story "The Eyes of Pride."

There was another reason, probably more fundamental, which drove him to finish the story. His quarrel with Missie immediately before leaving London had given him considerable distress; and once away from her he reflected on the reasons which had brought it about in order to find an explanation if not a justification for his part in the situation. The lines from Number XXIV of George Meredith's *Modern Love:*

> Pluck out the eyes of pride; thy lips to mine?
> Never, though I die thirsting! Go thy ways . . .

struck him as applicable to the situation, and using them as the basis for the title of his story and its motivation, he built up a narrative which invites autobiographical interpretation. That the story was dedicated to Missie when it appeared in the January issue of *The Savoy* lends additional encourage-ment to one who attempts to interpret it in the light of his recent quarrel with her.

She, on her side, [we are told in the story] was exacting, jealous of his past life; he was faithfully her lover, and he felt aggrieved, perhaps unjustly, that woman-like she took constancy too much for granted, and was not more grateful that he did not lapse. And neither could make concessions: they hardened their hearts, were cold of eye and tongue when a seasonable softening would have flung them into each other's arms.

Seefang, the man of the story, left Rosalind to travel for two years on the Continent and to devote himself to his writing, which, by reason of his unrequited love for Rosalind, he had neglected. But after a brief time away from her, he realized that only pride was keeping them apart. On his return he found Rosalind unwilling to make concessions; and the story ends with the lovers in anguished separation because of their pride.

The autobiographical significance of the story must not be carried too far, but it must at least be recognized. When "The Eyes of Pride" appeared in the first issue of *The Savoy,* few of its readers knew anything about "A.F.," to whom the story was dedicated, and who undoubtedly had a share in its motivation. To its author, however, the story was not whipped off to give Symons and Smithers the promised contribution to the magazine, but it was written out of his own distress, and with the thought that possibly there would be a time when Adelaide would read it and understand.

The poignant cry in "Impenitentia Ultima" also grew out of the distress he experienced when he thought of the gulf which lay between them. In spite of the fact that he wrote bravely to Smith in December 1895: "I have just answered my *damigella's* last letter and we are on the most affectionate terms—at least I think so—that we have been on for years," he often gave himself reason to believe that the circumstances under which he had left Missie were enough to ruin any chances which he might have had with her. His love might have been "pure fantasy" as O'Riordan believed, but the fact remains that the uncertainty which gripped him when he thought of what might result from their quarrel gave him real distress. When he cried out:

> One day of the great lost days, one face of all the faces,
> Grant me to see and touch once more, and nothing more to see . . .

he surely had Missie in mind. And when in the last stanza, he wrote:

Before the ruining waters fall, and my soul be carried under,
And Thine anger cleaves me through, as a child cuts down a flower,
I will praise Thee, Lord! in Hell, while my limbs are racked asunder,
For the last sad sight of her face and the little grace of an hour.

he was not performing an exercise in bold rhetoric. Whether Symons detected the sincerity of the poem cannot be determined, though by January
1896 he was aware of the situation at Poland. But he took "Impenitentia
Ultima" for the first issue of The Savoy, along with "The Eyes of Pride"
with the assurance that the beauty of Dowson's contributions would be
recognized.

The two pieces which Dowson contributed to the first issue of The Savoy
are not among his best-known works, but in spite of the fact that they
stood alongside the contributions of W. B. Yeats, Havelock Ellis, Selwyn
Image, Arthur Symons, and George Bernard Shaw, their inclusion undoubtedly added to the literary value of the first number of the magazine.
When Dowson received his copy of The Savoy, he was proud of the company he kept in it and pleased at the thought that he had contributed a part
in making the magazine the substantial and beautiful quarterly that it was.
When he reflected on the motivation of his story and poem, he was satisfied
that they fulfilled the standards which Symons stated in the editorial note
to the first issue:

We intend to print no verse which has not some close relationship with poetry,
no fiction which has not a certain sense of what is finest in living fact. . . . We
have not invented a new point of view. We are not Realists, or Romanticists,
or Decadents. For us, all art is good which is good art.

Although much of Dowson's time and energy was consumed in saturating
himself with the atmosphere of what he believed was Bohemia, he had
sufficient pride in his role as contributor to The Savoy, and a sufficient sense
of obligation to Smithers to apply himself occasionally to his work. Then,
too, with the example of O'Riordan's diligence in finishing his novel before
him, he attempted to prove to his friend and himself that he was not always
the victim of lagging inspiration. Before the winter was spent he had finally
submitted his translation of Balzac's La Fille aux Yeux d'Or to Smithers.
The publisher had shown importunate concern about what was happening
to the work on which he had already advanced Dowson money; and this,
combined with the momentum he had attained while writing his pieces for
The Savoy, led Dowson to forsake the cafés for a few nights in order to
apply himself ceaselessly to his assignment. When the book was issued from
the House of Smithers, with its handsome binding and the Conder wood-

cuts, both he and Smithers were pleased by its appearance and reception. The quality of the prose undoubtedly enhanced the decorative printing and illustration of the volume, and in part justified the delay.

Dowson had come to Paris presumably to work. At least that was the reason he gave his friends to whom he insisted that London tormented him to such an extent that it was impossible for him to settle down to any consistent application. Although Paris afforded him distraction from the cheerless memories which London provoked, it also put obstacles in the way of his intention to settle down to work. He was prone to consider as blessings the obstacles to work which Paris provided in abundance, and in some measure they were; but when inquiries came from Smithers concerning assignments which he had suggested, and the next issue of *The Savoy* was reaching the deadline for contributions, he saw the wisdom of O'Riordan's decision to leave Paris for the country.

Even before Christmas, O'Riordan found that he could not work amid all the distractions which surrounded him at 214 rue St. Jacques, and in order to apply himself to his novel he determined to retire to Mons-par-Donne-Marie, Seine et Marne. Out of fondness for his friend, and with the thought that he too would be able to apply himself more assiduously to his work if he left his companions of the cafés, Dowson visited O'Riordan over Christmas, at which time he finished the Balzac story. According to O'Riordan, however, "the country quiet was too much for him. He said he was afraid he might marry a dairymaid." Leaving O'Riordan at Mons, he returned to Paris where, in a garret room in the Hotel de Medici, he tried to settle down to a regular life and work. His intentions, however, were futile. Now that O'Riordan was gone, he found it impossible to sit alone and try to write. After a few weeks in Paris, during which time he contributed nothing to his work or his self-respect, he again came to the conclusion that if he could find a quiet place in the country, not too distant from Paris to make an ocasional evening with his friends impossible, he would be ideally situated. In a letter to Smithers, written soon after he had submitted the completed Balzac story, he described his plans.

214 rue St. Jacques
Paris

My dear Smithers,

Thanks for cheque. I am going to stir up my solicitor & will arrange to have the money lodged with you & draw it weekly. I hope you will come over here soon. It is lovely now & I always take my dejeuner in the open air. But I am beginning to hanker after the flesh pots of Egypt. I am afraid my simple tastes have been corrupted: a dirty, or no table-cloth has come to distress me & I often hanker for a good dinner with you chez Foyot & the taste of decent wine. I am thinking of moving out of Paris shortly to Fontenay aux Roses. I have found a very cheap & comfortable place there & as I should be the only pensionnaire & no one ever goes there except on Sundays I should be undisturbed. My landlord, however, may stick out for his pound of flesh: i.e. his next fortnight which I have encroached on. If he does not I shall wire to you to send me £2. I shall not wire until I have arranged to leave the following day so do not fail me, I pray you, as I shall want money for my demenagement & will try & do without anything further the week following.

My neuralgia has gone I am glad to say, but I am quite worn out with want of sleep. Your remedy is more appetizing than mine but I fear the brandy. Excellent stout is to be had for 40 centimes at the American bar in the Rue Soufflot & I often sample it.

There is a rumour that Douglas is in Paris: somebody saw him in the Bois. I suppose that this is not true. I have only seen Aubrey twice. I gather that he is rather *lié* with Whibley whom I greatly dislike & do not want to meet. Is O'Sullivan coming to Paris soon?

Votre bien dévoué

ERNEST DOWSON

Fontenay is about half an hour from Paris from the Luxembourg Station. There is a last train about 12.50 so that I shall be able to pass an occasional evening here.

It is the general opinion of his friends who were intimate with him at the time that his plan to go to Fontenay aux Roses was never carried out. Perhaps by reason of the fact that his landlord at the Medici held out "for his pound of flesh," he felt that it would be a needless extravagance to pay for lodgings at two places at the same time. It is more likely, however, that his indecision, augmented by his fondness for Paris night life, kept him at the Hotel de Medici. Mindful of his promise to contribute regularly to *The Savoy,* and eager to show Smithers that he was deserving of the cheque which the publisher had sent him, he found sufficient ambition and energy to finish another story and two poems which he sent to Symons for the April issue of *The Savoy.* Symons took the story "Countess Marie of the Angels," and of the two poems which Dowson submitted, he selected only one, "Saint-Germain-en-Laye." Neither the story nor the poem is among Dowson's more memorable works. They show excellent craftsmanship, but otherwise they are interesting only in so far as they show his willingness to fulfill his obligations to *The Savoy.*

His contributions to the April issue of *The Savoy* and his occasional dabbling with some of the assignments which Smithers had suggested were scarcely enough to keep him occupied constructively. He had not returned from his visit with O'Riordan for long before an urge for companionship seized him. He had acquaintances of all sorts in the cafés, but since O'Riordan's departure he was lonely. So long as he had friendship, he felt that life still had something to offer; alone, he was oppressed with thoughts of the past and visions of the future. He had started to work on a collection of his poems, which Smithers assured him he would handle advantageously to him, and he had assignments in translating which beckoned for his steady application; but after an evening with his work, loneliness, heightened by illness and fatigue, left him desperate. Time and again he was tempted to return to London, but his pride and the recollection of the sufferings of recent years caused him to lift his shabby coat from the bed where it had served to help keep him warm in the hours before dawn, and go out in search of company—anyone. A pony of absinthe at the café adjacent to the hotel, another, and still another, and he was ready to go over to the rue Corneille to see who was moving about after the play. He was fortunate if he encountered one of the staff of the *Mercure* or, lacking such a meeting, found someone at the D'Harcourt with whom he could talk. Leopold Nelkin, the young Slav who was studying medicine, was occasionally there, and with him he could talk about the Poles he knew in London. There were chance acquaintanceships, too, with men who were probably quite as lonely as he. But when the goodnights were finally said, again there was an emptiness which cut to the soul.

Away from O'Riordan, he realized what the association had meant. Not many weeks after he had returned from his Christmas visit with his friend, he suggested that they go to Brittany together. O'Riordan, however, had had almost enough of France, and if truth be told, he probably felt that he had had almost enough of Dowson. He admired his verse and liked him, but he realized that if he were to do his work it was impossible to put up with the irregularities which such an association was bound to present. When he told Dowson that he would be unable to go to Brittany with him, Dowson at the time regarded his friend's unwillingness to leave Mons-par-Donne-Marie as desertion. Had O'Riordan realized the desperate loneliness of his friend, it is possible that he might have changed his plans to a sufficient extent to go with him for a short time to Brittany. But to all appearances, Dowson already had more companionship than was good for either his health or his work; and without feeling inconsiderate, O'Riordan saw no immediate necessity for giving up his regular life in order to accompany him to Brittany.

Even before he had tried to interest O'Riordan in a Breton sojourn— in fact, while O'Riordan was still in Paris—Dowson had written a long letter to Edgar Jepson which illuminates much of his attitude toward his life in Paris.

Rue Saint-Jacques . 214
Paris

My dear Jepson

It was charming to hear from you, and I ought to have written before but Connell had written to you (he does most of our correspondence) only a day or two before I received your letter, so that I gathered you had news of me. My own news is of the scantiest; beyond the obvious fact that I am, and have been, for some 5 weeks in Paris, and that j'y probablement resterai. That is to say unless you feel inclined to try Britanny with me in another month. The Hotel Gloanec, Pontaven, Finisterre, (recommended strongly by Moore and sundry Parisian painters I have met) offers board and lodging, including cider for 85 francs a month. I should be strongly tempted to try this for 2 or 3 months in company; therefore think it over. I doubt if I could stand it alone. Connell has made arrangements with a married couple to whom I have introduced him who live about 2 hours from Paris, to be taken in as a boarder, and I think will be more comfortable there than he has been here. He leaves me in a 4tnight. For we have rooms in a *hotel meublé* where nothing can be got in the house and Connell's notion of comfort is as deeply rooted in a sense of being able to eat and drink entirely on his own premises as mine is in the opposite facility.

Failing a companion, therefore, to the Breton shore, I shall probably remain in Paris which suits me excellently. I know a heap of persons and get as many cards for private views as if I were a celebrity.

I was uneasy at first over your remarks on the Symons libel action. He is— (*don't show this to anyone*)—a silly b—r. But I should think he must get a verdict, and even if he doesn't, Smithers is so little disturbed about it, that he has inspired in me something of his own security.

In any case, I doubt if the "Savoy" will be materially affected. I have sent off my story to it, and am tolerably satisfied with it—in fact it is the best I have done—except perhaps that in the "Yellow Book." By the way, Harland has been in Paris and we met curiously enough at Bullier's, on the very day on which both he and Smithers had arrived in Paris. I introduced the rivals and for the rest of their common sojourn here we foregathered and got on famously. Teixeira also turned up here and called on me. I have heard news of you and frequently of Edward, from Davray who is now de retour. Write to me soon and tell me London news and if it would not bother you too much send me an occasional *Daily Chronicle*. I have not seen a single English paper since I left England—how many years ago? Also, if you have Smith's address would you send him mine and ask him to write to me—or send him this letter. I have lost his but I should like to write to him.

I find I can do considerably more work here than in town and if I am to keep it up and do not find it too expensive would prefer to remain here than hibernate in the country. If I had been alone, indeed, I should have come away here straight, and avoided our useless and expensive Belgian campaign of which doubtless you have heard from Connell. I have run across Verlaine, quite by chance, and am going to call on him next week. Also Vaughan and Conder are living here. Although one never quite escapes from the "horror of life" one avoids it better here. No more now: write soon—by return if you are not too busy—and tell me how things move, and if there is any chance of your joining me. If you see Moore tell him that I am writing tout de suite—but I am really working very hard and find almost every moment occupied. Remember me affectionately to all the brethren.

Tout à toi

ERNEST DOWSON

This letter, written before the novelty of life in Paris had begun to fade, indicates his dread of doing anything alone. And as the winter drew slowly to a close, he felt his loneliness acutely. It is true that he had company. Smithers turned up occasionally for a few days, O'Sullivan returned to Paris after a brief stay in London, Sherard was often to be found at the better cafés near the Place de l'Opera; and Davray, who lived within a stone's throw of the Medici, was almost certain to be found at the gathering places around the Odeon. But in spite of the fact that groups of les jeunes kept the cafés lively at night, and that Englishmen were numerous in Paris, Dowson suffered from an increasing recognition that he was not quite English nor was he entirely French in interests and ideals. Smith, Moore, and Smithers were fairly regular correspondents. Lionel Johnson, who sent him occasional messages "with promises of speedy letters," failed to write. Missie wrote to him at rare intervals, "friendly letters," he called them, "which give me sleepless nights and cause me to shed morbid and puerile tears." But the letters from Missie and his friends in London and the acquaintances, both French and English, whom he encountered at the cafés, were poor substitutes for the intimate companionship which he craved. "In my sick and sorry old age," he wrote to Plarr in the early spring of 1896, "I begin to be dependent on society." What he really meant was that he needed friendship.

His loneliness during the first winter in Paris was no doubt heightened by his ill health. He suffered much during the winter. The neuralgia and sleeplessness of which he had complained to Smithers were the least of his ailments. Even before O'Riordan had left him, he was often seized with attacks of coughing which left him breathless and weak. The table of his room at the Hotel de Medici was filled with bottles of assorted cough "cures," most of which had the ingredients and efficacy of patent medicines. There were probably hemorrhages during that winter, though no one observed such grisly manifestations of his malady, nor did he report its progress to his friends. And no one observed the nights when he tossed on his cot in the garret of the Medici, struggling for breath and wishing for the stroke which would end it all; or the mornings, when with the rising sun, he would feel for a while renewed hope and strength to finish a story for *The Savoy*. His teeth, to which he had never given care, were responsible for the racking neuralgia of the winter of 1896, and one by one he had them extracted until he had only a few discolored lower teeth left. His eyes, once luminous, began to take on a shade of lifeless green; and his complexion, always pale, had assumed an unhealthy pallor which attracted attention even among those who were themselves little given to self-preservation.

With the first signs of spring, he decided that he had had enough of Paris for the time. In spite of the fact that he could get no one to accompany him, he would go to the Hotel Gloanec at Pont-Aven in Brittany where he could get "board and lodging including cider for 85 francs a month." There he believed he would find a better climate, agreeable companionship with the artists who made a colony in Pont-Aven in the spring and summer, and an added incentive to work. By March his mind was made up. Even when he learned that Smith would be in Paris for a few days in late March, he held to his plan to go to Brittany. "Yes," he wrote to Smith, who had informed him of his intention of coming to Paris, "I deeply regret that I shall not be in Paris to receive you; but let us hope it is only the postponement of a reunion we shall have here." By Easter 1896, he was at the Hotel Gloanec, Pont-Aven.

VIII

PONT-AVEN

TO HIS friends who were concerned about his health and reputation, the news that he had finally gone to Brittany was encouraging. Accounts of his excesses in Paris—most of which no doubt had been heightened in the retelling—had reached their ears during the winter, and they were naturally led to believe that Paris exercised an unhealthy influence on him. When the information circulated in London that he had left Paris for Brittany, Moore, Jepson, and O'Riordan, who had by this time finished his novel and returned to London, were encouraged to think that he would settle down to a life which would be more beneficial to his talents and health. Nor would he be without companionship, for English and French poets and painters were sojourning along the Breton coast, and he was familiar with the country from past visits.

Although his feeling and that of his friends concerning the benefits which Pont-Aven might hold for him was somewhat optimistic, the fact remains that he had brief intervals of serenity and hope after his arrival in Brittany. "I think he was happiest in the remote Breton villages," wrote Edgar Jepson in "The Real Ernest Dowson" which appeared in *The Academy*, November 1907, "whither he now and again withdrew himself, and from which he wrote his most delightful letters. They used to give me the impression that the world went well with him there . . . as well, at any rate as it ever could go with him." To Davray he wrote soon after his arrival:

Hotel Gloanec
Pont-Aven
Finisterre

My Dear Davray,

Me voici at the world's end (finis-terrae) at last. I am sorry that I could not come and say au revoir (not good-bye) to you but I was in such a rush to get off. I have left your books and also one of Lautrec's with my Russian friend Leopold and have asked him to send them round to you. This is an adorable little town all shut in by hills except where an estuary of the sea runs up. The weather is glorious and yesterday at Quimperlé, I took coffee in an arbour in a garden. Write to me, I will write shortly. Shall be here for at least a month.

Ever yours
ERNEST DOWSON

About the same time he wrote a postcard to Victor Plarr.

Mon Cher Vieux,

Many months have I meant to write to you and give you of my wandering news. But arriving here, after passing through these Breton lands, which are so associated with you, makes it incumbent on me to send at least a post-card. I will follow it up with a letter when I am settled down, but write to me in the meantime. I shall stay here at least a month. I wish you could come too and leave your fogs and bask in baking sunshine as I did this afternoon, taking my coffee in a garden of my hotel at Quimperlé. I feel I shall do much work here: it is an adorable place and, much as I love Paris, where I have lived now for some time, I felt rested and restored to some prospect of reasonable health directly I came here. Write and believe me in spite of all my shortcomings as a correspondent, always yours,

ERNEST DOWSON

His feeling that he would "do much work" was not without foundation. For long he had entertained the notion of collecting his poems which had appeared in the Rhymers' Club anthologies and in the London magazines, and after augmenting their number with verses which remained unpublished in his "Poesie Schublade" and incidental pieces which he had written in letters to his friends, he felt that he would have enough for a little volume. Even before he left London, he had made some sort of arrangement with Elkin Mathews; and Mathews and Lane, who had published his collection of stories Dilemmas in the autumn of 1895, assumed that the volume would be theirs to issue when Dowson had finally submitted enough poems to make a sufficiently sizable book. The project, however, had been interrupted during Dowson's distracting experiences at home and by his journey in Flanders and life in Paris. In the meantime, his literary fortunes had become so much involved with the House of Smithers that all thought of publication began and ended at Arundel Street. Smithers, pleased with Dowson's work for The Savoy and the translation of the Balzac story, despite the tardiness with which the copy had been submitted, encouraged him to get the poems together, and promised to issue them to Dowson's advantage. Beardsley, he was assured, would do the cover design, and possibly the initial letters.

During the late winter, while Dowson was still in Paris, the prospect of issuing a volume of his own, without any contributions of Plarr or Lionel Johnson, stimulated in him sporadic energy which led to the preliminary work of selection and assembling. Thirteen poems he selected from his manuscript book; the others which were to compose the slender volume he took from the verses already printed. But with ill health and indecision undermining his energy at every turn, he kept putting off the apparently simple task of arranging and revising the poems. The work of arrangement was apparently easy enough, but his sensitivity to the value of his poetry caused him to deliberate long and earnestly over each phrase and even each mark of punctuation. All evidence points to the fact that he was meticulous in the revision of his verse, even to the point of spending considerable time on the varying degrees of effect which could be gained by the use of a semicolon instead of a comma.

The work of arranging the poems in the order in which he wished them to appear was perhaps a more trying problem than is generally recognized. Thomas, his Oxford friend, remarked that the poems in the volume constitute a cycle "whose unity needs emphasizing. Two numbers, Soli Cantare and A Friend's Child, have crept in by mischance, but, when these are removed, a sequence of intimate verses remains that can hardly be paralleled. Shakespeare's sonnets, Meredith's Modern Love, and Housman's Shropshire Lad are all artificial beside this real thing." Thomas' opinion in this instance is definitely subject to question. There are poems other than "Soli Cantare" and "A Friend's Child" which seem to be irrelevant to the unity which Thomas detected. The fact remains, however, that the position of "Vitae Summa Brevis Spem Nos Vetat Incohare Longam," "A Coronal," and "Chanson Sans Paroles" in the published volume was carefully deliberated.

Thomas' belief that there is a definite unity in the poems which made up Verses is given support by Dowson's dedication of the volume. The dedication of the individual pieces to Dowson's friends surely shows an indiscriminate selection which could have caused the author no great pains. To dedicate "Beata Solitudo" to Sam Smith, "Spleen" to Arthur Symons, and "April Love" to Arthur Hillier was surely no tax on the author's sense of appropriateness. One suspects that Dowson was eager to mention his friends without trying to associate the sentiment of the particular verse with the person whose name stood under its title. Perhaps in time commentators will spring up who will try to show how singularly appropriate "Beata Solitudo" was to Sam Smith, but at present there is no necessity for making an issue of such a topic. It is enough to observe that whereas Dowson was little concerned at the time with the appropriateness of his dedication of individual poems, he was greatly interested in the dedication of the entire volume.

Although it was not until he came to Brittany that he was ready to submit the poems in revised form to Smithers, he had made up his mind concerning the one to whom the volume was to be dedicated before he left

Paris. His decision, however, left him uneasy. While the poems were still in proof, he wrote from Pont-Aven to Smith:

I hope the dedication of my poems will be understood of her and accepted— as, although there is no name, nor initials even, it will doubtless be understood of others—who will not, I hope, think it extravagant. It is very literally true.

His concern over whether Missie would be assured that she was the one to whom the volume was dedicated led him immediately before the book went to press to use her first name—Adelaide. O'Riordan, amongst others, probably found the use of her name and the dedicatory epistle at large in poor taste, for Dowson continued to concern himself about his tact. Immediately before the book was issued, he wrote to Smith: "I have asked Smithers to give you a copy of 'Verses' which may be out by the time this reaches you. Let me know how you find them, and if you think the 'Preface' is indiscreet."

The dedicatory epistle, written at Pont-Aven a little before Easter, read:

IN PREFACE: FOR ADELAIDE

To you, who are my verses, as on some very future day, if you ever care to read them, you will understand, would it not be somewhat trivial to dedicate any one verse, as I may do, in all humility, to my friends? Trivial, too, perhaps, only to name you even here? Trivial, presumptuous? For I need not write your name for you at least to know that this and all my work is made for you in the first place, and I need not to be reminded by my critics that I have no silver tongue such as were fit to praise you. So for once you shall go indedicate, if not quite anonymous; and I will only commend my little book to you in sentences far beyond my poor compass which will help you perhaps to be kind to it:

'*Votre personne, vos moindres mouvements me semblaient avoir dans le monde une importance extra-humaine. Mon coeur comme de la poussière se soulevait derrière vos pas. Vous me faisiez l'effet d'un clair-de-lune par une nuit d'été, quand tout est parfums, ombres douces, blancheurs, infini; et les délices de la chair et de l'âme étaient contenues pour moi dans votre nom que je me répétais en tachant de le baiser sur mes lèvres.*

'*Quelquefois vos paroles me reviennent comme un écho lointain, comme le son d'une cloche apporté par le vent; et il me semble que vous êtes là quand je lis des passages de l'amour dans les livres. . . . Tout ce qu'on y blâme d'exagéré, vous me l'avez fait ressentir.*'

There is no record of Smith's response to the Preface, but many of his acquaintances, including O'Riordan and Symons, were of the opinion that the book would have profited by its omission. The quotation from Flaubert's

Education Sentimentale only heightened the impression expressed in some
circles that Dowson was casting pearls before swine. Had his friends been
uninformed about the girl to whom the epistle was written and the circumstances surrounding Dowson's attachment, they would have accepted
Dowson's pleading tone as one common to all lovers. Then it would have
been interpreted as a sort of Petrarchian cry to his Laura or Astrophel's
yearning for Stella. But to many of Dowson's friends, Adelaide of Soho
was a most infelicitous Laura or Stella. Had she been other than a restaurant keeper's daughter on Sherwood Street, there would have been small
significance attached to his tribute; but the notion, current in some circles
then and even today, that the Poles of Soho had led him on and then cast
him aside, gave additional support to their feeling that if Dowson insisted
on caring for the girl he should keep his love affairs to himself. To plead
with such a girl to read his poems and regard them kindly was, in their
opinion, only another demonstration of Dowson's lack of a sense of the
fitness of things.

In spite of the fact that some of his friends who were unsympathetic to
his attachment at Poland found the dedication indiscreet, the poems in the
volume which he had modestly chosen to entitle *Verses* were without exception highly commended. He was himself satisfied with the book, both
as a representation of his talent and as an indication of his ability to complete a task under difficulties. Soon after the book was issued he wrote to
Smith:

I am glad you like the volume. Do you like Aubrey Beardsley's binding-
block? I am very pleased with it. There are no reviews yet, but I have had
very charming letters from [John] Gray, Teixeira [de Mattos] and [Arthur]
Symons, the last of whom, as also Yeats, are going to write about it. Perhaps,
you are right in your remarks about my preface. Conal [O'Riordan] is dedicating to me his new novel 'A Fool and His Heart' and I fear the dedication
is appropriate. But it is too late to convert me now; I am idolatrous for the
rest of my days. Idolatrous to the extent that Keats was when he wrote from
Rome to his friend Browne: " the lining which she put in my travelling cap
scalds my head"—and like Keats I can not open her letters for a day or so
after they reach me. There is nothing in the universe which you can do, which
will give me more pleasure than to pay the visit of which you speak. I have
not yet sent her the volume, as the large-paper copies will not be bound for
another week.

Well, enough: it grows near post-time. Go and see my Missie I beseech
you: and tell me how she takes my 'Preface'—if she reads it. I only ask that she
does not *m'en vouloir* for it, and that is a little thing to ask for as absolute an
adoration as any girl or woman has ever had from anyone.

The review that Yeats was going to write apparently was never done, and the notice of Arthur Symons did not appear until the August 1896 issue of *The Savoy*, at which time the editor devoted three pages to Dowson, rather than to his *Verses* in the article entitled "A Literary Causerie." The London newspapers were prompter in their recognition of *Verses,* and as the reviews appeared, Smithers relayed copies of them to Dowson. He was pleased to learn that the critic in *The Daily Chronicle* had said: "Mr. Dowson had a genuine talent. Indeed he has several talents. A classic propriety of epithet, rising at moments to remarkable distinction; a full, rich melody, and . . . an occasional dignity of thought and feeling." From the object of the dedication, however, he did not hear. "The very future day" of which he spoke in his preface had not come. She had written to him since his arrival in Brittany, however, for in a letter to Plarr, written sometime in May, he told his friend: "My young lady writes to me fairly often, friendly letters, which give me sleepless nights and cause me to shed morbid and puerile tears. But she is very kind. . . ."

The publication of *Verses* and the novelty of Brittany kept him in good spirits for a time, but it was not more than six weeks after his departure from Paris that he again began to regard his prospect without cheer. His letter to Plarr, written in May soon after he had spoken of the appearance of his poems, indicates that his delight in being in Brittany was short-lived.

My dear Victor,—

I am ashamed of myself for not having long ago answered your charming letter, from Pont-Aven, but constant ill health and depression of spirits have made me a sorry correspondent. At least, I will not go away from this place, with which we both have had pleasant associations, without putting myself in touch with you. You will remember the room (salle à manger) in which I am writing. This visit of mine has not been a success; I came up from Pont-Aven only two days ago, to see if the change of air—from Pont-Aven to Faouet is really an enormous change, though it may sound ridiculous to you—would do me any good, and to spend a fortnight. But the ineffable *tristesse* of the place is too much for me and I am returning to what is more or less my permanent home and address (Hotel Gloanec, Pont-Aven, Finistère) to-morrow. Faouet is charming in the daytime. One can work without interruption, and, tired of work, one can bask in the blazing sunshine by Sainte-Barbe. But the evenings, the cold-bleak desolation of the evenings! Perhaps Pont-Aven, where I know everybody, and have many friends, French, English and Breton, has spoilt me; perhaps Le Faouet has changed, more likely I have. But I have not the courage to stay here by myself. It is more beautiful, however, now than in the full summer. There is no one in either hotel. Our old friend Jeanne has retired and Madame Mitouard (who asks to be remembered to you) is shaky on her pins.

Marie-Joseph has gone to Paris. Miss or Meese Rose, who spoke English, is post-mistress or tobacconist at Vannes. The two little twins, whom Moore and I admired much at the *billiard,* are grown into ugly and farouches girls of twelve. And the two trees, whom (? which) Moore christened the 'Sisters Limejuice,' are cut down. Eheu fugaces! But it is probably I, who have changed, more than Faouet, and doubtless if I was here with you and Moore I should love the place again. But in my sick and sorry old age I begin to be dependent on society: so I am off to Pont-Aven *après demain,* and there I hope you will write to me.

I hope you and yours prosper. It is long since I have heard news of you. My poems will be out in a day or two—perhaps are out now. You must forgive the freedom I have taken with yours and your wife's name in my inscription to my poem on Marion. I am full up with work of various kinds and I suppose I ought to be satisfied with myself, for it is all work that pays. But as I have no lungs left to speak of, an apology for a liver, and a broken heart I may be permitted to rail a little sometimes.

Write to me soon, mon Vieux. I shall be at Pont-Aven for two or three months and winter probably in Paris. Smith, Smithers and Moore are my only regular correspondents. Johnson sends me messages, with promises of speedy letters, but has not written as yet since I started on my wanderings. With J—[*] I have seriously quarrelled; and I am afraid H—[*] is annoyed with me because I have published my verses out of the series. . . . With all remembrances to all, affectionately yours,

ERNEST DOWSON

In spite of the fact that he had felt on his arrival in Brittany that he was restored "to some prospect of reasonable health," and that he should do much work, the change from Paris evidently had only temporary benefits. Even in Le Faouet, where, in July 1892, he had told Plarr that he expected sometime to live permanently on account of its picturesqueness and tranquillity, he now felt "an ineffable *tristesse."* The loneliness which had oppressed him during the winter in Paris again left him disconsolate. The unwillingness to do anything alone, which he had expressed in Paris, began to extend to a dread of even being alone. As he told Plarr, he had not the courage to stay in Le Faouet by himself. The prospect of seeing his poems in print, beautifully bound and with decorations by Beardsley, gave him temporary encouragement; and his reflections over Missie's response to the dedicatory epistle gave him an occasional ray of hope. Such thoughts, however, could not support an abiding serenity of mind, especially when he was regularly forced to an acute realization of his infirmities. He was more aware of his physical condition than most of his friends believed, and

* Possibly he refers to Edgar Jepson and Herbert Horne.

this knowledge, along with an ever-increasing life-weariness, made him crave company in order to escape from his own thoughts.

After his seemingly endless fortnight in Le Faouet, he was ready to return to Pont-Aven in spite of the dampness of the sea air, for there were acquaintances to whom he could attach himself when he felt he needed sanctuary from his thoughts. There he could see enough of provincial life without being completely detached from his other world in London. Although he had been away from England for almost a year, homesickness for London had rarely contributed to his loneliness. There had been times, to be sure, when he wanted to read the *Chronicle,* and when he would have sacrificed the little he had to offer for the company of someone who would tell him what was going on at the Crown, in the Temple, and in Soho. Though he never spoke of the searing thoughts which came to him when he recalled the "Rabbit Warren" at Queen's, the long nights after the Rhymers' meetings with Johnson, and the little restaurant with its perennial smell of garlic on Sherwood Street, one can read much between the lines in some of his letters to his friends. Much as he tried to convince himself that his ideals were essentially French, he still retained a few British loyalties. In Pont-Aven there were English folk; and after a fortnight in Le Faouet, he was eager to hear and speak his native tongue again, even when it was spoken by the bourgeois group who went to the more respectable of the two hotels which the town afforded.

The Hotel Gloanec, which he told Plarr was to be "more or less my permanent home and address," was in ill odor among the patrons of the other hotel, which catered to family trade, for the majority of men who took up residence at the Gloanec were of the Bohemian sort who occasionally brought their mistresses along with them from Paris or London, and spent more time conversing over their bottles than in application to their art. To be sure there were on occasion men of solid respectability who stayed at the Gloanec, but their presence had no perceptible effect on the tone of the hotel. Dowson, however, was definitely part of the Gloanec's atmosphere.

By the early part of the summer, most of his countrymen who patronized the family hotel on account of its respectability considered Dowson pretty much of a wastrel. One story especially had gained wide circulation, and on account of the heightened construction which the episode took in the retelling, Dowson was *persona non grata* among a goodly number of the English colony. Mrs. Gertrude Atherton, who spent part of the summer of 1896 in Pont-Aven, reported that when she arrived Dowson was in dire disgrace. Only a short time before her arrival, so the story runs, Dowson, filled with something stronger than the cider which was included in the pension at the Gloanec, developed a consuming desire for the wife of the town baker. So impatient was he to reach the object of his desire that he leaped through an open window of the baker's house and insisted on declaring his amorous intent even in the presence of her agitated spouse. A fight naturally ensued, the outcome of which found Dowson in the town jail where, during a period of two weeks, he was given the opportunity to allow his ardor to cool in a cell.

Yeats, writing from hearsay, told how Dowson had sent a letter to Effingham House in which he described the life of industry he was leading in order to keep up with his assignments and provide stories and poems for *The Savoy*. Before the letter arrived, however, those who sat at the House of Smithers received a telegram which read: "Arrested, sell watch and send proceeds." But before Smithers could dispose of the watch, which evidently Dowson in a moment of precaution had left in London, another wire arrived, "Am free." According to Yeats, who admitted that he heard the tale ten years after the episode occurred, Dowson "had got drunk and fought the baker, and a deputation of villagers had gone to the magistrate and pointed out that Monsieur Dowson was one of the most illustrious of the English poets. 'Quite right to remind me,' said the magistrate, 'I will imprison the baker.' "

Jepson, too, has given a version of the story, in which, as in the Yeats story, there is no mention of the reasons for the quarrel or of the baker's wife. "Only once," said Jepson,

did Dowson plainly look too long on the wine when it was red, and then in a petulant moment he beat the village baker, and the impudent fellow hauled him before a magistrate. Fortunately, being French, the magistrate had no patience with such actions, and taking the proper view that if a poet might not beat a baker, what might he beat? censured his fellow-countryman and dismissed the case.

Even this account, though lacking the picturesque details of the others and obviously compressed in Dowson's favor, is readily subject to question. The picture of the fragile Dowson, filled with the *vin du pays*, thrashing anyone—especially a Breton baker—is pretty difficult to conceive. It may easily be believed that Dowson had a fight, for many of his acquaintances have reported his pugnacity when he was drinking. Sherard recalls that there were times, even when he was completely sober, when he would antagonize men to whom he had taken a sudden and unreasonable dislike, and as often as not call them out for a fight.

He would snap his fingers in their faces, make nasty noises with his mouth in derision of them, and then propose an immediate bout of fisticuffs, which seeing his physical weakness, was the very last thing he should have attempted and would have resulted in his immediate discomfiture. He once thus insulted, provoked and challenged a guardsman from the Knightsbridge Barracks, who could have smashed him with the first blow.

The guardsman, so the story runs, seeing Dowson's slender frame, but also realizing that he was in earnest in his intention to try to thrash him, pacified him finally by telling him that he could not fight him in uniform, but that if he would appear at the barracks on the following morning, they would put on the gloves and Dowson would get his satisfaction.

This episode occurred sometime in 1898 on one of Dowson's visits to London, but even in the summer of 1896 he was scarcely the sort of adversary who could give anyone a sound thrashing. That he tried to beat the town baker is another question. In the light of all the stories which have been told about the affair, it seems likely that some sort of difficulty arose which brought Dowson to the attention of the magistrate, and that the trouble was largely of his own making; but until someone can present evidence which is more substantial than tales which are admittedly reported from remote and idle hearsay, we may conclude that the details of the fight with the baker belong to the very wide class of apocryphal anecdote.

It was in the summer of 1896, a month or so after the story of Dowson's fight with the baker began to circulate, that Mrs. Gertude Atherton, according to her own report, tried to "reclaim" him. Her interest in Dowson was aroused by her friend Horace Annesley Vachell, the novelist who was staying at the Hotel Gloanec with his cousin in order to get interesting "copy" of which the place was full. Vachell at the time was eager to try to do something to give Dowson a new lease on life. "It hurts me to see him so cowed and wretched," he told Mrs. Atherton soon after her arrival.

He really is a genius—and what a fate! Only twenty-nine and already an outcast! If one could only keep him from drinking he might pull up and become a brilliant figure in London. He is terribly poor, but what he has written has been received with such acclaim by the critics that anything he wrote would be well paid for, and he could soon reinstate himself. But he won't even write. . . . If you would only let me bring him over. It must be years since he has spoken to a decent woman—if he ever knew one! If he thought you took an interest in him . . . who knows? . . . it might mean a rebirth.

In the *Adventures of a Novelist,* Mrs. Atherton has told her side of the story of her attempt to reclaim Dowson. She, who had never looked at herself in the light of a reformer, was familiar with some of his works, including the "Cynara" poem and his translation, done with Teixeira de Mattos, of Couperus' *Majesty*. Realizing that he was one of the most lyric of poets, she told Vachell that she would see what she could do. Vachell was uncertain about the best method for bringing them together, for he knew Dowson to be naturally shy, and at the time especially sensitive to the advances of strangers. He had watched him slink into the hotel with averted eyes, but Vachell was convinced that Dowson regarded him as a friend, and as a result he felt that ultimately Dowson would yield to his invitation to meet Mrs. Atherton if the matter were arranged in the proper way. It took Vachell several days before he accomplished his purpose, and then the results were only partially satisfying. It was, however, a start. While Mrs. Atherton and a friend were seated on the terrace in front of her hotel one afternoon, Vachell appeared accompanied by a small man who had nothing of youth in his bearing. He wore a black sweater somewhat dusty; he was unshaven, and he showed at his first greeting a mouth without front teeth.

After the strained amenities of the introduction were exchanged, Dowson sank into a chair. His shifty eyes moved like a wild creature's, though when Mrs. Atherton offered him coffee he accepted politely. When she spoke flatteringly of his verse, and mentioned the London poets whom she felt he must know, he seemed confused. Apparently he was unable to carry on a conversation. So ill at ease he seemed that Mrs. Atherton deliberately turned to chat with a lady at an adjoining table in order to give him an opportunity to excuse himself. This he did as soon as there was a lull in Mrs. Atherton's talk. His coffee remained untouched.

Vachell, however, was not so easily discouraged. At his request, Mrs. Atherton was persuaded to make a second effort. A Mrs. Trulow, an American artist, had a studio in the "good" hotel, and it was to a little gathering at Mrs. Trulow's that Dowson was invited. Contrary to her expectations, he accepted graciously, and on the appointed afternoon he appeared with white collar and cuffs attached to his sweater, a clean pair of white shoes, and freshly shaven. There were only four in the group: Mrs. Atherton, her sister Aleece, Mrs. Trulow, and Horace Vachell. When Dowson entered, he seemed very shy, but at once Mrs. Atherton and Vachell produced a volume of his recently issued *Verses,* and commented on the beauty of the little book. Evidently the manner of procedure was tactful, for according to Mrs. Atherton, he began to show signs of being at ease. He drank three cups of tea before he left, and finally consented to read his "Cynara" poem, which he recited "in a low monotone that never varied for an instant." All the group commended him for the poem, and he left after a time apparently pleased by their praise. Evidently he was prevailed upon to read the poem a second time at a later gathering, for Michael Holland has told me that he remembers well an autumn night in 1896 when outside of Julie's Inn at Pont-Aven Dowson repeated the four stanzas in the moonlight to a small group including Mrs. Atherton, Horace Vachell, and himself.

Inspired by what she believed to be his need for proper companionship, and with Vachell's constant encouragement, Mrs. Atherton did her best to cultivate his friendship. They went on walks together, on which she allowed him to open her parasol and to assist her over difficult places in the road. When she pretended to be frightened at the cows which at times stood on the road, he drove them away with a fine show of his ability to offer her protection. He always appeared for these walks with his collar and cuffs, and freshly shaved. They talked about contemporary authors and painters, and according to Mrs. Atherton, he showed considerable interest when she told him about the delights of California. When Vachell was obliged to leave Pont-Aven, he told Mrs. Atherton:

I leave Dowson to you as a solemn responsibility. You have accomplished wonders; he hasn't been drunk since that day in the studio; but there is much to do yet. Try to persuade him to return with you to England. I know that he is writing again.

Mrs. Atherton, however, was only partially successful in fulfilling her "solemn responsibility." Her willingness to look after Dowson was hampered by the insistence of Aleece that they return to London. Before she yielded to Aleece's eagerness to be off she had given Dowson something to contemplate—a sort of dream, which possibly she felt might be realized. One afternoon she and Dowson passed a vacant stone house which in the vicinity was called a chateau. It was for rent—and cheap—and out of idle curiosity, they explored the interior. When she exclaimed that in such a place she could write, and began to consider renting the house for the winter, Dowson seemed immensely pleased. They both had a vision of a comfortable interior in which they could write and judge each other's work. When she asked him whether he would come every day if she rented the house, "he stared about him as if the bare little room held a vision of paradise. 'Will I! Last winter I had no one to talk to.' "

There were practical objections, however, to her renting the house, not the least of which was Aleece's hostility to such a plan; and reluctantly she had to bid Dowson goodbye. She dared not offer him money, for she knew he had refused Vachell's offer to pay his bill at the Gloanec. When she tried to persuade him to return to London, he shook his head: apparently he felt that he could afford to live only in Pont-Aven. On the day that the *diligence* carried her away, he stood watching it until it disappeared in the distance. She wrote to him from London, but he answered none of her letters. A few weeks after she had gone to London, Mrs. Trulow wrote to her: "Your poet has been drunk ever since you left, and no longer sports his collar and cuffs. Too bad your influence was not more lasting." And later from Mrs. Trulow: "Your poet left today to pay a farewell visit to Aubrey Beardsley, who is said to be dying. His only luggage was an extra sweater, which he carried under his arm. He may have had a toothbrush in his pocket, but I doubt it."

Despite the resentment which many of Dowson's friends have expressed toward Mrs. Atherton's account of her brief association with Dowson, her record undoubtedly has much truth. There is adequate evidence from substantial sources to support her observations that he was lonely, shy with strangers, and extremely negligent of his appearance. O'Riordan had observed his untidiness already in Paris, and Vincent O'Sullivan, who saw Dowson in both Paris and Pont-Aven, remarked:

Dowson's neglect of his personal appearance went to lengths I have never seen in anybody else still on the surface, and hardly in bums and beats and down-and-out tramps forced by hardship to a condition which they have not the means to remedy. The thing about Dowson was that he did not want to remedy it.

At the time, however, Dowson was not the completely "lost soul" which Mrs. Atherton and O'Sullivan saw. Vachell had given her a clue to his character which hampered her open-minded judgment of him as a man. In the "sad-looking object" who had not spoken to a decent woman for years, as Vachell had put it, she saw only what she wanted to see. In spite of the fact that Dowson was in sore need of the right kind of friendship at the time, he would have resented even a less calculated attempt than Mrs. Atherton's to "reclaim" him. Mrs. Atherton undoubtedly presented Dowson as she saw him, but her general air of patronage and her well-deliberated flattery give to her record a tone which has caused several of Dowson's friends to rise in his defense. When her account was brought to Jepson's attention, he remarked that he knew "a different Dowson"; and John Gawsworth in "The Dowson Legend," read before the Royal Society of Literature, called Mrs. Atherton's recollections of Dowson "monstrous reading."

Lonely as he often was in the late winter and spring, he was by no means friendless during the summer of 1896, nor did his shabby appearance make him an outcast. Men of extreme respectability and literary attainment wrote to him during his stay at Pont-Aven and joined him for brief periods on their holidays in France. Michael Holland met him at Julie's Inn late in the summer, and after forty years he has told me that Dowson was one of the most friendly and charming men he ever met, perfectly honest and natural, and with a genius for friendship.

In 1896 Dowson was not down and out. He drank too much at times, but when sober was a most delightful companion. When I left Pont-Aven, he came with me as far as Rennes, and we entertained a party of French cavalry officers, who were on manoeuvers, at our hotel. They dined with us, and I remember Dowson making an excellent speech in French which was appreciated and applauded by the French officers.

Hillier and Greene were in touch with him over the translation of the last volume of *The History of Modern Painting*. Arthur Moore was still trying to get chapters from him for *Adrian Rome*—in fact, Moore spent two weeks in August with him in Pont-Aven—and Charles Conder, when he tired of painting fans and trying to amuse Germaine, spent considerable time with him. O'Sullivan, who stayed at the Gloanec for a while during the summer, frowned on Dowson's shabby appearance, but he did not try to avoid him. And when Smithers on his periodic visits to France came to Pont-Aven, he showed no concern at being seen in public places with Mrs. Atherton's "sad-looking object." Of course Smithers was impervious to the effects of wagging tongues; in fact, he rather liked to be seen with men and women whom the ultra-respectable class considered flotsam. There were French artists, too, including Toulouse-Lautrec, whom Dowson had known intimately during the preceding winter in Paris, and Loiseau, both recognized for their achievements if not for their exemplary lives.

There was other company which, if it did not contribute to his reputation as a man of good taste and respectability, at least kept him from spending his evenings alone. He probably had nothing to do with "the independent lady of commerce" who helped to provide company for the lonesome Londoners who were spending their holiday in Brittany, but he had at least one attachment which for a time he followed with an unreasonable seriousness. Always possessed of an interest in loose women, more for their company than for their wares, he had a curious and even amusing acquaintanceship with a lady of alleged literary interests who had long since become indifferent to her reputation. He was unwilling to have his friends believe that his interest in her was other than platonic, and he tried to make plain that his attachment had literary ties and utility. Yeats and others recalled that one of Dowson's well-wishers, upon seeing him in a public place with the

trollop, later suggested to him that he might find choicer company else-
where. Dowson, promptly on the defensive, is reported to have exclaimed:
"What? Give her up for some of these b—s? Our association is like that of
Robert and Mrs. Browning!"

Although Mrs. Atherton's company would have undoubtedly proved
more beneficial than that of some of the people with whom he was driven
to consort by reason of his loneliness, it must be observed that during the
summer and early autumn of 1896 he was not exactly an outcast, nor had
he lost all ambition and hope. When Horace Vachell told Mrs. Atherton
that he would no longer even try to write, he based his statement on a very
limited knowledge of what Dowson was doing at the time and what he
planned to do in the immediate future. The reception which had greeted
the publication of *Verses* encouraged him to start on new projects. Smithers
had given him another commission during the spring, a verse translation of
Voltaire's *La Pucelle d'Orléans,* a long and difficult piece of work. Other
suggestions for possible translations for Smithers were regularly exchanged,
including *Les Liaisons Dangereuses* of Choderlos de Laclos. The letter
which follows, written during the summer of 1896, indicates clearly that
Dowson was neither without ambition nor a completely "lost soul."

Hotel Gloanec,
Pont-Aven.

My dear Smithers,

Just a line to ask you not to *forget me & to send a hundred francs* if you have
not done so already. I missed the post with the 'Pucelle,' but you will receive it
before this letter & also the proof of story.

I have done a poem in my Breton manner which I will send you when I
have worked it up a little, & am getting on, though slowly, with my story &
the "Pucelle."

But I am working regularly & only drinking just enough to keep me in
reasonable spirits. Have been feeling better than usual the last two days,
having had three good nights; yesterday got a boat which I took down the
river (with Cremnitz—Jean de Tinan's friend in it) nearly to the sea. Missed
the tide, or forgot about it, & had to scull up four miles, unaided—Cremnitz
being ignorant of the art of rowing—against a tide of seventeen horse-power.
With the result that today my legs are so stiff that I can barely move. But the
exercise was no doubt salutory.

Ever yours,

ERNEST DOWSON

In addition to the projects which he had under way for Smithers, he was
encouraged to believe that there was always space for him in *The Savoy.*

Hôtel Gloanec,
Pont-Aven,

My dear Smithers,

Just a line to ask you not to forget me & to send a hundred francs if you have not done so already. I missed the post with the 'Pucelle' but you will receive it before this letter & also the proof of story.

I have done a poem in my Breton manner which I will send you when I have worked it up a little, & am getting on, though slowly, with my story & the "Pucelle".

But I am working regularly & only drinking just enough to keep me in reasonable spirits. Have been feeling better than usual the last two days, having had three good nights; yesterday got a boat which I took down the river (with Cremnitz — Jean de Tinan's friend in it) nearly to the sea. Missed the tide, or forgot about it, & had to scull up four miles, unaided — Cremnitz being ignorant of the art of rowing — against a tide of seventeen horse-power with the result that to day my legs are so stiff that I can barely move. But the exercise was no doubt salutary.

Ever yours,
Ernest Dowson

A LETTER FROM DOWSON TO LEONARD SMITHERS

The success of the first two numbers of *The Savoy* had been so pronounced that Symons, Beardsley, and Smithers decided to make the magazine a monthly instead of a quarterly. The policy of the magazine was to remain otherwise unchanged, save for the intention of including a serial which a monthly issue would permit. In fact, arrangements were being made with George Moore for the serial publication of *Evelyn Innes*. Dowson welcomed the change from quarterly to monthly, for not only did he have the best interests of the magazine at heart, but he also felt that the more frequent issue would give him additional opportunity to supplement his income and widen his literary reputation.

In the July issue he was represented by only one poem, "Breton Afternoon," but by the time the August issue went to press he had submitted the poem "Venite, Descendamus" and the prose study "The Dying of Francis Donne." To the September number he contributed the Song which began "All that man may pray," and in the October issue he had the poem "The Three Witches." In November there appeared the fine poem "Epilogue," and in the December issue, the last number of *The Savoy*, only Arthur Symons contributed to the literary contents.

The poem entitled "Epilogue," if Dowson listed the date of its writing correctly in his Manuscript Book, was finished more than ten years before it appeared in *The Savoy*, and it is possible that some of the other pieces were finished long before there was an immediate necessity that he submit work if he wished to be represented in a particular number of the magazine. With the exception of the poems to which he assigns dates in his Manuscript Book, there is no means of determining exactly when some of the pieces which appeared in *The Savoy* were written; but it seems likely that most of them were turned out immediately before the magazine went to press.

This would seem especially true of such a poem as "Breton Afternoon" and the prose study "The Dying of Francis Donne." To be sure, he had been in Brittany in 1890 and again in 1892, but it is improbable that he should have kept "Breton Afternoon," and "In a Breton Cemetery" which Symons rejected and which was later printed in *The Pageant*, for the time when he should again be in Brittany and when he should need poems to make good his promise to contribute faithfully to *The Savoy*. Certainly there is sufficient evidence to support the assumption that these Breton poems were written after his arrival in Pont-Aven.

The prose study "The Dying of Francis Donne" was also probably written during the period in which Vachell reported that "he won't even write." It is possible—I offer the suggestion hesitantly—that his loneliness and despair while he was spending the fortnight in Le Faouet were in some measure the substance out of which the story grew. He, like Francis Donne,

> . . . had lived so long in the meditation of death, visited it so often in others, studied it with such persistency, with a sentiment in which fascination and horror mingled; but it had always been, as it were, an objective, alien fact, remote from himself and from his own life. So that it was in a sudden flash, quite too stupefying to admit in the first instance of terror, that knowledge of his mortality dawned on him. . . . "I, Francis Donne, am going to die," he repeated, and, presently, *"I am going to die soon;* in a few months, in six perhaps, certainly in a year." . . . Was it his fancy, or, perhaps, only for the vague light that he seemed to discover a strange gray tone about his face? . . . Since death is coming to me, said Francis Donne to himself, let me meet it, a stranger in a strange land, with only strange faces round me and the kind indifference of strangers, instead of the intolerable pity of friends.

In the light of what Dowson was experiencing at the time immediately before the study appeared, and of what was to follow, "The Dying of Francis Donne" becomes not only a curious study in the psychology of the contemplation of death, but a searching revelation of Dowson's attitude as well. To my knowledge, it has never been reprinted from *The Savoy;* but anyone who wishes to know the essential voice of Dowson at the time at which his dread malady was tightening its grip about him should reflect on the significance of this study.

Such a piece, and the poem "Epilogue," his last contribution to *The Savoy,* were curiously applicable to the waning fortunes of the mgazine. In fact, the sentiment and tone of "Epilogue," especially the lines

> . . . Vain things alone
> Have driven our perverse and aimless band

have led commentators to interpret the poem as Dowson's judgment of the last phase of the esthetic movement of which *The Savoy* was a part. The poem, which Dowson had written before he went up to Oxford, has a broader meaning; but he, too, must have felt that its lines were appropriate to the decline of *The Savoy.*

As early as October 30, 1896, Hubert Crackanthorpe reported to Grant Richards from Paris: "I have just heard from Arthur Symons that the *Savoy* is to cease in December." Crackanthorpe, sometime editor of *The Albemarle,* felt that if Richards would take over the publication, and he take over Symons' role as editor, the magazine could be revived. Richards, however, felt that the magazine could not be saved. "The reaction," he observed, "had not spent itself."

What he meant is clarified by Arthur Symons' own account of the reasons for the magazine's failure. Symons, the sole contributor to the final issue, expressed himself bitterly about what he believed to be the causes.

Our first mistake was in giving so much for so little money; our second, in abandoning a quarterly for a monthly issue. The action of Messrs. Smith and Son in refusing to place "The Savoy" on their book-stalls on account of the reproduction of a drawing by Blake, was another misfortune. And then, worst of all, we assumed that there were very many people in the world who really cared for art, and really for art's sake. The more I consider it, the more I realize that this is not the case. Comparatively few people care for art at all, and most of these care for it because they mistake it for something else.

Yeats had another explanation:

We might have survived but for our association with Beardsley; perhaps, for his *Under the Hill,* a Rabelaisian fragment promising a literary genius as great as his artistic genius; and for the refusal of the bookseller who controlled the railway bookstalls to display our wares. The bookseller's manager, no doubt looking for a design of Beardsley's, pitched upon Blake's "Anteus setting Vergil and Dante upon the verge of Cocytus" as the ground of refusal, and when Arthur Symons pointed out that Blake was considered "a very spiritual artist," replied, "O, Mr. Symons, you must remember that we have an audience of young ladies as well as an audience of agnostics." However, he called Arthur Symons back from the door to say, "If contrary to our expectations the *Savoy* should have a large sale, we should be very glad to see you again."

Although Robert Ross observed that "Quite wrongly Beardsley's art had come to be regarded as the pictorial and sympathetic expression of an unfortunate tendency in English literature," the stories which were circulated about Beardsley's planned insinuations in his drawings did the magazine no good. According to Edgar Jepson, a heated argument raged at Effingham House before the publication of the first issue of *The Savoy.* The original cover was a Beardsley drawing in which John Bull was represented in a state of sexual excitement. The implication of the drawing was to point out to potential purchasers the nature of the contents. Beardsley, either misled, or in one of the moments of devilishness which were common to him, had made the implication clear. That *The Savoy* was to reach artistic heights on which morals were unquestioned was the current belief among at least a few of the writers whose contributions were sought. Weeks before the first issue of the magazine appeared, Dowson wrote to Jepson: "I should like to have an opportunity of meeting you and telling you of a new and very advanced review which is being founded and where perhaps some of your Barbadian Idylls—it wouldn't matter how swarthy they were—

might be *casé.*" But when Beardsley contributed his "swarthy" illustration, Jepson and many of the other contributors to the first issue were plainly hostile to its being used; and after a short meeting in Jepson's rooms, they went to Effingham House to insist to Smithers that a totally different drawing be submitted. Smithers was delighted with the idea of the original cover, but Jepson, together with Shaw, Image, and Horne, was sufficiently vigorous in his opposition to cause the publisher finally to decide to use another drawing, despite the fact that he continued to insist that the John Bull which Beardsley had drawn was precisely the John Bull for which the readers were aching. A few demurred when it was finally agreed to change the cover, with the thought that Smithers knew what he was doing and that he was paying them for supporting his notions of how such a magazine could be successfully managed. Although Smithers listened to the reasoning of Jepson and his faction, the report gained wide circulation before the first number appeared that *The Savoy* was to be "very advanced" indeed.

Soon after the first issued appeared, readers and critics thought they were able to detect fragrances in the magazine which bore out their assumption that it would be a distillate of the patchouli of *The Yellow Book.* Punch said of it: "There is not an article in the volume which can be put down without feeling the better and purer for it . . . it should be on every schoolroom table; every mother should present it to her daughter, for it is bound to have an ennobling and purifying influence." Such a statement, though amusing in its irony, was in no way an accurate description of the tone of the contents of the first issue of *The Savoy,* nor were the other reports which pointed to its so-called decadence more than preconceptions. According to present-day standards at least, the description of its contents which appeared in *Punch* might readily be taken literally. But the report was out that *The Savoy* was "very advanced"; and, as result, everything which bordered on the unconventional was promptly exaggerated by those whose tastes were peculiarly Victorian. The accounts of Oscar Wilde's trial, Aubrey Beardsley's reputation, and Leonard Smithers' policy of insinuation, all gave the early issues of the magazine a notoriety which can at present be only partially understood.

In all these discussions concerning the "morality" of *The Savoy,* Dowson had no part. He had left London before Beardsley's original drawing became an issue, and he was not of the sort to take a strong stand had he been in London. But even at a distance, he followed the fortunes of the magazine with interest. In a letter to Jepson written from Paris sometime before the second number appeared, he showed his concern over a libel action which was impending, and expressed at the same time his confidence in Smithers.

With all the difficulties which beset *The Savoy* in its brief existence, Dowson had little to do. He liked to believe that he was one of its chief supporters, but by reason of his absence from Effingham House and Symons' quarters in the Temple he was unaware of most of the struggles which attended the birth of the magazine and its short life. He probably would have sided with Image, Horne, and Jepson in their objection to Beardsley's original drawing for the first issue of the magazine, for surely there was nothing in his contributions to *The Savoy* or in his idea of what a good art magazine should be which would bear out the implication which Beardsley had put into his drawing. On the other hand, he surely would not have raised his voice against the reproduction of the drawing by Blake, to which Messrs. Smith and Son objected so strenuously. He was eager to support the change of policy which provided for a monthly instead of a quarterly issue, though he failed to see how a serial by George Moore, which was one of the reasons advanced for making the change, could improve the magazine.* Although he was never consulted by Smithers and Symons concerning their policies, he was led to believe as a regular contributor that he had a hand in shaping the destiny of the magazine. To his promise that he would submit poems and stories regularly, he remained faithful. It was to only the last issue that he submitted nothing, and at that time it was generally understood that *The Savoy* was to be discontinued.

Dowson watched the approaching death of the magazine with regret, for its very existence had been good for him. It gave him a feeling of responsibility, it provided a ready receptacle for his work, and it helped to widen his reputation as a writer. And his contributions had been good for *The Savoy*. Nothing which he submitted ever caused the editorial staff the slightest disquiet. In the stories and poems which he submitted there was nothing that could possibly be construed as unfit for Messrs. Smith and Son's "audience of young ladies." Although his contributions to the magazine are not on a plane with his finest work, they fulfilled more than adequately Symons' expressed requirement that "We intend to print no verse which has not some close relationship with poetry, no fiction which has not a certain sense of what is finest in living fact. . . ."

Had *The Savoy* flourished for another year, it is likely that Dowson would have broken his promise to contribute something to each issue, especially had Arthur Symons continued as literary editor. Symons and Dowson, although both of the Rhymers' and of the inner circle at the Crown, had

* Moore's *Evelyn Innes* never appeared even in part in *The Savoy*.

very little in common. They were incapable of understanding each other when topics other than poetry were considered. "To Symons," said Jepson, "his harmless enough life among the poets and artists who foregathered at the Crown was a patch of the most purple, and he saw their peccadilloes as the sins of imperial Rome." Although his early poetry would seem to indicate that he played with fire along with other young men of his generation who followed the pleasures of London and Paris nights, his training in youth and his instinct toward moderation and regularity kept him more the observer than the active participant. Quite naturally he saw much in Dowson's life which was anomalous. An admirable critic, he found Dowson's verses very fine; and in an effort to present his readers with an evaluation of Dowson's poetry in the August issue of *The Savoy*, he overstepped his role in a way which gave the poet considerable distress.

"A Literary Causerie: on a Book of Verses" which Symons probably intended as a tribute to his friend and contributor was scarcely the sort of notice which could gladden Dowson's heavy heart. No name was mentioned in the "Causerie," but most of the readers of *The Savoy*, if they did not recognize the subject of the article at once, were soon informed about whom Symons had written. It is impossible to realize what Dowson must have felt when he picked up the issue of *The Savoy* to which he had contributed "Venite, Descendamus" and "The Dying of Francis Donne" to read:

A book of delicate, mournful, almost colourless, but very fragrant verses was lately published by a young poet whom I have the privilege to know somewhat intimately. Whether a book so essentially poetic, and at the same time so fragile in its hold on outward things, is likely to appeal very much to the general public, for which verse is still supposed to be written, it scarcely interests me to conjecture. It is a matter of more legitimate speculation, what sort of person would be called up before the mind's eye of any casual reader, as the author of love-poetry so reverent and so disembodied. A very ghostly lover, I suppose, wandering in a land of perpetual twilight, holding a whispered "colloque sentimental" with the ghost of an old love:

> "Dans le vieux parc solitaire et glacé
> Deux spectres ont évoqué le passé."

That is not how I have seen my friend, for the most part; and the contrast between the man as I have seen him and the writer of verses as I read them, is to me the most attractive interest of a book which I find singularly attractive. He will not mind, I know, if I speak of him with some of that frankness which we reserve usually for the dead, or with which we sometimes honour our enemies; for he is of a complete indifference to these things, as I shall assure myself over again before these lines are printed.

I do not remember the occasion of our first meeting, but I remember seeing him casually, at railway stations, in a semi-literary tavern which once had a fantastic kind of existence, and sometimes, at night, in various parts of the Temple, before I was more than slightly his acquaintance. I was struck then by a look and manner of pathetic charm, a sort of Keats-like face, the face of a demoralized Keats, and by something curious in the contrast of a manner exquisitely refined, with an appearance generally somewhat dilapidated. That impression was only accentuated, later on, when I came to know him, and the manner of his life, much more intimately. I think I may date my first real impression of what one calls "the real man"—as if it were more real than the poet of the disembodied verses!—from an evening in which he first introduced me to those charming supper-houses, open all night through, the cabmen's shelters. There were four of us, two in evening dress, and we were welcomed, cordially and without comment, at a little place near the Langham; and, I recollect very hospitably entertained. He was known there, and I used to think he was always at his best in a cabmen's shelter. Without a certain sordidness in his surroundings, he was never quite comfortable, never quite himself; and at those places you are obliged to drink nothing stronger than coffee or tea. I liked to see him occasionally, for a change, drinking nothing stronger than coffee or tea. At Oxford, I believe, his favorite form of intoxication had been haschisch; afterwards he gave up this somewhat elaborate experiment in visionary sensations for readier means of oblivion; but he returned to it, I remember, for at least one afternoon, in a company of which I had been the gatherer, and of which I was the host. The experience was not a very successful one; it ended in what should have been its first symptom, immoderate laughter. It was disappointing, and my charming, expectant friends, disappointed.

Always, perhaps a little consciously, but; at least always sincerely, in search of new sensations, my friend found what was for him the supreme sensation in a very passionate and tender adoration of the most escaping of all ideals, the ideal of youth. Cherished, as I imagine, first only in the abstract, this search after the immature, the ripening graces which time can but spoil in the ripening, found itself at the journey's end, as some of his friends thought, a little prematurely. I was never of their opinion. I only saw twice, and for a few moments only, the young girl to whom most of his verses were to be written, and whose presence in his life may be held to account for much of that astonishing contrast between the broad outlines of his life and work. The situation seemed to me of the most exquisite and appropriate impossibility. She had the gift of evoking, and, in its way, of retaining, all that was most delicate, sensitive, shy, typically poetic, in a nature which I can only compare to a weedy garden, its grass trodden down by many feet, but with one small, carefully-tended flower-bed, luminous with lilies. I used to think, sometimes, of Verlaine and his "girl wife," the one really profound passion, certainly, of that passionate career; the charming, child-like creature, to whom he looked back, at the end of his life, with an unchanged tenderness and disappointment: "Vous n'avez rien compris à ma simplicité," as he lamented. In the case of my friend there was, however, a sort of virginal devotion, as to a Madonna; and I think had things gone happily, to a conventionally happy ending, he would have felt (dare I say?) that his ideal had been spoilt.

But, for the good fortune of poets, things never do go happily with them, or to conventionally happy endings. So the wilder wanderings began, and a gradual slipping into deeper and steadier waters of oblivion. That curious love of the sordid, so common an affectation of the modern decadent, and with him so expressively genuine, grew upon him, and dragged him into yet more sorry corners of a life which was never exactly "gay" to him. And now, indifferent to most things, in the shipwrecked quietude of a sort of self-exile, he is living, I believe, somewhere on a remote foreign sea-coast. People will complain, probably, in his verses, of what will seem to them the factitious melancholy, the factitious idealism, and (peeping through at a few rare moments) the factitious suggestions of riot. They will see only a literary affectation where in truth there is as poignant a note of personal sincerity as in the more explicit and arranged confessions of less admirable poets. Yes, in these few, evasive, immaterial snatches of song, I find, implied for the most part, hidden away like a secret, all the fever and turmoil and the unattained dreams of a life which has itself had much of the swift, disastrous, and suicidal energy of genius.

The man who, according to Symons, was "now indifferent to most things," and was living "in a sort of self-exile . . . somewhere on a remote foreign sea-coast" was in regular correspondence with the editors of *The Savoy;* he had recently seen some of his London friends in Pont-Aven, and he had by no means as yet sunk into the "deeper and steadier waters of oblivion." Symons knew exactly where Dowson was when he wrote the article, and he also knew that Dowson was planning to contribute additional pieces to *The Savoy* and to Smithers' list of translations. Perhaps in order to try to conceal Dowson's identity and whereabouts, he deliberately spoke of "somewhere on a remote sea-coast"; but it is more likely that he wanted to make the picture of desolation complete.

Those who had been in recent correspondence with Dowson or had seen him during the summer were plainly annoyed by the inaccurate picture which Symons had drawn. Edgar Jepson was later to state his dissatisfaction unmincingly.

Mr. Symons' early years in the constrained atmosphere of the Midlands unfitted him for the task [of portraying Dowson] by confusing the values. When Mr. Symons states that Dowson felt strangely at home in that squalid part of the East End, Stepney, "drinking the poisonous liquors of those pot-houses which swarm the docks," he is writing nonsense. Dowson always made the greatest possible haste, a daily haste, to get out of the East End to the society of his kind, and the liquor in Stepney came from the same manufacturers as that of the Crown. When he describes him as afflicted by a morbid shyness, he is again talking nonsense: in all the years we perused London together, I never saw Dowson shy. Mr. Symons was exuberant, Dowson reserved; very likely more reserved than usual in the society of Mr. Symons, with whom his intimacy was slight.

No less nonsensical is Mr. Symons' statement that Dowson loved the sordid. He was merely indifferent to externals and though, most unwisely, he took a cold bath of a morning, he paid as much attention to his personal appearance as did that Englishman of Englishmen, Dr. Johnson himself. But in his hour of prosperity, in the hour when he loved Dulcie, Dowson wore a frock-coat from Saville Row and a masterpiece of Mr. Henry Heath, and more beautifully dressed than any other poet I have known, was fit to walk Bond Street with Teixeira himself.

With regard to his drinking, on which Mr. Symons lays such stress, during the years we perused London together Dowson would get drunk now and then. But who did not? Nevertheless for weeks together he would be sober enough. The craving for liquor which at times came upon him was a malady natural to a man with the nerves of a consumptive. Neither he nor Lionel Johnson could stand the strain of life, and at times liquor alone could give them relief. Naturally a couple of whiskies and sodas came to have as intoxicating effect on them as half a dozen on the average man.

Jepson's spirited defense against what he considered to be Symons' attack Dowson never saw. It is possible that he would have been grateful for the spirit which motivated it, but it is unlikely that he would have been pleased to have recalled to his mind the hour of his prosperity, or to have his excesses in his cups justified on account of his congenital malady. Suffering, and detached as he was from his friends, Dowson was by no means indifferent to Symons' statements concerning his personal affairs and the oblivion which would soon overtake him. He was too ill and dispirited at the time to strike back, and furthermore there was little of the polemic in his nature when it came to such deeply affecting matters; but Yeats and others have reported that he wrote a letter of protest in which he stated that his life was not devoid of industry. A letter has turned up, probably the one mentioned by Yeats, in which Dowson writing directly to Symons who had evidently sent him the proofs of the "Causerie" asked him to tone down some of the detail. Among other things, Dowson objected to Symons' describing his appearance as dilapidated.*

*See John M. Munro's "A Previously Unpublished Letter from Ernest Dowson to Arthur Symons," *Etudes Anglaises* XVII:3 (1964).

There is, however, sufficient evidence to indicate that despite his ill health and despair he was not consistently without hope. The thought of a new magazine with Hubert Crackanthorpe as editor pleased him, and he still regarded his commissions in translating for Smithers as worth-while, not only for the income they provided but also for the interest which they brought to him in their fulfillment. It is a mistaken notion that Dowson performed his assignments for Smithers perfunctorily. While he was at work on *Les Liaisons Dangereuses* he made inquiries concerning other works by Laclos which he could read for his own enjoyment if not for a translation for Smithers' list. When Smithers did not appear completely satisfied with parts of Dowson's translations, he was willing to do them over. His verse translation of *La Pucelle* he found fatiguing, but he never despaired of finishing it.

Although his contemplation of work well done provided him with sufficient energy and hope to abide his suffering, he had sources other than his work on which to rely when his spirit needed bolstering. Missie was slowly becoming older. A year had passed since he had last seen her, but their quarrel had been patched up by letters even before he had left Paris. But he, like Seefang in his story "The Eyes of Pride," was still unwilling to take the initial step toward a complete reconciliation. Both pride and indecision kept him from going straightway to her, to tell her that she was now of age and that she must marry him. Fear that she might have changed entirely in her attitude toward him made him pause at the thought of going to London, but he had in no way given up hope. She had written to him occasionally, and he knew that she had ample directions for communicating with him at Pont-Aven. With each post from England his spirits rose in the expectancy that perhaps she had written more than a friendly letter in which he would find sufficient encouragement to return to London to marry her. Symons had written in his *Savoy* article as if the attachment had been permanently broken, but in the autumn of 1896 Dowson still was hopeful that his affairs at Poland would be ultimately straightened out.

Then, too, another ray of hope came to him in the sere days at Pont-Aven which helped him to regain for a time his small zest for life. During the late summer he had struck up an acquaintanceship with the French painter Loiseau out of which evolved a plan which had much appeal to him. The details of the plan are by no means complete, but in a letter to Smithers, written sometime in the autumn of 1896, he told the publisher half-gaily about how he and Loiseau were on the lookout for a gypsy cart in which they would proceed in easy stages into the south of France and spend the cold months in the salubrious and picturesque towns on the Riviera. "He

[Loiseau] will do the cuisine," he wrote. "I am charging myself with the care of the horse . . . I think he underrates the eating capacity of the steed, even the sort of old screw we could buy for 100 francs. . . ." He added that he had been sitting for Loiseau for his portrait, but that the artist, being an Impressionist, had made violet and brick-red the dominant colors, and that no likeness between the sitter and the portrait was discernible. "I have begged him," he continued, "to inscribe it as the 'Portrait of a Murderer' and not of 'Ernest Dowson'!"

Such a letter, written not long after he had finished "The Dying of Francis Donne," undoubtedly indicates that in spite of all of his afflictions Dowson still retained a little zest for life as well as a little of the sense of humor about which he had written to Smith in the early winter of 1895. The prospect of acquiring a gypsy cart in which to move across France to a sunnier clime brought him out of his lethargy, and he and Loiseau spent pleasant evenings together mapping out their itinerary and anticipating the pleasures that were in store for them on the way and after they had reached their destination. In southern France he could escape from the rigors of a Breton winter, and with Loiseau as a companion he would never be oppressed by loneliness, for the young Frenchman was of lively spirit, if not of pronounced energy and ambition. In the coast towns of the Mediterranean, however, Loiseau would paint and he, with energy and health restored, would write more than Smithers could handle.

But the plan for going to southern France never became more than a pleasant prospect. Neither he nor Loiseau was sufficiently endowed with determination to make such a dream a reality; and the hundred francs which Dowson felt they needed in order to buy an "old screw" was not the least of the obstacles which stood in the way of its fulfillment. Already well in arrears with his bill at the Gloanec, and with no prospect of a sufficient advance from Smithers or from what he believed to be his interest in the Dock, he watched the plan collapse before it had fully developed. Loiseau was no better off than he in either possessions or ability to surmount obstacles.

With the collapse of the plan to go to the Riviera, a depression of spirit seized him which left him incapable of deciding on any course of action. The summer had passed, and Pont-Aven had begun to take on its autumnal bleakness. Most of his countrymen who had come for their holiday to Brittany were back in London, and the French artists had gone, one by one, back to the left bank of the Siene. The days of fête were over, the *bois d'amour* where on summer nights the young Bretons pledged their vows was deserted, and a cold wind swept across the cemetery close by in which were buried the widows of those who had failed to return from the *grande pêche*. The prospect of another winter in northern France without the companionship of a friend caused him to sink into a lethargy of mind and spirit out of which no plan for the future could evolve.

Suicide, with which he had a grim familiarity, fascinated him, but it demanded a kind of decision to which his enfeebled spirit could never rise. He was later to reprove himself for putting up with a life which he had come to loathe. "I ought to have drowned myself at Pont-Aven," he wrote to Smith in the spring of 1897. But in spite of the fact that William Rothenstein once said that he doubted "if Dowson wanted to live," in the autumn of 1896 he was neither willing nor able to die. When the gray prospect of Pont-Aven became unbearable, he mustered together the little decision which was left him, and after making his peace with the proprietor at the Gloanec as best he could, he went to Paris.

⁂ IX ⁂

IN SEARCH OF THAT WE KNOW NOT

D OWSON'S movements in Paris during the winter of 1896-97 cannot be traced clearly and consecutively. With a few friends he kept
up an irregular correspondence; but with the exception of Smithers, none of his acquaintances in London knew more than vaguely where he
was and what he was doing. His friends of the Rhymers' Club—Plarr, Hillier, and Lionel Johnson—had lost track of him altogether. To the few
inquiries which came to them concerning his whereabouts, they could only
answer: "Somewhere in France." Even Smith and Jepson, with whom he
had kept in fairly regular touch during the previous winter, were uncertain
of his movements and plans; and Conal O'Riordan could only assume that
he was in Paris. If the letters he wrote to Leonard Smithers during the
winter of 1896-97 are ever brought to light, it is possible that they will
illuminate this stage of his life considerably. They will surely not be pleasant reading, for it may readily be concluded that this period was filled with
suffering and despair.

There are reasons for the paucity of materials which might shed light
on his movements in Paris which are in themselves a faint illumination of
the sort of existence he led. He knew he had a fatal malady, in spite of
the fact that he was successful in leading his acquaintances to believe that
he had no notion of the seriousness of his affliction. It is idle to try to prove
that one who had been with tuberculous people all his life was unaware
of the seriousness of his condition. That he spoke of having colds and
influenza to his friends does not mean that he believed his ailment was
trifling. Like Francis Donne in his study for *The Savoy,* he knew he was
going to die "in a few months, in six perhaps, certainly in a year"; and he
wanted to meet death "a stranger in a strange land, with only strange faces
round [him], instead of the intolerable pity of friends." Everything points
to the conclusion that his convictions about meeting suffering and death
were those of Francis Donne.

He had relatives and friends in England who would have given him the
physical comforts he so sorely needed, and encouragement to struggle
against the odds which beset him, but he suspected them all of "intolerable
pity." It is possible that he felt that he might be too great a burden on
them; but it is more likely that he felt that his life had grown so different
from theirs that they would not welcome any proposal of his to visit them.

Devoid as he was of moral sense, he still realized that his relatives cherished standards of conduct which were different from his. Despite the fact that there had never been a quarrel between them, he was unwilling to go to them for comfort or sympathy, or even to let them know of his condition. To them, he had always been an odd sort of young man, and when they did not hear from him they had no reason to believe that there was anything extraordinary in his silence.

With the progress of his affliction he had become more and more sensitive to the thought that he might be imposing on the good nature of his relatives and friends if he wrote to them of his troubles. His spirit was supported by a pride of which his very silence to his friends is proof. He had by no means reached the point at which he was willing to give anyone concern about him. There were still a few interests around which his spirits could rally. In Davray and his staff, Toulouse-Lautrec, and Loiseau, he found company which pleased him and in which he detected no annoying solicitude concerning his appearance and health. Then, too, he still possessed the inclination to write. When his energy permitted, he worked on the translation of *La Pucelle* and *Les Liaisons Dangereuses*. Smithers had evidently informed some of his friends that Dowson was translating *La Pucelle* in verse for him and that he felt the book would create considerable interest. In a letter written sometime in January 1897, Beardsley remarked to Smithers: "Good old Dowson. I have today re-read *La Pucelle* with infinite pleasure and shall look forward more than ever to your edition." The dependability which is implied in Beardsley's "good old Dowson" was undoubtedly ironic, for Dowson had reached a stage in his translating for Smithers in which it was generally concluded that he would be late in finishing his assignments. *La Pucelle,* on which he had started to work as early as the spring of 1896, was not ready for publication until 1899. It was probably in the winter of 1897 that Smithers, irate at the failure of his translater to get to work, made a hurried visit to Paris "to kill Dowson." Dowson, however, could be driven with neither threats nor promises; and Smithers, appreciating his value to him, continued to keep him supplied with a little money and to provide him with commissions.

Smithers' indulgence with Dowson was worth much to the ill and despairing man who would seek no favors from his relatives and friends. It is probable that Smithers had more generosity and tact in his nature than the prevailing trend of opinion concerning him would indicate. He knew of the tragedies in Dowson's life, and he knew that Dowson was ill. Some of his comments to his friends seem to prove that he did not expect Dowson to turn out grist for his mill with the regularity and despatch of a professional hack. On one occasion when a friend spoke sorrowfully about the death of the young French poet, Jean de Tinan, Smithers is reported to have ejaculated: "Damn puny Frenchmen. They can't stand anything. Look at Dowson. Is he dead?" In spite of the fact that Dowson's irregularities in fulfilling assignments on time caused him to fly into an occasional rage, he was sympathetically disposed toward his translator to the extent of indulgence.

It was Smithers' interest in Dowson's work rather than any insistence on the author's part which led to publication of *The Pierrot of the Minute.* Early in the year Smithers had decided that the play would have a sufficient appeal to warrant the manufacture of a small edition. Although Dowson never cared much for the play even while he was working on it in the autumn of 1892, he was pleased at the prospect of having the piece published, especially when he learned that Beardsley had consented to illustrate it. The two manuscripts of the play were legible, and few changes were necessary to get it ready for the press. But in spite of the small amount of work which was demanded of him, the time between Smithers' decision to issue the play and its appearance was inordinately long. On February 4, 1897, Beardsley wrote to Smithers: "I have only just remembered today that I had made pictures for a play of Dowson's." And three weeks later he inquired impatiently: "When does that foolish book 'The Pierrot of the Minute' propose to be ready?" Of course, the fact that Dowson was away from London at the time contributed to the delay in publication, but the few changes which were necessary for bringing the play into print he put off until Smithers, finally losing patience, did a considerable amount of the preparation himself. The many variations between the two manuscripts and the first edition are probably as much the result of Smithers' knack of preparing manuscripts for the press as of Dowson's revisions of the proof. When the book finally appeared, with the frontispiece, vignette, cul-de-lampe and cover design by Beardsley, it was one of the most beautiful volumes ever issued from the House of Smithers. Dowson was pleased with the elegance of the book and with the reports which came to him of its circulation, but there is no evidence to support the notion that his energy and spirit rose on account of the handsome manner in which Smithers had brought the play to London readers. He was appreciative of Smithers' eagerness to help him get his work into print, and he certainly must have felt some of the satisfaction of achievement. But for long he had failed to find more than a temporary stimulation to his energy in the publication of any of his works. Already in 1894, he had written to Smith: "One lives and talks as if the making of many books were the end and aim of all

things. I am afraid they are the straws one chews to cheat one's appetite."
By the time *The Pierrot of the Minute* appeared his convictions about the
satisfaction of bookmaking had become more pronounced.

There were objectives other than those offered by Smithers around which
his spirit rallied. He was informed about Hubert Crackanthorpe's plan to
revive *The Savoy;* and in spite of the fact that he and Crackanthorpe moved
in different circles in Paris, he was led to believe that when the new *Savoy*
appeared with Crackanthorpe as editor, there would be space for any contributions which he might submit. Crackanthorpe had printed one of his
poems in *The Albemarle,* and evidently thought highly of him as a writer.
Of the details of Crackanthorpe's plan to revive *The Savoy* he knew little.
It is unlikely that he knew that both Symons and Smithers would have
nothing to do with the new magazine, and that Grant Richards had been
asked to become the publisher. His loyalty to Smithers would have been
severely tested had the prospect for a new *Savoy* become a reality. But his
loyalty was never tested, nor was his talent ever requested, for before the
arrangements for the new magazine had ever reached any sort of finality,
Crackanthorpe committed suicide in Paris.

Decay was in the air. The novelty of Paris had worn off, and Dowson
was left with few straws on which to try to cheat his appetite. Against his
suffering and despair, he struggled in the only way he knew: the forgetfulness and false energy and lightness of spirit which absinthe produced.
Frequently during the winter of 1897, he must have experienced all of
that which his prose poem "Absinthia Taetra" records.

Green changed to white, emerald to opal . . . and that obscure night of the
soul, and the valley of humiliation, through which he stumbled were forgotten.
He saw blue vistas of undiscovered countries, high prospects, and a quiet,
caressing sea. The past shed its perfume on him, today held his hand as it
were a little child, and tomorrow shone like a white star. . . . He drank
opaline. . . . The man had known the obscure night of the soul, and lay even
now in the valley of humiliation; and the tiger menace of things to be was
red in the skies. But for a little while he had forgotten.

It is impossible to see in these lines only their dark beauty. One cannot
help feeling that this is the voice of a man who had lived in the obscure
night of the soul and the valley of humiliation, who had for a little while
forgotten. Plarr saw him intoxicated only once, but that was at the carefree time of "the Bingers" when "a young poet just down from college"
was sowing his wild oats with other young fellows. Jepson saw him drunk
often, but he was eager to inquire, "Whom didn't we see drunk?" Sherard
know him most intimately when Dowson's body and spirit were entirely

crushed, when absinthe was his only escape from suffering. It is true, as all substantial evidence indicates, that Dowson even in his early twenties drank more than his weak body could stand. It is idle to observe that he was one of the unfortunates who cannot stand up under a few ounces of brandy, and that proportionately he drank less than many a man who never could be called a drunkard. That may or may not be the case; the quantity necessary for one's escape from illness of body and soul need not be considered. It is enough to say that Dowson sought and found temporary escape from his suffering in drink. Such temporary escape only hastened his end. That he "literally drank himself to death," as some of his commentators have observed, is a statement which lacks both accuracy and charity. Dowson's malady was aggravated by his excesses; but his intemperance was a result, not a cause. He drank because he was ill.

There are no records of his movements about les Halles in search of escape, but evidently his excesses were neither sustained nor of the sort which made recovery impossible. O'Riordan, who saw him after the winter of 1897, has said that no one, with the possible exception of a specialist, could have seen in Dowson the symptoms of a dipsomaniac. Furthermore, his activities during the few remaining years of his life indicate plainly that he could still manage to keep a grip on himself for fairly long intervals. With the coming of spring, he realized that "for a little while he had forgotten" and that "the blue vistas of undiscovered countries, high prospects, and a caressing sea," were cheats, and that "nothing had changed." And instead of trying to recapture his period of forgetfulness, he began to contemplate the future with clear eyes, grim as the prospect appeared.

He had been away from England for almost two years. With the coming of spring, something of Browning's "O, to be in England, now that April's here," must have stimulated in him the desire to return to London. Much as he always insisted that he preferred Paris to London, there were times that he must have experienced a feeling of homesickness. The relentless loneliness which he had felt during his second winter in France had left him willing to see many merits in London. There were acquaintances in London with whom he could revive friendship if he wished; and there was Missie who was now almost eighteen. Then, too, in spite of Smithers' payments, he was desperately poor. Perhaps his interest in the Dock—some £600, he believed—he might now be able to recover if he set himself to it. London, under any circumstances, would not tax his income more than Paris. "Poverty can hide in London better than anywhere else," he once told Frank Harris; and although he probably held no strong convictions concerning his ability to live more cheaply in London than in Paris, his suffering during the winter just past was enough to cause him to seek a change.

By May 1897, after an absence of almost two years, he was back in London. Among his first inquiries were those about Missie who, according to the reports of his friends, had lost interest in him and was planning to marry Auguste, the waiter. An impulse which grew out of desperation led him to Sherwood Street to learn the worst. The response of Missie and Madame to his visit confirmed his fears: Missie was to be married to Auguste in September. His anguish at the discovery of what he must have felt all along is revealed in the letter he wrote to Smith soon after his return to London.

I know you must think me a fool, but I am suffering the torture of the damned. I ought to have drowned myself at Pont-Aven, or having come back to London, I ought to have had the strength of mind to have kept away. Now, if I change my rooms or go to the Arctic Pole it is only an increased intolerable Hell, and except yourself, and slightly Morse,* there is not a person I come across who realizes that I am being scorched daily, or does not put down my behavior to sheer ill humour. *Quousque tandem, Domine, quousque tandem?*

No one put down his behavior to sheer ill humor, although some of his friends who had not seen him since he had left London in the summer of 1895 were concerned about the changes which had come over him. Plarr, with whom he had been so friendly in the Rhymers' Club days and to whom he had once written: ". . . of all men I know you are the most likely to find me intelligible," passed him on Arundel Street when he was coming from Smithers' rooms:

So ill and absent-minded, so pale and, to me, forbidding did he look that I could not summon up enough courage to address him. *Cui bono?* Of course I am quite wrong, but we all know this state of feeling. . . . I had no idea that Ernest Dowson was then in London or how long he would stay. He had received a facial injury, easily remediable, which may have partly accounted for his unwillingness to revisit old and faithful friends. He was musing as usual, and seemed to see nothing, his eyes almost bulging from his head. He was wrapped in a heavy coat and had a larger cigar than of old in his mouth. I forgot the incident, which pained me at the time, as such things do.

Neither Plarr nor Dowson can be blamed for the failure to revive the old friendship. They had drifted far apart; and Dowson, sensitive to his friend's conservatism and changed order of life since he had become a

---

* He possibly meant Moore, but the spelling is unquestionably "Morse." I have been unable to find evidence of Dowson's friendship with any one named Morse.

librarian, and failing to realize that he had been largely responsible for bringing to an end a correspondence which had lasted for over five years, was unwilling to take the initiative in bringing Plarr back as a friend. He felt that he had lost caste, and until Plarr and others were willing to re-assure him that all was at it once had been, he would make no advances.

A morbid sensitivity, which grew out of his physical condition and the realization that his life in the past few years had been different from that of his old friends, kept him from finding the companionship in London for which he yearned. He who at one time had been impatient to leave Stepney in order to be with his friends at the Crown and the Café Royal now tried to avoid the places where he might encounter friends who, he felt, might pity him. Despite the fact that save for a brief time he had always been indifferent to his appearance, he surely realized that after his two years in France his features and dress were scarcely those of a healthy and prosperous Londoner. Sometime after Mrs. Atherton's departure from Pont-Aven— and possibly at her suggestion—he had procured a set of false teeth, but they were so ill fitting that they annoyed him. "The clip and grip of them had caused him torture," he is reported to have said, "but what was that?" "It was true that he could scarcely speak while wearing them, but that, too, was a mere trifle. Also, he could not masticate, or even entertain his food at all," said Rosamund Langbridge, "but that, too, might have been worse. But when it came to smoking, and he found that he could not hold his pipe—that, said Dowson, finished it, and he 'threw the teeth away.' " Toothless, with a scar on his forehead which had been received in a fight, and with obvious signs of ill health on his lined and pallid face, he was scarcely able to feel completely at ease at the better places in the West End in spite of his indifference to his appearance. Then, too, he coughed at times in a way which caused others to watch him with alarm and pity. His clothes were of the sort which were far more appropriate in the cheap cafés around les Halles than on the Strand. Though he was not totally aware of the shabbiness of his appearance, his sensitivity led him to detect a certain constraint in some of his erstwhile acquaintances.

It was scarcely *nostalgie de la boue* which drove him to the cabmen's shelters and to the East End during his last years in London. Limehouse had never detained him for long in the years in which he had worked at Bridge Dock; in fact, he had always been impatient to leave its boundaries in order to get to a section in which people dressed well, spoke well, and lived well. And with the passage of years, he no doubt still preferred Yvette Guilbert to Kitty Gresham, and Henekey's back-parlor on the Strand to the ill-lighted, reeking pubs of Poplar. In his nature there was no fondness for squalor. It is true that he was indifferent to material luxuries, but he never sought squalor for its own sake. Possibly during his early twenties, when he was caught by the idea of *la vie de Bohème,* he tried to cultivate deliberately some of the negligence of garb which he associated with the French artists he admired, but in the later years of his life, his apparent fondness for cabmen's shelters and cheap pubs was forced on him by poverty and sensitivity.

Save for a few brief periods of attempted rehabilitation, from 1897 until his death he went to the green cabmen's shelters because in their dimly lighted interiors he was conscious of neither his poverty nor "the intolerable pity of his friends." The habitués of these make-shift refuges from cold and loneliness were not, as a general rule, the dregs of London; most of them were cabbies whose lives were probably more exemplary than those of some of the loungers in the cafés around Piccadilly; and despite the fact that the talk and food dispensed were scarcely refined, there was little that was unwholesome about the cabmen's shelters. Within their small confines, Dowson could sit in the warmth of a pot-bellied stove, eat bowls of gravy soup and coarse bread, and find a sort of respite from his loneliness with men who were neither reproachful nor pitying.

There were a few of his old friends whom he did not suspect of pity or of attention to his condition and welfare. Arthur Moore, though impatient with him for his failure to contribute his share of *Adrian Rome,* was always kindly. And Lionel Johnson, who saw men's minds and souls rather than their ill-kept, suffering bodies, was also one to whom Dowson went. Johnson, himself, was rapidly declining in health. He was about to enter that stage in his brief life to which Plarr referred as the "mythic phase." His fondness for company and lengthy discussion had waned somewhat, though of Dowson's company he apparently did not tire. There had been no correspondence during Dowson's absence, but the bond of friendship had not been broken. When Dowson returned, although they were both changed men, they picked up their friendship where it had been interrupted. There is no record of what the poets discussed on the nights of their reunions; but in spite of the fact that they both probably drank more than was good for them, the renewed friendship was more constructive than harmful to them both. To Dowson, at least, the evenings spent with Lionel Johnson were more salutary and agreeable than were he to have gone to one of the dives in Limehouse. Although there is no evidence to support the surmise other than the fact that Johnson always had a great admiration for Dowson's verse, it is possible that Johnson, who had read *Verses* in his friend's absence, encouraged him to get another volume ready for the press. Even to

the end of his life, Johnson, like his poetry, conveyed a quality which
Yeats referred to as "hard energy"; and it is possible that some of this
quality was brought over to Dowson on those long nights that they talked
together in Johnson's ill-kept rooms in Lincoln's Inn Fields.

Dowson had another friend in London who had energy of a different
sort from Johnson's and with whom he was generally at ease—his publisher,
Leonard Smithers. Smithers encouraged him to settle down to work, not
only by assurances of rewards for the fulfillment of assignments, but also
by his forthright friendliness. In Smithers, Dowson must have found a
companion with whom he could feel free to look and do as he pleased
without being made an object of pity and reproach. The friendship between
them after Dowson's return from Paris undoubtedly had disadvantages to
Dowson, for the publisher lived a life which was conducive to neither good
health nor good reputation. The nights which Dowson spent at Smithers'
home were occasionally devoted to such harmless pastimes as chess and
cards, but more generally there were heavy drinking and debilitating excesses for which Smithers was notorious. Unwholesome as the publisher's
influence on Dowson was, he was by no means responsible for the irregularities and enfeebled condition of his contributor. It is only those who find
difficulty in explaining the real reasons for Dowson's decline who point to
Leonard Smithers as his chief perverter. Although Smithers undoubtedly
helped Dowson to hasten his end, it is unfair to point to him as the principal cause of Dowson's suffering. Dowson's health and habits were already
pretty well determined before he became one of the Smithers people. Perhaps he would have been more continently disposed at an East End music
hall; but when Smithers, who had many acquaintances on whom to depend
for an evening's revel, was hospitable to Dowson, who was ill and lonely,
he is not to be blamed for the effects of his well-intended friendliness.
Furthermore, while associating with Smithers, Dowson was never permitted to forget for long that he had literary obligations to fulfill.

It was soon after Dowson's return to London that Oscar Wilde finished
his sentence in prison. On May 19, 1897, he was released after a confine-
ment of two years. From the time that Dowson had met Wilde at Herbert
Horne's rooms in the Fitzroy settlement, he had admired Wilde. In fact,
when Wilde, shortly after the meeting at Horne's, invited Dowson to have
luncheon with him at the Café Royal, he made no effort to conceal his
pleasure. On the day that Wilde was convicted at the Old Bailey, he had
accompanied Sherard to the scene of the trial, and it is probable that he
was with Sherard in the courtroom when the verdict was read. Although
he had never visited Wilde during his imprisonment and had never written

him any letters, he had in no way lost his admiration for the brilliant play-wright and poet on account of his misfortune. Long since indifferent to his own reputation and eager to show his loyalty, he learned of Wilde's refuge on Oakley Street and visited him there before he took flight for France.

Wilde received him hospitably, not only because he was happy to have anyone show kindness to him at the time, but also because he had a sincere admiration for Dowson's genius. He had told Sherard, among others, that of the younger poets Dowson's work pleased him greatly. Then, too, Wilde had considerable respect for what he believed to be Dowson's erudition. The younger poet's handling of Latin phrases had caused Wilde to believe that Dowson was not only a master of the Latin language, but an authority on Roman culture history as well. He was familiar with Dowson's transla-tions from the French, and he liked them. He must have been startled to see some of the changes which had come over the young poet since he had had luncheon with him at the Café Royal, but he was willing to believe that he too was different from the man Dowson knew at the Fitzroy settle-ment.

Despite the changes which each detected in the other, and perhaps on account of them, they were drawn together. Both of them were lonely and in ill repute, although for totally different reasons. It was their loneliness as well as their common interest in literature which drew them together in the late spring of 1897 and provided Dowson for a time with one of the few friendships which his later years afforded. When Wilde went to France to take up temporary residence at Bernaval, Dowson, feeling that he could be of service to Wilde in his attempt to regain his ambition and spirit, made the crossing in early June to take quarters at Arques so that he could be near his friend. The fact of the matter was that Dowson needed care and friendship far more than did Wilde at the time, for the latter's spirit was not so completely broken after his release from prison as some of his biographers have stated. In a letter to Davray written from Dieppe soon after he had gone to visit Wilde, Dowson reported: "He is in excellent health and spirits . . . even a pessimist like myself is infected. . . ."

It was while they were in Dieppe that Dowson tried to press on Wilde the necessity for acquiring a "more wholesome taste." Wilde finally agreed to accompany his friend to a brothel. The results have been recorded in variant ways, but as Yeats recalled the episode from hearsay:

They emptied their pockets onto the café table, and though there was not much, there was enough if both heaps were put into one. Meanwhile the news had spread, and they set out accompanied by a cheering crowd. Arrived at their destination, Dowson and the crowd remained outside, and presently Wilde returned. He said in a low voice to Dowson, "The first in these ten years, and it will be the last. . . ." . . . and then aloud so that the crowd might hear him, "But tell it in England, for it will entirely restore my character."

Some of the details of this story are subject to question, including the statement that Dowson had to contribute money to the experiment. All evidence indicates that Wilde at the time was under no necessity to depend on advances from Dowson. In fact, it was generally the other way round. With the generous permission of Captain Vyvyan Holland, Wilde's son, I quote in full a series of twelve hitherto unpublished letters from Wilde to Dowson in which the course of their brief friendship is clearly traced. The first letter was written soon after Wilde took up residence in France.

de la part de
M. Sebastian Melmoth
Hotel de la Plage
Bernaval-sur-Mer
Dieppe
(June 1897)

Cher Monsieur le Poête,
    It was most kind of you coming to see me, and I thank you sincerely and grateful [*sic*] for your pleasant companionship and the many gentle ways by which you recalled to me that, once, at any rate, I was a Lord of Language and had myself the soul of a poet. Of course I am lonely after the departure of my three friends—le Poête, le Philosophe, and le Peintre—but I have no mourning suit, so all I can do is to wear my red tie 'with a difference'—!
    I am breakfasting with the Stannards at Dieppe on Wednesday and will be at the Café Suisse at 3.15. If you happen to be there it would be kind of you to introduce me to Jean who has the boats or knows about them. I have a wild desire for the sea. I feel that water purifies, and that in nature there is, for me at any rate healing power.
    Of course don't put yourself out to come in from your Forest—but if you happen to be in Dieppe, I would like to be introduced to Jean.
    There is a sea-mist today, and my fishermen have not come up the chalk ravine in search for me. I long to get your poems. The sea's 'Restless chime' makes me hungry for poetry.
                    Sincerely yours

OSCAR WILDE

Dieppe.
Monday: 11 Juin 97

Dear Ernest:

I must see you: so I propose to breakfast at St. Martin L'Eglise tomorrow at 11.30 and you must come: take a voiture and be there. I want to have a poet to talk to, as I have had lots of bad news since you left me. Do try, like a good chap, to be there, and wear a *blue* tie. I want to be consoled.

SEBASTIAN MELMOTH

From M. Sebastian Melmoth

[*Dieppe*]
Monday, June 21st. (1897)

My dear Ernest,

I arrived, not safe, but very unsafe, at Bernaval in pouring rain at 10.30. There was only one lantern to the voiture, so one wheel of the Carriage was always in the air. On my arrival I found André Gide who had come from Paris to see me.

Madame Bonnet made me drink *two* hot grogs, so I came to life at 11.15 and had a wonderful evening. André left yesterday at eleven oc. He was most charming and had heard of you and your work.

All my invitations to my Jubilee Garden Party were issued yesterday through Marcel, the little grandson of Madam Darcy of the Café de la Paix, Bernaval-le-Grand. He supervised the invitations and struck off several names on the perfectly right grounds that he did not like them. The list was strictly limited to twelve—as the garden only holds *six* at the most, I felt that *twelve* would be sufficient. I hate crowds. Today I go to order strawberries.

I still hope you may come. A green coat always lights up a garden so well. I intend to wear my turquoise coloured shirt.

Finally I have found my overcoat. A dear woman at Belleville picked it up on the road. So I now *"know Joseph"* again.

Wednesday at any rate, at 3 oc. Café Suisse. Wear your blue tie.

Yours

OSCAR

Café Suisse,
Dieppe. (1897)

Dear Ernest,

I arrived safe under a cold white moon, at 1 oc. in the morning. My servant was asleep, so I woke him up and enquired about his early life, which, as I expected, was quite uninteresting.

There is a fatality about our being together that is astounding, or rather quite probable.

Had I stayed at Arques I should have given up all hopes of ever separating from you. Why are you so persistently and perversely wonderful?

Do I see you tomorrow? Try to come over. I hope Thompson and Socrates (*his* Socrates) will come. It was delightful meeting Varsity men again. I like them both so much. But I intend to send them both to Oxford, especially Thompson.

Come with vine leaves in your hair.

I suppose I shall see you in ten minutes from this. I am looking out for the green costume that goes so well with your hyacinth locks.

I decided this morning to take a 'Pernot.' The result was marvellous. At 8.30 I was dead. Now I am alive, and all is perfect, except for your absence.

Tout à toi
SEBASTIAN MELMOTH*

Café Suisse, Dieppe. (1897)
Wednesday 6:30

Dear Ernest,

I write a little line, whose only excuse is its entire illegibility, to tell you how charming you are (at Bernaval) and how much I like *your* friend, *and mine*, the dear Achille. He is a most noble and splendid fellow, and I feel happy to have his esteem and friendship.

Tonight I am going to read your poems—your lovely lyrics—words with wings you write always—it is an exquisite gift—and fortunately rare in an age whose prose is more poetic than its poetry. Do come soon and see me.

The youthful costermonger returns on Friday with the price of a pony and cart in his pocket. I have given him a costume idea, but I hope he will survive it—the effects up to this, are not so promising as I could wish. But he means well.

His calling you Ernest was awful. It is the effect of vegetables on the mind.

I am now going to write poetry, as soon as the 'coster' leaves us. Poor fellow, I hope he will be all right.

You and Achille and Achille's friend and I must *all* be at Bernaval together. I am making arrangements.

Give to Achille my sincere friendship; you have it, and other things, always

S.M.

Café Suisse, Dieppe. (1897)

My dear Ernest,

Do come here at once: Monsieur Meyer is presiding over a morning meal of absinthe and we want you.

---

* A comparison of the implications in this letter and others in the series with those in the letters which Wilde wrote from Cannes early in 1898 to Jerome Pollitt supports the conclusion that they are Wilde mannerisms. Mr. J. Harlin O'Connell, who has the original Wilde-Pollitt correspondence, insists that Wilde never so much as saw Pollitt.

I am a wreck of course, but la belle soeur is like the moon.
You were wonderful and charming all last night.

Yours

OSCAR

(Dieppe)

Tuesday August 9. (1897)

My dear Ernest,

I send you your letters. I have not read them! but I have cut open the envelopes on account of the postal arrangements. I also send you your cahiers.

I hope you will be able to send me what you owe me in a few days, as I have no money. Your bill with Monsieur Bonnet was £11 and then in Dieppe of course there were huge expenses, and I also lent you money—it comes to £19—which I hope to receive within a week as I cannot pay M. Bonnet and he is getting offensively tedious.

I have lost many pleasures in life—one is the pleasure of playing the hosts's part. I have not the means: nor do I know how to live at all.

Vincent O'Sullivan came here on Sunday and dined: he spoke of you with much affection, in which I joined I need not tell you.

Yours

O.W.

Bernaval-sur-Mer

pres Dieppe

August 18 (1897)

My dear Ernest,

I think your translating *Aphrodite* a capital idea: I do hope you will get someone to make good terms for you—why not Smithers? The Bacchic, the Dionysiac!

You should make a lot of money by royalties—the book if well published, might be a great success.

Bobbie Ross is here with me, and Sherard left on Saturday. Smithers is devoted, and breakfasts here every Monday. I like him immensely. He is a most interesting and, in some respects, a charming personality.

I have not yet finished my poem—but I hope to do so soon. I wrote four splendid stanzas yesterday. I am going to try to get a lot money for it from the *New York World*. Robert Sherard will, he says, manage it for me.

Vincent O'Sullivan has been here twice to dine. I *now* like him; at first I loathed him.

As for the cheque I know, dear Ernest, you will send it as soon as you can. I scramble on somehow and hope to survive the season. After that,—, rags and haschish!

Yours

O.W.

Villa Giudice,
Posilipo
Naples.
Monday (October, 1897)

Dear Ernest,

Thank you very much for your nice letter—my poem is finished at last—and is now with Smithers. I have added a good deal to it.

What you owe me is between £18 and £20—whichever you choose—I am thinking of telegraphing to you today to wire it, or as much as you can afford, through Cook's Agency. They wire money like angels—and cheques and P.O. orders are difficult to cash. If I can find the money I will—for at present I am quite penniless—and Smithers has not behaved well to me at all—I wanted a paltry £20 in advance for my poem—secure on its sale and the American rights—and for three weeks he has put me off with silly promises—never realised of course—I feel it, because when he offered me the entire profits in a moment of dramatic generosity I refused to take his offer and insisted on his sharing half. Also I have refused an offer from "The Musician" to publish the poem as I felt that previous publication of the poem would spoil Smithers' edition. So I made all these sacrifices and at the end he refuses a petty sum in advance. Smithers is personally charming, but at present I simply am furious with him and intend to remain so—till he sends me the money.

I am delighted to hear you finished your novel and are writing stories. I have begun today the tragedy in one-act I told you about at Bernaval with the passages about clothes in it. I find the architecture of art difficult now, it requires sustained effort but I must do it.

The Neapolitan papers have turned out to be worst form of American journalism. They fill columns with me and write interviews of a fictitious character. I wish the world would let me alone and really I thought that at Naples I should be at peace. I dare say they will tire of this nonsense soon.

I hope you will do a good thing with 'Aphrodite' and that when you make lots of money, you will be able to find time to come to Naples—which I know you would like. The museum is full as you know of lovely Greek bronzes—the only bother is that they all walk about the town at night. However, one gets delicately accustomed to that—and there are compensations.

Yours

OSCAR WILDE

Hotel Royal des Etrangers
Naples October. 19. 1897
Tuesday.

My dear Ernest,

Why you should have given Smithers the £10 to send to me I cannot understand. You should have sent it to me yourself. I have heard nothing about it. I asked you in my telegram to wire what you owe me through Cook; had you done this, or sent me a portion of it, I would not be in the absurd position in which I am placed. There is no reason that Smithers should receive the money—the person to receive it is myself.

The whole business is most irritating and silly. I am now going to telegraph to Smithers.

If you see Davray as of course you are sure to do, will you tell him that I have received no drawing of any kind from Hermann (?) and that consequently I have to bring out my poem without design of any kind, as I cannot wait too long.

Later on if the poem is a succes I may bring out an adorned edition—but I know nothing of Hermann's views at all.

Do try and pull yourself together, and close an annoying money-account— a thing I hate, because it is so so painful to me.

                                                            OSCAR

> *Villa Giudice*
> *Posilipo*
> *Naples.*
> *(October, 1897)*

My dear Ernest,

I have just received a letter from Smithers dated *last* Monday; he says nothing in it of having received any money from you for me. From the date of your letter you seem to have entrusted him with this £10 on Saturday or Friday last.

I have written to him again on the subject. Would you kindly write yourself? There seems something strange—almost improbable—in his retaining money entrusted to him for me.

However, Psychology is in its infancy as a science. I hope, in the interests of art it will always remain so.

                                            Yours
                                                            OSCAR

> *Villa Giudice*
> *Posilipo*
> *Naples*
> *(October, 1897)*

Dear Ernest,

The fault was the fault of the post. They took 12 days to deliver Smithers' letter.

I am much obliged to you for what you have sent me. I am afraid I wrote irritably to you—but I have been terribly worried by the want of money—the most sordid and hungry of wants.

I hope your translation will be a great success—tho' of course I like you to do your own original work best.

The negotiations over my poem still drag on as yet—no offer and no money in consequence. Still I keep on building castles of fairy gold in the air—we Celts always do.

Pray let me know how you are getting on in Paris—and whom you see.

Yours
OSCAR

I have retaken my own name—as my incognito was absurd.

Although Dowson's correspondence with Wilde during their brief period of friendship cannot be produced, Wilde's letters do much to shed light on Dowson's movements and condition at the time. It is plain that he underwent a period of temporary rehabilitation during the early summer, for Wilde, despite his recent experiences, was scarcely given to consorting with those whose appearance offended his sensibilities. The picture of Dowson and Wilde, two outcasts, slinking into the ill-smelling waterfront cafés because they felt that neither their reputation nor appearance would permit their admission to better places, is completely refuted by Wilde's letters to Dowson during June 1897. Wilde had what he called a Jubilee Garden Party at the Café de la Paix at Bernaval, to which he invited twelve of his friends, including Dowson. Every detail in the letters indicates that they lived pretty well during their brief association, and that they both spent some time with literary projects.

It is possible that Wilde tired of Dowson's inability to pay for his share of the evenings they spent together; at any rate, a strain had grown between them which by August caused Dowson to avoid Wilde's company. But during the following October, when Wilde had gone to Naples and Dowson had returned to Paris, the breach was closed, for by that time Dowson had sent Wilde some of the money he owed him, and Wilde was solicitous about how Dowson was getting on in Paris with his work. Although their intimate association lasted for six weeks at the most, it had more advantages than disadvantages to both of them in spite of the fact that the friendship ended in discord. Much as Wilde disliked his friend's dilatory manner of paying his debts, and much as Dowson deplored some of Wilde's tastes, they admired each other's poetry and enjoyed each other's company at a time when they were both in sore need of friendship.

Dowson returned to London sometime in July, for what particular reason inquiry has not disclosed. His experiences in Dieppe evidently had done little to restore his health and spirits. "In July, 1897, he called on us, dined and stayed the night," wrote Plarr.

Hardly a word could be drawn from him. He seemed frozen to stone. It was dreadful. As a family we were longing for sympathy, for congratulations. We had a charming new house; our little child was at the pretty age of five; I had been appointed to my life's work. He nodded wearily in reply to every question. He would tell me nothing of himself. I have no sort or recollection of how we got through that evening. Did he go out—did he stay at home? I forget.

Next morning I left him in my book-room. I was going for the first time, if I remember rightly, to visit my official Library as Librarian elect. It was an exciting occasion. Would he come too? Oh no!' He waved the subject aside as though he were an Indian General repressing the family poet. I left him among my old books, of which he used to be so fond. At about four o'clock I returned. He had smoked innumerable cigarettes: they lay all around him in saucers and trays. And with dreaming eyes he was viewing my little child, who stood in front of him and seemed puzzled by his demeanour. He appeared to be looking through her, while she gazed at him. It was the child whose birth he had hymned.

Very shortly afterwards, he arose briskly enough, borrowed a new suit of clothes, of which I rarely possess an exemplar, and announced curtly that he was going yachting off the coast of Ireland. I congratulated him on his fashionable occupation. He never smiled, seemed to be painfully repressing something— he had seemed ill at ease and in a state of self-repression throughout his visit— shook hands, briefly, in a most matter-of-fact way, left no exact indication of his future whereabouts, was gone!

Plarr's observations bear out those of several of Dowson's friends who saw him during the summer and early autumn of 1897. Lonely he doubtless was, but when he managed to bolster up sufficient assurance to lead him to visit his old friends of the Rhymers', he seemed in what Plarr called a state of self-repression. His brief period of rehabilitation while he was with Wilde in Dieppe had restored some of his confidence in mingling with old acquaintances, but they, like Plarr, found him ill at ease, and nodding wearily in reply to their inquiries. It is possible that after he had taken the first step to revive friendship, he detected what seemed to him "intolerable pity."

That he went yachting off the coast of Ireland after his short visit with the Plarrs is unlikely, but during late July and August he spent at least six weeks in Limerick. Sometime in August he wrote to Plarr: "The climate is rather trying and utterly destructive of all energy. But it is a dear country. . . . I quite understand [Lionel] Johnson's enthusiasm and if I wasn't already so wedded to France I should feel inclined to take up my abode in it."

It was from Fairy Hill, the house at which he stayed near Parteen in Limerick, that he wrote to Henry Davray:

Mon Cher Ami,

I wonder if you are still in Paris. I have been staying with friends here for the last six weeks & remain sometime longer. It is a charming place and very wild country & as there is little society I have plenty of time for work. I am writing now to ask if you would mind putting me in communication with the Mercure de France as I shall not be in Paris myself for another month, perhaps. I enclose a letter which Pierre Louys sent me respecting a translation of "Aphrodite." I wrote to him telling him I would undertake the translation with pleasure but I have not heard any more from him. I should be much obliged then if you would tell Vallette that I am ready to translate the book at once. Perhaps, you would advise me as to the "conditions" I should propose, or obtain an offer for me from Vallette. However, any "conditions" could stand over until I come to Paris, if you can obtain an assurance that my translation will be published. I hope this is not troubling you overmuch but I know that you are often at the Mercure de France and I have only met Vallette once. I am anxious to do the book even if the "conditions" are not good. Oscar Wilde thinks a translation by me ought to do well.

My own plans are only vague in the matter of dates. But I expect to come to Paris in October or November & shall take an apartment for a year & furnish it, although I do not intend to spend all the winter there. It will be charming if you and your wife, to whom convey all my compliments will assist me in the matter of furnishing. Autrement je serai sur d'acheter rien que des choses absolument inutiler.

I hope to have two volumes (roman & Nouvelles) in the press by the beginning of next year. I trust you are both well & that I may see you soon. I stayed with Victor Plarr whilst in London. He & his wife were delighted at having met you.

Bien a toi,

ERNEST DOWSON

Who the friends were with whom he stayed at Fairy Hill he failed to state, and Rosemond Langbridge, who recalled seeing him while he was in Ireland, spoke only of a comrade "who lived some miles outside the city of the Broken Treaty." It was at the home of one of the friends of Dowson's "comrade" that Rosamond Langbridge first saw him. "I remember perfectly the air he brought with him into the house," she wrote in *T. P.'s Weekly* on January 30, 1915,

as of some gracious gentleness which the buffetings of Fate had beaten back and crushed into himself. He seemed to shelter himself against the friend he brought with him, like some wind-tortured plant beneath a sturdy tree. His shyness, and that sense of pain that he brought with him, made one's heart ache, and I remember now with a mature remorse that as I sat by him I gave vent to some childish "smartness" which made him wince, not because it was aimed at him, but rather because it came from a region of crude flippancy that his bruised soul had shrunk away from long ago.

He sat crouched down in his chair, and in his face was the luminous pallor of the drug taker; but in his eyes, the eyes of a woman in pain, there was the light that never shone on land or sea. What eyes had Mr. Plarr himself to say that Dowson's eyes were merely "amiable"? He spoke very seldom, and then in the subdued voice of one to whom the world about him has become a troubled dream; but he listened with shy interest to the table talk, and when his buoyant friend broke out into some Celtic witticism, Dowson's face lit up.

Dowson's hands were frail, but his brillantly orange thumb and forefinger— he was a prodigious smoker of cigarettes—leapt to his eyes as their most striking characteristic, before one took stock of their fluttering nervousness. . . . It was when he laughed—the laugh of a shy boy—under his breath that one made the discovery that this young man with the poet's lips had not a tooth in his head. . . .

Until there are more adequate records on which to base a conclusion, it is impossible to determine what took Dowson to Ireland in the summer of 1897. The yachting cruise of which he spoke to Plarr has no evidence, save his expressed intention, to support it. Were it to be established that Lionel Johnson made a trip to Ireland in the summer of 1897, it might be suggested that Dowson went along with him for companionship, or paid him a visit. Johnson, however, spent most of that summer reading, scribbling, and drinking in his rooms in Lincoln's Inn Fields—or so it would seem from the reports of his acquaintances who are hesitant about committing themselves on Johnson's movements at the time. Desmond Flower has written to me that "Dowson had friends in Ireland" but that he "had not identified the friends." Others, including Michael Holland, who knew him well at the time, have been unable to determine the exact reasons for his sojourn in Ireland and the friends with whom he stayed.* The only conjecture which can be offered is that Johnson's enthusiasm for Ireland had caught Dowson, and he, eager to keep moving about to distract himself from his ills, sought in Ireland the respite which novel scenes afforded. The interest in things Irish which Jepson detected on the evenings which he spent with the Rhymers' Club may have had some influence on Dowson's decision to seek sanctuary in Limerick. Then, too, the nameless

---

* An undated letter from Fairy Hill to Elkin Mathews, now in the possession of J. Harlin O'Connell, has a return address in care of I. De Courcy MacDonnell, Esq. MacDonnell, according to Conal O'Riordan, was the Librarian at Marsh's Dublin. He admired Dowson's work sufficiently to order six copies of *Verses*.

comrade whom he had possibly met on his nightly rounds in London, or even in Paris, may have encouraged him to try Limerick instead of returning to Brittany.

He was in urgent need of distraction in the late summer of 1897, for he was not only oppressed by an increasing life-weariness, but there was also an event in the offing which he felt he could not meet unflinchingly. Missie was to be married in September to Auguste. From the time that he had learned that her love was pledged to another, he had tried to build up sufficient resignation to take the blow without wincing. Dieppe, Arques, and then Limerick afforded him detachment and occasional distraction; and when the blow fell, he felt its impact at a distance. He was too broken in spirit to attend the ceremony, but at his earnest request Arthur Moore went to the wedding, bearing Dowson's gift to the bride.

The years of waiting, filled with hope and anguish, were spent. The wedding did not come as a shock to him: it was only a confirmation of what he knew in his more discerning moments was ultimately going to happen. That which he had long dreaded had come to pass. Missie was lost to him forever. The effect of her marriage on him was without grave consequences. If his poem "To A Lost Love," which was to appear in *Decorations,* is in any way a revelation of his state of mind at the time of Missie's marriage, he was resigned to her union with another. It is a persistent though ill-founded notion that his life was broken up by his unhappy love, but there was no great heightening of his suffering and despair in the months immediately following the wedding. His letter to Smith, which had been written soon after he learned that Missie was to be married to Auguste in which he ended, *"Quousque tandem, Domine, quousque tandem?"* indicated that he knew the worst and was suffering, as he said, "the torture of the damned." By the time of the wedding, however, he had fortified his spirit to the extent of laying plans to furnish an apartment in Paris and to settle down to work on Pierre Louÿs' *Aphrodite.*

Those who knew him in only his late years and were unaware of the circumstances surrounding his life before Missie's marriage were misled by reports and by Symons' article in *The Savoy* to believe that all of Dowson's suffering could be readily traced to his unhappy love affair. Guy Thorne, in a brief sketch of Dowson in *T. P.'s Weekly* for July 1913, gave momentum to the belief that Dowson was a victim of unrequited love.

There was a "lounge" [he wrote] in the center of the Strand called "The Bun Shop," kept by an old actor who played with Ellen Terry, and who merged the artist in the publican, where poor Ernest Dowson, the poet, was constantly seen toward the end of his short and tragic life. I knew him well. Very few of us had then read his poems or suspected the hidden genius which was to flower in such dainty splendor after his death. He seemed a lost creature, a youthful ghost strayed amongst the haunts of men, an object of pity. Pale, emaciated, in clothes that were almost ragged, poor Ernest flittered from bar to bar in search of someone with whom to talk. When he found a friend, his face would light up with a singular and penetrating sweetness that made one forget his untidiness—to use no other word—which verged on offense. He was never penniless, was always the first to pay for others, and when the drink was served he would sometimes furtively take a little gold cross from his waistcoat pocket and dip it in the glass before he drank. Someone who did not know the circumstances said, "Ernest, were you ever in love?" The poet answered in the words of Voltaire. "Vous me demandez si j'ai aimé: oui! c'est une historie singulière et terrible." While I live I shall never forget the wan smile, the haunted look in the poor fellow's eyes.

There is no doubt that to the habitués of "The Bun Shop" and to many others who knew little of his life Dowson's tragedy was one of unrequited love. He himself did nothing to change the impression. Even after Missie's marriage, he tried to defend her and his love for her. In *Contemporary Portraits,* Frank Harris reported a conversation which he had had with Dowson soon after Missie's marriage. "Fancy," said Harris to him, "that little French girl [Harris was misinformed about her nationality] calling forth such a passion in you! It astounds me that you can't see her as she was and is with nothing to her but the beauty of youth. She had nothing in her, Dowson, or she'd never have preferred a waiter to you."

"What did Keats see in Fanny Brawne?" interrupted Dowson wearily.

"But don't you know," continued Harris, "that you'd only have to take hold of yourself for a month and go out among the better class girls in London to find someone infinitely superior to her in body and mind and soul; someone worthy of you and your genius. For God's sake, man, give life a chance to show you what jewels it holds!"

"I've lost the one pearl," said Dowson. "What's life good for but to be lived to the full; the whole meaning of it is in the moment when you reach the ultimate in feeling and can throw life away as meaning nothing higher. To me passion is the way to Nirvana, love the supreme sacrament, the perfect chrysolite. . . ."

"You can find a dozen finer gems, incomparably more lustrous, more—" interrupted Harris.

"More to your taste, I dare say—" said Dowson, "not to mine. Can't you see that I loved her just because you and the others could find nothing in her; no beauty in her curving white neck and the way the dark tendrils curled on it; no sweetness in the pure eyes and mocking gay laughter:

ERNEST DOWSON

(*From a drawing by Charles Conder*)

nothing. But I saw, and I knew that she was mine, made for me and me alone to love and possess; can't you see that the less she was yours, man, the more she was mine; all mine—mine alone; no one else could know her and her shy, elusive grace. Ah, God, how did I lose her? Why?"

The reports which possibly came to his ears about Missie after her marriage found him generally willing to speak in her defense. According to rumor, her marriage brought her little happiness. Auguste, who had been a tailor before he came into the employ of Joseph Foltinowicz, began to find the restaurant unprofitable and only a makeshift until he could establish himself in his original trade. A Continental tailor in London, however, had little to expect by way of patronage, and it was not long before he and Missie were brought to the realization that a restaurant at least provided its keepers with meals. Stubbornly Auguste kept his tailor's shop in the rooms above what had once been Poland. Two children were born to them who apparently did little to bring happiness into a poverty-stricken home. It is possible that Missie rued her choice, for report has it that she left Auguste and Sherwood Street before 1900. Another rumor would seem to indicate that she and Auguste, realizing that his tailoring business would never flourish, left Soho to take up residence in one of the industrial suburbs where Auguste secured employment in a mill. The most sinister gossip which has circulated is that Missie, tiring of her husband, left him to make her living as best she could, and that she died in 1910 in the free ward of a London hospital as the result of a crude abortion. Such a report possibly had its origin with those of Dowson's acquaintances who felt that they needed complete corroboration for their original estimate of her character.

The chagrin which heightened Dowson's anguish at Missie's marriage to Auguste provoked no expressed resentment toward her and the man of her choice. His spirit was never avenging. To his friends, he was more inclined to defend her and her choice than to deplore her taste in marrying a waiter. Those who knew him intimately during the months following Missie's marriage are as one in their belief that he was willing to shoulder much of the blame for the unhappy outcome of his love affair. He often spoke of the deserts of his own indecision and his inability to cope with the problems which beset him. He probably asked himself, as did Philip Rainham in *A Comedy of Masks,* "Whether in love, as in life, his error had not been the same; and his passion, like the rest, a thing without conviction, and thereby foredoomed to fail." Although he never said disagreeable things about Missie, Madame, and Auguste to his friends, with the passage of time he probably was willing to agree in part with those who had told him that his love for the girl was little more than a sentimental attachment, and that she was not "the one pearl" which life had to offer him. He was never willing to confirm openly the opinions of his friends concerning the nature of his attachment and to state that he possibly had been blinded in his judgment of her character; but in *Decorations,* his last volume which appeared in 1899, he included a brief piece of lyric prose which surely had some relationship to his attitude toward Adelaide in the years following her marriage. "The Princess of Dreams," which was probably written in the autumn following the wedding, may readily be interpreted as more than an exercise in poetic prose.

THE PRINCESS OF DREAMS

Poor legendary princess! In her enchaunted tower of ivory, the liberator thought that she awaited him.

For once in a dream he had seen, as they were flowers de luce, the blue lakes of her eyes, had seemed to be enveloped in a tangle of her golden hair.

And he sought her through the countless windings of her forest for many moons, sought her through the morasses, sparing not his horse nor his sword. On his way he slew certain evil magicians and many of his friends, so that at his journey's end his bright sword was tarnished and his comeliness swart with mud. His horses he had not spared: their bones made a white track behind him in the windings of the forest: but he still bore her ransom, all the costly, graceful things stored in a cypress chest: massed pearls and amethysts and silks from Samarcand, Valance of Venice, and fine tapestry of Tyre. All these he brought with him to the gates of her ivory tower.

Poor legendary princess.

For he did not free her and the fustian porter took his treasure and broke his stained sword in two.

And who knows where he went, horseless and disarmed, through the morasses and the dark windings of her forest under the moonless night, dreaming of those blue lakes which were flowers de luce, her eyes? Who knows? For the fustian porter says nothing, being slow of wit.

But there are some who say that she had no wish to be freed, and that those flowers de luce, her eyes, are a stagnant, dark pool, that her glorious golden hair was only long enough to reach her postern gate.

Some say, moreover, that her tower is not of ivory and that she is not even virtuous nor a princess.

Even were this allegory to be entirely rejected as evidence that he was finally willing to believe that the tower was not of ivory and that Missie was neither virtuous nor a princess, the fact remains that during the months immediately following her marriage he settled down to work. Missie could not be entirely forgotten, but in his more deliberative moments he must have realized that the blow which had finally fallen was better for his peace of mind than the tormenting expectancy of it. Her marriage, in spite of the immediate suffering it caused him, freed him from the shackles of uncertainty which had bruised his spirit for years. As with Seefang in his story "The Eyes of Pride," "he began to think of his work, and was surprised how utterly he had neglected it. . . . He went to bed, vowing to make amends."

In so far as his energy permitted, he made amends. By late September he was in France, for London since Missie's marriage had become more tormenting to him than it had been before. It was probably soon after his departure from London that he wrote to Davray:

> *Hotel de Chateau d'Arques*
> *Arques-la-Bataille*
> *Seine, Inferieure*

Mon cher Ami,

Je suis ici pendant quelque temps en train de reposer apres le train de Londres. Conder est egalement ici et nous travailons tout les deaux. Il a deja fait plusieurs charmants eventails et un tableau—et moi je traduis come un moulin. Par example, voulez vous etre assez aimable de me faire une faveur. C'est de me procurer et m'expedier ici un exemplair, n'importe quel pourvu que ca ne coute pas trop cher des 'Liaisons Dangereuses.' J'aurai fini demain ie travail que j'ai apporte ici, et je voudrais continuer ma traduction des 'Liaisons.' Si vous voulez faire ca pour moi vous m'obligerez beaucoup. Je crois qu'il doit etre une edition moderne a 2. ou 3.50.—mais vous me direz la prix et vous enverrai un mandat.

Je suis tres fache de vous n'avoir pas vu encore pendant votre sejour a Londres, mais j'ai parti tout d'un coup pour voir cet en droit et quand j'etais a Londres je vous ai cru parti.

Un de ces jours, peutetre, je viendrai serrer votre main a Paris, mais pour le moment je n'ai ni le temps ni l'argent.

Mes compliments a Madame Davray.

> Tout Votre
> ERNEST DOWSON

Conder 'sends his remembrances to you.'*

In spite of the fact that he had Conder's company and that he was working, as he wrote, like a mill, Arques-la-Bataille could not keep him content. Possibly he was handicapped by his inability to gain the materials

---

* Throughout this letter I have preserved the spellings which appear in the copy of the original letter which John Gawsworth kindly made for me. I have been unable to compare the original letter with Gawsworth's copy.

which he needed for his translations promptly; but whatever the reason, by mid-October he was in Paris. The apartment which he had told Davray in his letter from Limerick he was planning to furnish on his arrival in Paris evidently was not taken. Davray and his wife were never called upon to assist him "in the matter of furnishing." His plan for fitting out an apartment so that he could be comfortable for the winter was in some measure similar to the proposed trip in the gypsy cart to the Riviera with Loiseau: he lacked the determination to overcome the obstacles which promptly confronted him in its fulfillment. In quarters at the St. Malo which were no more commodious and comfortable than those which he had formerly occupied at the Hotel de Medici, he set out to finish his commissions for Smithers, who had promised to pay him three pounds a week so long as he had the assurance that he was at work, with an additional sum on the satisfactory completion of the assignments.

During the autumn of 1897 and the winter of 1898 he did a considerable amount of work which, though not always of the creative sort which Wilde had begged him to do, was at least a demonstration of his willingness to complete what he had undertaken. *Les Liaisons Dangereuses*, on which he had been at work as early as December 1896, he had ready for Smithers by March 1898. He was also at work on a two-volume translation of the *Memoirs of Cardinal Dubois* by Paul Lacroix, and the even longer work of the Goncourt brothers, *The Confidantes of a King: the Mistresses of Louis XV*. To the verse translation of *La Pucelle*, on which he had started to work in the spring of 1896, and which he never liked, he began to apply himself with renewed vigor. In spite of the fact that he had told Davray that he was eager to do Pierre Louÿs' *Aphrodite* "even if the 'conditions' are not good," he evidently found on his arrival in Paris that Vallette had made other arrangements for the translation, and that Davray's friendship and influence, and even Louÿs' belief that he was eminently qualified to translate the work well, were not sufficient to secure him the assignment. It is possible, to be sure, that he dallied over the "conditions" with Vallette, or that he had given up the project before his arrival in Paris. He had enough on his hands with his assignments for Smithers without trying to fulfill commissions for Vallette.

Then, too, he had sincere intentions of doing a considerable amount of creative work. He had written to Davray from Ireland in the late summer that he hoped to have two volumes "roman & Nouvelles" in the press by January; and to Wilde, who was in Naples, he wrote from Paris that he was engaged in writing stories. It is possible that he referred to the little poetic prose pieces which were later to appear in *Decorations*, but it seems more likely that what he referred to as "stories" were the beginnings of narratives such as those which had appeared in *Dilemmas*. Although his letter to Wilde in which he referred to his story-writing has not been brought to light, one can readily see through Wilde's return letters what Dowson had told him about his literary activities. Quite evidently Dowson told Wilde that he was engaged not only in writing stories, but also that he had finished a novel, for sometime in October, Wilde expressed his delight at the information that Dowson had finished his novel. The only novel to which he could have referred was *Adrian Rome*. According to Moore, however, Dowson had become so dilatory in submitting his share of the work that Moore found it necessary to complete the novel himself. It is possible that Dowson felt that after submitting a few additional chapters to Moore his part in the collaboration was finished, that Moore would see to it that the concluding chapters were written, and *Adrian Rome* would be sent to the publishers.

Although his energy was not equal to his intentions, during the late autumn and winter of 1897-98 he worked with a sort of feverish zeal. When Smithers seemed dissatisfied with certain passages in *Les Liaisons Dangereuses*, Dowson promptly insisted that he would revise them. Long sections of *La Pucelle* and *The Confidantes of a King* began to arrive in London with surprising frequency. The report began to circulate among the Smithers people that Dowson was working like mad, that he was not only turning out copy as rapidly as a professional hack, but that he was also eagerly inquiring after additional assignments. And instead of complaining to his publisher of the conditions in which poverty forced him to live, as he had written in the winter of 1895-96, he told Smithers to send him only a part of his earnings. The rest Smithers was to keep as a sort of savings fund. This in itself was an encouraging sign to those who had his best interests at heart: the dilatory contributor was not only working steadily, but he was also conserving his scanty resources. To all outward appearances, Dowson, like Seefang, was "making amends."

His greatest achievement in 1898 was his work on a second volume of poems. Lionel Johnson and Wilde had both encouraged him to devote his energy to what Wilde called his "own work," and with the encouragement of men whose taste he admired and the assurances of Smithers that a second volume would be well received, he set out to realize that which had long been an intention. There is sufficient evidence to indicate that by November 1897 he had started a second "Poesie Schublade," a manuscript book which he possibly felt would attain in time the same volume and quality as the one from which he had drawn most of the poems for *Verses*. Although many of the poems which were to appear in his second volume, *Decorations: in Verse and Prose* (1899), had been written long before a second book was contemplated, there were poems in the collection, including the poems in prose, which were surely written in Paris during the winter of 1897-98. Were it not for the fact that many of the poems which were to appear in *Decorations* had been printed in the London magazines much earlier, and the dates of composition of some of them were clearly written in the first manuscript book, one might readily be led to believe, after examining the verse at the beginning, that the contents of the entire collection were written very late in Dowson's life, and represented, as Plarr observed, the sad song of "a man who is done with the world and is dying disillusioned." The first poem in the volume entitled "Beyond," for instance, with its opening lines:

> Love's aftermath! I think the time is now
> That we must gather in, alone, apart
> The saddest crop of all the crops that grow
> Love's aftermath. . . .

and

> Love that is love at all,
> Needs not an earthly coronal;
> Love is himself his own exceeding great reward,
> A mighty lord!

was probably written after the poet had been a victim of love's defeat; but with the exception of "Dregs" and "To a Lost Love," few of the poems in the collection were in keeping with the proposed title *Love's Aftermath*. It was possibly for this reason that immediately before the poems went to press he decided to change the title to *Decorations*. It is also possible that the change in title may have resulted from his belief that he had already identified his work too strictly with Adelaide, and that his friends would welcome a less personal sentiment in the title.

It was not until August 1899 that the corrected proof sheets were returned to Smithers, but it may be assumed that the principal work on the collection was done during the winter of 1898, when Dowson's industry reached a peak which had been equaled only by his work in 1893-94. It is true that the poems in *Decorations* show an appreciable falling off in quality, but they show no more disillusionment than the earlier poems. A careful examination of the contents reveals clearly that the life-weariness so frequently found in his earlier work had in no way become sufficiently

pronounced to exclude a variety of themes. "To His Mistress," with its
Herrick-like note, "Exchanges," and the "Rondeau" which begins

> Ah, Manon, say why is it we
> Are one and all so fain of thee?

indicate that the volume represents far more than the sad song of "a man
who is done with the world and is dying disillusioned." The "lassitude
and sorrowfulness" which Plarr detected are there, no doubt; but both in
variety of theme and beauty of melody and sentiment *Decorations* added to
Dowson's stature as a poet.

THE WELCOME VISITOR

THE industry which Dowson showed in finishing his assignments in translating for Smithers and in getting poems ready for a second volume was mistaken among his London acquaintances for an about-face in his attitude toward his work and a sign of increasing energy. The fact of the matter was that Dowson's days were numbered. It was a feverish instinct which drove him to try to complete what he had set out to do, for he himself must have had more than vague intimations that his time was short. In his more hopeful moments, he planned to build up a sufficient amount out of his savings with Smithers to permit him to go to Italy, about which Wilde had written glowingly; and if Italy could not be managed for a long sojourn, to go to the Riviera and bask there in the sunshine with the comforting thought that he had done his work well. It is touching to reflect on his recurrent plans to go south on the surplus which he was building up with Smithers and on the income which he continued to believe would soon come to him from his interest in Bridge Dock. There were times, however, when his body and soul were so besieged by suffering that he realized that it was too late to entertain any hope. It was probably at such a time that he wrote "The Visit," of which no manuscript or record of the date of composition has been brought to light. With a prescience given only to those who have long lived in the shadow of the contemplation of death, he wrote:

THE VISIT

As though I were still struggling through the meshes of some riotous dream, I heard his knock upon the door. As in a dream, I bade him enter, but with his entry, I awoke. Yet when he entered it seemed to me that I was dreaming, for there was nothing strange in that supreme and sorrowful smile which shone through the mask which I knew. And just as though I had not always been afraid of him I said: "Welcome."

And he said very simply, "I am here."

Dreaming I had thought myself, but the reproachful sorrow of his smile showed me that I was awake. Then dared I open my eyes and I saw my old body on the bed, and the room in which I had grown so tired, and in the middle of the room the pan of charcoal which still smouldered. And dimly I remembered my great weariness and the lost whiteness of Lalage and last year's snows; and these things had been agonies.

Darkly, as in a dream, I wondered why they gave me no more hurt, as I looked at my old body on the bed; why, they were like old maids' fancies (as I looked at my gray body on the bed of my agonies)—like silly toys of children that fond mothers lay up in lavender (as I looked at the twisted limbs of my old body), for these things had been agonies.

But all my wonder was gone when I looked again into the eyes of my guest, and I said:

"I have wanted you all my life."

Then said Death (and what reproachful tenderness was shadowed in his obscure smile):

"You had only to call."

Viewed in the light of the circumstances which had surrounded him for years, "The Visit" cannot be dismissed as mere rhetoric. Even were its date of composition to be traced to August 1896, the time at which "The Dying of Francis Donne" had appeared in *The Savoy,* its lines must be read and envisaged with the somber background in mind. Like Francis Donne, his awareness of approaching death became increasingly poignant: he knew he was going to die "in a few months, in six perhaps, and certainly in a year." This knowledge stimulated and depressed him in turn. During the winter of 1898, when he, like Keats, had fears that he might cease to be, he drove himself to work until his feeble body could stand no more; and there were times, when the charcoal smoldered low and a great weariness came over him, that he looked into the countenance of the visitor who had come to him on lonely, anguished nights, and said, "I have wanted you all my life."

He still had long to wait. The "Welcome" which had formed itself on his lips could not be spoken. Days of suffering and despair were followed by brief intervals of hope in which he worked sporadically on his translations and read the proof for *Decorations. La Pucelle,* which Smithers had intended to issue in a completely new translation, Dowson had disliked from the start; and now, with his energy rapidly waning, he was satisfied to rely more and more on earlier translations. When work was once put aside, he had increasing difficulty in returning to it. By the autumn of 1898, the sporadic energy which had driven him to work during the preceding year was virtually spent. He had long since given up regular correspondence with anyone save for an occasional note to Smithers, and even Smithers, according to report, was uncertain of his movements. Loneliness, illness, and despair were his regular companions, and at their insistence he sought in absinthe the only refuge he knew.

He kept up his acquaintance after a fashion with Davray and some of the staff of the *Mercure de France,* and occasionally he mingled with his countrymen who were in Paris and were not given to reproach. Wilde was back in Paris after his sojourn in Italy, and in spite of the fact that the old friendship of 1897 of Bernaval and Dieppe was not resumed, they saw each other at the small cafés along the Boulevard St. Michael. Dowson, however, could not forget the breach which had grown between Wilde and himself over the money he had borrowed in Dieppe. In a letter to Frank Harris, written sometime in the winter of 1899, he said:

I met severally & separately yesterday afternoon Oscar, Strong & Sherard— all inveighing bitterly against one another and two of them discussing divers fashions of self-destruction. Oscar was particularly grieved because of a Swedish baron (whom he had met at Marlotte [?] and of whom he had hoped much) who had borrowed 5 francs from him on the Boulevard.

In Dowson's case surely borrowing had dulled the edge of husbandry; but even had there been no strain over Wilde's advance of funds at Dieppe, it is unlikely that they could have resumed their friendship. Both Wilde and Dowson had reached a stage in which they had little to offer to each other.

They both could still be gracious, and they were not unmindful of the fact that they had once been poets. On New Year's Day, 1899, a Miss Ida Battye or Baltye brought Dowson her copy of *The Pierrot of the Minute* or an autograph book of the same size page in which she requested him to write something for her. Over the date of January 1, 1899, he wrote:

> For Miss Ida Battye [Baltye]
> >   This piece of moonshine
> >   with the hommage of the author
> >   ERNEST DOWSON
>
> >   In the days of the good, gay people,
> >   Of the little folk in green,
> >   The moon shone clear in Fairyland,
> >   Or ever the world was seen.

This little piece, which was included by Desmond Flower among the "Hitherto Unpublished Poems" in his *Poems of Ernest Christopher Dowson,* was copied from the original sheet for me by John Gawsworth; but save for the date of writing which appears below the quatrain, there is no detail which might shed light on the recipient of the verse or what the nature of her association with Dowson was. It is possible that she had had Dowson pointed out to her while she was in Paris, and being an admirer of his poems, she had asked him to write something for her. That he was gracious and compliant is indicated by his response.

Trifling as such admiration probably was, it helped to lead Dowson to feel that he had not written altogether in vain; and when he learned that he might receive some sort of decoration for his work from the Belgian Court, he must have been pleased at the prospect of such an honor. The information, which had come to him from Arthur Symons, made him curious about its origin. Among the few notes he wrote in the winter of 1899 which have been brought to light, there is a card to Arthur Symons, written from the Hotel de St. Malo, Paris, dated March 7, 1899, which reads:

I am intrigued by your card. It is from a serious Belgian consulate or a jest from Dublin? If it is the former, I can only imagine that Leopold has discovered my merit and decided on decorating me. Toulouse-Lautrec, you will be sorry to hear, was taken to a lunatic asylum yesterday.

Whether or not the information that he was to be decorated by the Belgian Court was a jest from Dublin cannot readily be determined, but it is the opinion of those who knew Dowson that there had never been a serious intention on the part of the Belgian Court to decorate him. If the information that came to him was the result of facetiousness on the part of Symons or another, it was a hapless sort of humor. Dowson had enough trouble during the winter of 1899 without being made the victim of a practical joke.

With the coming of spring he was back in London, spending his nights in cabmen's shelters and the retreats with which he had become familiar in the East End. Occasionally he dropped in on Smithers to deliver a few pages of work, to ask for money, or merely to ease his loneliness. Evidently Smithers gave him the surplus which had gathered, or advanced him money on a new project, for there was a brief period of rehabilitation and of revived hopes soon after his return to London. Upon meeting O'Riordan by chance, he asked his old companion of the Flanders journey to accompany him to Brittany for the summer. He said he planned to do a great deal of work. O'Riordan, however, found it impossible to leave London, though he knew that his company would be good for Dowson. Since their journey together in 1895, Dowson had felt that O'Riordan was one of the few men who could help him regulate his life. But when he learned that his friend would be unable to join him, he construed O'Riordan's response as an evasion and a desertion. With his sensitivity heightened by suffering, he readily made himself believe that his other friends had drifted away from him, and he was still sufficiently proud to keep his distance from those who might look at him reproachfully and pityingly. When his sensitivity had been mitigated by absinthe, he occasionally made the rounds of the pubs on the Strand. It was at this time that Ranger Gull often saw him, "a lost creature, a youthful ghost strayed amongst the haunts of men, an object of pity."

Evidently he had sufficient money and will to live to go back to France in the late spring. The meager evidence available indicates that he went alone with the thought that he would be able to find an acquaintance to whom he could attach himself; and that after spending a few weeks in Dieppe and Arques, restlessness again seized him, and he moved on to Paris. He had no definite objective save to keep moving. As soon as he settled in one place, he already contemplated a change. He probably had learned from much experience in moving about that one place was no better than another for him, but the very thought of change gave him respite from despair. He himself had said in a fragment of a poem that the crossing of seas and the changing of lands were vain, and that the search was without purpose; but he was helpless to resist the avenue of escape from himself which constant change provided.

In Paris he took a room in the Hotel d'Odessa near the Gare Montparnasse to which he went only when the green-aproned bistro keepers were preparing for the day that had dawned, or when he could no longer find company at the cafés or on the streets in the vicinity of les Halles. It was in the summer of 1899 that Robert Sherard found him one night in a small café, slumped far down in his chair over a table sticky with absinthe. Sherard, who had met Dowson as early as 1894 in Teixeira de Mattos' rooms at the Temple when the translation of Zola was under way, and had seen him occasionally in London in the days of his apparent prosperity, was distressed at the condition to which Dowson had fallen, and promptly tried to give him all the assistance which was in his power to give.

Sherard and Dowson had never been especially intimate in London. In fact, Dowson had reported to Plarr that Sherard was charming, "but the most morose and spleenful person I have yet encountered." It was not until Wilde's trial that a bond had sprung up between them. When Sherard saw Dowson's loyalty to Wilde, in the face of all the hooting crowd which stood on the outside of the courtroom on the day of the verdict, he decided then and there that the young poet was one to respect. Sherard's devotion to Wilde as a man of letters was enough to cause him to see in Dowson a kindred spirit. After Wilde's release, and Dowson's return to London after a two-year sojourn in France, Sherard saw Dowson occasionally, and at one time accompanied him to Limehouse for a night. When on that night Dowson got into a fight with a stevedore from which he emerged with a deep gash on his forehead, Sherard sensed something unusual in the young poet, but his liking for him increased.

To find him in a dingy café obviously ill and poor, and much the worse for absinthe, touched Sherard to such a point that he took him along to his quarters on the Boulevard Magenta where he did his best to give him the attention he so sorely needed. Sherard's account of Dowson's condition in Paris in the summer of 1899 may readily be accepted as an accurate description of the depths to which Dowson had been brought by illness and despair.

Although Sherard's quarters on the Boulevard Magenta were far from commodious and well appointed, they did afford an extra cot and the comforts to which Englishmen who visited in Paris were accustomed. Of these comforts, however, Dowson would not avail himself. He slept with his boots on and avoided generally the bowl and pitcher. His spirit was so completely broken by his illness that he was no longer mindful of what anyone thought of him. His pride in trying to keep away from what he believed would be "the intolerable pity of friends" had finally been shaken. Once established with Sherard, he showed no signs of going back to the Hotel d'Odessa to gather his few belongings. He was afraid to go to his room, he told Sherard, for in its dingy confines all manner of tormenting spirits lurked. A statue in his room had taken on a sinister import. "I lie awake at night and watch it," he told his friend. "I know that one night it means to come down off its shelf and strangle me." To go into a shop filled him with dread. He would go for hours without making a necessary purchase in order to avoid the slight ordeal of talking with the shopkeepers. He sought to avoid people, especially strangers who might seem inquisitive about his health. His most harassing thought was that he was about to be paralyzed, or fall into an epileptic fit, as he had heard that confirmed absinthe drinkers sometimes did. But from absinthe he would not desist, even with the menace of paralysis before him. On the mornings that he stayed with Sherard in Paris, he would have the attendant go out for absinthe, which taken on an empty stomach had prompt effect. Persuasion was useless, for he had neither the strength to resist an emollient to his suffering, nor the sort of self-pity which has on occasion been known to cause men to escape self-destruction. "Self-pity never entered Dowson's psychology," Sherard told me. "Hang-overs never induced in him commiseration of self. He took immediate recourse to the hair of the dog which had bitten him." Although rarely completely intoxicated, he gave himself small opportunity to see to what a pass he had come.

He showed all the symptoms of acute neurasthenia. For a reason which baffled Sherard, he was unwilling to go to the Odessa when he knew that letters probably awaited him there in which there might be money. Sherard recalls that on one occasion a letter lay at the Odessa for four days without being opened, and that finally Dowson, after being persuaded to get his mail, thrust the letter into his pocket, slowly to work the envelope open. At last, after his face had been contorted with apprehension, he cried out: "It's all right! I feel the frill of a check." The amount, however, meant little to him. For days he would go with a few francs in his pocket when all the while he had a draft for a hundred tucked away in a book. To apply for money, even that which was owing him, apparently required too much effort and exacted a strain on him which he tried to avoid. The few nourishing meals he had while he was staying with Sherard were taken at a small café adjoining the hotel and at Sherard's insistence that he must eat. So long as Sherard remained in the room he could not be persuaded to venture out; but the moment his friend had left to do some of the work which had brought him to Paris, Dowson would go out into the streets in order to seek escape from his thoughts.

Reports of his condition had reached London. Plarr was under the impression that these reports galvanized one of the poet's friends into action, and that straightway the friend, whom Plarr failed to name, went to Paris to bring Dowson back to London. This nameless friend, according to Plarr's report, invited Dowson on their return to London to have dinner with him at a good restaurant. To which Dowson replied despairingly: "I cannot face a dinner at ————'s." Evidently the friend felt that his mission had been satisfactorily fulfilled when he brought Dowson back to London, for there is no record of anyone's giving the poet sanctuary in the early autumn of 1899. Smithers provided him with a little money—thirty shillings a week, so report has it—and also with his usual hospitality; but Dowson found only a temporary refuge with his publisher. Smithers knew he was ill, but to him Dowson had always been ill; and there seemed to be no particular necessity for taking strict care of him. Furthermore, Smithers had difficulties of his own. His own health, reputation, and finances had suffered considerably in 1898. He gave Dowson an additional commission in translating which was to be the last. Arthur Moore saw Dowson during the autumn, but in spite of the fact that his friend was coughing a great deal, he did not feel that his condition had materially changed.

Soon after his return to London, Dowson took lodgings in a garret on Euston Road, opposite the Church of St. Pancras. His landlord was an Italian music master, who no doubt had some of the kindliness of his race, but who in time tired of his tenant's failure to pay his bill and sent him off, deathly sick, to his publisher to try to get money. Smithers evidently was not to be found when Dowson arrived. He dragged himself back to Euston Road to stop on his way at a bar to get something to drink. It was here that Sherard, who had befriended him a few months earlier in Paris, felt a tap on his shoulder and turned to see Dowson, with a face like soiled parchment, smile wanly at him. Sherard saw that he was desperately ill. After Dowson had drunk off two brandies, Sherard learned his plight. His landlord had threatened to evict him, and Smithers, who had promised him thirty shillings a week upon the completion of work, could not be found. He admitted to Sherard that he had not been able to turn in work to Smithers for several weeks on account of an enfeebling influenza which had kept him bedfast. The little nourishment he had taken during his illness was of the sort which he had been able to procure at a confectioner's shop on Euston Road—pastry and occasionally milk.

It was on a Friday in late December that Sherard found him at the pub on Bedford Street, and together they went to the garret on Euston Road to make peace with the Italian music master. When Sherard left him, he promised to return on Sunday. Good as his word, he returned on Sunday to find Dowson in bed, from which he had not stirred since the Friday on which Sherard had left him. In the meantime he had had no nourishment save that which the now partially pacified landlord saw fit to send up to him. In Sherard's mind there was no doubt that he needed attention. In spite of the fact that he was by no means comfortably situated at the time, he invited Dowson to come to his home where he should have at least the assurance that he would never be evicted and where Mrs. Sherard could give him nourishing food. Dowson was no longer capable of making up his mind. At Sherard's insistence, he consented to go with him, for he felt that he could not face the landlord when another bill was due. "But," he said, "you must take me down first-class to Catford, for I cannot bear to be with people."

There was some difficulty in getting him to rise and dress, for he was so weak that he could scarcely stand. A cab had to be summoned to take him to Charing Cross Station from which they could catch a train for Catford. On the train, Dowson slumped down in sheer exhaustion. From the Catford Station they again rode in a cab to Sherard's house at 26 Sandhurst Gardens, now a part of Sandhurst Road, where he was promptly put to bed.

Sherard was in no way prosperous in 1900; in fact, he had been glad to accept the commission to write a pamphlet on some new process for making white lead. He and his wife had sublet the ground floor of their small house to a bricklayer and his family in order to help to pay their rent. Although the second story was adequate for the modest needs of Sherard, his wife, and their adopted child, Paul, it afforded no such luxury as a guestroom. The Sherards, however, did everything in their power to make Dowson comfortable. During the day he sat in the armchair in the front room, which, when the weather was at all agreeable, was a sunny, cheerful place; and at night he slept on a comfortable cot, which was as much as his host could offer.

Lacking as they were in comfort for themselves, the Sherards nevertheless wanted to call a physician to attend him, but he insisted that he was suffering only from the weakness which followed an attack of influenza, and that in a few days, or a week at most, he would recover his strength and no longer impose on their kindness. And so it seemed, for after a week with the Sherards, he apparently regained a little strength and spoke as if his complete recovery would be only a matter of a few days. He never could be induced, however, to leave the house even for a short walk on a mild, sunshiny afternoon; and when anyone knocked on the door below, he would jump up from his armchair, and lock himself in the back room. At times he would send Sherard out to the chemist's to have prescriptions compounded for him which he had found in such publications as *Health in the Home*. He scanned the sections of the papers which were devoted to advertisements of different remedies and to discussions of health. Sherard humored him in his requests for patent medicines, though he had little money to spare at the chemist's and no confidence in the efficacy of the specifics for which he was sent. He and his wife felt that a physician would be of infinitely more use, but at their slightest intimation that a physician should be procured, Dowson rose from his chair and began to get himself ready to go into the street.

Several weeks passed, with few positive signs of renewed strength. There were times at which he seemed cheerful enough, especially when he spoke of his plan to find an agreeable companion and leave London for the Riviera. With the money which would come to him when settlement was made of his holdings at Bridge Dock, he would have ample means to satisfy all of his desires. Sherard suspected, if he did not know, that the £600 which Dowson thought were coming to him would never materialize, but he encouraged him with the plan, for the illusion he felt was strengthening to Dowson's body and spirit. Sherard read to him passages from books which he had written and on which he was writing at the time, and Dowson produced a French novel, which he had carried along from Euston Road, on which he said he was working for Smithers. The title of the novel has slipped Sherard's memory, but he recalls a few indelicate passages in the opening chapters and a memorably indecent frontispiece. They talked about Paris and the old nights at the Temple and the bar parlors on the Strand. There were times when Dowson smiled at the reminiscences which such conversations brought forth, and on a few occasions he laughed. Undoubtedly he was somewhat improved, for he ate with appetite, and was generally eager to read or talk. But his strength seemed unusually long in returning, and in spite of the fact that there was no sign of hemorrhage, he had paroxysms of coughing at night which left him bathed in perspiration.

Four weeks passed with no conspicuous changes in his condition. Sherard, who had been trying to follow his own work during the month, was at times away for most of the day, but Dowson had the attention and company of Mrs. Sherard and the little boy. After a month had passed, Sherard found it necessary to leave London for a time in order to fulfill a commission which called him to Paris. He tells how he took leave of Dowson, repeating to him that he would soon return, and went to the Catford Station to take a train for London to get his passage for France. At the station, however, as he was waiting for his train, a sort of premonition came over him. He could not well afford to neglect his work, nor could he with a clear conscience leave Dowson for even a week. The feeling that he should return to Sandhurst Gardens became so strong that he threw his ticket away and went home. When he arrived, Dowson greeted him smilingly, saying that he had expected him to return. Sherard was touched by the warmth of his greeting, and told him that he would put off his trip to Paris until his guest was able to go back to London. Dowson had often mentioned a friend who had rooms in Bromley who wanted him to stay with him, but evidently the friend was unable to come for him, for Dowson continued to stay in Catford.

The fifth week passed, with Sherard often in London trying to keep up with his own work. While he was away, Dowson read *Henry Esmond*, for which he expressed a great admiration; and for the first time in his life, he read Dickens. When he was tired of reading, he talked with Mrs. Sherard and little Paul. At the beginning of the sixth week, his condition was such that the Sherards were alarmed. Instead of continuing to regain his strength, he had become so weak that he was no longer able to sit in the armchair for more than a short time. He was alert, however, to what the

Sherards said in a subdued tone about him. The moment he felt he detected in their talk or expression the summoning of a physician, he rose and with a sudden display of vigor, began to put on his clothes. When they had reassured him that no doctor was coming, he would sink back on the bed and drop off into an exhausted sleep.

On the evening of February 22, 1900, he asked Sherard to write a letter for him to Arthur Moore. When Sherard inquired of him what he was to say, he could not phrase so much as the beginning. "I feel too tired," he said. And still he remained in his chair, to which he had come in the afternoon, eager to talk about *Oliver Twist*. When Sherard tried to get him to go off to bed, he insisted on continuing the conversation. They discussed Bill Sikes's murder of Nancy, and when Sherard observed that Sikes killed Nancy without being influenced by anything that Fagin had said about her, Dowson was in complete agreement. He expressed the opinion that if Fagin had spoken ill of her, Sikes would "have gone for Fagin." They sat up until five in the morning, and even then Dowson was unwilling to go to bed. He insisted that they continue their discussion over what was left in a bottle of Gilbey's port wine. Finally he went to his cot but he kept calling to Sherard to come in and talk with him.

Dawn had broken before he was quiet, with the promise of another gray, cold day. At about eight o'clock he started to cough. Sherard went into his room to raise him from his pillow so that he might breathe more freely. Between racking coughs, he made plain to Sherard that he was to go to the chemist's for some ipecacuanha wine which he believed would relieve him. But the wine failed to bring relief. Realizing that a doctor was absolutely necessary, Sherard left his wife with Dowson and sent a neighbor for the nearest physician. On approaching Dowson's room on his return, he called out: "You had better get up, Ernest, and sit in the armchair. You will breathe more easily." In the room it was strangely quiet. His wife pointed to the silent figure on the cot. He moved over to raise him, and as he lifted the emaciated form to a sitting position, the head sagged forward on his shoulder. Ernest Dowson was dead.

Although Sherard has given a lucid and touching account of Dowson's last days, there are details which he could not record by reason of the fact that he was often away from Catford during the six weeks in which Dowson stayed in his home. His wife, however, was in almost constant attendance during that time, and it was she who was with Dowson when he died. It is her story which not only supplements Sherard's account of Dowson's last days, but also illuminates some of the recesses of the poet's nature.

The manner in which I found the woman who took care of Ernest Dowson in his last days and who was with him when he died is a story in itself. Mrs. Dillon-Jones—she married again after she and Sherard were separated—at the age of seventy-seven retained much in her memory of her experiences of January and February 1900, in spite of the vicissitudes of a checkered life. When I saw her at the Poplar Institution in August 1939, I found her, despite her suffering and the atmosphere of her surroundings, a woman of considerable attractiveness and charm. To my written request that I should like to have her talk with me, she answered in a legible hand on the back of an envelope as follows:

Dear Doctor:

Please come, as soon as you can. I am very unhappy here. In these glorious institutions, one can get in, but not out. I have been 2 years here, kept a prisoner, surrounded by the lowest scum of humanity. Their singing is shrieking, their dancing is stamping on their feet. You can pity me, a Latin and Greek scholar, surrounded by such people. Please come, as soon as you can. I am kept as a prisoner and I have committed no crime.

Do not be afraid for yourself. You would be a visitor and they are safe.

We are supposed to get patrons through begging letters. We get no sugar in our tea, nor milk. I will tell you more when I see you.

Yours very sincerely,

MRS. DILLON-JONES

With the sociological import of this letter we need not be concerned. It is enough to observe that the matron and attendants seemed kindly and thoroughly interested in the welfare of the inmates of the poorhouse. Although there may be those who question the retentiveness of Mrs. Dillon-Jones's memory, no one can question her authority. I was impressed by the clarity and consecutiveness of her story which, save for a few changes in wording made necessary by my inability to take down the narrative as rapidly as she told it, I repeat in substance and largely in phrase:

I have known great poets: Ernest Dowson died in my arms. Little Paul, my adopted son, was playing with the tin toys which we had got him for Christmas— it was only a few days after Christmas when my husband came home with a sick young man. He was very sick. He was nothing but a skeleton, and I remember that I heard coughing before I saw that my husband had brought anyone home with him. He was getting over the influenza, he said apologetically when we took him in. My husband at the time was very poor, but he was sure that he would soon have money—he was always sure that he would soon get money— so we arranged to keep Mr. Dowson for a while, for no one attended him in his rooms on Euston Road. I could not protest, although I knew that the young man needed nourishment and medical attention which were not within our means to provide. But he stroked the head of little Paul so kindly, and looked into my eyes as if he were frightened. I gave him the most comfortable room in our small house, one of the four which we had, for we had taken in a family on the ground floor. The young man was put to bed, and I recall I gave him some weak tea which he did not drink. He spoke to me in French, a language which I knew very well, and after he had finished what he was saying, he would often burst into a sort of laugh, as if the sound of his voice amused him.

That was the beginning of his stay with us, which lasted till his death. He had brought no clothes, nothing, I recall, save a French book with some evil pictures, which he said he was translating for a very fine gentleman who had many rich friends. His clothes were very old and dirty. In his waistcoat, which bore the label of a French tailor, and which was all spotted, he had a few pennies. He had no gloves, and his coat was frayed at the lapels and threadbare at the sleeves. He had a black hat such as those worn by the artists in Paris at the time. He always spoke to me in French during the early days of his stay, but after a week or two he spoke English, probably because he wanted to talk so Paul could understand him. He showed a great fondness for little Paul, who was too small to be frightened by his appearance.

I knew that he was going to die, but he kept saying that he was much better, and my husband said that he had always looked as if he were going to die. But I knew that he had something worse than influenza, and I told my husband that we must have a doctor at once. He was willing that I get a doctor, but Mr. Dowson became very angry when I told him that we would have a doctor come in to attend him. He said that if he were not much improved in a few days, then I could bring a doctor. He was not much improved, in a few days or in a few weeks. I expressed my fears to Robert that we should have a doctor not only for the young man but also to relieve the strain of a coroner's inquest, which I felt sure would soon be held. My husband was not frightened at the thought of an inquest, for he had no thought that the young man was soon to die, nor did he see that there would be any disgrace in having a coroner come to the house.

I made up my mind that we must have a doctor, and I knew exactly for whom to send. Paul had recited a poem at a Christmas party which Mrs. Shillingforth wanted her little daughter to learn. Mrs. Shillingforth's husband was a doctor, and I thought that if I could get Dr. Shillingforth to come for the poem, I could get him to look at Mr. Dowson. I told Dr. Shillingforth about Mr. Dowson, and he said that if only I could manage to let him see him several times, or even only once, we should need have no fear about an inquest.

I told Robert about the arrangement which I had made with Dr. Shillingforth to come to get the poem which Paul had recited, and then, without saying that he was a doctor, to look at Mr. Dowson, and prescribe some remedy for his cough. My husband was sure that the plan would not work, but he, too, was beginning to be distressed over Mr. Dowson's continued and even increasing weakness. Dr. Shillingforth came one noon. Mr. Dowson was in his bed, reading I believe a story of Thackeray's. Though the doctor and I talked in a subdued tone at the door, Mr. Dowson must have overheard us, or at least believed that a stranger was about to enter the house. Excusing myself from the doctor in order to explain to Mr. Dowson that a friend had called for a poem for his small daughter, I went above to find him half-dressed, pacing about the room, his eyes burning with fever and anger. "Mrs. Sherard," he said, "if you bring that man in to see me, I'll leave you and go out and die in the street." His manner frightened me, so I told him that the man had only called for a poem and that I should not permit him to come upstairs.

That was about two weeks before he died. I had become a member of the Church of England, and knowing that he was a Catholic, for he had a little medal on which there was stamped the image of a French saint, I asked him about his religion and whether he would not like to have a priest come to see him. He had been in a more cheerful mood than usual when I brought up the matter, and I thought that I was finally going to get his consent to see someone beside us. There was a long pause after my inquiry, but after staring at the ceiling for a time, he turned over on the bed with his face to the wall, mumbling: "No, no, no one is to see me." His hand, over the covers, clenched and un-clenched again and again.

It was the following day, or perhaps the day after, that my husband and I believed that he was mending. He talked brightly about going to southern France, and perhaps to Italy. He told me that his dream was to go to southern France, and he asked me what my dream was. I told him that I would like nothing better than to go over to the West End and have a fine dinner with fine people at a brightly lighted restaurant, for I was a charming woman, and I was often irked by the life I had to live in Catford. Of little Paul, too, he inquired his dream. As I recall, the child had heard about a train, which upon winding a spring, would run by itself—better than the tin train which he had been pushing around on the floor. The child's eyes, always large, grew wider with joy as he pictured the shining toy. It was on this day that the sun had stolen into the room for a brief hour that Mr. Dowson put his hand on little Paul's head to say: "You shall have your train, Paul, and you"—and he smiled at me so kindly—"shall have the finest dinner at the finest place in the West End when my ship comes in." The prospect of being a kind of St. Nicholas appar-ently pleased him. I remember how he lay there staring at the ceiling, often re-peating: "When my ship comes in."

Robert had changed his mind about going to Paris at the last moment, and returned to us after he had gone to the Catford Station. Upon his decision to remain in Catford, Mr. Dowson's spirits revived very much. Every night after my husband had come home the two of them would talk about books, and their discussions were often filled with disagreement, for I know there were nights that long after midnight they would still be shouting at each other, my husband in his deep bass voice, and Mr. Dowson in a high-pitched tone like a wail. It was after one of these nights of talking about books that Mr. Dowson had a bad attack of coughing. I remember that my husband tried to get him to sit up so that he might breathe more easily, and that, when the coughing continued and he could no longer get his breath, Robert went downstairs, for what I do not know. He said later that he had gone to send for a doctor. I held the young man in my arms, and for a moment he seemed to catch his breath. "You are like an angel from heaven," he said. "God bless you."

When my husband came upstairs, he was trying to say something, but I knew that it was the end. Robert took the limp body in his arms, but he was already dead. We placed pennies on his eyes, and later they were replaced with silver coins by a friend of the young poet who came down on the evening after he died. That I, or any woman who was in the house, took the coins and went off to get drunk at the nearest bar, as my husband is reported to have said, I am sure is not the case.*

This account, of which I am not the sole possessor, though it was probably told me with more completeness than to the one or two others who found Mrs. Dillon-Jones, needs small commentary. It is the record of a woman who had been a constant observer of Dowson's last days. It is some satisfaction to know that the woman who saw Ernest Dowson in his last moments, and to whom he spoke his last words, could, in spite of her own wrecked life, still recite passages of "Cynara" and approach her inquirer with the statement: "I have known great English poets: Ernest Dowson died in my arms."

The Sherards were relieved of any discomfiture for their kindness in giving the dying poet sanctuary by the appearance of Dowson's uncle, Stanley Hoole, whose address Sherard found in one of Dowson's pockets. It is true that the police came from the coroner's office in order to determine the circumstances of his death. Curious neighbors gathered in front of the house in Sandhurst Gardens to wag their tongues uncharitably about what they thought had gone on within. For a time Sherard's motives in taking care of the poet did not seem satisfactory to the police; but when Stanley Hoole appeared, he was able to assure the police that Sherard's service had been without thought of income, that the poet had died with nothing which could be of value to those who had sheltered him. The police were finally convinced. They left with the remark that there was "no reasonable cause for suspicion in the case."

Sherard, who never exaggerated his role of good Samaritan, sent notices

---

* I am fully aware that Miss Ada Swan, the poet's aunt, reported that she visited him in the New Cross Hospital near Lewisham three days before his death. Although Miss Swan's statement that she visited him in the hospital is not to be discounted, it would seem that Dowson recovered sufficiently after her visit to leave the hospital and take a room on Euston Road. The balance of evidence indicates that Dowson died at Sherard's home, 26 Sandhurst Gardens, Catford.

of Dowson's death to the London papers in which he remarked frankly that the poet had died destitute and friendless. When Sherard's notices appeared, Plarr exclaimed: "Ye gods! our doors had stood open for him, our lamp had been trimmed for him for years!" Sherard reports that he had to hear over and over again, "If I had only known." The fact of the matter was that no one knew what had happened to Dowson. When his aunt, Mrs. Holford Secretan, said: "Without ever any shade of quarrel or disagreement he dropped away—till his relations never knew if he were dead or alive—or he need not have been in the state he was . . ." she expressed the state of affairs very truthfully indeed.

The funeral was well attended by reason of Sherard's notices in the papers. Smithers showed surprise and sorrow when he learned of Dowson's death, but neither he nor Arthur Symons was at the funeral. Many elaborate wreaths were sent by old friends, some of whom had not seen Dowson since 1894; and the hearse, starting from the Catholic Church in Lewisham, was followed up the hill to the Ladywell cemetery by at least eight carriages. When the coffin was lowered, Lennox Pawle, a Bensonian who had moved about with Dowson on many a night in 1893-94, broke into tears. "The most exquisite poet of the age to have died thus," he lamented. There were those standing nearby who were either too moved to express sadness, or too detached from any sincere feeling to become articulate. Among this group there were those who were later to say that Pawle was first, last, and always an actor. To one observer, the tributes paid to the dead poet after the coffin was lowered seemed to have nothing but their conventionality to distinguish them. The "intolerable pity" which Ernest Dowson had tried to escape in life surely did not oppress him in death.

Stanley Hoole had made the arrangements for the funeral. Mr. Nairne, of the law partners Baker and Nairne, at the time was a clerk of the firm which for long had had charge of the Dowson interests. He recalls that he was sent at short notice to Somerset House to get funds for the immediate expenses of the funeral. In spite of the fact that the financial affairs of the Dowsons were involved and unpromising, adequate money was secured without a request for contributions. On the night following the funeral, Dowson's uncle wrote to Sherard:

Lloyd's,
London, E.C. 27 Feby.

Dear Mr. Sherard,

I had not time to say anything to you this morning, or to introduce you to my son as we had to catch a train. I need hardly say how deeply grateful we all feel to you and Mrs. Sherard for all your kindness to poor Ernie. It was nice to see so many of his friends there today. Please give my kind regards to Madame. You will hear from me again in a day or two when I have had time to look a little in Ernie's affairs.

Believe me

Very gratefully yours

STANLEY HOOLE

The notices which appeared in the papers after the funeral were largely perfunctory and misleading. *The Daily Telegraph* reported on February 28, 1900 as follows:

Mr. Ernest Dowson, whose death has just taken place, was a writer of verse which had the true poetic touch. Since he went up to Queen's College, Oxford, some fourteen years ago, he proved an inveterate Bohemian, without any attempt at posing in that uncomfortable rôle. He was quite genuine and simple, loved by his friends, but difficult to live with by reason of his vagabond temperament. His long and intimate acquaintance with French town and country life, together with his keen literary sense, well fitted him for his task of translator. The books which he put into English from the French had especial merit, the last being "The Memoirs of Cardinal Dubois." It is said that some of his most charming verses were inspired by the daughter of a café-keeper in a little town in Brittany. The poet, rumour has it, wanted to marry her, but she declined the honour, and instead chose as husband one of her father's waiters.

Seventy years after the poet was born, *The Daily Mail* carried the brief notice:

POET'S NEGLECTED GRAVE

Five people yesterday laid wreaths on a neglected and overgrown grave in Lewisham cemetery, S.E.

It was that of Ernest Dowson, writer of the love poem "Cynara" who was born exactly 70 years ago yesterday, and died in 1900.

His grave was rediscovered by Mr. Thomas Burke, the writer about London, only a few weeks ago.

Of those who stood by his grave on his seventieth anniversary, only Edgar Jepson had been an intimate friend. The others were Thomas Burke, Clare Cameron, Frederick Carter, and John Gawsworth, who has done much to bring Dowson to his proper rank amongst English poets. In fact, it has been through Gawsworth's splendid energy and enthusiasm that the Dowson Club, of which Victor Plarr spoke as early as 1914, has begun to take shape.

There are those, however, who have not brought wreaths to his grave and know not where he is laid who have done much to arouse interest in

Dowson's poetical worth. Before the flowers had withered on the grave in the Ladywell cemetery tributes began slowly to gather. Plarr in his "Informal Epitaph" wrote:

> The critics seized on you the very day
> They laid you deep within your Kentish clay.
> That skilled young person who discovered "Art,"
> Proclaimed you Chatterton without delay.

And with the progress of the century his friends have done much to perpetuate his memory by portraying him in different attitudes and by editing and commending his verse. Arthur Symons was the first to erect a memorial to his name in an edition of his works which included *Verses, Decorations,* and *The Pierrot of the Minute.* The biographical notice which served as a preface to the volume, in which Symons used much of the material of *The Savoy* article of August 1897, aroused the ire of some of Dowson's relatives and friends by reason of its inadequacies and inaccuracies, but it stimulated interest in Dowson; and when all is said, it undoubtedly rendered a service to the poet's name. And when T. B. Mosher issued an edition of Dowson's poems in America, he paid a substantial tribute to the poet by bringing his verse to a group of readers who promptly recognized its beauty. Victor Plarr's "Informal Epitaph on a Young Poet," which appeared in *Poetry and Drama* in June 1913; and his *Ernest Dowson: 1888-1897, Reminiscences, Unpublished Letters, Marginalia* (1914), though inadequate as a penetrating biography, were of considerable worth in their kindly estimate of Dowson's personality and works.

Edgar Jepson, who spent at least four nights a week with Dowson in a period extending over several years, in his article "The Real Ernest Dowson" which appeared in *The Academy* in November 1907, and in his *Memories of a Victorian,* 1933, undoubtedly did much to preserve Dowson's name, not only by correcting Symons, but by illuminating the lineaments of his personality. It was Jepson who said:

Dowson was a gentle dreamer with a keen sense of beauty. He was out of place in the world and wisely lived, most of the time, in an aloof beautiful world of his own. He had the air of being submerged in a dream, and plainly enough he rose out of the dream only when you called him into the world in which he was actually moving. But he was really not concerned with it, and I think that a great deal of his uncommon charm came from that attitude to life: he never cared enough for this world to pose before it. It was the charm of an uncommon simplicity and sincerity, and the charm of extraordinary gentleness. He was always just Ernest Dowson. It was a delightful person to be.

I think the full truth about him is set forth in the words he gave me to write opposite his name in a curious birthday book I kept:

"The small things of life are odious to me, and the habit of them enslaves me; the great things of life are eternally attractive to me, but indolence and fear put them by."

Indolence and fear undoubtedly played an important part in Dowson's inability to cope with the great things of life. He understood the devastating effects of indecision which grew out of his own indolence and fear when he reflected on the character of Philip Rainham in *A Comedy of Masks.*

Certainly, the world was full of persons [he observed] who had been broken on the wheel of their proper audacity, because they had sought so much more than was to be found; but might it not be equally true that one could err on the other side, expect, desire too little, less even than was there, and so reap finally, as he had done, in an immense lassitude and disgust of all things, born neither of satiety nor of disappointment, the full measure of one's reward? Perhaps success in the difficult art of life depended, almost as much as in the plastic arts, upon conviction, upon the personal enthusiasm which one brought to bear upon its conduct, and was never really compatible with that attitude of half-disdainful toleration which he had so early acquired.

The indolence, the fear, the indecision, and the attitude of half-disdainful toleration which marked his regard for the struggle with the great things of life were forces over which he had small control. There is no doubt that he was weak in both body and will, nor is there doubt that he aggravated the weaknesses which were thrust upon him by birth and training by irregularities in living which were in some measure of his own devising. But out of the bludgeonings of circumstance which would have left many a man stronger than he mumbling incoherent blasphemies, Dowson fashioned a dark beauty which leaves one fascinated; and out of the dissonances of a life which was apparently without plan he captured melodies which one hears only in dimly remembered dreams. Perhaps it was a sincere discipleship to beauty which gave objective to a life which to him had no apparent purpose or plan; possibly there is some law of compensation of which man knows little. At least, out of a life filled with suffering and despair, there have come poems which have a secure place in that hall which is reserved for those whose names cannot be effaced by war and the smoky wake of progress. Time and sea-change can only add to the beauty of

> You would have understood me, had you waited . . .

and

> Last night, ah yesternight, betwixt her lips and mine
> There fell thy shadow, Cynara! . . .

APPENDIX

Bridge Dock,
Limehouse, E.

Cher Vieux,

I was grieved, indeed, to miss you the other day: I had gone down to Chadwell rather early. You must give me another look in when you are returned from Devon, before you take up your abode in the Library. Let me hear how you fared there—& how the family are getting on. "The Comedy of Masks" appears on Friday—nominally—but I see no reason now why it should be actually any further delayed. You must command it from Mudies. I tremble at the prospect of being reviewed—I am painfully conscious of the innumerable blemishes & alas! the weakest points are in the first volume so that I fear sleep will overcome the reviewer before he reach any of our less banal passages. What fools we are to write—or rather to publish! Mercifully Lionel does not review novels—and as to the opinion of the average novel-reviewing LeGallienish animal—"we will not think of it." Peters has turned up in town again very redolent of the States and very enthusiastic over the Highlands.

Commend me to Walton if this should reach you in his neighbourhood.

Ever yours

ERNEST DOWSON

How shall you call la petite? This will be an exercise almost as difficult as the choice of a book title. En passant can you suggest a name for notre prochain roman—wh. is just half completed. "A Mesalliance" is, I fear, bad English. "The Opportunist"—occurs to me, also "The Interlopers"—but none of these is good. It's better than "Masks" we both think but vindictive, savage, spleenful, libellous almost, to the last degree. Heaven knows when it will be finished.

To Victor Plarr

Bridge Dock,
Limehouse, E.

Cher Vieux,

What must you think of me for this ungrateful silence? But I have been so beset with inevitable correspondence that I have not possessed my soul since I saw you. I interviewed Warr on Sunday concerning l'affaire Williams & learnt from him what I heard in your letter of Monday that a musician was required. But he was charming and I was glad to have met him. Also I believe secretly I was glad that the matter had fallen through for I have not the courage I fear, after all to absent myself from Sherwood St. for so long.

You will have seen perhaps some of our reviews. Their benevolence has taken my breath away. The "Speaker," "Daily Chronicle," "Telegraph,"—"Scotsman" all favourable, some of them gushing—this weeks "Graphic" wh. has just come to hand. So far the only downright bad one was in the "World."

I was staying with Teixeira last night in the Temple & sat up for long talking to Sherard who is there & who came over with Zola & is writing a biography of him for Chatto & Windus. He is charming but the most morose & spleenful person I have yet encountered. His conversation is undiluted vitriol—like the man—nescio quem in "La Première Maitresse." Also this morning Gray who is finally leaving the Temple—quantum mutatus ab isto—fat but friendly, I fear incurably given over to social things & about to take up his abode in Park Lane! This is sad. May we meet soon—I have to return you your Spenser. I send all my compliments to the family wh: I trust prospers.

Ever thine
ERNEST DOWSON

TO VICTOR PLARR

Bridge Dock,
Limehouse,
Thursdy.

Mon cher Victor,

I hope you have not been misapprehending this long silence: only I have not been sure of your being able to read letters, and I felt pretty certain at least that you would not care to be writing them. Recent reports, however, have been more favourable, and so with no more preamble, I start on this epistolary adventure. It is delightful to think that you are really to be roofed in Fitzroy St: I hope I shall see much of you then, and that you will be perfectly, if you are not already, recovered. It will be nearer for me in a month: for I am thankful to say, we move into our new house (Bristol Gardens, Maida Hill) at the end of Aout. The station is Edgware Rd: which is a matter of a few minutes only from Portland Rd: you must often dine with us.

I suppose you have heard from Lionel of my Gascon adventures: it is a charming country, though not more so than Brittany, whither I go with Moore on Monday next. If it is not too bad for your eyes, you must let me find a letter from you there. Address me

Hotel du Lion D'Or
L'Faouet,
Morbihan.

We shall stay there for a 4ᵗnight. Have you been able to write anything lately? And are you to be in our Booke of Rymes? I have a story, but not at all a satisfactory one in the current "Macmillan." It treats of Poland and Poles; Paris, Violins and Soho!

But I have been dreadfully lazy, and without any excuse for it. You are to be felicitated on your absence from London, which has been dreary and desolate to a degree. But I hope you will come back soon. I hate it, when I am here; and go away anywhere, thankfully; but alas! such is my inconsistency, that when I have been but a little while from it, as says Johnson, that great lexicographer whom you blaspheme "I take the first convenient opportunity of returning to a place, where, if there is not much happiness, there is, at least such a diversity of good and evil, that slight vexations do not fix upon the heart."

Please commend me to your people, who are well, I hope: and write, if you may.

Yours ever

ERNEST DOWSON

TO VICTOR PLARR

15 Bristol Gardens, W.

Cher Vieux,

I have had a great many tedious things to do; I have also had a cold: they are both now arranged to a certain extent, and I am able to do what I should have done before, thank you for the charming night you allowed me to spend at Middleton last week. Were you at the Rhymers last night? I wish I could have managed to be of the party. I suppose it is settled that we are to hold the Laurelship as a corporate office, and present the bull of Canary to the patron du Cheshire, as a composition for free drinks. I am sorry that Tennyson has crossed the bar: if only, that it leaves us so much at the mercy of Sir Edwin, L. Morriss, Austen et Cᵢᵉ. But he was un grand poete, tout de même. Above all I love him because he did sacredly hate the mob—which whether it be the well dressed mob whom Browning pandered to, or the evil smelling mob to which William Morris does now to the detriment of his art and of his own dignity still pander, I hold alike to be damnable, unwholesome and obscene.

Write to me, as I suppose I shall not very often see you now; and send me anything you have written. My muse awoke from her torpor of many months yesterday: here is her feeble utterance, but she may run to another verse by and by.

IN AUTUMN

Pale, amber sunlight falls across
  The reddening, September trees,
  That hardly move before a breeze
As soft as summer: summer's loss
  Seems little, Dear! on days like these.

Let misty autumn be our part!
  The twilight of the year is sweet
  Where sunshine and the darkness meet,

Our love, a twilight of the heart
Eludes a little time's deceit.

Are we not better and at home
In dreamful autumn, we who deem
No harvest joy is worth a dream?
A little while and night shall come,
A little while we have to dream.

T à t
ERNEST DOWSON

With very kind regards to your mother
& Mme Victor

To Victor Plarr

Bridge Dock,
Limehouse, E.

Cher Vieux,

How are you all finding yourselves, and where; and when are we going to meet again? The whirling of time has taken my people to the world's end, which is called by the sublunary Chadwell Heath—& there I suppose for the present I must pass penetential Sundays—with much regret for your ancient, hospitable supper table. I suppose you are away from town: most people are, I think, now. I have had a prolonged epistolary paralysis or I would have afflicted you with a letter before. In fact I have only just reminded myself today that Greene's letter demanding rhymes is still unanswered & likely to remain so. But I am trying to hunt up the necessary half dozen & will dispatch them: though I should think the Star Chamber will have decided by this time to dispense with me. The weather is—well, too damned hot to write about for fear of burning the paper with expletives. I imagine you in Devonshire, drinking cider, playing skittles & eating cream *du pays.* Write to me & assure me that this is so, or if not that you are at Middleton & will look in upon me here one afternoon. I am verily I believe "alone in London." The darkness of the unknown has swallowed up Hillier, the provincial stage, Marmie. Did you ever interview Lane, and with what result? I called at his shop t'other day but like every one else he was campaigning. I do not even attempt to write any longer, not even verses. My mental horizon doesn't extend beyond cooling drinks and cigarettes. Forgive this tedious letter.—It is too hot to write letters: but on the other hand they are the only literature that is light enough for one to read—so I may conclude with an apt enough citation from a prince of letter writers though a most vile poet—(*pace* Mathew Arnold!)

"To be tiresome is the privilege of old age and absence; I avail myself of the latter and the former I have anticipated. If I do not speak to you of my own affairs, it is not from want of confidence, but to spare you and myself. My day is over—what then?—I have had it. To be sure I have shortened it, and if I had done as much by this letter, it would have been as well."

Always yours

ERNEST DOWSON

To HENRY DAVRAY

Hotel Gloanec,
Pont-Aven,
Finistère.

Mon cher Davray,

(Mais pourquoi—should I write to you in bad French when you understand so well English?)—I was very glad to hear from you, & that you have got back the books which you were kind enough to lend me.

I am also much obliged for your offer of papers. I should be very grateful if you will send me from time to time any French or English paper which is likely to interest me. (*Except* the "Journal" to which I am *abonné*.) Here in this pastoral place I can get no papers except the "Petit Journal" which is not inspiring though I can foresee that if I stay here long, I shall begin to take an absorbing interest in all the accidents at Dijon and in the intrigues of M. Xavier & Montepin's feuilleton.

Could you, without much trouble procure me 2 exemplaires of the Courier Français in which was Lautrec's article on the Savoy? I enclose a mandat for the price & postage, & shall be much obliged if you can get them & send them here.

I am glad to be here, I am working fairly hard, & find the people pleasant—chiefly painters, French & American. But there are moments when I have a very strong desire to take the next train back to Paris. Have you seen Beardsley? I hear he has returned to Paris & will stay there for two or three months. If you have not yet met him I will, as soon as I get his address—put you into communication with him. He was very amusing on my last Sunday at Paris. We went to see Lautrec, & Beardsley took some haschish for the first time. There was no result for some hours: then suddenly, while we were dining with Smithers at Margary's the haschish began to work very powerfully. Luckily we were in a *cabinet* or I think we should have been turned out—for Beardsley's laughter was so tumultuous that it infected the rest of us—who had *not* taken haschish & we all behaved like imbeciles.

I am glad you have come across Léopold Nelken. C'est un charmant garcon with a particularly suave & gentle manner, which I find essentially Russian.

My poems are now in the press. I will send you the volume when it appears. Write to me when you have time, & commend me to our friends, Ramborson [?], Lautrec etc. & to Madame Davray. O'Sullivan is likely to be in Paris soon, after which he intends to join me here.

Tout Votre

ERNEST DOWSON

To Henry Davray

Hotel Gloanec,
Pont-Aven,
Finistère.

My dear Davray,

I had long been meaning to write to you when your welcome letter came to "hurry me" up. I heard of Osman Edward's visit to you from Smith who was in Paris and ran across you at Bullier's I believe.

Beardsley as, perhaps, you have heard has been *very seriously* ill at Bruxelles. He went to see Smithers off at the Gare du nord & quite in the spirit with which we used to retire to Dieppe last summer decided at *the station* to go with him. Then he was attacked with congestion of the lungs & has been nursed by his sister and the good Smithers. From this last who is once more in England, I hear that he is now getting better.

I am doing a fair amount of work now, chiefly stories & the interminable "Pucelle." I am daily expecting the volume of my poems to arrive, & you will receive one at the same time at the *Mercure de France*. It is charming of you to write about me in your series. Any "documents" you may require I shall be delighted to send you. I have also sent a copy to Lautrec. Life is very charming here & I feel no inclination to move. A friend of Jean de Tinan's, le *nommé* "Cremnitz" was here for a quinzaine. There are also some half a dozen of painters, French & English, very excellent fellows—especially Loiseau, whom I knew before slightly, & whose work is exquisite. Séguin is expected & perhaps Goquain [?]; also later on some of our English comrades. Smithers, however, is very anxious that I should meet him in Paris, so that I may *possibly* come for ten days in May, when he will be there: in which case I shall hasten joyfully to press your hand. But in any case I shall return here for the summer and remain till October. Then—heigh ho for Paris—or perhaps Bruxelles & perhaps— very much perhaps, for it involves the question d'argent, Alger, et les jolies femmes arabesques. Here, I have no petites amies. C'est la vieille Armorique et pas la jeune qui me retient ici.

I was delighted to hear of Louÿs' success: I have written to him. Imagine Coppée!! Je viens de lire un livre d'Edouard Rod. "Dernière Refuge" qui me semble très bien écrit mais assez fade et fatiquant.

The "Savoy" ought to be "out" today. I have a story & poem in it, & am busy with a story for No. III. Symons has sent me his new book, which *entre nous*, I find disappointing. Connell O'Riordan's new roman "A Fool & his Heart," will appear in a day or two. I believe he has dedicated it to me. Tell me how I can get into communication with "Jean Thorel" (Bouthors), who I see has just produced a play at the Odéon. Five years ago, he sent me a book of his published by Vannier "La Complainte Humaine," & his brother Louis Bouthors was, when he was in England, for a year my most intimate friend. When I last wrote to him, at Dresden, my letter came back by the post & I should like to find out from his brother what has become of him. Would a letter to the Odéon reach Thorel? Of Horne I have had no news for a month. O'Sullivan was in Bruxelles with Beardsley, and in Paris for one day, en route for Pont-Aven. But in Paris he became alarmed about his health and returned to London, since which time I have received no news of him. I fear he also is ill. Alas! we are a *degenerate* and *maladive* race. My own health is of the worst. The life and the early hours are no doubt good for me, but the actual climate suits me less well than that of Paris.

Write soon and tell me all the news. Do you ever see Léopold Nelken? My friend Smith seems to have had a most debauched and frivolous quinzaine under his ciceronage.

Commend me to Ramborson [?] and all our connaissance.

Votre bien devoué
ERNEST DOWSON

I have not yet had time to write anything for "Tomorrow" but when Louys sends me "Aphrodite" I hope to write an appreciation upon it there.

To HENRY DAVRAY

Hotel Gloanec,
Pont-Aven,
Finistère.

Just a line to thank you very much for the various reviews & mag⁵. O'Sullivan had already sent me the *Senate* with 2 excellent portraits of Verlaine. Thank you also immensely for your offer to write of my poems in the "Hermitage." You shall have them as soon as they are out. I have just finished a *nouvelle* for the "Savoy" but fear it may arrive too late for the forthcoming number. I had a letter from Symons a day or two ago, also from Horne, from Florence. He— Horne will be in Paris about May. I expect Vincent O'Sullivan here in about a week. When he leaves me, which I hope will not be soon, he also goes to Paris. Go and see Beardsley at the Hotel St Romain, Rue St. Roch. Smithers was also there last week. I will write at greater length shortly. The "cuttings" are admirable. Quel fou, ce Buchanan. Mes amitiés à Mᵐᵉ, à toute la bande et à toi-même.

To LEONARD SMITHERS

Hotel Gloanec,
Pont-Aven,
Finistère.

My dear Smithers,

Your letter gratefully received & the 50 francs; but I am truly grieved to hear that you also have fallen a victim to treachery of the skin. You are welcome to pass it on to me if you like, for one more malady, more or less, makes no difference in my museum of ailments. It is a fête again today—curse these fêtes which seem to occur every other day—& in consequence I have found the post shut after déjeuner & am unable to send you my story which is ready, until tomorrow. I hope it will reach in time. In any case, I fear it has spun out to too great a length for one number, especially, as I presume the Savoy, having taken to menstruation, will be less in volume than of old.

It is a great & admirable institution the "Savoy," & held in high esteem here as elsewhere. I hope it will succeed as well in its monthly aspect as I presume it has as a quarterly. May the hair of John Lane grow green with Envy!

When may I expect my verses? I am grieved about "Lot's Daughters." I have mislaid both my manuscript & the original but I will have a search this afternoon amongst the mass of letters, proofs & manuscript which have accumulated in my room. I am quite resigned to spending my life at Pont-Aven like the other exiles who have drifted here: except that I want to see your classically sin-stained countenance, I should not even think of a week in Paris.

In its monthly stage will the "Savoy" take chronical notice of literary events? If so I should like to write a short notice say a couple of pages on the three most notable recent publications in Paris—Louÿ's "Aphrodite," Zola's "Roma" & Tinan's "Erythrée."

I have no more to say, except that I hope my study will satisfy you & that I will now resume the "Pucelle" like a trojan.

On the 10th of the ensuing month, unless I am with you in Paris, I shall be let in for my landlord's wedding, which will be an infernal nuisance as it occurs some 15 miles from here, & a Breton wedding is kept up for two days,—two days of riotous gaiety & compulsory drinking, which finishes up with a ball at our Hotel! Write soon.

Always yours,
ERNEST DOWSON

I sent you a little book.

To Elkin Mathews

c/o I. De Courcy MacDonnell Esq.
Fairy Hill,
Limerick,
Ireland.

Dear Mr. Mathews,

I shall be much obliged if you will send me a copy of "Dilemmas" to the above address.

I should be glad also if you would let me have an account at your earliest convenience as to how the book has gone as it is now more than 18 months since I heard any news from you about it.

Yours truly,
ERNEST DOWSON

LETTERS TO CONAL O'RIORDAN

Dowson's association with Conal O'Riordan (whose early novels were written under the name Norreys Connell) was long and profitable. Of all the men, French or English, with whom the poet moved during his first autumn and winter in Paris, none provided him with more salutary companionship than the young novel-ist with whom he had made a walking trip in Flanders in the summer of 1895. (For a detailed record of their acquaintanceship, see pp. 187-189.) From the late summer of 1895 until a few days before Dowson's death on February 23, 1900, they were in irregular correspondence. Mrs. Olga O'Riordan, widow of the novel-ist, has generously provided me with copies of the Dowson Letters which were among her husband's effects.

*Since Dowson dated few of his letters, an accurate chronological arrangement is virtually impossible. From the contents, however, and the infrequent notations made on them by O'Riordan, I have tried to arrange the eighteen letters in some sort of sequence. Nine of them were written in the fall and early winter of 1895-96; three from June to September, 1897 (surely after Wilde's release from gaol); four which O'Riordan places sometime in the fall of 1897 or the spring of 1898; and then two short letters in February, 1900, the second of which O'Riordan believed to be Dowson's last letter. In almost all instances, they are highly auto-biographical, and rich in detail that reveals. Misspellings and irregularities in punctuation, syntax, and French accents are retained as they appeared in the letters.—*ED.

214 Rue Saint Jacques,
Paris.

My dear Connell,

By some oversight you have run away with the key of No 15. The proprietor has asked me to write to you & remind you of this: I feel that with my natural propensity to put off, unless I write at once I shall get into trouble with my pro-prietor. This must be my excuse for writing shortly. Further news at a more con-venient season,

T   à   t
ERNEST DOWSON

Brasserie des Femmes-en-Reet

Café d'Harcourt,
Tuesday.

Cher Vieux,

I have been lunching here, money having arrived, & must send you a line to wish you an happy inauguration in your new home. I was very seedy all yesterday —lit my fire & stayed at home, drowsing, all day until 8. when I went dined at a very decent place in La Boul. Miche. which I found, for 1.25. Then I came back, went to bed, had, for once in my life, a fairly decent night, & actually rose & breakfasted at our Crémerie at 8.0 AM. I then went for a walk to the Gare Montparnasse, looked at the hole in the station & returned to find Smithers' letter.

I have bought a conical hat—black—& think of having my hair cropped very short so that it will suit me better. I fell much better today except for my specific disease which increases by leaps & starts. Have heard no news of my fracas with the Snailmer-chant: so trust it is all happily over.

I saw Léopold in here just now, but he has received "a little money from Petersburg" so has gone off to the races. Write me a line to say how you are getting on, if you,have not done so already—or even if you have & remember me "mes meilleures amities" to the Noblet. I hope you lunched today as well as I did.

> Tout à toi
>
> ERNEST DOWSON

This was written about the last week of November 1895.

C
[O'Riordan's Note]

> D'Harcourt (Café)
> Heure d'apéritif.

Dear Exile,

Your letter agreeably to hand. I am sorry the Mons-par-Donnemarie food is not all that it should be, but I had my suspicion that the dejeuner we partook of was a sample one to inspire confidence. (Par exemple, don't leave this letter about—) I rather emmerde myself since your departure. Was seedy yesterday & stayed in bed & sent for the ordinary litre of milk. Today got up early, took the steam train from the Odeon to Bourge-la-Reine & had a charming walk to Antony where I lunched, returning by the train to the Gay-Lussac station. The country was charming, but the trees more decayed than at Donnemarie. I have had a letter at last from my young lady. She tells me that there is a "Trilby boom" in London now—everything, hats, collars, coats & mantles a la Trilby. It is also on at the theatre quelque part. I have also had an ennuyeux letter from Horne: Jepson has, I fear, successfully embroiled me with everybody. I have just written to ask what the devil he means by it! Have received a line from Smithers & the proofs of my story. He says he is simply waiting for money to come over. Léopold, for whom I am now waiting, received certain roubles from Russia, the day before yesterday & promptly got extremely drunk here & retired with a most exceptionally ordinary woman to whom he probably gave £100. By the way there is an amusing paragraph dealing with us, inserted by Rambosson, in the "Nouvelle France" & I am told also in the Echo de Paris describing an imaginary reception by "M. Henri Davray l'orientaliste dans son appartement superbe aux glaces, Rue Fléurus, pour fêtes les poétes anglais Ernest Dousog et O'Connell Norreys" at which assisted X. Y. Z. et Marcel Schwob, Gabriel de Lautrec, Yvanhoe Rambosson, le Docteur Charrier (I put down the names I remember but there were many more). The honours were done by "Mme. D. Davray resplendissante dans une robe noir et or." And music was played by the "pianiste anglaise bien connue Miss Ethel Jepson et le compositeur

Ruschoff Bey". I will send you the paper—show it to Noblet, but let him take it au serieux. He will then probably realize what great men we are & either give you decent food or reduce your pension.

I ran across Lautrec the other night & am going to lunch with him on Sunday.

I have no other news that I can think of to consummate this page. Write me a letter by return. I am consumed with ennui, & start for Auvergne at the end of my month.

By the way I am devoutly thankful, much as I miss you that I was not idiot enough to share your rustication except for one thing which your letter informs me of—your visit to the Curé. It is hard lines after all my efforts and ambitions, that you should be moving—you who probably don't appreciate it—in the best ecclesiastical society while I do not even know a seminarist. I feel towards you, as you would towards me, if I had dined with the General Saussier & he had talked to me for hours on the art of fortification & sent me a MSS on "The right employ-ment of cavalry in a siege"

Write at once, dear Rusticus, & I am, always

Yours,

ERNEST DOWSON

As this letter-journal extends over several days, I number it for your conven-ience. E.D.

214 Rue Saint-Jacques,
Monday.

Very dear Gossip,

Delighted to receive your letter. Here too, the cold—but only yesterday and today has been biting, and a high N.N.E wind has prevailed. I am in an awful state of penury & unless Smithers or someone else (a debtor) to whom I appealed on Sat. has paid by tomorrow I know not how I shall exist. I dined en famille on Saturday with the Davrays, & yesterday called on the most noble Vicomte de Lautrec, who insisted on my staying to dine with him. It was a most charming & original dinner; his younger brother shares his apartment, & cooks & apparently does all the house work. The other guests were, the poet Wattein, an anonnymous poet, & an elderly professor at the Lycee of which Lautrec is also a professor. After dinner which was most creditable to Henri de Lautrec's culinary talent we drank rum & worked hankey-pankey with *planchette* at which Lautrec & the pro-fessor are adepts. We got a message from Satan but he appeared to have nothing of the slightest importance to say. We then took haschish, & eventually all, with the exception of the elderly professor, slept on sofas & mattresses at Lautrec's. A charming evening, but today I have felt a little worn & weary. You will like Lautrec extremely though, & I am sorry we had not the energy to seek him out before you left. But Passy is a hell of a way off. I write this at the D'Harcourt & Leopold has just entered, so I must cut it short. If he asks me to dine I shall not refuse, for I have just 1.50 in the world. I hope & pray money arrives tomorrow:

if not & you have any spare cash would you send me 10 francs. Do this unless I wire to you: I will wire if money reaches me. Au revoir, carissime Rustice. Write —write—write. It is not in my disposition to write letters but see how voluminous I get.

T à t
ERNEST DOWSON
of Paris

I will send you a most amusing Caran d'Ache "Journal" with a military story in it if you will not mind after perusing it sending it on to

Arthur Moore Esq.
5 Loudoun Rd
London N.W

He adores Caran d'Ache.

(Continuation)

Leopold was called away by a friend so I have returned chez moi to dine on the most frugal scale that I have yet contrived—I don't count my litre of milk days when I lie in bed. My dinner is one longish roll 5ᶜ one Brie cheese 20ᶜ ½ bottle red wine 50ᶜ· I had an absinthe at the D'Harcourt & I have spent something on tobacco & cigarette papers. And curiously enough I do not feel depressed at this meal in my room, although I would sooner be dining at the D'Harcourt. I have a splendid fire, twopence in the world, & only complain—(but Heaven or Smithers send me some money tomorrow!) that I am in such bad company—the only company I can not stand—my own! I feel like working too. Curiously enough also & secondly the exact opposite in the matter of my hours & habits to what I anticipated after your departure has happened. It is probably owing to the fact that when you were with me I depended on you for all knowledge of the time of day & knew you would call me when you were ready for dejeuner, whereas now I am utterly at sea when I awake as to whether it is 8 or 12—but the fact remains, I am almost invariably up & out by nine o'clock now. This is not an economy to me, because it means that after a petit dejeuner at the Cremerie I get hungry again & have to indulge in a 1.15 dejeuner at 1.0. But I will pause, (this descriptive passage has reminded me that I must dine)—when I have finished my sumptuous repast I will continue.

[*There is a sketch here of the table laid with the meal described.*—ED.]

Wednesday night

I did not send this letter because no money came—the gales in the channel having disorganized the postal service—& I preferred to spend my twopence on bread, rather than on a three sou stamp. I confess I did not enjoy yesterday!!!! But I had philosophy enough yesterday, even yesterday!—and can you imagine from my previous Monday's beginning, what yesterday was like? to quote in anticipation "Forsan et haec olim meminisse furabit.". . . . And this morning lo there was a letter & £1 & I went out with tears of gratitude in my eyes and had an absinthe & afterwards a breakfast a f1.25 at my recently discovered rest[nt.] My seclusion of yesterday had given me a sort of letch of adventure so I took a return ticket to Sceaux (80[e], & the third class carriages are sumptuous!) & walked thence some kilos to Fontenay-aux-Roses: is it not an adorable name? And the place too is adorable: I felt inclined to look about for lodgings. The east wind of yesterday had utterly gone; except that the trees were a little worn & weary, it might have been a very fine day in spring. And I drank my beer outside a rural cafe & wrote a letter, & concocted verses and generally basked for an hour or so: then strolled back to Sceaux & so back to Paris to dine. One has one's fortunate days sometimes —do you remember "Marius"?—so that after my expansion of the afternoon I was not surprised that I should strike, quite by accident on the most attractive of cheap restaurants that I have yet encountered—a little place in the Place St. Andre des Arts, near the Place St. Michel. The cuisine was wonderful: it was a la carte, & including coffee my bill reached the sum of f1.75. When you come back—you must run up for a day soon, we will dine there. Apres, I fell in such a Christian mood—even towards my relations, (because it suddenly struck me that however prosperous & well conditioned they may be, their malice & meanness, even from a purely pagan point of view hurts them far more than it ever can me) apres I took an omnibus to the Bourse and got into Notre Dame des Victoires just at the fag end of the sermon before the Benediction. I had never been to the Church before,—only known of it from Huysman's marvelous novel, which, by the way, you should possess, if your novel deals with a reconciliation to Catholicism. But I was immensely impressed by the sort of wave of devotion which thrills through the whole crowded congregation,—I had fancied Huysman had exaggerated it—: but the reality exceeds his description & I can imagine no other church in Paris, no other church anywhere, perhaps, except Lourdes, where one may have the same experience. It makes me afraid to go back there, for fear it should move me too much. Because—although I know sooner or later I must put on the dust & ashes there are things I care about so much, which I want to do first. And I am afraid, or rather certain, that after all this long time of abstinence, when I once do bring myself to the point of reconcilation, it will be so horribly serious, and it will be all up with my work and so on . . . However, let us return to our muttons. I an writing this very unnecessary scrawl, which I hope won't bore you too much, in an arm chair, by a noble fire, in No. 14, my paper being supported by an exercise book on my knee & this fact, & the uncertain light must excuse sundry blots & uncertainties in the writing. It is not very late for I came straight back here from N.D. de V. but I suppose it is the middle of the night with you. I wish you were back here. My plans are utterly vague, but probably after Smithers' visit, which he tells me in his letter that arrived today, may be at any moment, I shall decide something. I don't think I shall stay here; I may go to Florence; I may get a room like this at some convenient suburb—the suburbs here are not in the least like anything within thirty miles of London—such as St. Germain, Chantillon, Sceaux or

Fontenay; I may go to Cannes where I am told I can get a room for about f40-50. If you get tired of Mons after your month or arrange definitely to get tired of it by the end of Dec. I will go to Brittany with you & postpone my other projects: but I can not face it alone. Of these things we will talk however after Smithers' visit. Write soon, not to say immediately: I quite realized Noblet was economical as it is only in the nature of the bourgeois French to be—I told you so in Paris—& I can see with my own eyes how he waters the ink. But send me a sample menu of dej. & dinner. It will be instructive. And also describe to me your personal relations with "Mons, Madame et Bebe" not to mention the dogs.

Always yours,

ERNEST DOWSON

214 Rue Saint Jacques,
Paris.

My dear Connell,

Forgive my tardiness: but you must know by this time how ingrained & incurable is my habit of procrastination. I got your letter last night—or rather this morning for I entered after a night with notre Leonard at 7 AM. The storm of which you send so graphic a description must have coincided with the one which conveyed Smithers from England. You will have heard of his arrival here. I am writing this in the Rue Druont while he deals with a bookseller across the street. The "Savoy" business was very foolish "much ado etc" but I gather from a letter reaching me today from Jepson that he & the other objectors believed themselves entirely in the right. I have conveyed to them my own opinion in the frankest terms: viz that they are a parcel of idiots. We have pursued our usual courses since Smithers arrived—varied by a visit to a prison to call on his friend who is confined in St. Pélagie. We go & *lunch* with the said prisoner tomorrow: is it not a charming idea? I shall certainly write an article on it. Nothing could be more pleasant than the surroundings of the captives of that grisly dungeon. Except that two rather sleepy gaolers sit at a little table by the door & object to our friend's leaving he is entirely free apparently to wander where he wills. His room is one for which one would pay 50 francs at the Hotel de Médicis: he gets it free. His meals are provided by the state and are sent in from a restaurant. He is apparently free to ask his friends to lunch. He is not stinted in society—for instance when we called yesterday his three children, his mother-in-law & his wife were sitting with him. There is a library in the gaol & a benevolent government provides him with 12 newspapers daily! (This is *literally true* although it seems incredible). And a climax which will especially appeal to you, he burns *wood* logs in his stove & has a pile of them enough to stock a fortress. He can smoke also—not only in his room—but about the establishment. Why, oh why am I not a prisoner of Saint-Pélagie? I thought of Oscar & marvelled at the quaintness of this adorable country.

No more now. I must join Smithers. Write soon. I will write again tout de suite. Love to the Noblets.

T à t,

E.D.

P.S. I suppose it was owing to the improper overtures which you made to Maxime that the poor boy was sacked? If it had been a chamber maid it would have been only excusable.

214, Rue Saint Jacques,
Paris.

My dear Conal,

I enclose this line in a letter answering Noblet's invitation which of course I have gladly accepted. I was thinking of asking you to come up here for Xmas, but it will be just as well *chez vous*—not that I approve as a rule of celebrating that fete, *a l'Anglais*—it should rather be celebrated, at least in my case, & perhaps with you, as the *jour des morts*—All Souls Day. But it struck me that we two might seasonably spend it together. I haven't heard from you but your key has arrived. Smithers, Leopold & myself had a very gay evening together before he left last Friday, & our two friends got very friendly; even Smithers accepted a loan of twenty francs from Leopold, as he had run short. To day, when I was in bed, who should arrive but John-Paul-Emmanuel-Ashworth, very drunk,—the Newhaven-Dieppe boat having taken nine hours instead of four in crossing & J.-P.-E.-Ashworth having spent the extra five hours in standing whiskey to the crew & himself. John Paul Emmanuel was commissioned by Smithers to repay Leopold his twenty francs & we consequently called there. J.P.E.A. repaid the debt, & told Leopold thirteen times at intervals of three minutes that he was "one of the best"; he also told him that Smithers was "one of the best" & that I was "one of the best". We then went out and had drinks at the D'Harcourt & elsewhere & at ten fifteen I succeeded in taking Jean-Paul-Emmanuel-Ashworth back to the Hotel d'Athenes & putting him to bed. I then, feeling responsibility was over—for Ashworth was really so drunk that I was in terror of a row—came back here—the German beer cafe in the Rue Soufflot & had a *demie* & wrote these letters. I will turn up, as Noblet suggests on the 24th—that is if I have the money for my fare.

The "Fille aux Yeux D'Or" is now in the printers' hands. I spent an entire night in writing the preface (from midnight—8.30. AM) & Pierre Louys has allowed it to be dedicated to him as the greatest authority in Europe on Lesbianism except myself.

Why, by the way, did you bugger up Smithers so much about me over your lunch the other day? We are both fond (unduly) of "fire water" & you know that, but the result was that I had to spend the rest of the day in defending you on the ground of your being, as I believe you are, really one of my best friends, &

explaining your remarks away, as an indiscretion of friendship. And, *seriously* you were wrong in talking like that, because I might easily have interpreted what you said as a sort of treachery, & resented it; & with anybody else except Smithers you might have done me serious harm. As it was, I refused to regard you as a sort of (Jepson + Teixeira), put down your animadversions as kindly meant, & as Smithers declared your conversation had given him a thirst we drank that day more heavily than ever. Of course, I should not write like this unless I knew you were really a friend of mine—one whom I look forward to meeting in a day or two. Jepson's interference I have satisfactorily dealt with. I have not answered his last two letters but I have written to Moore (my collaborator) who sees him every now & then & asked him to give him (Jepson) a hint. He answers me that he will give him the "hint". He puts it with the quotation marks. I forget if you know Moore, but he has the most polished manner & can be more infernally rude in an urbane way than any man I have ever known in my life. As Jepson, with all his faults is subtile, & Moore dislikes him personally, apart from my own resentment with him—I gather Mr. Jepson & I, have made a happy consummation of our correspondence. His last letter was most impudently familiar . . . But enough of an unpleasant subject. The students have invaded this cafe & are beginning to *"sing"*. Therefore it is time for me to go. Until the 24th,

> Tout à toi,
>
> ERNEST DOWSON

> *214 Rue Saint-Jacques,*
> *Paris*
> *31 Dec. 1895.*

Mon bon Vieux,

   I must send a line to wish you all my good wishes for the year which opens tomorrow. It can easily be more prosperous to you & to me than the one which is over. Vincent O'Sullivan is over here now, has called on me, & been banqueting me at the Café de Paris. He is a very nice fellow & improves on acquaintance. I hope you are better than you were when I left. Convey my necessary compliments to the Noblets. Write soon: I have but a moment or two to catch the post & am besides, too profoundly triste to write at length.

> Poignee de main,
>
> ERNEST DOWSON

> *214 Rue Saint Jacques,*
> *Paris.*

My dear Connell,

   I hope you have not *m'en voulu* for my silence, and that your own is not due to the same reason as my own—that is to say to persistent & increasing lack of health. Make my excuses to Noblet for not answering his letter & tell him that I will send the papers he wants & the addresses in a day or two. For the last ten days I have been more or less decrepit—sometimes well enough when pricked by the stings of starvation to get out of doors as today, but never of sufficient robustness to cross the river & reach the kiosques whereat I can buy the papers he wants. Write & tell me how you get on & when I may expect you here? I have arranged to leave at the end of my term i.e. by the 5th Feb. but I may go before. I merely wait to see Smithers who may arrive any day & when he leaves I leave also—for *Brittany,* not for Aix-les-Bains as I had intended—but in Brittany certain people have promised to come & see me, & my horror of my own company increases with my infirmities. I hope you will turn up here, however, before I go. I would come down to see you if it were possible, but I am saving myself for the journey to Pontaven, which I begin to think will be my last journey. *En effet* you who have known me when helas I was *plus gai et plus brillant* will hardly believe that now a walk from the Hotel des Medicis to the Place St. Michel is an adventure which knocks me up for two days

What, however, more I think than my physical collapse is really killing me is the conviction that has come to me—justified by the news I get from England of how my affairs are going—of the monstrous way in which I have been exploited and swindled and ruined by the very people who, from their near kinship to me, I thought I could depend on—at least *not* to rob me flagrantly:—I never expected justice or generosity from them. But you can have no conception of how I have been exploited: I have only recently realized it myself. And, as perhaps you will understand, this feeling (multiplied by my temperament) lights up a sort of intense flame of hatred and loathing which destroys the peace of my days, & the sleep of my nights & deprives me of any chance that remains to me of getting cured. For I have been told particularly that my one chance depends on my ability to avoid any strong emotion or excitement. But this thing grows on me, though I know that even if I had the money I should not have the energy to take the necessary legal proceedings to make the bloodsuckers disgorge. Forgive me, for boring you with these allusions to my personal affairs; but I am acquiring such a profound distrust for everyone—the result of my unhappy experiences—that except Smithers and yourself I can think of nobody to whom I can speak of these matters without fear of treachery. Even Langdale, who, I know means me very well, & who has been profuse in his offers to serve me, writes to me about an uncle of mine, whom he knows, as if it was a sort of testimonial to me that the said uncle speaks "kindly" of me, & is anxious to do anything in his power for me. I told Langdale in reply that it was quite indifferent to me whether my uncle was kind or unkind, but that he (my uncle) should feel intensely grateful to me for having recognized the fact that he was only weak & not *méchant,* and so having refrained from prosecuting him for culpable negligence.

Keep this letter, my dear Connell, & send it, at a future date, to persons whose address will be given you. I am settling up my affairs just now & am making you —if you don't mind—& Smithers my executors. Give all the necessary compliments (& don't tell him how very little I want to meet his friends) to Noblet. I *will* deliver that card of introduction to the deaf & dumb power, when I am in better health. At present, I avoid everybody, except Leopold Nelken, who is awfully nice to me: & write soon.

Tout à toi,
ERNEST DOWSON

-----

*214 Rue St. Jacques,
Paris.*

My Dear Conal,

You must be thinking me a fearful brute, but I did not get your letter until yesterday, having been seedy & in bed and yesterday also I was a prisoner in my chamber. Rambosson came to see me & I gave him my letter—a long one, to post wh. probably has reached you. Today I am all right again & I enclose a *mandat* for 20f. I have kept the balance 5f to buy the guides, which I will do tomorrow or on Monday. I hope this involuntary delay on my part hasn't seriously inconvenienced you, but if so you have all my sympathy (moi qui sait la veche)—at any rate you have had your food, but I during the 24 hours which—if Rambosson posted my letter—you will dimly imagine from the "........" was practically foodless.

By the way I hope you will succeed in cashing the enclosed document in less time that it took me to obtain it. It is the first time I have ever "dealt" with a French postal order & I took *half an hour* without exaggeration getting it: and I signed enough documents to have set me up in London for some years in a promising Chancery suit. Write soon.

T à t
ERNEST

I don't write at length now for fear of missing the post.
I dined with Strong last night, & tonight go to dine with Lautrec.

-----

*Hotel du Château d'Arques
Arques-la-Bataille
Seine-Inferieure
France.*

My dear Conal,

Have you balm in Gilead for me? I write in a grand desespoir to beg you for old days' sake to sound Tiemons [Symons?] to see if he is open to any suggestion of work from me. For the hour has come, which I have long forseen when Smithers' & my arrangement has ended. Perhaps, it is a good thing for me, in some ways; or will be, rather, if I can get a little money to go along with. Conder was with me here for long, in similar terrible straights, & then I bore up. But a good Samaritan, Dal Young came to his rescue, bought a picture which enabled him to pay his Hotel bill & took him back to England. The same Young, who is a marvel of good nature is busying himself with selling or mortgaging through his solicitor a small share of mine in an East India Ry. which brings me in £18 a year & on which he is sanguine of raising £300. But he has not written today, & it will take time, & my credit will expire & I shall not soon have the money for tobacco & stamps, & I feel as if all the world have abandoned me—& Crackanthorpe's ghost is calling to me from the other side of Styx. Write to me by return, mon cher ami; send me a little money if you can, but *write, write.* Siemens [Symons?] once asked me to write a short novel & hinted that he would finance me to some extent while writing it. If he were of the same mind today, & would advance me something on it, I would write one in a month. I have the idea, but in this state of worry & distress how can one write? If once this £300 reaches me, I shall take a little house for about 500 francs in the country, pay my debts, a years rent in advance & make the balance last me for at least a couple of years, while I write, write, write. But this waiting kills me. I write this dismal appeal in an enchanting garden, on an enchanting day—et j'ai envie de pleurer. And it angers me to think that I have never felt so physically well, or so morally fit to work & not to drink as I do at present. The other day I met Oscar & dined with him at his seaside retreat; I had some difficulty in suppressing my own sourness & attuning myself to his enormous joy in life just at this moment—but I hope I left him with the impression that I had not a care in the world. He was in wonderful form, but has changed a good deal—he seems of much broader sympathies, much more human & simple. And his delight in the country, in walking, in the simplicities of life is enchanting. When Conder had left he described, by the way, Conder's delightfully inconsequent mind & manner of conversation, which you will remember to perfection. "Conder's conversation, he said "is like a beautiful sea-mist". N'est ce pas, que c'est le trait?

Adieu, my dear friend; writing to you has somewhat cheered me, but all my *misères* will return in a moment. *Please* do not delay to write.

affectionately
ERNEST DOWSON

By the way, I need not say that Oscar does not want his retreat generally known; nor his pseudonym.

[*There is an enclosure with this letter:*]
Mon Conal,

Since writing this long & lugubrious scrawl—I have had a letter to cheer me. I am saved; although it may be a week or so before I have any money.

Dal Young writes to me, after interviewing my solicitor as follows: "You have no need to be anxious in the least. He (Nairne) spoke very nicely about you & absolutely assured me that there was no difficulty in getting some money on your East India Ry property. He wanted to know the exact amount you wanted as, apparently £300 wd not quite exhaust the whole value of your share. If £200 wd do for you now, for instance, you could leave the rest to be realized at some future time". Of course I wrote to Young that £200 *would* do & I await in hope for a letter from Nairne. Meanwhile, as I have but a few francs left I should be immensely grateful if you could procure a pound or so—or a few shillings even & send me the same here. As you will gather from the quotation from Young's letter there is no hitch about the money, I am sure to be able to repay it to you within a week or ten days.

I am going to take a house near Rouen.

I am so poor that I hope you won't mind posting enclosed letter to Moore. 2½d a letter is awful—& yet I am rich!!!

Adieu, cher vieux

Postmark June 1897
[*O'Riordan's Note*]

Hotel du Chateau d'Arques,
Arques-la-Bataille,
Seine, Inf.

My dear Conal,

My most hearty thanks for the 50 francs received today & your letter yesterday. I hope things will soon right themselves, although since I wrote to you with my usual luck it turns out that one of the trustees of the fund, my share of which my solicitor is to realize for me, is *non compos mentis,* so that an order of the Court (?of Chancery) will have to be got. This I fear means delay. I am writing, however, to see if I can not obtain an interim advance of £50 while this is being done. I hope to get a small house somewhere near Rouen, which is not too far from London to enable me to treat with publishers & stay there for a year, paying a year's rent in advance & living of course most frugally. The MacDonnells of Fairy Hill, Limerick have sent me a truly Irish invitation to come & stay all the summer with them & fish salmon, but although this is tempting, I fear lest Irish hospitality should be too little conducive of the hard work I propose for myself.

Oscar came over & lunched with me the other day & carried me back with him to Bernaval. His gorgeous spirits cheered me mightily. I was amused by the unconscious contrast between his present talk about his changed position & his notions of economy, & his practise, which is perversely extravagant. He does not realize in the least that nobody except himself *could* manage to spend the money he does in a *petit non de campagne.* He is a wonderful man.

You tell me nothing of your own doings: I hope they are rosy. I saw Rothenstein the other day, on his return from a pilgrimage to Bernaval, & he told me that Teixeira was leaving Henry's? I hope this is not true, or that he is doing it merely to "better himself". Once more, my many thanks. I hope you will write soon, as I don't hope to escape from Arques for another ten days & I shall have sundry relapses into the blues until something is settled.

Affecly yours,
ERNEST DOWSON

Moore highly approves my idea of taking a house over here. Thanks for the review: it is charming. Do you know who wrote it? You have, doubtless, heard that Beardsley has become a papist & is living surrounded by images & crufixes at St. Germain.

_____

Received 13/9/97
[*O'Riordan's Note*]

c/o J. de Courcy MacDonnell Esq.
Fairy Hill,
Parteen,
Limerick.

My Dear Conal,

How wags the world with you, Sir? I gather from some journal or other that you have retired to some country estate of yours to write a very readable work. I have been staying here with the MacDonnells for the last month for the same end, and am to stay here until October when I hope fortune will allow me to proceed to Paris for the winter. I interviewed my solicitor on my way through London & expect to get £300 out of him shortly. I will send you the £2 you so kindly lent me the moment I have it. At present, I am utterly stony. I am trying to write sundry things but this is a terribly lazy though very charming place. I was staying with Oscar for some time before I left France. I introduced Smithers to him, who had turned up at Dieppe, & they have struck up an alliance. Conder & Beardsley, the Dal Youngs etc. were also at Dieppe: I lacked only you and Symons to reproduce the former occasion. Only some of us being wrecks & some of us ruined a good deal of the joy of life had departed.

Let me hear soon of your news. Are you a member of the "Author's Club"? If so I will ask you to put me up later on as a foreign member as I want a London address. I am going to take an apartment in Paris & furnish it. I have given up the idea of the house at Pont de l'Arches. I was only in London two days en route here. I dined with O'Sullivan, saw Johnson & stayed with the Victor Plarrs. They were in a mighty fury over a letter of Jepson's in "Tomorrow" which you doubtless saw. I suppose that man of sin still flourishes? Tell me what has become of Teixeira? DO write soon

Tout a toi
ERNEST DOWSON

Who is editor of Pearson's?

_____

Autumn of '97 or Spring '98
[*O'Riordan's Note*]

Sophia House,
Bloomsbury.

My dear Conal,

Of course I shall be delighted to be translated into the Dutch. I am only sorry that my rudimentary knowledge of the language will prevent me from appreciating the proper values of your friend Van Houten's translation.

I am still in London—still waiting for the completion of my interminable financial transactions, which, however, cannot be spread out beyond another week or two,—then I hope to fly away to some peaceful place in France or Italy & be at rest for a little.

You must come & dine with me if you will before my departure—my really very last departure & we will talk of Ypres.

T à toi

ERNEST DOWSON

You will excuse the flippancy of my note-paper & my language if you can guess the sadness of my heart.

---

c/o S. Smith Esq.
46, Preston St.,
Faversham, Kent.

Private

My dear Conal,

Behold me here in England again, for how long I know not, but for longer I fear than I had hoped when I arrived. I am staying for the next day or two with Smith. Forgive my asking you, and don't my dear old chap inconvenience yourself if you are in evil case, (for I know nothing of how you are situated) *but* if you could let me have a sovereign & send it here as soon as possible I should be very grateful. Smithers has not abandoned me but I have to get back to town, & I am anxious not to have to ask him for money immediately. If you would not mind writing by return I shall be relieved.

I am anxious to see you again but am too busy at present to arrange a meeting or make any plans: nor am I quite certain where you are.

Affectionately,

ERNEST DOWSON

P.S. Please treat this as confidential.

[*Since Dowson's financial straits are well known, I, like O'Riordan, have ignored his request to treat this letter as confidential. It is difficult to account for his sensitivity in this instance, for usually—at least after 1896—he showed little hesitancy in informing his acquaintances of the condition of his purse.*—ED.]

---

6 Featherstone Buildings
High Holborn,
W.C.

My dear Conal,

I am dreadfully remiss: I wrote to thank you for the very acceptable sovran, but in my oblivion did not post the letter, nor did I call at Royal Arcade & find your letter till yesterday. Note my address & let me know when & how I may see you.

I am starting on a new & monumental translation for Smithers, which may neces-
sitate my staying in London, & have many other schemes of work in my hand. I
have seldom felt in more industrious mood; & seldom felt more pessimistic or
unsociable. But I should greatly like to see you again, if you can come to town.

Ever yours,

ERNEST DOWSON

1, Guilford Place
Bloomsbury, W.C.

My dear Conal,

Forgive my delay in answering you. I was hoping to have raised the money. I
am awfully sorry that I must ask you to wait another fortnight. I have had infinite
worry & difficulty since June owing to the very complicated legal difficulties in the
way of realizing my money. But when I saw my solicitor on the 6th ult. he told me
definitely that the matter would be finished in a month's time. I shall then have
some hundreds at my disposal & will discharge my debt to you at once. For the
moment I have only just enough to carry me through the period of waiting. I am
on the very best of terms with Smithers, however, which has cheered me & he has
promised me further work. I hope you are well & prospering & that we may meet
some day.

Votre bien de voué

ERNEST DOWSON

Our novel (Moore's & mine) is now with Heinemann. It will be called probably
"The Arrangement of Life".

------

26 Sandhurst Gardens,
Catford, S.E.
Wednesday

Dear Connell,

Ernest Dowson is here with me in my little cottage. He is not well enough to
write to you himself & of course unable to go to see you. He would much like a
chat with you & so I am writing to ask you if you would come over here to-morrow
afternoon on your bicycle at any hour that may best suit you.

Sandhurst Gardens is up a lane to the right just before you come to the Black
Horse pub, which is opposite the Catford Fire Station. At the corner of the lane
is a wine & spirit merchant. Our fashionable residence is in a row of cottages
about 200 yards up the lane. The lane is a mud swamp. You pass a big tree before
you reach Sandhurst Gardens, also some cottages in course of construction.

Anyway drop him a line.

Yours faithfully

ROBERT H. SHERARD

I am glad to see you so busy & successful.

Sandhurst Gdns.
26 Sandown Rd.
Catford. Tuesd.

My dear Conal,

Thanks many times for your kind letter and remittance. It is a great comfort to me to feel I can come to you now at any time but I fear I am too weak to do it tomorrow. Sherard will not go to Paris this week & Mrs. Sherard is most kind in urging me not to leave until I am a little stronger—so I will not inflict myself upon you just yet. Perhaps if the weather improves you will be able to come over and see us. We shall all be delighted to see you. Forgive this short scrawl but it is the first letter I have tried to write & my hand is "nowhere".

Always yrs affectly
ERNEST DOWSON

---

26 Sandhurst Gardens
Catford

My dear Conal,

I was going to write & say how grieved I was at the news in your 1st letter when the second came to relieve my mind, of course my dear old chap nothing you said hurt me & when I get to you & I can't say how much I want to I shall ask my uncle to come & see me. I am deeply grateful for the sums you can send me as medicines are so dear & I accept them with less reluctance as I had better news from my solo[r] the other day & fancy that my money is now within measurable dist. of coming—at any rate I have consented to an arrangement which avoids the necessity of lunatic proceedings & think the affair is now so settled that one of my uncles will at any rate advance me something.

Come over & see us soon, we all wish it

Yrs

ERNEST DOWSON

[A note on this letter reads:]
N.B. Probably the last letter he ever wrote.
C (20/2/00)

---

26 Sandhurst Gardens
Catford,
S.E.
Friday

Dear Connell,

You will not be able to be kind to Ernest any more. You will be very glad you were the last friend to be good to him. He died suddenly at 10 to 12 to-day. He steadily refused to see a doctor, putting it off until he got to your house. I am to have a Coroner's officer here.

Yours ever
R.H. SHERARD

26 Sandhurst Gardens
Catford,
S.E.
Sunday

Dear Connell,

I presume from not hearing from you, you are still in Holland & did not get my letter notifying Dowson's happy release. He is to be buried at Lewisham (Catholic Chapel at 11 a.m.) on Tuesday. But I fear you won't get this in time. I send it to Dulwich as it is useless to write to Holland, though I have your address.

Yrs ever,

R. H. SHERARD

3, Plowden Buildings,
In the Temple.
24/2/00

My dear Connell,

I don't know if this will find you in Holland; but I have to give you very sad news. A friend to whom we were all very much attached, who had long been very ill, died suddenly yesterday at mid-day. I need hardly say that I refer to poor Ernest Dowson. He died of syncope, while still at Sherard's, and is to be buried on Tuesday at noon, at the Catholic Cemetery at Lewisham, if an inquest can be avoided. As he refused, however, to see a doctor, I fear that an inquest may have to be held.

The pity that he was allowed to die so young—you will feel this as much as I do; for was it not you who wrote of the land of Bohemia and the Ulysses who stops his ears?

Ever yours,

A. T. DE M.

[ALEXANDER TEIXEIRA DE MATTOS]

If the Simonses are still in Holland, give them my best wishes.

BIBLIOGRAPHY

A CHRONOLOGY OF DOWSON'S WORKS

1886 "Sonnet of a Little Girl," *London Society*, November 1886.

1887 "Moritura," *London Society*, March 1887. Reprinted with slight changes in *Decorations: in Verse and Prose*, 1899.

1888 "Souvenirs of an Egoist," a tale in prose, *Temple Bar*, January 1888.

1889 "April," a sonnet, *Temple Bar*, April 1889. Later reprinted in *Verses*, 1896, under the title "My Lady April." Many unsigned contributions to the short-lived periodical *The Critic*.

1890 "The Diary of a Successful Man," *Macmillan's Magazine*, February 1890. Reprinted in *Dilemmas*, 1895.

1891 "The Story of a Violin," *Macmillan's Magazine*, August 1891. Reprinted in *Dilemmas*, 1895, under the title "An Orchestral Violin."
"A Case of Conscience," *The Century Guild Hobby Horse*, April 1891. Reprinted in *Dilemmas*, 1895.
"Non Sum Qualis Eram Bonae Sub Regno Cynarae," *The Century Guild Hobby Horse*, April 1891. Reprinted in *The Second Book of the Rhymers' Club*, 1894; and in *Verses*, 1896.
"In Praise of Solitude," a series of three poems: "Fleur de la Lune," "The Carmelite Nuns of the Perpetual Adoration," and "Amor Umbratilis," *The Century Guild Hobby Horse*, October 1891. "The Carmelite Nuns of the Perpetual Adoration" and "Amor Umbratilis" were reprinted in *The Book of the Rhymers' Club*, 1892, and all of them were reprinted in *Verses*, 1896. In *Verses*, the title "Fleur de la Lune" became "Flos Lunae," and "The Carmelite Nuns of the Perpetual Adoration" became "The Nuns of the Perpetual Adoration." This poem also appeared in the *Mercure de France*, March 1892.

1892 "To One in Bedlam," *The Albemarle*, August 1892. Reprinted in *The Second Book of the Rhymers' Club*, 1894, and in *Verses*, 1896.
The Book of the Rhymers' Club contained six of Dowson's poems: "The Carmelite Nuns of the Perpetual Adoration," "O Mors! Quam Amara Est Memoria Tua Homini Pacem Habenti In Substantiis Suis," "Amor Umbratilis," "Ad Domnulam Suam," "Vanitas," and "Villanelle of Sunset." All were reprinted in *Verses*, 1896.

1893 "Villanelle of His Lady's Treasures," *Temple Bar*, August 1893. Reprinted in *Verses*, 1896.
"The Statute of Limitations," a prose tale, *The Century Guild Hobby Horse*, January 1893. Reprinted in *Dilemmas*, 1895.
"A Roundel," *Temple Bar*, September 1893. Reprinted in *Decorations: in Verse and Prose*, 1899, under the title "Beyond."
"The Dead Child," *Atalanta*, February 1893. Reprinted in *Decorations: in Verse and Prose*, 1899.
A Comedy of Masks, a novel, with Arthur Moore, 1893.

1894 "Villanelle of the Marguerites," *Temple Bar*, September 1894. Reprinted in *Verses*, 1896.

The Second Book of the Rhymers' Club, 1894, contained six of Dowson's poems: "Extreme Unction," "To One in Bedlam," "Non Sum Qualis Eram Bonae Sub Regno Cynarae," "Growth," "The Garden of Shadow," and "You Would Have Understood Me Had You Waited." All of them were reprinted in *Verses*, 1896.

"Apple Blossom in Brittany," a prose tale, *The Yellow Book*, October 1894.

La Terre by Emile Zola. Translated by Ernest Dowson for the Lutetian Society.

Majesty by Louis Marie Anne Couperus. Translated by Teixeira de Mattos and Ernest Dowson.

1895 *Dilemmas: Stories and Studies in Sentiment*, contained "A Case of Conscience," "The Diary of a Successful Man," "An Orchestral Violin," "The Statute of Limitations," and "Souvenirs of an Egoist."

1896 "Impenitentia Ultima," *The Savoy*, January 1896. Reprinted in *Verses*, 1896.

"The Eyes of Pride," a prose tale, *The Savoy*, January 1896.

"Countess Marie of the Angels," a prose tale, *The Savoy*, April 1896.

"Saint-Germain-en-Laye," *The Savoy*, April 1896. Reprinted in *Decorations: in Verse and Prose*, 1899.

"Breton Afternoon," *The Savoy*, July 1896. Reprinted in *Decorations: in Verse and Prose*, 1899.

"Venite, Descendamus," *The Savoy*, August 1896. Reprinted in *Decorations: in Verse and Prose*, 1899.

"The Dying of Francis Donne," a study, *The Savoy*, August 1896.

"All That a Man May Pray," a song, *The Savoy*, September 1896. Reprinted in *Decorations: in Verse and Prose*, 1899, under the title "A Song."

"The Three Witches," *The Savoy*, October 1896. Reprinted in *Decorations: in Verse and Prose*, 1899.

"Epilogue," *The Savoy*, November 1896. Reprinted in *Decorations: in Verse and Prose*, 1899, under the title "A Last Word."

La Fille aux Yeux d'Or by Honoré de Balzac. Translated by Ernest Dowson.

Geschichte der Malerei im neunzehnten Jahrhundert by Richard Muther. Translated by G. A. Greene, A. C. Hillier, and Ernest Dowson.

1897 "In a Breton Cemetery," *The Pageant*, 1897. Reprinted in *Decorations: in Verse and Prose*, 1899.

The Pierrot of the Minute, a Dramatic Phantasie in One Act.

1898 *Les Liaisons Dangereuses* by Choderlos de Laclos. Translated by Ernest Dowson.

1899   *Adrian Rome*, a novel, by Arthur Moore and Ernest Dowson.
       La Pucelle d'Orléans by Voltaire. Translated in Verse by Ernest Dowson.
       Memoirs of Cardinal Dubois by Paul LaCroix. Translated by Ernest
       Dowson.
       Decorations: in Verse and Prose.
1902   *The Poems of Ernest Dowson*, including *The Pierrot of the Minute*,
       edited by T. B. Mosher, Portland, Maine.
1905   *The Poems of Ernest Dowson*, with a Memoir by Arthur Symons. Sixth
       edition, 1915. Reprinted 1929.
1907   *Cynara, a Little Book of Verse*, edited by T. B. Mosher, Portland, Maine.
       The Confidantes of a King: the Mistresses of Louis XV by the Gon-
       court brothers. Translated by Ernest Dowson.
1908   *The Story of Beauty and the Beast*, a fairy tale. Translated by Ernest
       Dowson.
1915   "The Passing of Tennyson," *T.P.'s Weekly*, January 8, 1915. Reprinted
       in *The Literary Digest*, March 27, 1915.
1928   *The Poems of Ernest Dowson*, The Medusa Head, New York.
1932   "Fantasie Triste," *Known Signatures.*
1934   *The Poetical Works of Ernest Christopher Dowson*, edited by Desmond
       Flower, London.

BIOGRAPHICAL AND CRITICAL REFERENCES

Athenaeum, The: Review of *Adrian Rome*, February 1899.
     Review of *Decorations: in Verse and Prose*, April 1900.
ATHERTON, GERTRUDE: Cassell's Weekly, March 21, 1923.
     Adventures of a Novelist, London, 1932.
Bookman, The (London): Review of *A Comedy of Masks*, November 1893.
     Contains in the same issue brief biographical notices of Dowson and Moore
     Review of *Adrian Rome*, April 1899.
     "An Estimate," November 1905.
BRÉGY, KATHERINE: "Ernest Dowson: An Interpretation," *The Catholic World*,
     November 1914.
BURDETT, OSBERT: *The Beardsley Period*, London, 1925.
CHARASSON, HENRIETTE: "Ernest Dowson," *Mercure de France*, CVII (1914),
     239-54.
COLBY, FRANK M.: A review of Plarr's *Ernest Dowson* with biographical annota-
     tions, *The New Republic*, July 15, 1915.
Current Opinion: "A New Glimpse of the Mysterious Author of Cynara," un-
     signed, March 1915.
Daily Telegraph (London): An Obituary Notice, February 28, 1900.
EVANS, B. IFOR: *English Poetry in the Late Nineteenth Century*, London, 1933.
FLOWER, DESMOND, ed.: *The Poetical Works of Ernest Christopher Dowson.*
     London, 1934.

FLOWER, NEWMAN: "Two Interesting Sinners," *The Bookman* (London), October 1926.

GAWSWORTH, JOHN: "The Dowson Legend," *The Transactions of the Royal Society of Literature of the United Kingdom*, London, March 1939.

GIBSON, FRANK: *Charles Conder: His Life and Work*, London, 1914.

Golden Book: Reprints of some of Dowson's poems with brief notes. "Cynara," October 1925; "Valediction," May 1926; "Statute of Limitations," a story, March 1927; "Song Without Words," October 1927; "Epigram," March 1928.

GRIBBLE, FRANCIS: *Seen in Passing*, London, 1929.

GRIERSON, H. J. C. *Lyrical Poetry from Blake to Hardy*, London, 1928.

GULL, RANGER (GUY THORNE): "The Strand Twenty Years Ago," *T.P.'s Weekly*, July 11, 1913.

HARRIS, FRANK: "The Swan Song of Youth: Ernest Dowson," *Pearson's Magazine*, March 1917.
Contemporary Portraits, Second Series, New York, 1920.

JACKSON, HOLBROOK: *The Eighteen Nineties*, London, 1914.
A critical note, *T.P.'s Weekly*, January 8, 1915.

JEPSON, EDGAR: "The Real Ernest Dowson," *The Academy*, November 1907.
Memories of a Victorian, Volume I, London, 1933.

KENNEDY, J. M.: *English Literature: 1880-1905*, London, 1905.

LANG, ANDREW: "Decadence," *The Critic* (London), August 1900.

LANGBRIDGE, ROSAMUND: "Ernest Dowson in Ireland," *T.P.'s Weekly*, January 30, 1915.

LE GALLIENNE, RICHARD: *The Romantic Nineties*, London, 1926.

LOCKETT, JOHN: A critical note, *T.P.'s Weekly*, February 8, 1928.

MAY, JOHN LEWIS: *John Lane and the Nineties*, London, 1936.

MOSHER, T. B., ed.: *The Poems of Ernest Dowson*, Portland, Maine, 1902.

MUDDIMAN, BERNARD: *The Men of the Nineties*, London, 1920.

MURDOCH, W. G. B.: *The Renaissance of the Nineties*, London, 1911.

O'SULLIVAN, VINCENT: *Aspects of Wilde*, New York, 1936.

PALMER, HERBERT: *Post-Victorian Poetry*, London, 1938.

PERCIVAL, M. O., AND ANDREWS, C. E.: *Poetry of the Nineties*, New York, 1926.

PLARR, MARION: *Cynara: The Story of Ernest Dowson and Adelaide*, a novel, London, 1933.

PLARR, VICTOR: "An Informal Epitaph on a Young Poet," *Poetry and Drama*, June 1913.
Ernest Dowson, 1888-1897: Reminiscences, Unpublished Letters, and Marginalia, London, 1914.

QUINN, JOHN: *The Catalogue of the Quinn Library*, edited by Mitchell Kennerley, New York, 1933.

REID, FORREST: "Ernest Dowson," *Monthly Review*, XIX (June 1905) 107-13.

RHYS, ERNEST: *Everyman Remembers*, London, 1931.

RICHARDS, GRANT: *Memories of a Misspent Youth*, London, 1932.

Author Hunting, London, 1934.

ROBERTS, MORLEY: A critical note in *John o'London's Weekly*, September 30, 1933.

ROTHENSTEIN, SIR WILLIAM: *Men and Memories*, Volume I, London, 1931.

ROTHERY, AGNES: "Mad Poets in Spring," *The Virginia Quarterly Review*, April 1927.

SHERARD, ROBERT HARBOROUGH: "Dowson's Last Days," *The Author*, May 1900.

Twenty Years in Paris, London, 1905.

The Real Oscar Wilde, London, 1911.

STONEHILL, C. A. AND H. W.: *Bibliographies of Modern Authors*, Second Series, London, 1925.

Sunday Express (London): An article unsigned, May 1928.

SYMONS, ARTHUR: "A Literary Causerie," *The Savoy*, August 1896.

An article in *The Athenaeum*, March 3, 1900.

An article in *Current Literature*, September, 1900.

An article in *The Fortnightly*, June 1900.

The Poems of Ernest Dowson, with a Memoir by Arthur Symons, London, 1905.

THOMAS, W. R.: "Ernest Dowson at Oxford," *The Nineteenth Century*, April 1928.

UNTERMEYER, LOUIS: *Modern British Poetry*, New York, 1936.

WALKER, R. A.: *Letters from Aubrey Beardsley to Leonard Smithers*, London, 1937.

WEYGANDT, CORNELIUS: *The Time of Yeats*, New York, 1935.

WHEATLEY, KATHERINE: "Ernest Dowson's 'Extreme Unction,'" University of Texas, *Modern Language Notes*, May 1923.

WILLIAMS, TALCOT: "Ernest Dowson," *The Book News Monthly*, April 1907.

WINWAR, FRANCES: *Oscar Wilde and the Yellow Nineties*, New York, 1940.

YEATS, W. B.: *The Trembling of the Veil*, London, 1922.

The Listener (London), October 14, 1936.

ADDENDA

ALBERT, EDWARD: *A History of English Literature*, Third ed., London, 1955.

ALFORD, NORMAN: *The Rhymers' Club: A Study of Its Activities and Their Significance*, University of Texas Dissertation, Austin, 1966.

BATHO, EDITH (See also DOBREE, BONAMY): *The Victorians and After*, Second ed., London, 1950.

BECKSON, KARL, ed.: *Aesthetes and Decadents of the 1890's*, New York, 1967.

BUCKLEY, JEROME: "The Decadence and After," *The Victorian Temper*, Cambridge, Massachusetts, 1951.

CECIL, LORD DAVID: "Fin de Siècle," *Ideas and Beliefs of the Victorians*, ed. Harman Grisewood, London, 1949.

CHEW, SAMUEL: "Aestheticism and Decadence," *A Literary History of England*, ed. Albert Baugh, New York, 1948.

DOBREE, BONAMY (See also BATHO, EDITH): *The Victorians and After*, Second ed., London, 1950.

DURRELL, LAWRENCE: *A Key to Modern Poetry*, London, 1951.

GARBATY, THOMAS: *The Savoy, 1896: a Re-Edition of Representative Prose and Verse, with a Critical Introduction, and Biographical and Critical Notes*, University Microfilms, Ann Arbor, Michigan, 1957.

GAUNT, WILLIAM: *The Aesthetic Adventure*, New York, 1945.

GOLDFARB, RUSSELL: "The Dowson Legend Today," *Studies in English Literature*, IV, No. 4 (Autumn 1964).

HARRIS, WENDELL: "Innocent Decadence: the Poetry of the Savoy," PMLA, LXXVII (December 1962).

HEATH-STUBBS, JOHN: *The Darkling Plain*, London, 1950.

HOUGH, GRAHAM: *The Last Romantics*, London, 1949.

HOUGHTON, WALTER, and G. ROBERT STANGE, eds.: *Victorian Poetry and Poetics*, Cambridge, Massachusetts, 1959.

KLINGOPULOS, G.D.: "The Literary Scene," *Pelican Guide to English Literature*, VI, 67, Hammondsworth, England, 1958.

LHOMBREAUD, ROGER: *Arthur Symons, a Critical Biography*, London, 1963.

LONGAKER, MARK, ed.: *The Stories of Ernest Dowson*, Philadelphia, 1947.

———————————: The Poems of Ernest Dowson, Philadelphia, 1962.

MUNRO, J.M.: "A Previously Unpublished Letter from Ernest Dowson to Arthur Symons," *Etudes Anglaises*, XVII (1964).

RODWAY, A.E.: "The Last Phase," *Pelican Guide to English Literature*, VI, 67, Hammondsworth, England, 1958.

RYALS, CLYDE: *Decadence Before the Fin de Siècle*, Philadelphia, 1957.

SWANN, THOMAS B.: *Ernest Dowson* ("Twayne's English Authors Series"), New York, 1964.

TILLOTSON, GEOFFREY: "Ernest Dowson," *Essays in Criticism and Research*, Cambridge, England, 1942.

INDEX